Race & Family

To Claudia Sevgi and Sage Sibel
Daughters and Muses, who amuse, bemuse,
and infuse me with their humor, curiosity, and potential

Race & Family

A Structural Approach

ROBERTA L. COLES
Marquette University

SAGE Publications
Thousand Oaks ■ London ■ New Delhi

For information:

Sage Publications, Inc.
2455 Teller Road
Thousand Oaks, California 91320
E-mail: order@sagepub.com

Sage Publications Ltd.
1 Oliver's Yard
55 City Road
London EC1Y 1SP
United Kingdom

Sage Publications India Pvt. Ltd.
B-42, Panchsheel Enclave
Post Box 4109
New Delhi 110 017 India

Printed in the United States of America on acid-free paper.

Library of Congress Cataloging-in-Publication Data

Coles, Roberta L.
Race and family: a structural approach/Roberta L. Coles.
p. cm.
Includes bibliographical references and index.
ISBN 978-0-7619-8864-9 (pbk.)
1. Family—United States. 2. Minorities—United States—Family relationships.
I. Title.
HQ536.C714 2006
306.85′089′00973—dc222

2005005279

12 13 14 15 16 9 8 7 6 5 4 3

Acquiring Editor:	Jim Brace-Thompson
Editorial Assistant:	Karen Ehrmann
Production Editor:	Sanford Robinson
Typesetter:	C&M Digitals (P) Ltd.
Copy Editor:	Taryn L. Bigelow
Indexer:	Julie Grayson
Cover Designer:	Janet Foulger

CONTENTS

Preface ix

1. Introduction 1
    - Overview of the Text 5
    - Discussion of Key Concepts 6
        - Race 6
        - Ethnicity 7
        - Racial-Ethnic Labels 8
        - Minority and Majority 9
        - Family or Kin 10
2. Approaching the Study of Race and Family 13
    - Economic Factors 15
        - Occupational Structure 16
        - Income and Wealth Distribution 16
        - Poverty 18
        - Education 19
    - Demographic Factors 20
        - Sex Ratio 20
        - Age Structure 22
        - Geographic Distribution 23
    - Historical-Legal Factors 24
        - Manner of Entry 25
        - Immigrant Status 27
3. A Brief History of the American Family 31
    - American Families Through the Centuries 33
        - The Agricultural Era (Colonial Period 1500 to 1800) 34
        - The Industrial Era (About 1800 to 1970) 37
        - The Service Era (Since the 1970s) 41

4. Cross-Cultural Comparisons 47
Social or Legal Marriage 49
Marriage Types and Choices 49
Marriage as a Family Affair 51
Arranged Marriages 51
Exchange of Resources 53
Family Power Systems 54
Descent 54
Family Roles and Titles 55
Residence 56
Family Functions 57
Reproduction 57
Regulation of Sexuality 58
Socialization of Children 59

5. Family Structures 63
Extended Family Households 64
Multigenerational Extended Households 66
Simple Extended Households 67
Stem Family Households 67
Attenuated Extended Households 68
Laterally Extended Households 69
Extended Families as Systems of Exchange 70
Nuclear Family Households 73
Single-Parent Families 75
Female-Headed Households 77
Nonmarital Births 77
Teen Births 78
Explaining the Racial Gap in Nonmarital Births 79
Outcomes for Female-Headed Households 81
Male-Headed Households 82
Noncustodial Parents 83
Nonfamily Households 84

6. Gender Relations and Sex Ratios 87
Gender Stereotypes and Roles 89
Adult Roles 95
Sex Ratios 96
African American Gender Issues 99
Latina/o Gender Issues 101
Asian American Gender Issues 103
Native American Gender Issues 104
Domestic Violence 105

7. Intergenerational Relationships: Parent and Child 111
Individual and Communal Orientations 112
Effects of Socioeconomic Status on Children's Well-Being 116
Parenting Styles and Class 117
Parenting Styles and Environment 119
Corporal Punishment and Abuse 122
Parenting Styles and the School System 124
Racial Socialization 126
Cultural Rituals That Contribute to Racial Socialization 129

8. Intergenerational Relationships in Late Life: The Elderly, Their Adult Children and Grandchildren 135
Intergenerational Interaction 138
Living Arrangements of the Elderly 138
Caregiving for the Elderly 140
Nursing Home Use 140
Informal Home Caregiving 141
Caregiver Stress 142
Elder Abuse 143
Social Interaction and Resource Exchange 143
Grandparenting 144
Illness and Death 146
Illness 146
Death 147
African Americans 148
Native Americans 148
Latino Americans 149
Asian Americans 149

9. African American Families 153
How Did Slavery Shape Black American Families? 156
African American Families After Slavery 160
African American Families Today 165

10. Native American Families 171
Looking Back in History 174
Removal and Reservations 175
Assimilating Native Americans 177
Increased Tribal Sovereignty 179
The State of American Indians and Their Families Today 180
On or Off the Reservation 180

Tribal Structure 181
Cultural Values 182
Current Family Trends 183

11. Latino American Families 189
Manner and Timing of Entry 191
Mexico 191
Puerto Rico and Cuba 193
Puerto Rico 193
Cuba 194
Similarities Among Hispanic Families 198
Divergent Trends Among Latino Ethnic Groups 200

12. Asian American Families 207
East Asians in America 209
Chinese Americans 210
The Japanese American Experience 214
Asian Indian, Filipino, and Korean Americans 216
Southeast Asians in America 218
Asian American Families Today 221

13. Acculturation and Multiracial Family Issues 231
Acculturation 232
Factors Hindering and Helping Acculturation 234
Effects of Acculturation on Family Life 237
Multiracial Issues 239
Interracial Dating and Marriage 240
Dating and Cohabitation 240
Interracial Marriage 241
Race and Gender Influences on Interracial Marriage Rates 242
Generation, Education, and Residence as Influences on Interracial Marriage 245
Why Marry Interracially? 245
Social Acceptance and Outcomes of Interracial Marriage 246
Bi- or Multiracial Identity 247
Trans- or Interracial Adoption 250

References 255

Author Index 289

Subject Index 299

About the Author 319

PREFACE

Talking about race and ethnicity is akin to strolling through a minefield. Americans have not been socialized to easily converse in public settings about politics, and talking about race and ethnicity tends to get political. Americans also espouse apparently contradictory values about race and ethnicity. On one hand, we seek to judge and be judged without regard to skin color; on the other, we wish to acknowledge and celebrate diversity. Americans yearn for colorblindness while we proactively integrate people of color into the nation's economy and educational system.

At the same time, American behavior clearly indicates that White Americans have been valued more than Americans of color—both in the sense that White Americans have held a disproportionate share of the country's wealth and resources and in the sense that their lives have been valued more. Criminological studies, for instance, find that a perpetrator of a violent crime against a White person has a much greater chance of receiving a severe sentence than does the perpetrator of a similar crime against a person of color (Weitzer, 1996). Moreover, it would be almost unheard of for a child of color who disappears or is murdered to garner the same degree of media attention as a White child victim, such as JonBenet Ramsey or Elizabeth Smart. Such are the hidden injuries of race in diverse America.

Although family issues appear less contentious, they also have controversial political repercussions. How we define family informs society about who is obligated to whom. For instance, are biological ties more important than adoptive ties? Does a stepparent have visitation rights to a stepchild in the case of divorce? Should a grandparent who is rearing his or her grandchild be able to make medical care decisions as would the child's parent?

How we define family has consequences for the distribution of limited societal resources. Should a single-parent family, a cohabiting couple, and a childless married couple all have equal access to family housing at a local university? Should all members of an extended or polygamous family household have access to family coverage on their health insurance benefit? Should poor married couples without children and single-parent families have the same access to public assistance? Such questions are periodically debated throughout the nation.

When a society values certain ethnicities or families more than others, it may pass laws or policies to hinder the creation of less valued family types. For instance, in the 1800s, threatened by the presence of people of color, many states passed laws prohibiting interracial marriage and creating racial segregation. In the early part of the 1900s, eugenicists believed that certain people, such as poor, disabled, and "promiscuous" people should not be allowed to reproduce. Consequently, an estimated 60,000 sterilizations were performed from 1900 through the 1970s, with Black and Native American women disproportionately represented in that group (New York Academy of Medicine, 2003). More recently, concern over America's high divorce rate led several states to pass "covenant marriage" options constricting the grounds for divorce (Hawkins, Nock, Wilson, Sanchez, & Wright, 2002). Although a few states have legalized civil unions among same-sex couples, another 28 states either have passed or are considering bans on same-sex marriage (Human Rights Campaign, 2004). Moreover, at least 23 states recently implemented family caps, provisions denying or reducing assistance to welfare recipients who have additional births (Joyce, Kaestner, Korenman, & Henshaw, 2004). These policies and others (such as family leave, tax law, child care, or education) all affect and are affected by the ebb, flow, and hue of family trends.

These cultural and political battles over race and family values frequently merge and are manifested in the vacillating manner in which families of color are studied and portrayed. Both scholarship and the popular media are prone to pathologize or romanticize families of color. From the former perspective, families of color are presented as nonconforming, deviations from the traditional white-picket-fence American family. Poor, single-parent or polygamous families, for instance, are treated as dysfunctional, inferior, or in need of help. When romanticized, families of color are portrayed as embodying more culture, resiliency, and closeness than European American families. Articles about various ethnic families frequently commence with a statement similar to this: "The family is the most important social unit to *(fill in any ethnic group)*," implying that that's less true for other racial-ethnic groups.

Realistically, one can safely say that for most, if not all, racial-ethnic groups (Whites included), family is the most important attachment in life. How that attachment is expressed varies by ethnicity, class, gender, age, as well as individual temperament; but for the vast majority of people, family is the first social unit to which they are introduced. Moreover, family is the primary and, for most, probably the only warm and fuzzy social structure in which humans develop physically and psychologically. For the majority of people, family remains the source to which they return for succor and sustenance of one sort or another throughout their lives. At the same time, it would be naïve to conclude that the family serves only as an isolated haven, untouched by the vicissitudes of modern life. The family can also be a source of pain and a site of conflict and struggle over identity and resources. As one societal institution among many, the family is both facilitated and constrained by its institutional counterparts.

Rather than looking to this book to confirm perceptions that certain racial groups' families or ways of doing family are superior or inferior, I suggest that the reader approach the study of ethnicity and family with the following considerations in mind.

First, misconceptions about the family life of various racial-ethnic groups are not necessarily due to incorrect information but rather to how information is understood and interpreted. For instance, the percentage of households in America that are family households has declined from about 90 percent in 1950 to 68 percent in 2000. Some observers use those figures to argue that Americans have lost their family values; fewer people are forming families. But most people don't realize that the percentage of family households declined largely due to two major developments: young people now postpone marriage to attend college or settle in a career, and an increased life expectancy has multiplied the number of elderly. Both of these groups live alone or with roommates in what the census calls "nonfamily" households.

Second, the text covers a number of racial-ethnic groups in a limited space. Hence, my goal is to provide readers with an overview of each of the main racial-ethnic groups' historical and current social experiences and to facilitate understanding of the linkages between those experiences and each group's family dynamics. Because space limitations prevent me from detailing all the different ways that people can do family, this book will inevitably make generalizations.

Generalizations differ from stereotypes. Generalizations are based on empirical data and indicate a strong correlation between a particular characteristic or behavior and a certain population. Hence, phrases such as "on average," "more likely," and "tend to" will be used to illustrate that a particular ethnic group frequently practices a certain form of family or family tradition, without implying that every group member does so in the exact same way. For instance, it would be a generalization to say that Americans tend to celebrate Christmas by trimming trees and giving gifts. Most people would understand that not *every* American celebrates Christmas nor that every celebrator celebrates in the same way. The practice differs by one's age, socioeconomic class, gender, religion, and so on. Moreover, when the words "traditionally" or "historically" are used throughout this text to describe a certain practice, I intend to imply that that practice has probably declined some in recent years, but that it remains a strong influence.

Whenever possible, I have listed sources of further information, such as memoirs, scholarly research, videos, and websites, for those who want to delve more deeply into a particular racial-ethnic group or who desire more reader/viewer-friendly sources of knowledge. Although this book is primarily intended for student use in colleges and universities, those who see life as a series of educational opportunities will find it useful too. I invite reader feedback as well.

Third, as you read about racial-ethnic families, look for parallels in your own family or in American society generally. You will find that the various groups have much in common. For instance, Americans tend to find arranged marriages at odds with their ideas about romance and individual autonomy. But are arranged marriages much different from the growing use of newspaper personal ads or Internet dating services, where seekers delineate with great detail the characteristics they desire in a companion? Are they much different from blind dates, speed dating, or reality television shows, such as "The Bachelor"? Although important differences in experiences and statistics exist among all groups, universal human commonalities can be recalled to deepen one's understanding.

Finally, families in America and around the world exist in a constant state of flux, evolving and adapting to the demands of the social, economic, and political environments that envelop them, inventing new ways to meet old human needs. Families reconfigure in composition over their life course. Family members grow, leave home, and sometimes reenter; some members die and new ones are born. All of these changes have their advantages and disadvantages; some people benefit, whereas others are hurt. These macro and micro forces, along with the increasing racial-ethnic diversity in America, produce an ever-changing kaleidoscope of shapes and colors in American family life.

Acknowledgments

Deep appreciation goes to the many students who have made Race and Family a delightful course to teach. Their willingness to share their family experiences and struggles with me and others undergirds this project. Special thanks to students Kenna Bolton, Mary Chapman, Cynthia Schwartz, Michael Ugorek, and Mylou Vang, for their help in collecting data and citations and to my husband Selim Dogan for "taking over" when I made myself scarce to work on the book. Grateful acknowledgment is made to the reviewers for their incisive comments, to Taryn Bigelow, a patient and eagle-eyed editor; and to Karen Ehrmann for her diligence in the editorial department. Finally, I am fondly indebted to my Marquette University colleagues in the Department of Social and Cultural Sciences who, over the years, have graciously given me respite for the body and soul. They are a rare bunch.

CHAPTER 1

INTRODUCTION

America is one of the world's most racially diverse countries, and becoming more so each year. As you can see from Table 1.1, in 2000 White Americans, who are *ethnically* diverse, represented 69 percent of the U.S. population, whereas Americans of color accounted for 31 percent of the population. By 2050, assuming that fertility rates, the national origins of immigrants, and the rate of immigration remain stable, White Americans will constitute only a slim numerical majority. In fact, due to persistent segregation, White Americans are already a minority in California and in numerous counties around the country.

Some people fear this growing diversity; others view it as the creation of a multicolored montage. Either way, the fact remains that learning about one another—both our commonalities and differences—and interacting with each other on equal footing will benefit all Americans and future generations, enabling society to successfully sustain itself.

Table 1.1 Population of America 1990, 2000, and 2050[a] by Race and Ethnicity

	1990 Number	*1990 Percentage*	*2000 Number*	*2000 Percentage*	*2050 Number*	*2050 Percentage*
Total Population	248,709,873	100.0	281,421,906	100.0	419,854,000	100.0
Non-Hispanic White	188,128,296	75.6	194,552,774	69.1	210,283,000	50.1
Hispanic	22,354,059	9.0	35,305,818	12.5	102,560,000	24.4
Black	29,216,293	11.7	33,947,837	12.1	61,361,000	14.6
Asian & Pacific Islander	6,968,359	2.8	10,476,678	3.7	33,430,000	8.0
American Indian & Alaskan Native	1,793,773	0.7	2,068,883	0.7	—	—
Some Other Race	249,093	0.1	467,770[b]	0.2	22,437	5.3
Two or More Races	—	—	4,602,146	1.6	—	—

SOURCES: U.S. Department of Commerce (2001a); U.S. Department of Commerce (2003c), Table 15

a. The 1990 census did not include the option to check multiple races. The 2050 projections also do not include the multiracial or the American Indian and Alaskan Native categories.

b. In 2000, the vast majority of "Some other race" would have been categorized as "Hispanic."

As a sociology professor, I am occasionally asked why a separate course on race and family is necessary. After all, I also teach a general family course, so couldn't I incorporate related race data into that one? On the surface this seems merely a pragmatic question; but underlying it are assumptions that all American families vary only superficially, that they are all similarly impacted by current events and policies, and that the ways in which we vary merely reflect differences of personal choice and have little import. In other words, race doesn't or shouldn't make a noteworthy difference in the family experience.

On the contrary, adding race to any discussion of societal trends often reveals new elements or layers of understanding that would have otherwise remained obscure. Let me give two examples to illustrate. In my sex and gender course, I ask the class to describe some stereotypes of women. Students usually list many of the following adjectives: submissive, weak, emotional, irrational, vain, low self-esteem. But if I specify the request in terms of race or ethnicity—such as stereotypes of *Black* women—several adjectives change. Usually, "strong" or "aggressive" replaces weak and submissive. For reasons I will discuss in Chapter 6, Black women are frequently associated with "attitude" or high self-esteem.

Another topic of recent interest in the United States is eating disorders. Most Americans immediately think of anorexia or bulimia, which are 5 to 15 times more common among White women than Black women (Striegel-Moore et al., 2003). The primary explanation for the rise of these disorders is America's obsession with thinness, an obsession that is particularly common among White women, perhaps because they are the ones most likely to see women like themselves (only thinner, yet with ample bosom) reflected in the media.

Once again, overlaying race on the eating disorder issue changes the contours of the discussion. First, the definition of eating disorder broadens to include obesity caused by overeating or binging. African Americans, particularly women, have higher levels of obesity than do Whites. Obesity is higher among women of color because both are associated with low income. Low-income people tend to have more stress, less education about nutrition, less access to expensive organic and fresh foods, and fewer exercise venues, such as health clubs, tennis courts, and safe neighborhoods for jogging. When Striegel-Moore et al. (2003) controlled for socioeconomic class, they found that the rates of extreme disorder behaviors, such as vomiting, were nearly equal among affluent Blacks and Whites.

Second, the *causes* of eating disorders expand when race is included. One study (Thompson, 1992) that included women of color found that an obsession with physical appearance was only one possible cause. Among racial minority women, eating disorders also serve as (inadequate) psychological strategies to cope with poverty, discrimination, or sexual abuse.

These two examples illustrate that when race is unspecified, the subject (woman) is often assumed to be White (Landrine, 1985). Because Whites have been the majority in America, they are treated as the standard, the generic norm, as has frequently been the case with gender norms. For instance, news articles used to specify the gender of a professional, such as "the *female* doctor" or "the *female* attorney." If the article referred only to "the doctor" or "attorney," the reader usually visualized a man. Likewise, race, and the different life experiences that attend people of color in America, often needs to be denoted. Otherwise, people often assume the White experience is everyone's experience.

Until recently, the vast majority of research on families focused on White middle-class respondents. Therefore, Chapter 3 (the history chapter) and any generic references to the American family or to "national averages" largely reflect the White experience. Therefore, this book includes no specific chapter on White families. Whenever possible, however, specific statistics for White families are used for purposes of comparison.

Some scholars have expressed concern that comparing every racial minority group to Whites only buttresses the perception that Whites are the standard by which everyone else should be measured. Comparison and contrast, however, are essential elements in scientific inquiry. Let me offer an example to illustrate how making comparisons enables more in-depth analysis. If my fifth-grade daughter's teacher reports to me that my daughter reads at the fifth-grade level, I could say, "That's great" and leave it at that. But if the teacher provides a comparative overview of the performance of the whole class, indicating where my daughter's scores rank relative to her classmates, I might discover that all the other students are reading at higher levels. In and of itself, that reading gap wouldn't prove that a problem exists, but it would lead me to ask questions that I wouldn't otherwise ask: Does my daughter need glasses? Is the teacher treating her differently than she or he treats the other students? Are all the other students just smarter than my daughter? Does she not like reading? Did I not read to her enough as a toddler? Are all the other families using tutors?

Aside from making me look like a paranoid parent, the point of this example is that making comparisons prods us to ask questions and delve more deeply. Moreover, when race is the subject, we are inevitably talking about equity and fairness. Getting a sense of whether and why one group's experience is different from another's necessitates some comparison. Therefore, this book uses a comparative approach so that the reader can see both similarities and differences among America's racial-ethnic groups and, more important, can understand and interpret those differences.

Unfortunately, I cannot consistently compare *all* racial-ethnic groups on *all* aspects of family life. Because Asians and Native Americans are relatively small proportions of the American population and are very diverse within their racial groups, less research and fewer data sets have included these groups. More research has focused on Black and/or Hispanic respondents, but frequently not within the same study, so sometimes it is impossible to describe or compare the same aspects of family life across racial-ethnic groups.

Overview of the Text

Rather than merely describing each racial-ethnic group's family style in separate chapters, this book employs an integrated structural approach. Chapter 2 gives the reader an overview of various structural factors—historical, economic, and demographic—that impact family life. Understanding how these factors work and the likely effect they have on families will provide the reader with analytic tools to use when she or he encounters racial-ethnic families not addressed here.

Chapter 3 gives a brief overview of why and in what ways American family life has changed over the past 400 years. This historical look is intended to illustrate that families change not only because individuals change their attitudes or values, but also because they must adapt to circumstances beyond their control. This chapter will also help the reader understand that some perceptions of past American families are more fantasy than fact.

Chapter 4 reviews concepts common in anthropological studies of family systems throughout the world, from simple tribal societies to complex, post-industrial societies. More important than just learning the definitions of such concepts is appreciating the myriad of family structures, marriage forms, and child-rearing styles that have all successfully nurtured generation after generation of humans.

Chapters 5 through 8 explore specific aspects of family life—family structures, gender roles, and intergenerational relations—describing their varied manifestations across racial groups. Chapters 9 through 12 examine the historical experience and the current social status of major racial and ethnic groups in America. Obviously, one chapter cannot do justice to the history of each group; the focus here is on specific historical experiences that impacted the family life of each group and a brief overview of the group's socioeconomic status, common types of family structure and traditions, and trends in divorce, fertility rates, outmarriage, and so on. Chapter 13 concludes the text with a focus on acculturation, and multi- and interracial aspects of family relations, such as interracial marriage, transracial adoption, and multiracial identity. The percentage of multiracial people in America is increasing, causing related issues to rise to the forefront of American life and politics.

Discussion of Key Concepts

In most discussions, it helps to ascertain whether all discussants are defining their terms similarly. Frequently, friends can find themselves feuding over an issue, only to discover later that they actually agree on the overall principle, but they were using specific terms differently. This is particularly true when the discussion is about race. For example, I have witnessed arguments on television talk shows over who can be racist. Frequently, people of color on the show assert that only Whites can be racist, and Whites retort that anyone can be racist. The argument is often caused by the discrepancy in their definition of "racism." Many scholars define racism as discrimination by institutions and individuals who have the power to make policy. In America, those with such institutional power are mostly White. Whites, on the other hand, commonly use *racism* as a synonym for *prejudice* (anyone can be prejudiced to one degree or another), and they apply the term *racist* only to those who exhibit extreme behaviors, such as members of the Ku Klux Klan, Skinheads, or individuals who commit racial crimes. If the discussants in this case recognized their varied definitions, they might find they agree more than they presume. Therefore, the next section is devoted to clarifying terms used throughout this book.

Race

People often think of race as a biological concept. Throughout history, however, the concept of race has been a slippery one, mutating over time and space. Most sociologists now speak of race as a "social construction," meaning that people, usually unwittingly, define and redefine a concept so that it denotes something different in one society from another or in one era from another. For instance, in centuries past, people spoke of the "human race." In the 1800s and early 1900s, social scientists spoke of the French race, the American race, or the Jewish race (Dworkin & Dworkin, 1999). At various points in history, scientists classified humans into 150 different races, and many of you probably have heard the Sunday school hymn that categorizes humans into four racial groups: "Jesus loves the little children, all the children of the world. Red and Yellow, Black and White; they are precious in His sight. Jesus loves the little children of the world." Modern science now rejects the existence of distinct groupings of pure races. If pure races existed in the past, their biological borders are now blurred by centuries of intermixing.

Some have suggested, therefore, that the word "race" is useless and should be discarded. I would argue, however, that for centuries people acted on and lived their lives as if race had biological certainty. Many societies created policies based on race, and years of living under those policies created more social differences among "racial" groups than probably existed in reality. For decades, American society acted upon a "one-drop rule," which stated that anyone with any African or Negro ancestry would be considered and treated as a Black person. Those treatments included a myriad of Jim Crow laws that justified segregation in schools, neighborhoods, marriage, social services, and employment. Years of abiding by these policies prevented minorities from accumulating wealth and cultural capital that could be passed on to future generations (Oliver & Shapiro, 1999). Therefore, race, whether or not existing in reality, has had a real impact on the organization of societies and the lives of individuals. This book will continue to use the word "race," keeping its limitations in mind.

Ethnicity

People associate race with people of color, forgetting that White is a race too. White Americans, because of their majority status, often define themselves more in terms of ethnicity and overlook how race affects their lives.

Ethnicity refers to a person's cultural heritage. Frequently, but not always, ethnicity derives from a territorial association. That is, Italians hail from Italy, Australians from Australia, Brazilians from Brazil. But territorial boundaries change throughout history, so certain ethnic groups may no longer possess a legally bounded territory. The Kurds, for instance, live primarily in Iraq, Turkey, and Syria; there is no country called "Kurdistan." Likewise, ethnicity is not synonymous with citizenship or nationality. Kurds born in Turkey are Turkish citizens or nationals, though they may not self-identify as ethnically Turkish.

Unlike race, which prioritizes physical features, such as skin color and facial features, ethnicity refers to cultural elements—language, religion and other values and beliefs, dress, food, music, traditions, and holidays. Ethnic categories are not consistent in their cultural dimensions. That is, many, but not all, Asian Indians practice Hinduism as a religion and speak Hindi. Some Koreans are Protestant, whereas others are Buddhist or Catholic.

Because of the growing recognition that ethnicity and race are largely social constructs, the U.S. Census Bureau has in recent years allowed respondents to self-identify their racial and ethnic categories. Prior to 1960, census takers used certain criteria, such as physical features or blood quantum, to determine in which racial and ethnic category to place people. Since the first census in 1790, the racial and ethnic categories have adjusted to account for new immigrant groups, new ways of thinking about race and ethnicity, and the growth of interracial and interethnic mixing. For the first time, in 2000, the census allowed respondents to choose more than one racial category for their identity. This acknowledged the reality of racial intermixing in America, but it made life more confusing for social scientists who rely on census data. The census data used in this text usually is based on the figures for the respondents who chose only one racial category (more than 97 percent of Americans chose only one race).

Racial-Ethnic Labels

As the above discussion implies, race and ethnicity are not separate; they overlap. Black Americans have a culture that is partly generic American and partly their own developed through years of segregation. For instance, we speak of Black music or a "White way of acting." We also know that Black Americans have a culture that is different from that of Black Africans. Every individual has a race and an ethnicity, sometimes several. Therefore, I frequently use the term "racial-ethnic" to acknowledge the intersection of both elements.

In addition, for each specific group, I use racial-ethnic labels interchangeably to acknowledge the diversity of opinion within each group about which label is preferred. For instance, some people prefer the African American label to acknowledge their ethnic origins in Africa. Others prefer to be called "Black Americans," sometimes because their African origins seem distant to them or because the term "Black" arose in the 1960s as a way of acknowledging pride in their skin color. The terms "Negro" and "colored" had been used previously, but, as words often do, those terms acquired a negative connotation and were replaced by *Black*. Every label has its limitations. For instance, White Africans whose families have lived in various African countries for generations don't know what to call themselves upon arrival in America. "African Americans?" Also, many so-called African Americans are recent immigrants from non-African countries. Despite these drawbacks, I will use Black and African American interchangeably.

The census defines *Hispanic* as an ethnicity, not a race. Consequently, to distinguish Hispanics from Whites in data, the government and academicians frequently sort Hispanics into a separate category and refer to the remaining Whites as "non-Hispanic White." This is sometimes done for Blacks as well, but the majority of Hispanic Americans identify themselves as White, so the overlap between Black and Hispanic is small.

As with the Black and African American labels, I switch between *Latino* and *Hispanic,* which for some people carry different political connotations. Hispanic emphasizes the Spanish heritage, whereas Latino highlights the South or Central American origin. Moreover, many people of Latino or Hispanic origin prefer the label of their specific ethnicity; that is, they would prefer Mexican American (or Chicano) or Cuban American.

Similarly, Americans often lump all Asians into one category, but most Asians don't think of themselves as Asians until they arrive in the United States. They think of themselves in terms of their specific country or even in terms of a specific region in their country. Nevertheless, for practical purposes, when I'm making generalizations I use the term Asian American. The category Asian frequently includes Native Hawaiians and Pacific Islanders as well.

Native American, American Indian, indigenous people, or First Nations will be used interchangeably, but again keep in mind that many Native Americans see themselves primarily as part of their specific tribe (Cherokee, Lakota Sioux, Apache, etc.). Data on American Indians usually include Native Alaskans too.

Generally, I use the terms White and non-Hispanic White synonymously. The census includes people of European descent and also of Middle Eastern or North African descent in this category, despite the fact that the Middle East is geographically part of Asia and many North Africans are dark skinned.

Minority and Majority

Minority and majority denote the percentage of a population. The minority is 50 percent or less of a population, whereas the majority is at least 51 percent of a population. Racially speaking, White Americans are the majority because they currently constitute about 69 percent of the U.S. population.

These terms, however, carry political connotations as well. Politically, the majority, regardless of its actual numbers, possesses the most societal power, owns a disproportionate share of society's resources, and frequently is upheld as the standard to which minority groups are compared. On occasion, a numerical minority is the political majority. For instance, for many years in South Africa, White South Africans were the numerical minority, but they held economic and political power.

As mentioned earlier, it is forecasted that White Americans may become a numerical minority toward the latter half of this century. Whether that demographic shift results in a redistribution of political and economic power remains to be seen.

Family or Kin

These terms may seem self-explanatory, but as mentioned in the preface, the way we define family or kin has a number of political consequences. If families are defined by their legal relationships, the people included in that definition usually acquire more social privileges, such as access to tax deductions, health insurance, social subsidies, particular types of housing, and so on.

The U.S. government, for purposes of the census, defines families according to legal and biological relationships and also in terms of co-residence. Two or more people who are related by blood, marriage, or adoption *and* are living together are considered a family household. The census usually breaks family households into married-couple households (with and without children under 18) and male-headed and female-headed households (with and without children under 18). Although the government recognizes that people do have nonresident relatives, the census doesn't attempt to count all those relationships.

People living alone or with other non-related people, such as roommates or cohabiting homosexual or heterosexual couples, are considered nonfamily households. So your grandmother who lives alone may be your kin, but the census counts her as a nonfamily household.

While recognizing biological and legal relationships, many social scientists study families in terms of their social qualitative relationships, particularly because in a number of societies (more so in the past than now), few formal bureaucratic mechanisms existed to legalize a marriage or adoption. Therefore, social scientists often define families according to their relationships of exchange. When interacting individuals exhibit mutual dependence and exchanges of tangible (money, child care, possessions) and intangible (love, respect, and family roles) goods or services over an extended period of time, they may be considered a family. With this broader definition, social scientists recognize a form of kin they call *fictive kin,* which refers to family-like relations with non-related people. These can be formalized roles, such as the person who is appointed as a godparent for one's child, or more informal ones, such as my friend Pam who my daughters call "Auntie Pam" or your friend Paul who is "like a brother." In this text, I use the term fictive kin broadly to also include family members who have taken on an additional role. For instance, one's aunt and uncle may become one's godparents, or one's grandparents may take over the role of parents.

No one family model works for everyone; many factors contribute to a "successful" family. Moreover, no one analysis of any racial-ethnic family fully encompasses the variation existing within each racial-ethnic group by socioeconomic class, region of residence, educational levels, and individual uniqueness. This text describes major family patterns and trends exhibited by each major racial-ethnic group represented in America and provides analytical tools for understanding why those patterns and trends exist and change over time.

Resources

Books and Articles

Frankenberg, R. (2000). Whiteness as an "unmarked" cultural category. In K. E. Rosenblum & T.-M. C. Travis (Eds.), *The meaning of difference: American constructions of race, sex and gender, social class, and sexual orientation* (pp. 81–87). Boston: McGraw-Hill.

The author interviews 30 White women about what it means to be White.

Thompson, B. W. (1994). *A hunger so wide and so deep: American women speak out on eating problems.* Minneapolis: University of Minnesota Press.

Women from various backgrounds reveal that obsession with thinness is not the only reason for eating disorders.

Video

Adelman, L. (Executive Producer). (2003). *Race: The power of an illusion.* [Motion picture]. (Available from California Newsreel, Order Department, P.O. Box 2284, South Burlington, VT, or at http://www.newsreel.org)

This three-part documentary scrutinizes the concept of race from biological, historical, and political perspectives.

Websites

http://ssw.unc.edu/jif/
This is the site for the Jordan Institute for Families, sponsored by the social work department at University of North Carolina at Chapel Hill.

http://www.leveragingdiversity.com
This website has information about various cultural practices, communication behaviors, and holidays for different racial-ethnic groups.

http://www.search-institute.org/
This website is sponsored by a nonprofit group in Minneapolis, and publishes research, often done in conjunction with the YMCA, on family issues.

CHAPTER 2

APPROACHING THE STUDY OF RACE AND FAMILY

When people discuss the behaviors and practices of families from ethnic backgrounds different from their own, they often explain the behavior as due to the family's "culture." For instance, when an American child asks her parents why some Arabs practice polygamy, the parent might reply, "Well, it's part of their culture (or religion)." Or when a Latina immigrant explains why she doesn't use a nursing home for her aging parent, she may say, "In my culture (or country), we believe we should care for our parents at home." Culture then becomes a vast, vague term explaining everything and nothing. One might as well say, "That's just how they do it in that country," a statement that fails to clarify why that culture developed those particular beliefs or practices in the first place or why such practices are common among cultures geographically distant from one another.

Focusing solely on the cultural factor ignores the existence of structural factors, such as socioeconomic, historical, demographic, and legal factors. Such a narrow approach relegates family life to the private sphere, where all family outcomes appear to result from personal values and choices, overlooks the fact that families are impacted by public ideologies and policies, and frees the public sphere from any responsibility for family outcomes. To avoid these pitfalls and supply the reader with analytical tools that can be utilized beyond this book's bindings, this text stresses structural factors while not ignoring cultural ones.

Taking a "structural" approach to elucidate why groups form and conduct family life in the ways they do, according to sociologist David Newman (2002), entails surveying "the framework of society that exists above the level of individuals and provides the social setting in which individuals interact with one another" (p. 239). Such frameworks include statuses, roles, institutions, norms, and rules that organize one's life. Statuses refer to characteristics one is born with (ascribed statuses), such as age, class, race, and gender, or to positions one achieves, such as parent, occupation, income, and education. Some of those statuses have more prestige than others, and each status has a role attending it. In sociological lingua, a role is a set of expected behaviors, rights, and obligations. For example, one status a person might have is that of mother. Every society has a set of behavioral expectations about what duties and behaviors a mother should perform and what rights she has.

Institutions are arrangements of statuses, roles, and rules organized to meet the needs of a society; they include the economic system, legal system, government, religion, health care, education, and family. These institutions work together within a society to enable it to function for better or worse, and they connect to other societies in ways that produce historical events and political movements.

Because these structures are composed of and run by humans, they are dynamic, not static. The prevalence and importance of various statuses and institutional arrangements ebb and flow over time, influencing our lives in a myriad of ways. In fact, at times their influence is so pervasive, so taken for granted, that frequently we are oblivious to their presence and impact on us.

Growing up, you may have thought that all your decisions sprang solely from your unique individual characteristics, but they were also guided and constrained by these other social structures. Nevertheless, a structural approach does not imply that people lack agency or that they respond mechanistically to forces beyond their control. On the contrary, every individual is responsible for the choices she or he makes in life, but not everyone is presented with the same menu of options. A poor boy growing up in rural Arkansas will not have the same options as a wealthy lad in East Hampton, New York. A woman growing up in an earlier historical era faced a different set of options than does a woman growing up today. A Native American living on a reservation has different options than an African American in Atlanta. These menus of options are created by the structural forces beyond the individual's control. The individual still shapes strategies for managing his or her life within those constraints, and experiences the consequences of the choices made from among the options available, or perceived to be available, to him or her.

Taking a structural approach does not imply that we will have totally explained all the causes of certain behaviors, but it will provide a more detailed and realistic approach to understanding family styles. An endless number of structural or systemic factors impact families. I won't be able to cover all of them, and some have more import for certain ethnic groups than others. The main structural or systemic factors that I will consider can be classified in three large categories: economic, demographic, and historical-legal factors.

Economic Factors

Economic factors can be macro (broad society-wide) or micro (individual or group-level), and sometimes they overlap. Macroeconomic factors include transformations in the occupational structure of the economy (that is, whether the society is largely agricultural, industrial, or service-oriented in the types of jobs offered) and changes in income and wealth distribution throughout society. These macro-level factors are beyond the control of any one individual, but they make certain individual or group behaviors more likely to occur. Microeconomic factors are those related to the individual or group. For instance, what are the specific income and educational levels of an ethnic group? What occupations are prominent among individuals within a certain ethnic group?

Occupational Structure

If the United States had remained a less-developed agricultural society, we would observe different family trends than we do in an industrial or postindustrial society. Because of their high need for farm labor and reduced need for higher education, agrarian societies are usually associated with earlier marriage, higher birthrates, and larger households (Oropesa, 1997). In addition, infant and child mortality rates are higher in less-developed countries. Thus, families feel the need to produce more children, knowing that only a portion of them is likely to survive to adulthood. In one study of a West African tribe, Ukaegbu (1993) found that women who had lost none of their children had an average of three children, but women who had already lost two children to death, had an average of nearly seven live births; apparently, women who had experienced the death of a child overcompensated for their loss through more future births.

Development, on the other hand, leads to a reduced need for labor and an increased need for education. Laws mandating compulsory education and a minimum age for employment usually accompany development (Oropesa, 1997). Therefore, families need fewer children, and the country's fertility rate declines as education, income, and occupational status rise (Gonzales, 1998). An onlooker might interpret the higher fertility rate in one country as evidence that that culture highly values children and conversely assume that a lower fertility rate reflects a lower social valuation of children. One could, however, just as easily interpret the lower fertility rate to mean that a culture values its children more; the people have fewer offspring and invest more time, money, and education in each one. The point is that major changes in the birthrate are less a result of a change in values and more likely a response to economic changes. (Chapter 3 will illustrate in greater detail how America's family trends have been affected by changes in its economic and occupational structure.)

Income and Wealth Distribution

Although a country's class structure is not a visible physical structure, most people would not deny its existence and impact on their lives. People are organized in a class structure based on income and occupation. This class structure does not *determine* one's outcomes. That is, not every member of the working class is similar to every other working-class member, but a higher likelihood exists that they will have more characteristics and experiences in common with one another than with upper-class members. For instance, working-class members, on average, have a lower life expectancy, marry earlier, and have more children than middle-class members. They are also more likely paid hourly wages, have fewer employment benefits, and have less flexibility in their work schedule. Not every single working-class person will exhibit these lifestyle characteristics, but each has a higher probability of doing so.

Income and wealth are not synonymous. Income refers to any money (usually salary, but it can include public assistance, child support, social security, etc.) regularly coming into a household. As you can see from Table 2.1, income is not distributed equally across racial groups. The median household incomes for Black, Hispanic, and American Indian households are considerably less than White median household income. These income differentials are in part due to differences in education and occupation, but they are also due to differences in household and family structure. Higher rates of nonfamily households, found among Whites and African Americans, and higher rates of single-parent households, as found among African Americans, Native Americans, and some Hispanic groups, reduce median household income.

Wealth, on the other hand, comprises the assets one holds, such as real estate, stocks, and bonds; savings; businesses; and other property. Two families may have the same yearly income of $40,000, but they may not have the same wealth. If families have wealth in addition to income, they are more protected if trouble comes knocking. If a family member loses his or her job, encounters ill health, or experiences a natural disaster, that family's assets will cushion the fall.

Wealth inequality among racial groups is more severe than income inequality. For instance, in 2001 the median net worth of White families was $120,900, more than seven times that of families of color at $17,100 (United for a Fair Economy, 2004). The most prevalent form of wealth among American families, home ownership, is also less common among racial minorities (see Table 2.1). Although the 2002 ownership rates reflect increases over the past decade, these gains are weakened by mortgage foreclosures, which have also increased in the past few years, and by residential segregation, which weakens the effect of ownership by producing lower house values for racial minorities (Wellner, 2000). Moreover, past legal discrimination prevented people of color from obtaining other wealth-enhancing resources—such as education and high-paying jobs—that would have

Table 2.1 Median Household Income (2001)[a], Home Ownership (2002), and Poverty Rates (2000) by Race

	Median Household Income	*Percentage of Home Ownership*	*Percentage of Families in Poverty*
Non-Hispanic White	$46,702	74.5	8.0
Hispanic	$33,829	48.2	21.0
Black	$29,983	47.3	22.0
Asian & Pacific Islander	$55,474	54.7	10.8
American Indian & Alaskan Native	$32,143	54.6	25.9[b]

SOURCES: DeNavas-Walt & Cleveland (2002); U.S. Department of Commerce (2000e), Chapter 13

a. Median household income is based on a 3-year average, from 1999 to 2001.

b. The figure for American Indians and Alaskan Natives in poverty is based on a 1998 to 2000 average.

enabled them to save, invest, and transfer those assets to the next generation. Persistent inequalities in education and occupation, along with weakness in the current economy and rising costs of education and housing, continue to hinder wealth accumulation.

Income and wealth inequality have been increasing in recent decades. In 1980, the wealthiest 20 percent of the U.S. population received 43.7 percent of the nation's income; in 2000, its share had increased to 49.6 percent. During that same time period, the income share of the poorest 20 percent declined from 4.5 to 4.3 percent (Hurst, 2004). Because racial-ethnic minority groups disproportionately fall on the lower end of the class hierarchy, they have been more negatively impacted by the increasing inequality. For instance, in 2001, the bottom 20 percent of Black families took in 3.3 percent of Black income, whereas the bottom 20 percent of White families took in 4.8 percent (U.S. Department of Commerce, 2004).

Poverty

In 2001, 11.7 percent of the American population was in poverty, but, as you can see in Table 2.1, poverty is not randomly or equally distributed across the population. Contrary to common stereotypes of racial minorities, no racial-ethnic group has the majority of their population in poverty. But, on average, with few exceptions, racial minorities consistently have poverty levels two to three times higher than White poverty levels. Therefore, family trends associated with poverty will be more prevalent among racial minority groups.

Low income is highly correlated with a number of family structures and trends. Single-mother families have higher rates of poverty than do single-father families, who in turn have higher rates of poverty than do two-parent families. In addition, lower-income households are more likely to have extended family members living with them and to have higher birthrates, particularly nonmarital and teen births. Commonly, research finds that socioeconomic status and marital stability are positively related. That is, in general, families with higher socioeconomic standing experience more satisfaction, less divorce, and less violence (Eshleman, 2003). Again, it is not that divorce, family violence, single-parent households, and so on are nonexistent among middle- and upper-class families, just that their rates of occurrence are lower.

Education

Educational levels obviously impact the types of jobs that people can access, the kind of lifestyle they will lead, and the opportunities they can provide their children. One's level of education also influences the timing of marriage, the likelihood of divorce, and the number and timing of births. Generally speaking, people with a college education, on average, marry later, divorce less, and have fewer children farther apart than do people with only a high school education.

Education and income are highly correlated; higher income is associated with higher levels of education. As you can see from Figure 2.1, educational levels vary by race. Hispanic Americans have the lowest educational levels and highest drop-out rates, whereas Asians have just the opposite. In both cases, the educational status they hold at the time of immigration plays a pivotal role in those percentages.

Although people of color are legally eligible for any occupation, the income and educational factors just discussed make certain occupational categories more prominent among certain racial groups. In addition, for many minority families, the relatively recent application of antidiscrimination policies has resulted in this being their first generation of college graduates and/or holders of previously prohibited occupations. Consequently, you will find that most racial-ethnic minority groups have higher percentages of their workers in blue-collar or service-sector jobs—which pay less than professional—and in government jobs, such as the military, than do White Americans.

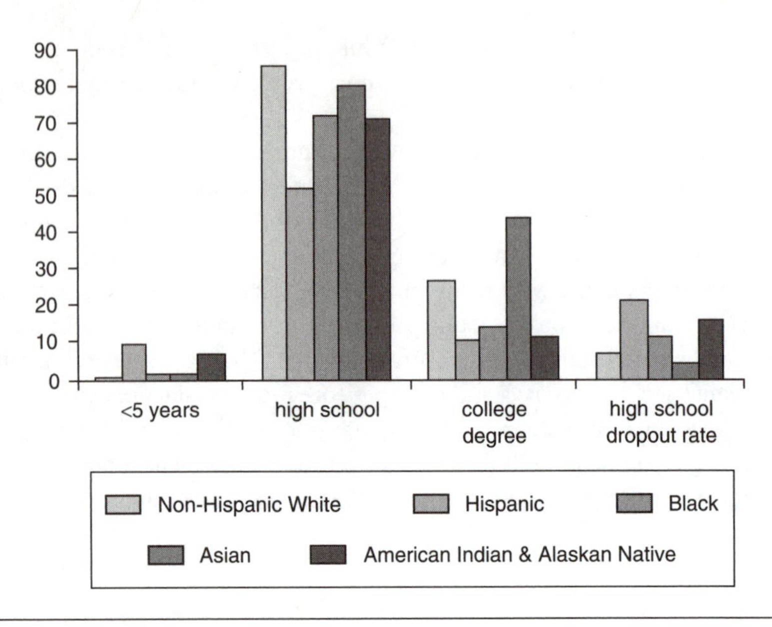

Figure 2.1 Educational Attainment Levels by Race for Population 25 Years or Older, 2000 (in percentages)

SOURCES: Cheeseman Day (2003); U.S. Department of Commerce (2003c), Tables 40, 43, 47

Demographic Factors

Demographic factors include vital statistics, such as the sex and age structure of a population, and the geographical distribution of various ethnic groups.

Sex Ratio

The sex ratio is usually expressed as the number of men for every 100 women in a society or group. A sex ratio of 106 indicates that men outnumber women, whereas a sex ratio of 97 reveals more women than men, and 100 indicates a balanced sex ratio. The sex ratio fluctuates throughout history and varies by country, and by age and ethnicity within a country. For instance, until World War II men outnumbered women in America, largely due to the significant role immigration played in the country's formation. Also, women frequently died in childbirth. Since then, health care and immigration patterns have changed, and today the sex ratio favors women, which is the case for the majority of countries around the world.

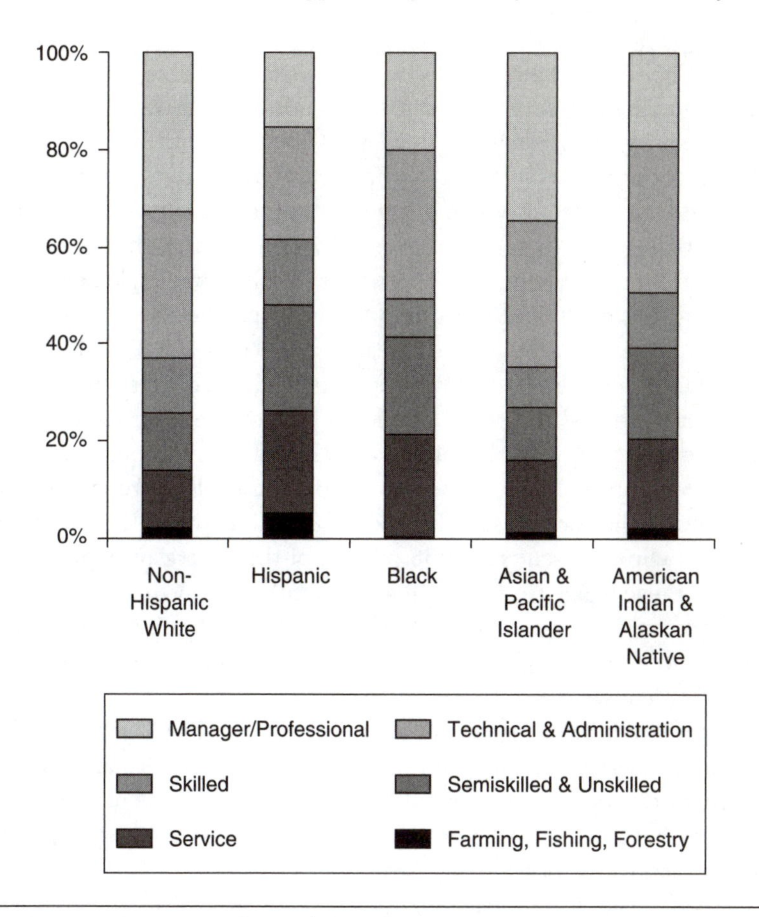

Figure 2.2 Occupational Distribution by Race, 1998

SOURCE: AmeriStat (2000)

Although the nation's current sex ratio (96.3 in 2000) favors women, the sex ratio varies by racial-ethnic group within the United States. In general, African Americans have significantly more women than men, whereas many Asian and Latino groups have more men than women. The former is due to higher mortality rates among Black men, and the latter is due to higher rates of immigration among Asians and Latinos.

When the sex ratio is imbalanced, which it is most of the time, family trends are impacted. When the sex ratio is highly skewed, one might conceivably find less marriage, more polygamy, more same-sex relationships, and/or more interracial marriage. Sex ratios and their effect on gender relations will be discussed more thoroughly in Chapter 6. Their effects on interracial marriage will be discussed in Chapter 13.

Age Structure

The age structure reveals how a population is distributed along the age scale; it tells us whether a group is relatively young or old. The age structure of a country or a specific group is impacted by birthrates, improvements in health, and immigration. When birthrates rise for a number of years, such as they did between 1946 and 1962 (the Baby Boom years), the median age of a country is shaped by the disproportionate number of people born in those years. Improvements in life expectancy will age the population as well. In 1900, life expectancy was 47 years; today it is 77 (U.S. Department of Commerce, 2003b). Because immigrants tend to be young adult age and have higher fertility, they tend to keep a country's age structure younger. Therefore, in 1900, when birthrates were higher, health poorer, and immigrants a larger proportion of the population, the median age was about 23. Today, with the increases in life expectancy and the aging of the Baby Boomers (who represent about 38 percent of the American population and currently range in age from early 40s to mid-50s), the median age of the U.S. population in 2000 was 35.3. That will probably continue to rise as the Boomers continue to age and health improvements continue to lead to life expectancy gains.

The age structure of specific racial-ethnic groups is illustrated in Table 2.2. Hispanics, American Indians, and Pacific Islanders, in particular, have young age structures, and every group but Whites and Asians have nearly one third of their population under 18. The White elderly population is two to three times the size of the other groups' elderly.

The differences in age structure among ethnic groups are due to the same factors mentioned earlier: variation in life expectancies, fertility rates, and rates of immigration. Relative to Whites, racial-ethnic minorities have higher

Table 2.2 Median Age by Race, 2000

	Median Age	*Percentage Under 18*	*Percentage 65 and Over*
Non-Hispanic White	38.6	22.6	15.0
Hispanic	25.8	35	4.9
Black	30.2	31.4	8.1
Asian	32.7	24.1	7.8
Pacific Islander	27.5	31.9	5.2
American Indian & Alaskan Native	28	33.9	5.6

SOURCE: U.S. Department of Commerce (2000a), Quick Table–P1, Matrices PCT3 and PCT4

fertility and immigration rates. Therefore, over the next few decades, with the aging of the Baby Boomers, the proportion of the American population in the 10-to-24-year age group will decline to about 16 percent; but because of their younger age structure, racial-ethnic minorities will make up a disproportionate share of that 16 percent (Pabon, 1998).

As with the sex ratio, the age structure impacts social and family trends as well. With an older age structure, elders are present to grandparent, and more three- or four-generation families exist. An older age structure is associated with higher median income for the group, because people in their 30s, 40s, and 50s have usually been in the workforce longer and received some raises and promotions. (Obviously, if the median age of a population became very old, lower median incomes could result because elderly people experience more non-income-producing years at the end of their lives.) The older age structure also leads to more family households without children (because their children have reached adulthood) and more elderly living alone.

On the other hand, populations with younger age structures have more "economic burdens" that need care and schooling and are not yet earning wages. Younger age structures are usually associated with higher marriage, divorce, fertility, and crime rates because a greater percentage of the population is in the age range when those behaviors are more common. Hence, one of the factors contributing to the increased divorce rate in the 1970s and its slight decline in the 1990s is the Baby Boomers' coming of marrying (and divorcing) age in the 1970s and 1980s, and aging beyond the peak marriage and divorce years in the 1990s.

Geographic Distribution

The U.S. population is not spread evenly across the states. Natural resources, economic development, climate, social connections, and so on make some parts of the country more residentially attractive than others. As you may suspect by now, racial-ethnic groups vary also in their geographic distribution in the United States. California and Hawaii are the most racially diverse states in the nation, whereas states in the Northeast, such as Vermont and New Hampshire, are the least diverse, with only about 3 percent of their populations being people of color.

Various social and economic trends vary by region. When a national recession occurs, for instance, not all parts of the country experience it to the same degree. Certain occupations or industries, such as the computer or auto industry, may be more severely impacted than others, and those industries may be more concentrated in certain regions. If certain ethnic groups live in regions suffering from an economic downturn, then those ethnic groups will exhibit higher rates of family trends associated with unemployment and/or poverty.

Also, certain regions have higher costs of living than others; therefore, average salaries are frequently higher in those regions than they would be for equivalent work in other regions. For instance, on average, salaries are higher in New York ($44,923 in 2002) or Hawaii ($50,565) than in Mississippi ($31,690), because the costs of food and shelter are higher in those areas (U. S. Department of Commerce, 2002c). If larger proportions of certain racial-ethnic groups reside in those higher-salaried regions, their median income levels may appear better (although they may be able to purchase less with it) than those who reside in lower-salaried regions such as the South. African Americans and Hispanic Americans each have a large portion of their populations in the southern states, whereas Asian Americans are highly represented in the West and Hawaii.

Other family trends, such as divorce or nonmarital births, differ by region as well. For instance, the Bible Belt of the country, contrary to what one may presume, actually has the highest divorce rate, about 50 percent higher than the national average (Harden, 2001). The coastal areas and urban areas, such as New York and California, have higher rates of divorce than does the Midwest.

Within major geographical regions, populations are classified as central city, suburban, or rural, which are likewise associated with various social trends. In 1900, only 40 percent of American families resided in urban areas; but by the 1990s, 75 percent of all American families were urban residents. Referring to Table 2.3 again, you can see that people of color, on average, are more urbanized than White Americans, who tend to live in suburban areas, reflecting America's continued high rates of residential segregation by race.

A related regional issue is whether racial-ethnic group members reside in proximity (density of population) to one another or are more dispersed among the mainstream population. More dispersion will facilitate acculturation and intermarriage, which will be discussed more in Chapter 13.

Historical-Legal Factors

In addition to demographic factors, families are affected by historical events and legal constraints. Historical events often determine who immigrates and how easily they are incorporated into the society. For instance, the Gold Rush in the mid-1800s and the Industrial Revolution attracted many European immigrants who then found jobs more easily than did people who

Table 2.3 Metropolitan-Rural Residence by Race, 2002

	Central City	*Suburb*	*Nonmetropolitan*
Non-Hispanic White	21.1	56.8	22.1
Hispanic	45.6	45.7	8.7
Black	51.5	36.0	12.5
Asian & Pacific Islander	41.4	53.5	5.1
American Indian & Alaskan Native	—	—	—

SOURCE: U.S. Department of Commerce (2002a), Table 20.1; U.S. Department of Commerce (2002b), Tables 21 and 22

NOTE: Data for American Indians and Native Alaskans were not available in these reports.

arrived during recessions. War also has a pivotal impact on who emigrates and the timing of their emigration. The Mexican-American War, the Spanish-American War, the Korean War, the Vietnam War, and the Cuban Revolution, to name a few, brought Mexicans, Puerto Ricans, Cubans, Filipinos, Koreans, Vietnamese, Cambodians, Hmong, Thai, and Laotians into America in large numbers.

The 1960s were a pivotal decade in American race relations. Congress passed civil rights legislation declaring segregation laws unconstitutional. At the end of that decade, laws prohibiting interracial marriage were declared unconstitutional. In the mid-1960s, modifications to immigration laws allowed Asians and others from so-called Third World countries to immigrate. In addition, those revised immigration policies gave preference to two groups of people: skilled, monied, and/or educated people and relatives of current American residents. Therefore, people who have immigrated here since the mid-1960s, which includes the majority of Asian Americans, avoided the earlier restrictions that would have limited where they could live and work and whom they could marry.

Manner of Entry

Sociologist Robert Blauner (1994) asserts that the manner of entry into this country greatly influences a racial-ethnic group's social and economic outcomes. Specifically, racial-ethnic groups arriving by force, conquest, or annexation will more likely have legal restrictions—related to jobs, education, residence, culture, and political rights—imposed upon them by the mainstream group than will groups who arrive by choice. Hence, those former groups end up concentrated in the least advanced sectors of the economy.

Applying this to the American case, we see that Native Americans and African Americans were incorporated into America by annexation and forced immigration. I will discuss specific restrictions on each racial group in Chapters 9 through 12, but to briefly illustrate, at least eight generations of Africans experienced the restrictions of slavery in America, which lasted more than 200 years in this country, before they were legally Americans. Several more generations of African Americans experienced Jim Crow restrictions, which limited occupational, educational, residential, and marital opportunities for another century. The effects of such restrictions linger long beyond their revocation.

The experience of people who arrive in a country by choice differs dramatically. Choice is not a clear-cut term; there are degrees of choice. People pushed out of their original country by war, political persecution, famine, and economic problems frequently arrive as "refugees." They have less "choice" than do immigrants who come to the United States for education or employment and decide to stay. Since 1820, at least 65 million people have immigrated to the United States. On average, their experience in the United States was a qualitatively better one than that of those who arrived by force.

To illustrate, many White ethnic groups, such as Irish, Italian, and Jewish Americans, arrived in America as immigrants from the mid-1800s through the early 1900s. They experienced much discrimination from Americans who were already here. People stereotyped them, refused to hire them, and sometimes murdered them. The 2002 film *Gangs of New York* portrayed some of the worst aspects of the conflict between Irish immigrants and the Europeans who were already here. Nevertheless, as a group, the Irish didn't experience widespread, long-term legal discrimination. They were able to establish churches, schools, newspapers, banks, and political parties. They could become citizens, vote, and run for office. They married freely, secured work, formed unions, and accumulated wealth. In addition, these ethnic groups, being lighter skinned, eventually became viewed as White and were more easily accepted and integrated.

Immigrants of color, who are more identifiable by their appearance or cultural traditions, experience more restrictions and discrimination than do White immigrants. However, due to their ability to choose the timing and location of their immigration and to self-select, even they are sometimes more successful than those who arrived by force. For instance, recent African immigrants who have entered the United States of their own accord have higher rates of educational attainment and income than do native-born African Americans. In 1997, 49 percent of African-born residents had a bachelor's degree, compared to 14 percent of American Blacks and 26 percent of American Whites (Wellner, 2000).

In addition to the fact that groups who arrive by choice avoid restrictions imposed by the native population, they are more likely than people incorporated by force to *desire* to be in the United States. Desire alone makes them more receptive to the new culture. They are also more likely to have made preparations to ease their integration; that is, they might have contacts in the United States waiting to help them; they might bring assets (money, job skills, education) with them; or they may already have a job awaiting them.

Individuals with assets are frequently the ones who choose to come to the United States in the first place, particularly if they are traveling a far distance. Therefore, immigrants to America are often the "cream of the crop" of other countries, a phenomenon called the "brain drain." Many countries complain that America is siphoning off their best and brightest.

Finally, those who arrive freely can also leave freely. If their experience is a negative one—say, for instance, they find the American lifestyle disagreeable, or they can't find work or they fail school—they are more likely to depart than those who came by force or with less choice. Although it is difficult to ascertain exact numbers, one study estimated that about 20 to 25 percent of immigrants return to their country of origin (Borjas & Bratsberg, 1996). For those groups who can't leave or have no place to go, all of their members—the successful ones and the so-called "failures"—remain, resulting in that group's average measurements of success (frequently income and education) being lower.

Even immigrants by choice, however, have experienced restrictions on the kind and number of people who could enter the United States. Such restrictions affect the gender ratio and age distribution of a group. For instance, in general, immigrant populations tend to have more men than women and more young adults than elderly because young men are more likely to make the trip to look for economic opportunities. This was particularly true for early immigrant groups when the trip itself was horrendous. In addition, for a number of decades the United States instituted restrictions that prevented some ethnic groups from immigrating or, once here, from bringing family members into the country. (I will discuss such immigration laws within each racial-ethnic group's history chapter.)

Immigrant Status

Immigrant status, that is, being a foreign-born American, influences family trends too. In 2000, the foreign-born represented 11.5 percent of the U.S. population, higher than in recent decades but still below the 15 percent they represented in 1910. The majority of America's foreign-born population resides in 3 states: California, New York, and Texas. Forty percent of them have become citizens. Despite the fact that many foreign-born Americans reside in high-salaried states, the foreign-born as a group have higher poverty rates than the native-born (16 percent versus 11 percent in 2002). The foreign-born have lower educational levels; 34 percent do not have a high school certificate, compared to 16 percent of native-born. The fertility rates of the foreign-born are higher, so that of the 4 million U.S. births in 2001, the foreign-born accounted for 22.5 percent of them, twice their percentage in the population (Martin & Midgley, 2003). They also have lower nonmarital birthrates, lower divorce rates, and more extended family household rates. Foreign-born Americans also tend to be healthier, exhibiting lower adult and infant mortality rates. Immigrant women, in particular, are less likely to smoke, more likely to be married, and less likely to have teenage pregnancies (Eshleman, 2003).

In conclusion, many noncultural factors help to explain why families come in a wide variety of configurations. Although all families are impacted by these economic, demographic, historical, and legal factors, and must respond and adapt to them in one way or another, each racial-ethnic group's unique characteristics and experiences mix with these factors and result in a multiplicity of family forms and dynamics.

Resources

Books and Articles

Blauner, R. (1994). Colonized and immigrant minorities. In R. Takaki (Ed.), *From different shores: Perspectives on race and ethnicity in America* (2nd ed., pp. 149–160). New York: Oxford University Press.

Blauner explains in more detail the effect of manner of entry on the status of racial-ethnic minorities. Takaki's entire book is useful as well.

Glusker, A. (2003). *Fertility patterns of native- and foreign-born women: Assimilating to diversity.* New York: LFB Scholarly Publishing.

The author considers a number of structural factors in exploring changes in fertility rates due to immigration.

Grieco, E. M. (2003). *Remittance behavior of immigrant households.* New York: LFB Scholarly Publishing.

This book examines how the remittance behavior of migrants is related to the family reunification process.

Taylor, R. D., & Wong, M. C. (Eds.). (1997). *Social and emotional adjustment and family relations in ethnic minority families.* Mahwah, NJ: Lawrence Erlbaum.

Many of the articles in this collection of research on a variety of racial-ethnic families address the role of structural factors.

Videos

Lennon, T., & Zwonitzer, M. (Directors). (1998). The Irish in America: Long journey home [Motion picture]. United States: Buena Vista Home Entertainment. (Available at http://www.rottentomatoes.com/m/irish_in_america_the_long_journey_home/dvd.php?select=1)

This four-part, nearly 6-hour documentary covers Ireland's history up to the Potato Famine and then tracks the new Irish immigrants in America.

Window on immigration [Motion picture]. (2001). (Available from Insight Media Inc., 2162 Broadway, New York, NY 10024-0621, or at http://www.insight-media.com)

This 20-minute film explains how immigration policy has changed since 9/11.

Website

http://www.prb.org
The Population Reference Bureau website provides up-to-date information on demographic changes in the United States.

CHAPTER 3

A BRIEF HISTORY OF THE AMERICAN FAMILY

Every semester for the last 8 years in my family class I distributed a survey. Two of the questions read:

> The state of my family is: (circle one) poor, fair, good, excellent.
>
> The state of America's families is: (circle one) poor, fair, good, excellent.

Without exception, every semester, the majority of students rank their own families as good or excellent and the nation's families as poor or fair.

So I ask them to account for that discrepancy. Initially, they frequently respond that Marquette University (a university in the Jesuit Catholic tradition) students originate from quality families. I point out to them that this response pattern is replicated at the national level as well. When national surveys ask respondents to rate their family, school, or neighborhood and then compare it to the nation's families, schools, or neighborhoods, the outcomes consistently indicate that Americans are generally satisfied with their own condition but think that everyone else's is dismal. The other common explanation proffered is that the students are lying; they don't want to admit that their families are bad too. Okay, that's a possibility and one I can't easily test, though most students swear they're not lying.

So then I ask them whether they think American families are deteriorating or were they always poor or fair. The answers are not so clear this time; but frequently, many, if not most, think American families have worsened. Typically, they point to divorce, teen and nonmarital births, single-parent families, working moms, and kids in day care centers as evidence of deterioration.

Most of these indicators are higher than they were 50 years ago, but some are lower than they were 10 years ago. Americans often think the rates of violent crime, teen births, and divorce continue to skyrocket when in fact each has been declining for at least a decade. Other indicators have improved as well. As *U.S. News & World Report* pointed out in 1997, more children finish high school and go to college than did in the 1950s; a lower proportion of children live in poverty than in the 1950s; today's teens are much less likely to smoke, be involved in alcohol-related traffic accidents, or die of drug overdoses than in the 1970s; a higher percentage of families have plumbing and electricity than ever before; and both infant mortality and life expectancy have improved (Whitman, 1997; also Skolnick, 1991).

The American public's propensity to depend on media sound bites for their information about the country's state of affairs exacerbates the tendency to idealize past family life. People rely on the headlines instead of the whole story, and by their nature the media focus on the exceptional or sensational.

It's cliché but true that the dog biting the man would not be considered newsworthy but the rare situation of the man biting the dog would make the news.

In short, the way one perceives the state of American families is in part affected by how one conceives the past, to which point in history one chooses to compare the present, and how well one understands the information presented in the media. This will become more clear as we go through the following historical overview of American families.

American Families Through the Centuries

American families are not stagnant entities. Rather, fluid and dynamic, they have adapted to a swiftly forming country encountering major social and economic transformations. These transformations are beyond any one person's control; they may even be beyond one's consciousness. Yet individuals and families are impacted by them and inevitably respond to them. Individual and societal values change, sometimes precipitating these transformations, sometimes subsequent to them. Frequently, however, what is perceived as a value change may merely be an adaptation in the means by which one fulfills the same underlying value. For instance, the median age at first marriage has risen in the last 50 years. As you can see in Figure 3.1, in 1950, women were about 20 years old and men were about 23 when they first married. In 2003, women were about 25 and men were about 27 when they married. Some might interpret this as evidence that young people no longer value marriage; they postpone it as long as possible to fulfill their own individualistic interests. But if we look back to 1890, we find that women married at 22 and men at 26. Were they more selfish than people in 1950 too? Maybe, but the most reasonable explanation was that in 1890, many men had to wait to inherit land before they could establish their own families. Others were immigrants who needed to settle before they could send for a wife. But in 1950, the post–World War II economy was such that men could obtain a decent-paying job and establish a family immediately after high school. In 2002, young people, women included this time, needed more education to ensure financial stability sufficient to marry. The underlying value remained constant; people want to start their family lives on the best financial footing possible. But the means to that end keep shifting. As we go through the history of American family life, keep in mind that societal forces, such as the economy, political events, and technological development, interact with human needs to produce various family forms and practices.

For simplicity's sake, I divide American history into three economic eras—agricultural, industrial, and service. These eras have no distinct time

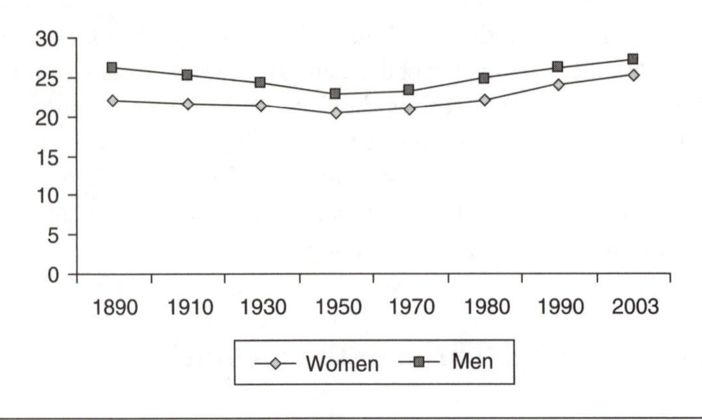

Figure 3.1 Median Age at First Marriage by Gender, 1890 to 2003

SOURCE: Fields (2004)

boundaries; the country gradually transitioned from one to another. For practical purposes, however, we can say that the agricultural era largely coincided with the colonial period in America, from the 1500s through the 1700s. Industrialization began in the early 1800s and experienced its demise by the 1970s, when manufacturing jobs were supplanted in significant numbers by service occupations.

The Agricultural Era (Colonial Period 1500 to 1800)

Even in the agricultural period, America was racially and ethnically diverse. At the beginning of this era, several million indigenous people lived throughout the territory. By the mid-1600s, Africans began entering the country primarily as slaves, and the Europeans who immigrated were largely from northern Europe. By 1790, when the first census was taken, Blacks were more than 16 percent of the U.S. population. The number of Native Americans had been greatly reduced through disease and fighting, so they were less than 13 percent of the population (Schaefer, 2004). The Europeans battled for political dominance and territory, and the English won. As the Europeans confiscated more Native American land, other Europeans were encouraged to immigrate for low-priced, sometimes free, plots of land. Near the end of this period, the American Revolution occurred, and the country changed in status from a British colony to the self-governing United States of America.

Most colonists made their living in agriculture, either by owning and farming land or working on someone else's. The majority of colonists would have been considered self-employed but fairly poor. Wages were not a significant part of the economy at this time, because most colonists ate what they grew and made their clothes and other products. They didn't need to purchase nearly as much as we do today, and frequently they could barter for commodities they needed. Their health was poor by today's standards. Life expectancy was about 45. Mortality rates (death rates) were high at most ages, especially infancy.

In these tumultuous times, a shortage of women resulted in high numbers of single men. Those who married formed what today's sociologists would call *co-provider* families. Essentially, the household was a place of production. Each member's labor was valued, as it helped to sustain the family. Although this was clearly a patriarchal society, with men having more legal power than women, wives' labor was valued as an economic contribution to the survival of the household as was the husbands'. Men sought strong, skilled wives who could make the journey across country and/or endure the rigors of a low-tech farming life. A gendered division of labor existed, with men usually plowing and planting the fields and hunting, and women tending gardens and chickens, processing foods, and milking cows. To bring in some cash, women and children often did piecework, such as sewing items for sale, in the home.

In such an economy, households were large, but not because they were multigenerational. In fact, contrary to popular myths, multigenerational extended households have never been a common phenomenon in the United States. The reasons should be obvious by now: People didn't live long, and the largely immigrant population was relatively young, as most elders remained in their country of origin. Once here, many families moved again, either west of the Mississippi River or from rural to urban areas. In those migrations as well, it was more likely the young who made the journey and the elders who remained in the rural areas.

Households were large because of high birthrates and the common practice of taking in non-related people. Families gave birth to many children for several reasons: First, they needed children's labor on the farm; second, high infant mortality rates meant a high probability that several of one's children would not survive to adulthood; and third, birth control was rudimentary or nonexistent. Also, families commonly took in "strangers"—boarders, hired hands, slaves, or servants; other people's children hired as apprentices; or people for whom institutions had not yet been invented, such as orphans, the ill, and "ne'er do wells."

Although households were large in terms of members, most American houses were small, only one or two rooms that served an array of functions. At one hour, people might cook and dine in a room, and the next hour sleep there. Privacy was scarce within the family as well as in the community.

Everyone knew what everyone was doing, and if someone violated social norms, punishment was public as well. The stocks, branding, dunking, and whipping were common ways of publicly shaming deviants.

During these centuries, childhood was short, due either to death or to taking on adult responsibilities early. It is estimated that about 10 percent of children died in infancy (one third in poorer communities) and another third died before their 10th birthday (Mintz & Kellogg, 1988). Those who survived became economic contributors at an early age. Children were often regarded as adults at the age they would now be starting elementary school (Demos, 1970). Therefore, they often did farm chores, cared for younger siblings, or did piecework on the homestead. Preteens were commonly "put out" to apprentice or serve in wealthier homes. Children were exposed to "adult" behavior. In fact, they often accompanied parents to observe local hangings on a Friday night (Coontz, 1997).

Ironically, the parenting of children was in some ways more egalitarian than it is today. The abbreviated childhood meant neither parent spent as much time doting on each child's development as modern parents do. Moreover, the extra individuals in the household helped supervise or train the children. In addition, because fathers were viewed as owners of their children, if children exhibited unproductive behavior, the father—more than the mother—was held accountable. Since men were more likely than women to have an education, they were the ones most likely to educate and train their children, particularly their sons. According to family historian Stephanie Coontz (1997), fathers emceed social gatherings, and the small amount of available child-rearing advice targeted fathers, not mothers.

Though divorce was uncommon (it was illegal until 1632), marriages were relatively short. Marriages were entered at relatively late ages (mid- to late 20s) and were frequently terminated by death, desertion, or separation; so the average length of marriage was about 12 years (Coontz, 1992; Laslett, 1971). Although arranged marriages were not practiced by the majority of families, some families advertised or hired matchmakers to locate spouses for their children. The basis for marriage was much more pragmatic than romantic. Unsupervised dating of the kind we know today was virtually nonexistent, but because of poor transportation, couples were occasionally allowed to "bundle," a practice allowing the couple to sleep together as long as one of them was encased in a duffle bag (Ingoldsby, 2003). Evidently, some of the sacks were threadbare, as it has been estimated that about one third of marriages were precipitated by a pregnancy (Demos, 1970).

Contrary to common perceptions of the past, single-parent families and remarriages creating step-relatives and half-siblings were also quite common, not because of divorce or nonmarital births, which are the main causes today, but because of the high mortality rates. It is estimated that in the late 1600s, most children in the colonies experienced single parenthood at some point in their childhood, and about one third lost both parents (Darrett & Rutman, 1979). In short, family life during the agricultural era was relatively unstable and unpredictable. One could not count on the presence or the support of one's siblings or parents into adulthood.

Of course, families varied along race and class lines. During these years, Native American families were declining rapidly due to disease and forced assimilation. The existence of African families was largely determined by slave masters' desires. (I will speak in more detail about Black American and Native American family histories in Chapters 9 and 10.) Life expectancy was longer and mortality rates lower among the middle classes, but this was a small segment of the American population.

The Industrial Era (About 1800 to 1970)

The Industrial Revolution started in Europe and then spread to America, accompanied by a number of other revolutions: technological, medical, and demographic. New scientific discoveries gave birth to new machinery, thus creating the Industrial Revolution, making wages the main source of income, and shifting residential patterns to the city. By 1900, 40 percent of the U.S. population lived in urban areas. These revolutions also produced new medical advancements, vaccines, and antibiotics, which, in turn, lowered the mortality rates of both infants and adults and lengthened life expectancy, thus creating exponential population growth and new stages in life development (childhood, adolescence, old age, retirement, grandparenting).

During this period, the United States expanded through land purchases and annexations to encompass most of North America and several islands off the continent. One of the largest additions was the annexation of half of Mexico after the 1848 Mexican-American War. This and the 1898 Spanish-American War introduced large numbers of Latinos into the United States. Two large waves of immigration also occurred during the industrial era, adding at least 38 million people to the United States. Although the vast majority of these immigrants were Europeans, from the mid-1800s through the early 1920s a significant number of Asians also entered the country. The Civil War and the end of slavery occurred in the 1860s, but they were followed by another century of legal segregation. Although new jobs proliferated with the Industrial Revolution, most of them went to new immigrants, rather than to the newly freed slaves who had resided and labored in America for generations. Two major world wars were also fought, with the United States on the winning side each time, thus catapulting America into a major geopolitical player and leading some observers to call the 20th century the century of "American Empire" (Smith, 2003).

Families reluctantly accommodated themselves to these rapid, sometimes painful, transformations in the lives to which they were accustomed. Many who had made their livelihood in farming and had expected their children would do the same were displaced by technological advancements that increased agricultural production while eliminating the need for so much human labor. If these displaced people wanted to survive (and most of them did), men who had seen themselves as autonomous, their own bosses, had to move to the city, where they attempted to sell their labor to new manufacturers in what seemed to them alienating working conditions. At first, women and children, especially among new immigrants, took similar jobs, though they were paid less. It is estimated that in a number of cities, children contributed 20 percent of family income (Mintz & Kellogg, 1988). Production became increasingly separated from the home, and the home became viewed as one's private haven in a dog-eat-dog world.

Consequently, a number of changes slowly occurred within American families. First, with the growth of unions, which fought successfully for increased wages and reduced working hours, many male laborers could make enough to support a family. Child labor laws were passed in the late 1930s to prevent children from working under harsh conditions. A mandatory public school system developed to teach new generations enough skills to obtain jobs in this new occupational structure. Eventually, children were considered children at least to the age of 16, when they could lawfully drop out of school. These social and economic changes transformed the children's role in their families from "economic contributors" to "economic burdens." Thus, childhood became viewed as a critical period of development, frequently divided into psychosocial stages: infant, toddler, preteen, adolescent, and so on.

The separation of work from the home, and the rise in wages, meant that many families became single-provider families. By the 1960s, about 60 percent of families were able to subsist on one income. More important, the single-provider family became the idealized version of the family; that is, most families strived to achieve that status. Wives and husbands both wanted to be able to say that the husbands made enough money to allow the wives to stay home to do unpaid domestic labor and socialize the children. But many families, disproportionately people of color and new immigrants, could not afford the luxury of one income.

Obviously, this shift in economic provision affected gender roles and responsibilities. Men's role in the family narrowed to the "breadwinner," the provider. Outside the home most of the day, husbands became honored, sometimes distant, visitors to their families. Essentially, the men's realm became the public arena, whereas the women's became more private and domesticated. Although certain domestic chores became easier, the standards for cleanliness and decoration of homes rose. Although the washing machine and dryer made cleaning clothes easier, people now bought more clothes and changed them more frequently. Unlike the former outhouse, indoor bathrooms had to be cleaned and color-coordinated. The invention of the car enabled women to become chauffeurs and to run errands for products and services that heretofore had not existed or had been delivered to their door. Unlike their husbands' new line of work, women's new form of labor was not compensated, and frequently its economic value went unrecognized. Women were told that their work was a labor of love with intangible rewards that would arrive later.

The increase in life expectancy and the separation of paid work from the home led paradoxically to both stabilizing and destabilizing trends. The potential length of marriage increased; people could celebrate silver and golden anniversaries. Families were generally more stable in the sense that they could count on their family members being around to support each other for longer periods of time. Fewer husbands and wives were widowed at early ages, and the need for orphanages eventually disappeared. Grandparents more often lived to see their grandchildren reach adulthood (currently, about half of grandparents have at least one adult grandchild [Bengtson & Harooytan, 1994]). People could plan for the future and reasonably assume their plans might actually materialize.

On the other hand, if a marriage was unhappy, the partners could no longer expect that they might be released from their marital discomfort through death (preferably their spouse's). As young adults relocated for work and no longer had to wait to inherit the family farm, they had more control over whom they married. And as it became clear that they might be with their spouses for a long period of time, attraction and mutual interests rose in importance on the list of mate selection criteria. But as companionship and romance became the primary motivations for marriage, the divorce rate gradually increased.

The prevalence of various family structures shifted. Single-parent households decreased with the decline of widowhood. And as life expectancy increased, multigenerational family households became somewhat more common, though they never represented a majority of households. At their peak in the mid- to late 1800s, the proportion of extended-family households reached 20 percent (Coontz, 1992). Most American households were family households, as young people remained in their parents' home until they formed their own family households.

Between 1900 and 1970, the average size of the industrial-era household decreased from 4.6 to 3.11 (Fields, 2004). With the decline in infant mortality, parents could have fewer children and still feel relatively confident that most, if not all, of their children would survive to adulthood. And, since most families no longer had their own farms, they didn't require as much labor. These factors contributed to the decline in birthrates and also to the decline of non-relatives in the household. Having boarders in one's home continued into the 1900s as a way for many homemakers to contribute to household income, but the need for hired hands, apprentices, and servants decreased. Slavery ended in 1865, which decreased the number of non-relatives residing in the home as well (though having a maid clean one's house weekly was common through the 1950s). Finally, other institutions, such as old-age homes, hospitals, orphanages, and prisons began accommodating people who otherwise might have been cared for by families.

Home and family life became more private. Ironically, though household population declined, houses became larger with more rooms and hallways separating those rooms, so the idea that kids could and should sleep separately from parents and eventually from one another developed. Old holidays, such as Christmas, Easter, and Thanksgiving, which frequently had been celebrated as a community, often in carnival fashion (Pleck, 2000), became private family gatherings. Wives prepared the house and cooked, while husbands sat at the head of the table to carve the meat. New holidays, such as Mother's Day and Father's Day, developed to honor new family roles, reflect romantic values, and bring dispersed family members together. All holidays became more commercialized, and the family increasingly became a site of consumerism rather than production.

These changes peaked in the 1950s, following the Great Depression and World War II. The economic boom and various government subsidies that followed the war shaped family trends for a period of time. The GI Bill enabled more men to attend college, thus widening the education gap between men and women. The booming economy and the need to make up for time lost during the depression and war led to a jump in the marriage rate and to marrying at earlier ages. New Federal Housing Association housing subsidies and highway construction funds resulted in an explosion of inexpensive suburban housing, which in turn facilitated "White flight" to the "burbs" and increased birthrates. Hence, the Baby Boomers, those born between 1946 and 1962, were largely a result of the postwar economic boom, and they currently account for 38 percent of the American population.

In addition, the divorce rate ebbed and flowed with political and economic upheavals, as you can see in Figure 3.2. The rate increased briefly after World War II (as seen in the 1950 rate), declined again in the 1950s (reflected in the 1960 rate) due to the improved economic situation and the fact that more women were economically dependent on their husbands, unable to consider divorce feasible even if they wanted to. Although the lower divorce and higher marriage and fertility rates of the 1950s are frequently proffered as proof of family values, it must be remembered that the conditions of the 1950s were unusual.

In many ways, the civil rights movement, the feminist movement, and the hippies of the 1960s were reactions to these changes. The 1950s were good for many White families, but racial segregation in jobs, schools, and public facilities was still enforced. Residential segregation increased with the movement of White families into these newly developing bedroom communities. Prominent women in these suburban communities complained that they felt undervalued, isolated, and disadvantaged educationally and economically. Youth, some of whom joined the hippie movement, saw their families as materialistic, their dads as uninvolved at home, and their mothers as depressed. Songs about the "ticky-tacky, little boxes" (houses in the suburbs) and about fathers who didn't have time for their kids ("Cat's in the Cradle") merged with anti–Vietnam War protests. The American public rode into the 1970s on the tails of these political movements.

The Service Era (Since the 1970s)

The service era derives its name from the fact that throughout the 1900s, more and more jobs were created in what is called service-sector occupations, such as retail, policing, banking, medicine, computers, social service, janitorial, and so on. Although the transition to service jobs began in the

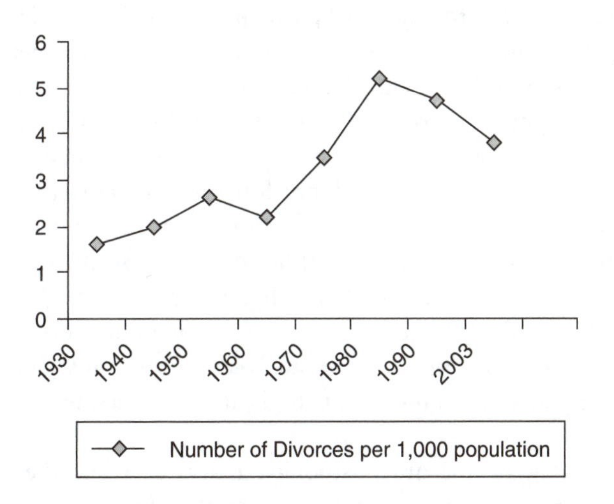

Figure 3.2 U.S. Divorce Rate, 1930 to 2003

SOURCES: Clarke (1995); U.S. Department of Health and Human Services (1988, 2003)

early 1900s, the process accelerated in the 1970s due to several political and economic events. The 1973 oil crisis increased the price of oil; changes in government policy favored globalization (the movement of jobs and money to other countries); and automation increased the use of computers and other technology and reduced the need for factory workers. The U.S. auto and steel industries declined greatly during the 1970s and 1980s.

Once again, like the transition from agriculture to industrial work, the transition from industrialization to service was a painful period that hasn't yet ended. In the first few years of the new millennium, America lost 2.5 million jobs; 90 percent of them were manufacturing jobs (Uchitelle, 2003). Unions have lost membership and influence. The relationship between worker and employer has eroded. Job security is nearly nil. In the 1940s and 1950s, men could graduate from high school or, for that matter, drop out of high school and still obtain a decent job making enough money to support a family; that is no longer the case. Many manufacturing workers who lost their jobs were forced to retire or re-skill for new service jobs that paid half of their previous hourly wage. It's true that some service professions pay high salaries, but those require more years of schooling, and American higher education is neither mandatory nor free.

Moreover, compared to the 1960s, men's real wages (that is, wages taking account of inflation) have declined. Even though a worker in the 2000s takes home a larger salary than did a worker in 1960, the 2000 salary doesn't purchase as much as the 1960 salary. Also, because service jobs are less physical and more mental, women can do those jobs more easily. These changes have again required families to adjust, whether they wanted to or not.

Consequently, in the last 40 years, we have seen a resurgence of some family patterns prevalent in the agricultural period and the continuation of a number of patterns from the industrial era. Most notably, co-provider (now known as dual-income) families once again are the majority. The percentage of married women in the labor force is now more than 60 percent (as compared with 43 percent in 1970). Although median family income has increased over the past few decades, it has only done so because women are putting in more work hours. Subsequently, gender roles are being renegotiated. Women are sharing men's provider roles; men, however, have exhibited more reticence in adopting domestic roles (as we will see in Chapter 6), thus precipitating a rise in the use of child care providers, maid services, and restaurants.

Second, young people are postponing marriage while they obtain the education necessary to provide financial stability for their families. About 27 percent of the population in 2000 had never been married (Kreider & Simmons, 2003). (Although this is higher than the 22 percent in 1950, it is lower than the 36 percent who had not yet married in 1900.) Subsequently, women are postponing childbirth by an average of 5 years. In 1980, women ages 20 to 24 had the highest birthrates. By the late 1990s, the majority of women were giving birth between the ages of 25 and 29 (AmeriStat 2003a).

Finally, single-parent households have risen again, representing a higher percentage of all American households now than they did half a century ago. In 1940, female-headed households represented 9.8 percent of all households (10.8 percent of family households); by 2000 they represented 12.2 percent of all households (18 percent of family households). Male-headed households, however, have not increased much as a proportion of all households, remaining stable at slightly over 4 percent (Fields, 2003).

Unlike in the agricultural era, today's single-parent households are precipitated by divorce and nonmarital births more often than by death. Women's increased access to paid labor has enabled unhappy wives to leave their marriages. Referring back to Figure 3.2, note that the divorce rate increased significantly in the 1960s and 1970s (peaking in 1980) but has since been declining. Nonmarital births, which will be discussed in greater detail in Chapter 5, have increased continuously throughout this period.

Other trends continue unabated. Household size has continued to drop over the last 25 years to 2.59 people in 2000. One factor has been that birthrates have dropped since the mid-1960s. The fertility rate reached its lowest point of 1.7 per woman of childbearing age in the 1970s. It has since risen a little to 2.1 (AmeriStat, 2003b), but it remains relatively low because working women reduce the number of births they have, and children's dependence on their parents has been extended into their mid-20s due to the need for college.

Nonfamily households have dramatically increased from 19 percent of all households in 1970 to 31 percent in 2000. These households are largely composed of marriage-postponing young adults or previously married elderly living alone or with non-related roommates or cohabiters. The number of elderly living alone has risen due to continued extensions in life expectancy.

Racial diversity also increased during the service era. Immigration laws modified in 1965 resulted in a shift in the racial composition of immigrants from mostly White European to "people of color"; that is, immigrants mostly from Asian and Latin American countries. More than merely reflecting a numerical increase, racial diversity became a more salient social issue as identity politics and multicultural education became more prevalent.

America is not unique in its experience. The service era trends outlined here typify those of many other developed countries as well. For instance, in Canada and many European countries, women now have higher rates of labor force participation than do American women. Consequently, age at first marriage for women is 25 to 30 throughout Europe. Whereas heterosexual cohabitation has increased in the United States, accounting for about 5 percent of all U.S. households, the 2000 cohabitation rates in European countries range from 8 percent in Portugal to 55 percent in Sweden. Divorce has increased in most countries, though the American divorce rate still ranks at the top. Although nonmarital births increased to about 33 percent of all U.S. births in 2000, this remains lower than the rates in most of Europe, where they represent up to 75 percent of all births. Divorce and nonmarital births have increased the proportion of single-parent families in most European countries as well. Fertility rates, which have fallen nearly 50 percent in the United States since the Baby Boom, are even lower in many European countries (Kiernan, 2004). Consequently, many European countries are experiencing a labor shortage and an aging population more severely than is the United States.

In sum, the vast majority of societies are in constant flux, forcing families to make subtle, sometimes sudden, adaptations. Even as I describe how a society does family, its way of doing it is changing. American families have responded to societal forces, sometimes unwittingly, other times grudgingly, complaining about how families just aren't the way they used to be while they attempt to hold tight to the old ways of doing things. For instance, even though most married women work outside the home now, many still try to single-handedly prepare the house and food for family holidays, even making the decorations by hand à la Martha Stewart. Most new millennium mothers are now advised to breastfeed their babies, despite the fact that during the 1950s, when most mothers were at home and could have breastfed more easily, formula was the popular method.

Eventually, to relieve the cognitive dissonance that occurs during these periods of transition, family members revise the way they think and feel about the changes. So some co-provider families have adjusted by making family gatherings potluck occasions, or by enlisting husbands' help, or by going to restaurants if they can afford it. Others recognize that divorce, although not the preferable resolution to a bad marriage, may have some advantages for unhappy or abused spouses and provide relief to children caught between inhospitable parents. Every change comes with its costs and benefits.

Taking a historical view "demythifies" family, enabling us to see that some of today's trends are reoccurrences of past trends and that family modifications are as much due to structural forces as they are to cultural values. Such a long-range perspective can help society deal more constructively with problems facing today's families.

Resources

Books and Articles

Coontz, S. (1997). *The way we really are.* New York: Basic Books.

Mintz, S., & Kellogg, S. (1988). *Domestic relations: A social history of American family life.* New York: Free Press.

Stacey, J. (1990). *Brave new families: Stories of domestic upheaval in late twentieth century America.* New York: Basic Books.

Videos

The changing American family: Decline or transition? [Motion picture]. (1997). (Available from Insight Media Inc., 2162 Broadway, New York, NY 10024-0621, or at http://www.insight-media.com)

This 30-minute video reviews some of the changes in the American family since industrialization.

Family [Motion picture]. (1999). (Available from Insight Media Inc., 2162 Broadway, New York, NY 10024-0621, or at http://www.insight-media.com)

This 53-minute video takes both a historical and cross-cultural look at family changes.

Website

http://www.census.gov/population/www/censusdata/hiscendata.html
The U.S. Census Bureau maintains decennial data since 1790 for population and housing.

CHAPTER 4

CROSS-CULTURAL COMPARISONS

Although this book is primarily concerned with families in the United States, it is useful to embed the discussion in a broader cultural context. Doing so builds awareness that the idealized American-style family is neither universal nor necessarily viewed as desirable by societies around the world. Moreover, because nearly 12 percent of the current American population originated in other societies, appreciation for the variety of family forms and processes in other contexts and understanding of their continued influence on families now in the United States is important.

Years of anthropological exploration have found that all societies develop family systems of one sort or another. Most of them have marriage as a basis for forming a family, but often it is not marriage as Americans know it. The marriage may be neither legal nor monogamous, and quite likely the marriage relationship does not play the central role in the family as it does in the United States.

Anthropologists have classified family or kin systems into several types. Two of concern here are *consanguineal* and *affinal.* In consanguineal (the root means "with blood") family systems, marriages are recognized but the married couple's relationship (the conjugal relationship) is less valued than are the biological relationships with extended family and children. The wife and husband are not considered independent individuals who marry for their own personal satisfaction; marriages serve the interests of the larger family, clan, and community as well. A person's relationships with one's parents, children, siblings, and extended family take priority over the marriage. Consequently, in consanguineal systems, extended family households, nonmonogamous marriages, and/or lack of co-residence between spouses are more common. For instance, the Nuer men in Sudan, a racial-ethnic group that has recently settled in significant numbers in Minnesota, traditionally sleep in men's huts separate from their wives' huts (Holtzman, 2000).

In affinal family systems, such as America's, the conjugal relationship is given priority. Marriage quality is valued. If a couple is not living together, the quality of their marriage is suspect. Child-rearing books and articles frequently advise parents that loving each other is the best thing parents can do for their children. For instance, in a recent *Wisconsin Women* magazine article on marriage counseling, a couple testified to the effectiveness of marital therapy. The wife stated, "We have learned [through a marriage enrichment program] to put our marriage first—over work, over hobbies, over the house, even over the kids" (Morrill, 2003).

Under such a conjugally oriented system, monogamy, spousal co-residence, and nuclear households are the norm. In most industrialized societies, marriage is now based on choice, voluntarily entered and ended, and motivated by emotional gratification of the couple. Although this creates a strong expectation and potential for companionship, intimacy, and personal fulfillment, it simultaneously creates a strong possibility for disappointment.

As you will see as we move through the text, racial-ethnic minorities lean more toward the consanguineal system than do White Americans, as evidenced in higher rates of extended households, arranged marriage, acceptance of polygamy, and single-parent households. Whether these trends are due to the retention of "old country" values and traditions or to the effects of discrimination and lower economic status in the United States remains under debate.

Social or Legal Marriage

When marriage exists without legitimation by law (what Americans might call *cohabitation*), it is a "social marriage." A number of tribal societies still lack bureaucracies that require licenses and fees for a marriage. In these societies, marriages usually occur when a couple cohabits after the performance of a social ritual. For instance, in Iroquois tradition, an exchange of corn bread and venison ratified the marriage.

Where social marriage is the norm, so is social divorce. That is, marriage termination may simply require that a spouse move out or a group of elders give approval. Although most Muslim societies now have developed bureaucracies that require legal marriages, traditionally a marriage could be terminated when the husband repeated "I divorce you" three times. Some countries, such as Ghana and Kenya, still allow the couple to choose whether they want to marry according to social custom or civil law. Civil law marriages may have different rules, such as prohibiting polygamy. In Ghana, 80 percent of couples choose to marry under social custom (Takyi, 2003).

Marriage Types and Choices

Whether social or legal, marriage can take several forms; I will focus on monogamy and polygamy. In monogamy, a person pairs with one other person. In polygamy, a man or woman pairs with two or more people. In 1967, George Murdock analyzed the marital structures of 1,157 societies. He found that monogamy was the sole permitted form of marriage in about 15 percent of the societies. Polygamy, on the other hand, was permitted in 85 percent of the societies. In nearly half of the societies that permitted polygamy, however, it was practiced in less than 20 percent of the marriages.

Since then, polygamy appears to be declining even more. For instance, a recent study in Kenya reported that in 1998, 16 percent of married Kenyan women were in polygamous marriages. That was a decline from 30 percent in 1977 (Wilson, Ngige, & Trollinger, 2003).

Most people associate polygamy with a man having several wives. Indeed, that is the most common form of polygamy, but the term itself means one person having several spouses. If a man has several wives, the specific term is *polygyny* (many women). If a woman has several husbands, the correct term is *polyandry* (many men). Frequently, in polygyny the husbands are free to choose among unrelated women for their wives, although one form of polygyny, called "sororal polygyny," encourages a man to marry a set of sisters. People may assume, therefore, that polyandry arises in a society where women have more power, and the women choose among men for their husbands. Most of the time, however, polyandry occurs within a patriarchal setting; the women have little to no choice about their spouses. In fact, sometimes, the husbands come as a package, as in "fraternal polyandry," when a woman marries a set of brothers. The eldest brother chooses the wife; the youngest brother may be just a toddler.

Although most Americans frown upon polygyny, thinking it degrades women or that it is contrary to Christian religious teachings, it has some practical aspects; it helps to distribute the workload of child rearing and housekeeping among several people. Hence, some women prefer, or at least see some benefits to, a polygynous system (Sorensen, 1996). The first wife usually has some authority over the new wives as well (Ingoldsby, 1995b). Polygyny also serves to keep divorces down. If a man is dissatisfied in his marriage, rather than leaving his wife (who in many societies would have difficulty remarrying or being self-sufficient), he can still support her and take a new wife. Polygyny also provides men with regular sexual outlets when there are societal taboos on having sex during a lengthy breastfeeding period.

Polyandry is most common in societies with high levels of poverty, where families have only small plots of land upon which to survive. In the Tibetan and Pahari societies of the Himalayas, polyandry is practiced primarily for that reason. Fraternal polyandry produces fewer children, on average, than would be produced if each brother married individually. If each brother inherited a piece of their family's land and set up separate households, each piece of land would be too small to sustain each family. And with each generation thereafter, the problem of limited resources would escalate. Marrying a set of brothers allows the extended family to keep the land intact and produce fewer heirs.

In America, the Morman church (the Church of the Latter-day Saints) allowed the practice of polygamy until 1890. Since then, splinter groups continue the practice in towns along the Utah-Arizona border and other western states. *Newsweek* reported that an estimated 20,000 to 50,000 people currently live in polygamous families. These cases, however, belie the fact that for most of American history monogamy has been both the idealized and legal form of marriage. Therefore, people who emigrate from countries where polygamy is allowed must either practice monogamy or social polygamy here.

Marriage as a Family Affair

Even in the United States, where individualism is highly valued, people recognize that, to one degree or another, the marriage of two individuals also involves family, friends, and public policies that support or hinder the union. In many other countries, the involvement of these "outside" characters is more overtly acknowledged through the family's participation in arranging the marriage, a formal exchange of resources, and the societal definition of appropriate marriage partners.

Arranged Marriages

Arranged marriages frequently reflect the priority of consanguineal relations. Their use stems from the idea that entire extended families gain or lose in a marriage. In many societies, the new wife leaves her family to live and work with her husband's family; hence, leaving marital decisions to inexperienced youth might jeopardize the families' welfare (Wong, B., 1998). Love marriages also threaten the authority and influence that senior family members have over their adult children (Stockard, 2002).

In fact, the marriage is so much about the extended family that it sometimes doesn't matter whether the bride and groom are present for the ceremony. Holtzman (2000) tells one story of a Nuer man who had immigrated to Minnesota, but his family arranged a marriage for him to a woman in Sudan. When he arrived back in Sudan to marry and bring back his wife, he became busy meeting with friends and relatives, so the ceremony was held without him. Since it was an arrangement between the families, his presence was incidental.

The degree to which the young couple can influence mate selection varies extensively in arranged marriages. In some cases, the couple has met and decided that they like each other. They then approach their parents who contact the potential in-laws and make arrangements. In other cases, the parents may locate a number of suitable spouses, and the child picks from among them. In extreme cases, the couple, particularly the daughter, may have no say in the arrangement. Though uncommon now in China, "spirit weddings" posthumously wedded one unmarried deceased man with a live woman. This wedding enabled the deceased to produce a lineage (not biologically) and eventually enjoy the company of a spouse in the afterlife. For instance, Louise Leung Larson (1989) recorded her mother's childhood recollection of an uncle who had died at age 14.

> The girl who had been chosen to marry him came to live at the grandmother's house. There was an elaborate ceremony in which the girl, just a child of 13, married the *gway* (ghost) of the dead boy. She even had to escort the body to the grave. (p. 6)

An unusual form of mate selection is "bride capture." Originally, the groom literally kidnapped his bride, but in most current practice, the capture is similar to elopement or to a ritual acting out of a kidnapping. A number of groups now present in the United States, in particular the Hmong and the Romas (gypsies), practiced bride capture. In fact, it is believed that the American use of bridesmaids and groom's attendants are remnants of bride capture. The bridesmaids try to protect the bride, while the attendants try to help the groom steal her (Fielding, 1942).

Love marriages, most prevalent in developed countries, where life expectancy is longer, divorce more acceptable, and fertility lower (Medora, 2003), are also on the rise in less-developed countries. Nevertheless, arranged marriages of one sort or another still occur fairly frequently in Asia, the Middle East, Africa, and among immigrants from those countries who now reside in the United States. Some young couples prefer this method to American-style mate selection, which to them looks daunting and, given the divorce rate, unsuccessful (Lessinger, 1995).

Immigrants in America may use the Internet, newspaper advertisements, such as in *India Abroad*, or marriage brokers to locate spouses of the same ethnicity for their children. Although some immigrants search in their original country for a spouse, others feel the marriage will be more auspicious if their child marries someone who is both accustomed to American society and still retains their cultural traditions. For instance, in his memoir of immigration to Canada from India, Tara Singh Bains (Bains & Johnston, 1995) recounted how he convinced a young Sikh man to marry a Sikh woman from Canada rather than one from India. He argued persuasively that a Canadian-born Sikh girl would bring education and professional earnings to the marriage, she would not require training to adjust to life in Canada, and the boy would not have to sponsor the immigration of her relatives.

Exchange of Resources

The formal exchange of family resources is another indicator that marriage is a family affair. A *bride-price,* the most common exchange, is a set of goods or money paid by the groom's family to the bride's family, usually in recognition of the loss of labor the bride's family faces when their daughter leaves home. A *dowry* is paid by the bride's family either to the groom's family or to the bride and groom. In the latter case, it frequently remains the property of the bride (especially when it consists of gold jewelry), although the groom may use it. In countries where women have low value, low labor force participation, and few inheritance rights, this dowry provides both an inducement to a potential spouse and leverage to the wife in her marriage. In countries where polygyny is allowed, being able to offer a bride-price facilitates finding a wife when some men monopolize several wives.

In some countries, the dowry has become a status symbol. For instance, in traditional China, the dowry would be paraded with fanfare through the streets from the bride's home to the groom's (Stockard, 2002). The dowry can be burdensome to the bride's family, especially in poor countries, and the anticipation of this future burden is one factor contributing to female infanticide. In India, for instance, disappointment in the size of the dowry has resulted in the grooms' families returning, abusing, maiming, or killing the bride. Bumiller (1990) estimated that at least 1,000 such incidents (usually setting the bride on fire) were perpetrated per year in India during the 1980s. Therefore, a few countries have outlawed the dowry.

Although the bride-price has not posed as much of a problem as the dowry has in many countries, many families of daughters will search for a potential husband whose family can offer a large bride-price. If a husband pays a healthy bride-price and his wife dies, her family may be expected to provide another wife for him. Or, as among the Nuer of Sudan, if the wife's husband dies, she would become the wife of his brother or another of her husband's male relatives (Holtzman, 2000). A number of studies (Hortacsu, 2003; Wilson, Ngige, & Trollinger, 2003) indicate that the use and amount of bride-price are declining in some countries, such as in Africa and Turkey, due to decreased resources and the increased value of education.

These forms of exchange signify the joint rights and obligations of two extended families and the commitment of the families to maintaining the marriage. If you think about it, these are not dissimilar to the American traditions of bridal showers and the bride's family paying for the wedding. These latter traditions are changing as well; bridal showers are becoming wedding showers, so that the gifts are to both spouses. Because couples are marrying at older ages, frequently after the bride and groom have reached economic independence, more couples are paying for the weddings themselves.

Family Power Systems

Although it seems unfamily-like, power is an integral element in family relationships. We like to think that families are cozy refuges untouched by the jungle of societal relationships. But such is not the case. Family systems establish hierarchal structures of roles and statuses. Differences in value and power among family members are reflected in and reproduced through rules governing distribution of resources and authority, descent, titles, and residence.

Most societies throughout the world and throughout time have been patriarchal, by which is meant that, on average, men have more access to societal resources, such as land, money, education, and power (legal, political, and social). In this case, men usually, but not always, have more authority within their family household as well. There is some debate about whether matriarchal societies have ever existed. Certainly, if they did, they were few in number. The word "matriarchy," however, has recently been employed to describe single-mother households or large extended families headed by a grandmother.

Descent

Descent or lineage refers to the family line of ancestors and determines who may inherit property and wealth and whose family name is passed down. In American society, lineage carries less import in an individual's social status, except on the few occasions when one's ancestor sailed over on the Mayflower or is a member of a famous or infamous family. But in many other societies, lineage plays not only an important role in social status, but also in religious practice, as we shall see when we discuss Asian families.

The United States is said to have a *bilineal* or cognatic system, as Americans recognize ancestors on both sides of the family, and both daughters and sons are able to inherit property from both sides of the family (though in practice sons frequently inherit more or certain types of property, such as businesses). The exception to American bilineality is the pattern of the wife and children taking the father's name.

Most systems of lineage around the world are *unilineal* systems—either *patrilineal* or *matrilineal*. In a patrilineal system, the ancestors on the mother's side are unimportant. Of course, everyone acknowledges their existence. Families may even recite heart-warming stories about them, but those ancestors don't carry the same social status for the family within their society. In most patrilineal systems, only the sons inherit the money and property or they inherit more than the daughters, and the children take the father's name.

Whereas patrilineal family systems are the most common around the world, and bilineality is the second most common, matrilineal systems do exist. Stockard (2002) estimates that about 15 percent of the world's cultures, usually horticultural societies, practice matrilineality. In America, matrilineal systems are most commonly found among several Native American nations, such as the Pueblo tribes. Again, keep in mind that matrilineality still occurs within a patriarchal society, but matrilineality does give women more leverage within the family, and sometimes within the society as a whole. In most matrilineal societies, wives are considered owners of the family property and children, so upon divorce, women are less likely to be impoverished. The husbands do not hold as much influence and power within the marriage, but many times the wives' brothers play an important role. Likewise, the husband plays a vital role in the lives of his sister's children.

Although there is some variation, in many matrilineal societies both sons and daughters (not just daughters) are born into their mother's lineage. This departs from many patrilineal societies, where the daughter is technically excluded from any lineage until she marries or perhaps until she bears a son.

Family Roles and Titles

The focus on lineage in many countries is reflected in the titles given to various family members. Americans, who generally follow a bilineal pattern, use the titles aunt, uncle, nephew, niece, cousin, and so on for relatives on both sides of the family. Societies that distinguish between the paternal and maternal sides of the family are more likely to use different titles for each side. For example, in China, paternal grandparents are called *zufumu*, whereas maternal grandparents are called *waisufumu*. The father's brother will be referred to as *bofu*, whereas the mother's brother will be *juifu* (Ng, 1998).

Rank and role within the family may also affect title. For example, a number of societies refer to older siblings by a title different from that of their younger siblings. In Chinese again, the title for older brother is *gege,* for younger brother *didi,* for older sister *jie jie*, and for younger sister *mei mei* (Ng, 1998). In Turkish, the older sister is called *abla*, a title that engenders in the younger siblings respect for their older sister and in the older sister a sense of responsibility toward the younger siblings. In Arab countries, when a wife and husband have a child, particularly a firstborn son, the parents gain new names. If they name their new son Ali, the mother is called *Umm Ali* (mother of Ali), and the father is *Abu Ali* (father of Ali). In turn, *Ali* may be called after his father's name as well. If his father's name is *Khalid*, the son is called *Ibn Khalid* (son of Khalid). In other words, one's individual identity becomes subordinate to the role one plays in the family.

Residence

Most societies have expectations about where a new family should live in respect to their families of origin. Most societies have been *patrilocal* societies; when a couple marries they live with, or very near, the husband's parents. If the society practices *matrilocality,* the couple moves in with the wife's family.

Bilocality allows couples to choose residence with either side of the family, and *neolocality,* historically one of the least common residence patterns, encourages newly married couples to establish a household independent of either extended family. The United States practices neolocality. That does not mean that no American couple lives with one of their parents, just that it is not the ideal to do so.

In 1949, illustrated in Figure 4.1, George Murdock surveyed 250 societies and concluded that the majority of the world's cultures were patrilocal; 15 percent were matrilocal, 9 percent matri-patrilocal (live with wife's family for the first few years, then with husband's family), 8 percent bilocal, 7 percent neolocal, and 3 percent avuncolocal (live with uncle's family). At that time more than 90 percent of patrilineal societies were also patrilocal, whereas the majority of matrilineal societies were either matrilocal or avunculocal. Increased urbanization and industrialization, mass education, transnational migration, and resource depletion have changed those figures drastically. Although extended family households remain more common in Asia, Africa, and Latin America than in America, neolocality is increasingly common (Stanton, 1995).

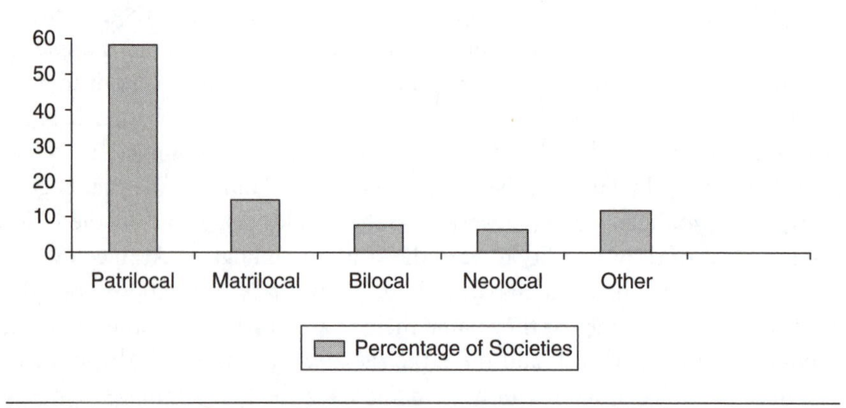

Figure 4.1 Cross-Cultural Prevalence of Types of Locality, 1949

SOURCE: Adapted from Murdock (1949)

In case you are still wondering what residence has to do with power, imagine who would have more power, leverage, or just comfort in a situation where the wife leaves her family to live with a husband she may have never met. She lives in his family's house, perhaps in a village where she knows no one. The husband's family now controls her daily chores, and her mother-in-law is frequently akin to an overseer. Or take the example of a multigenerational family household, where three generations are living in one household. In one case, the parent(s) and child(ren) have gone to live in the household of the grandparents and in another the grandparent(s) have come to live in the married daughter's household. Although each situation is unique, generally the permanent resident, the householder, will feel more comfort and control than the newcomer, who will feel the need to accommodate. In Chapter 8, we will see how these varying living arrangements can affect intergenerational relations.

Family Functions

Social scientists who study families cross-culturally agree that most societies utilize family systems to perform several functions. Although each society may choose different means to fulfill those functions, the functions usually include the following: (1) reproduce their society, (2) regulate sexuality, and (3) socialize children. Let's take each of these separately, illustrating how they can be fulfilled in myriad ways.

Reproduction

Most of the world has taken this function to heart. Consequently, we have a severe population problem, distributed unequally among the world's countries. The United States and much of Europe are reproducing at or below the 2.1 (about 2 children for every woman of childbearing age) replacement level. Unfortunately, most of the world's fertility rate is above replacement.

Consequently, some countries provide incentives to stimulate reproductive behavior, whereas others institute disincentives to stem the reproductive tide. Incentives usually include tax deductions, or outright payment, for children, whereas disincentives may include sterilization or reduction of social welfare for additional children. In 1979, China implemented a one child per family policy. After one child, women are encouraged to be sterilized or abort subsequent pregnancies. Chinese immigrants to America frequently have more than one child, whereas the pattern among other immigrants is to have fewer children in America than they would have had in their country of origin.

In addition to natural reproduction, the United States and many other countries, particularly in Europe, continue to debate the extent to which they want to maintain and shape their population and workforce through immigration rather than increased fertility. Therefore, as we will see in some of the history chapters, immigration policy has long been an effective tool for "managing" racial-ethnic immigrant groups in America.

Regulation of Sexuality

Related to reproduction is the regulation of sexual behavior. Although no country allows every member to have sex with whomever she or he wants at any time, most societies have had fewer sexual regulations than the United States, particularly in the past. Most people find that hard to believe, because Americans think of America as having an obsession with sex. Until fairly recently, however, we have had laws prohibiting premarital and extramarital sex, along with laws governing the types of sex we could partake in (such as vaginal, oral, or anal). Laws defining incest and limiting marriage to monogamy and heterosexuality also limit potential sexual partners.

In regard to incest, laws vary by country and, in America, by state. Anthropologists believe incest laws are intended to encourage societies to reach out to other societies, building networks of obligation and reciprocity. If people only married within their extended families we could easily deteriorate into narrow-minded tribal societies constantly in feud, such as the infamous Hatfields and McCoys or Shakespeare's Capulets and Montagues. Genetically, as well, diversity in reproduction protects societies from the proliferation of genetic disorders. A few bygone royal societies, such as the Hawaiian, Egyptian, and Incan, allowed royal brothers and sisters to occasionally marry to keep the wealth and the right of royalty contained (Bates & Fratkin, 2003); but most societies recognized the benefits of encouraging people to marry beyond the immediate family. Therefore, no society allows its members to marry grandparents, siblings, parents, children, aunts, uncles, nieces, or nephews. Islamic law adds foster mothers, foster sisters, mothers-in-law, stepdaughters, and daughters-in-law to the prohibited list, but American states vary in regard to in-laws, step-relatives, and cousins. Islamic law allows and sometimes encourages marriages between cousins (Korson, 1979). Taking incest proscriptions very seriously, the Cree Indians implemented infanticide for an infant resulting from an incestual relationship between a parent and child, stepparent and child, or brother and sister (Flannery, 1995).

Premarital sex is also accepted or expected in many societies (Murdock, 1967; Wen-Shing & Jing, 1991). In the Marshall Islands, for instance, sexual activity is expected to start around puberty, and it is normal to have numerous partners, cohabit, and have children outside of marriage (Ingoldsby, 1995c). Traditionally, the Hopi Indians also allowed late adolescent girls to have potential marriage partners visit their homes at night and sleep together. When the girl became pregnant, she would then select her favorite visitor as her husband, and their families would arrange the marriage (Queen, Habenstein, & Quadagno, 1985).

You have probably noticed that sex regulation tends to be more lenient for men than women; that double standard is a worldwide phenomenon. Moreover, anthropologists have noted that less-stratified societies exhibit lower levels of sexual jealousy, apparently a learned trait (Lee, 1982). In turn, less sexual jealousy often leads to more fluid ideas about socialization of children.

Socialization of Children

When there is less sexual jealousy and less concern about biological ownership of the child, such as in societies where women are allowed multiple partners and the biological father may be unknown, the parents are frequently viewed as only one of many appropriate socializers of the children. For instance, in polyandrous societies, a husband, not necessarily the biological father, is appointed father of all the children of the wife. Or in the Philippines' system of fosterage, young children might be loaned to older family members so that the older member can teach the child some skills and traditions, while the younger member provides help for the older one (Peterson, 1993). In particular, orphaned children or those with troubled parents are informally given to other family members. These exchanges mutually benefit the children, the "foster" parents, and the birth parents.

In colonial America, it was fairly common for families of meager means to lend out their children to work or learn a trade and for wealthy families to send their infants to wet nurses and their older children to boarding school (the latter is still common). Today, many would point to the increased use of child care among American families as a loosening of the rules about who the main socializers should be. Nevertheless, in some countries parents use other socializers not because they are unhappy with the children, but because they feel that others can provide better socialization than they can. For instance, in Israel, some families join kibbutzim, a type of communal living arrangement in which the children are reared separately from the parents by persons who have been trained in child development (Ingoldsby, 1995a).

In segregated African American communities, shared socialization of children has been a tradition as well. Charlayne Hunter-Gault, former PBS reporter, wrote in a foreword to James Comer's book *Maggie's American Dream* (1989) that when she grew up in her southern Black community, it was accepted "that anybody who saw you misbehaving could administer punishment on the spot—from a tongue-lashing to something more severe, without fear of reprisal from the otherwise-occupied parent" (p. xiv).

Today, with so many families migrating temporarily to other countries for work, it is common for young couples to practice what has come to be called "transnational motherhood" (Pyke, 2004). They leave their children with extended family for a year or two, so that the parents can devote their time to working and making money to send back.

In conclusion, this cross-cultural overview is intended to expose the reader to the myriad of family systems various cultures, under different conditions and different times, devised to nurture generations of humans. In 1963, William Goode suggested that over time family systems around the world would converge, taking on Western forms and ways of functioning. It does appear that many of the practices discussed above are declining. A number of studies indicate that in practice and attitude, families in other countries are becoming similar to families in North America. For instance, Schvaneveldt's (2003) study in Ecuador found an increase in love marriages. A number of studies in Africa (Hetherington, 2001; Meekers, 1995; Smith, 2001; Tayki, 2003) indicate that mate selection is becoming more individualized, with higher rates of self-selection, increased value of love and attraction, and later ages at marriage. Likewise, studies in Asia (Murray & Kimura, 2003; Xia & Zhou, 2003) found that arranged marriage is declining, while age at marriage is increasing in Japan and China. Studies in Korea, China, and Japan indicate that multigenerational co-residence is declining (Mabry, Giarusso, & Bengston, 2004), and studies in Africa find similar trends (Foster, 2000).

Many of these changes are responses to industrialization, urbanization, and the increasing value of education. In addition, intercountry communication has grown exponentially, with Western media and commercial marketing inundating other countries, influencing their lifestyles, and in many ways homogenizing the world. At the same time, as immigrants from other countries enter America and other Western societies, toting with them their traditions and ways of viewing kin relations, they in turn influence the way these countries do family. Although it is virtually impossible to clearly decipher the effects of cultural and structural factors, today's American families have witnessed a slight increase in extended-family households, a rise in social marriages and nonparental socialization, and increased interest in modified forms of arranged marriage.

Resources

Books and Articles

Hamon, R. R., & Ingoldsby, B. B. (Eds.). (2003). *Mate selection across cultures.* Thousand Oaks, CA: Sage.

Herdt. G. (2003). Coming of age and coming out ceremonies across cultures. In M. S. Kimmel (Ed.), *The gendered society reader* (2nd ed., pp. 39–57). New York: Oxford University Press.

Kassindja, F., & Bashir, L. M. (1999). *Do they hear you when you cry?* New York: Delta.

The true story of a young African woman who came to the United States to escape genital mutilation and arranged marriage only to be imprisoned.

Leeder, E. J. (2004). *The family in global perspective.* Thousand Oaks, CA: Pine Forge Press.

This book examines changing family patterns on several continents.

Perry, S., & Schenck, C. (Eds.). (2002). *Eye to eye: Women practising development across cultures.* London: Zed Books. Distributed exclusively in the United States by Palgrave.

This volume contains a collection of essays by women discussing how development processes affect them and advocating that development policy must respond to cultural differences.

Videos

Insight Media offers a wide variety of videos that take a cross-cultural look at different aspects of family. The following are all available from Insight Media Inc., 2162 Broadway, New York, NY 10024-0621, or at http://www.insight-media.com

Arranged marriages [Motion picture]. (1999).

This 50-minute film looks at patterns of arranged marriages in various countries, the relationships between parents and children in the arrangement, and whether couples consider themselves to be in love.

Four families [Motion picture]. (1960).

In this hour-long documentary, Margaret Mead looks at child rearing in four countries: India, France, Japan, and Canada.

In my country: An international perspective on gender [Motion picture]. (1993).

Using interviews with people from a dozen countries, this two-volume (91 minutes total) video set examines cultural attitudes about the household division of labor, discipline, control of money, elderly care, and other issues.

Kinship and descent [Motion picture]. (1983).

This two-part, hour-long documentary compares various classifications of descent in modern and traditional societies.

Without fathers or husbands [Motion picture]. (1995).

This 26-minute video investigates the Na, an ethnic group in southeast China that has a matrilineal social organization.

Longinotto, K. (2002). *The day I will never forget.* [Motion picture]. (Available from Women Making Movies at http://www.wmm.com)

This 92-minute subtitled video examines the practice of female genital mutilation in Kenya and the struggle of one African nurse to change the practice.

MacDonald, J., Gill, R., & Camerini, M. (1981). *Dadi's family* [Motion picture]. United States: Public Broadcasting Corporation, Odyssey Series. (Available from Documentary Educational Resources, 101 Morse St., Watertown, MA 02472, or at http://www.der.org/films/dadis-family.html)

This hour-long program follows a stem family in India.

Website

http://www.umanitoba.ca/anthropology/kintitle.html
From the Department of Anthropology of the University of Manitoba, Canada, this website provides details about cross-cultural systems of marriage, descent, and residence.

CHAPTER 5

FAMILY STRUCTURES

As mentioned in Chapter 1, we get most of our quantitative information about American family structures (essentially who resides with whom) from census data. As useful as these numbers are, they inform us little about the quality of relationships among the people in each household, and less about the relations between each household and other related or non-related households, such as those of their extended families, former family members, and fictive kin. In addition, census data only reveal the household structure at the time the census was taken. Since then, through death, divorce, aging, moving, remarrying, and so on, some of those same households may have changed structures. A household of two parents and children may experience a divorce and become a single-parent household. An adult child might move out and form a nonfamily household. A grandparent might move in to form an extended household. Lives change and so do family structures.

The distribution of family structure types also varies by race and ethnicity, as illustrated in Table 5.1. Non-Hispanic Whites and Blacks have about the same percentage of family households. The other four racial-ethnic groups have higher proportions of family households, because they have lower proportions of young and elderly people living alone or with roommates of one sort or another. Within family households, African Americans have the highest proportion of female-headed households, with and without children, whereas Asian Americans have the lowest. Male-headed households with children vary less; except for Asians, about 2 to 4 percent of households of each group are single-father households. Let's look at the variety of family structures more closely.

Extended Family Households

Lengthened life expectancy has increased the possibility that more generations of family members exist simultaneously, and they can co-reside in various configurations. Family households can be extended multigenerationally (vertically, three or more generations) or laterally (of the same generation, such as siblings); some combination of the two is possible as well.

The plethora of variations makes it difficult to ascertain exactly how many extended households of each type exist at any one point. Research on the use of extended households in the United States over the past few decades appears to show that extended households were decreasing in use until 1980 at which time they were about 10 percent of all households. That decade experienced about a 20 percent increase so that by 1990, 12 percent were extended (Glick, Bean, & Van Hook, 1997).

Table 5.1 Family and Nonfamily Households Total and by Race, 2000

		Percentage of All Households That Were Family							*Percentage of All Households That Were Nonfamily*		
	Number of All Households	*Total*	*Married Couple Total*	*Married Couple With Children*	*Female-Headed Household Total*	*Female-Headed Household With Children*	*Male-Headed Household Total*	*Male-Headed Household With Children*	*Total*	*Live Alone*	*Two or More*
U.S. Population		68.1	51.7	23.5	12.2	7.2	4.2	2.1	31.9	25.8	6.1
Non-Hispanic White	79,093,136	67.0	54.0	23.0	9.0	5.0	3.4	1.7	34.5	28.3	6.2
Hispanic	9,222,402	80.0	54.0	36.0	18.0	12.0	8.0	4.0	20.0	13.9	6.1
Black	11,862,087	68.0	31.0	16.0	31.0	19.0	6.0	3.0	32.2	27.1	5.1
Asian	3,101,668	74.0	61.0	34.0	9.0	4.0	5.0	1.0	26.0	19.0	7.0
Pacific Islander	94,361	77.0	55.0	33.0	16.0	9.0	7.0	4.0	23.0	15.0	8.0
American Indian & Alaskan Native	665,047	72.0	44.0	24.0	21.0	13.0	7.0	4.0	29.0	22.0	7.0

SOURCE: U.S. Department of Commerce (2000d), Quick Table-P10, Matrices PCT8, PCT17, PCT18, PCT26, PCT27, and PCT28

The recent increase in extended households is explained by the influx of immigrants from non-European, largely Asian and Latino, countries (Glick et al., 1997). Extended household living is a common tradition in these countries, but also temporary extended households serve as a strategy for adjustment and financial stability among recent immigrants. Foreign-born Americans have a much higher rate of utilizing extended households than do native-born Americans, and their use of extended households has increased over the past 40 years. In 1960, about 16 percent of immigrants resided in some type of extended household; by 1990, the use of extended households among immigrants, particularly among Mexican, Guatemalan, and Salvadoran immigrants, had nearly doubled to 30 percent (Glick et al.).

Even among the native-born, however, research indicates that families of color have higher rates of household extension than do White families. According to Glick et al. (1997), in 1910, 20 percent of White households were extended in the sense that they contained nonnuclear relatives (so they could have been lateral and/or multigenerational). By 1980, White extended households had declined to 7 percent. For Black families in 1910, 24 percent of households were extended, and by 1980 the number had dropped to 17 percent. In a study of 1990 U.S. census data, Koebel and Murray (1999) estimated that African Americans, Hispanics, and other racial minority groups were about twice as likely as Whites to live in extended households.

The greater use of extended households among families of color is due in part to the higher proportion of working-class and lower-income families in those racial groups. Among all racial groups, extended households decrease as income increases (Glick, 1999; Kamo & Zhou, 1994). When people are financially stable, they can afford their own households. This would explain why the majority of extended households are found in central cities, where higher rates of poverty are also prevalent.

In addition to financial need and immigrant status, factors such as marital status, age distribution, and gender affect the types of extended households used by various racial-ethnic groups.

Multigenerational Extended Households

As discussed in Chapter 3, multigenerational extended households have never constituted a large portion of American families, in fact, never more than 20 percent of family households nationwide. In 2000, multigenerational extended family households comprised less than 3.7 percent of all households; less than one percent were four-generation households (U.S. Department of Commerce, 2000d). These varied by state; for instance, in Hawaii 8.2 percent of its households were multigenerational and in Puerto

Rico 7.4 percent were. Using a broader definition of multigenerational—co-residence of two or more adults of different generations—Cohen and Casper (2002) found that 11 percent of White, 23 percent of Black, and 21 percent of Latino households were multigenerational. Several types of households are classified as multigenerational.

Simple Extended Households

A nuclear family living with grandma and/or grandpa is the extended household most familiar to people. In America, most simple multigenerational households consist of one grandparent and his or her adult children and grandchildren, because when both grandma and grandpa are still alive and married, they tend to live together independently of their adult children (Phua, Kaufman, & Park, 2001). When one of the grandparents dies, the remaining grandparent is more likely to move in with one of his or her adult children, though if his or her health is good, the majority of single healthy American elderly still live independently. Generally, research indicates that the grandparent(s) in multigenerational households are frequently the mother's parents. Paternal grandparents tend to play a stronger role in rural areas, particularly where a farming tradition is passed down from father to son (King & Elder, 1995; Pearson, Hunter, Cook, Ialongo, & Kellam, 1997).

Immigrating to America at older ages also makes multigenerational living more likely. Establishing economic independence at a late age in a new country is difficult, and frequently elderly immigrants come for the purpose of rejoining their families, not for seeking new economic opportunities (Angel, Angel, Lee, & Markides, 1999; Phua et al., 2001). Many older Cubans, for example, immigrated here with their families in the 1960s; consequently, Cubans have an older age distribution and for decades had a high rate of simple extended family households (Perez, 1994).

Stem Family Households

A form of multigenerational extension found most commonly in Asian and Middle Eastern countries, stem family households refer to a pattern where the adult sons—at least the oldest and perhaps all of the sons—and their families live with the sons' parents in the parents' household. Although this is a type of simple extension, it is distinguished by the fact that it is the son(s) and the paternal grandparents who make up the extension. Usually the grandparents maintain the headship of the stem family household, and the income is often pooled under the authority of the grandfather or the eldest son, who will eventually assume headship of the household when the grandfather dies. The grandmother will likely have authority over the daughter-in-law(s) until the eldest daughter-in-law assumes authority.

The practice of stem family extension has declined worldwide but especially declines upon immigration. Although varying by Asian ethnic group, according to Kamo (2000), in 60 to 85 percent of Asian American extended households, the grandparents reside in their adult children's households. Like other American elderly, when Asian American elderly have higher education and income, they are more likely to live apart from their children. When they reside with their children, employment of the elderly increases the possibility that the Asian American elderly will head the multigenerational household (Phua et al., 2001).

Attenuated Extended Households

Marital status as a single parent increases the likelihood of an attenuated extended household, which consists of a single-parent family living with a grandparent. This type of household has been most common among Black, Puerto Rican, and Native American families. In two studies comparing Blacks, Hispanics, and Whites, Aquilino (1990) and Crimmins and Ingegneri (1990) found that the higher overall use of extended households among African Americans could be accounted for by their higher rate of single-parent families living in attenuated extended households and their higher rate of poverty. Those studies, however, found that Latinos as a whole maintained a higher rate of extended households even when single parenthood and class were controlled. In 2000, the U.S. Census Bureau's *Current Population Reports* estimated that 14 percent of White single moms, 18 percent of Black, and 22 percent of Hispanic lived with other family members (Fields & Casper, 2001).

Pearson et al. (1997) conducted a small study of racial differences in co-residence with grandparents. Looking at children, matched for similar income backgrounds, in Baltimore schools, the authors found that the rate of living with grandparents was about the same for Black and White children. White children, however, were five times more likely to reside in households with both parents and a grandmother (a simple extended family). Although White children were less likely to reside in attenuated extended households, when they did they were twice as likely as Black students to live with a single father and a grandmother. Black students were more apt to live with a single mother and a grandmother.

Unlike grandparents in simple extended households, those in attenuated extended households frequently perform a more active parenting role. Therefore, a number of studies (Chase-Lansdale, Brooks-Gunn, & Zamsky,

1994; Cooley & Unger, 1991; Thomas, Rickel, Butler, & Montgomery, 1990) indicate that this type of household extension has many benefits for the single parent and her or his children. For instance, Dalla and Gamble's (1997) small study of Navajo teen mothers indicates that the majority were living with their mothers and reported that without the mother's assistance, many of the teen moms would not have been able to attend school, provide food and clothing for the children, or participate in any leisure activities.

Laterally Extended Households

When people of the same generation, such as siblings and/or cousins live together, the result is referred to as a laterally extended household. These households can be classified as (1) *simple lateral households,* in which perhaps two siblings co-reside or one nuclear family takes in a brother or sister or other distant relative; (2) *joint extended households,* in which two whole families of the same generation live together, such as two sisters and each of their families sharing a household; or (3) *augmented extended households,* in which families take in fictive kin.

Once again, these types are more common among families of color than among White families and more common among immigrants than native-born Americans. In a process called "chain migration," once young immigrants are settled, another brother, sister, or cousin (and his or her family) joins them, living together until they are established enough to move into a separate residence. For instance, in her study of 1990 census data, Glick (1999) found that recent Mexican immigrants were nearly three times more likely to reside in laterally extended households than were more established Mexican Americans (18.8 percent versus 6.4 percent, respectively). The latter, in turn, were twice as likely as recent immigrants to reside in multigenerational extended households (25.9 percent versus 12.6 percent). Another study of eighth- and ninth-grade children of Haitian immigrants in South Florida found that 18 percent had aunts or uncles in their household and 20 percent had other distant relatives (Perez, 1994).

Finally, I have been referring to extended households up to this point, but most people have extended *families;* they just don't live together. Even when they don't co-reside, some extended families live in proximity, interact daily, exchange goods and services, and basically nurture and provide a mutual aid system for several subfamilies. These *modified extended families* are frequently headed by a dominant figure, usually the maternal grandparents (Eisenberg, 1988) or a grandmother. Extended family activities frequently circulate around this dominant figure's home; for instance, all the individual families may gather at the grandparents' home every Sunday for dinner.

The larger an extended family is, such as in clan systems, where everyone with the same surname is considered a member of the extended family, the need for fictive kin, or even friends for that matter, may be reduced. For instance, Hmong Americans have 18 clans, meaning all Hmong (except those who have outmarried) have one of 18 surnames (McInnis, 1991). In her study of the Hmong community in Wausau, Wisconsin, Jo Ann Koltyk (1998) observed that Hmong families, although scattered around the city, socialized together and made joint economic arrangements. "One's friends are usually one's relatives [in the Hmong community]," she observed. "I rarely met individuals who had formed strong bonds of friendship outside of their own kinship circles" (p. 40).

Extended Families as Systems of Exchange

Extended family relationships serve a number of purposes and provide advantages and disadvantages for families. Primarily, they function as an extensive system of exchange. Although not exclusive to low-income communities, exchange practices are more common in less-developed societies, such as hunting and gathering societies, or among communities of low-income people in more-developed societies. Redistribution of resources may occur regularly or on an emergency basis and can include food, food stamps, clothing, furniture, and household or child care services. Carol Stack's 1974 classic ethnography, *All Our Kin,* a study of a Black community, referred to this as "swapping." Swapping may occur on a short-term basis, a couple of hours a day or week, or on a long-term basis, taking in a child for weeks or months until the parents can get back on their feet. This latter form of exchange is referred to as *informal adoption* and while practiced to some degree in all groups, Blacks and Puerto Ricans (who refer to it as *hijos de crianza*) are known for more frequent usage.

The main advantages of the exchange system in low-income extended families are that it ensures collective economic survival, levels inequality, and builds community. Extended family households are able to coordinate short-term labor needs, such as child care, and draw upon pooled resources to achieve economies of scale (Peterson, 1993). Everyone has something to offer, and when one family or individual is suffering, other families contribute to their sustenance. Although many family members give and sacrifice with no expectation of reward, ultimately exchanges come with a sense of mutuality. Once the recipient is back on his or her feet, she or he is expected to return the exchange, not necessarily to the same people who helped him or her but to someone in the community. Failing to do so might elicit some form of sanction, such as gossip, direct criticism, chastisement, or exclusion from further aid. One of the women in Stack's (1974) book illustrates this understanding. Speaking of her cousin, she said,

> Some people like my cousin don't mind borrowing from anybody, but she don't loan you no money, her clothes, nothing. . . . She don't believe in helping nobody, and lots of folks gossip about her. I'll never give her nothing again. One time I went over there after I had given her all these things and I asked her, "How about loaning me an outfit to wear?" She told me, "Girl, I ain't got nothing clean, . . . and what I do have you can't wear 'cause it's too small for you." Well, lots of people talks about someone who acts that way. (p. 35)

Although these extended kin exchanges ensure that everyone's minimum needs are met, they potentially can hinder some individuals from economically advancing. In capitalist America, where success is frequently measured in terms of income, education, and status, individuals must accumulate some of these resources to rise into the middle class. In situations of poverty, assisting family members with their daily needs can drain individuals economically. To achieve upward mobility, individual members occasionally must remove themselves to some extent from the exchange system. Most members refrain from cutting themselves off entirely, but many, particularly new immigrants, must make choices about the extent to which they will continue giving resources to other family members.

In Comer's 1988 biography *Maggie's American Dream,* the author's mother Maggie recounts how she migrated north leaving behind family members and a life of sharecropping in the South. She and her husband eventually made a conscious decision to discontinue the common pattern among new northern Blacks of traveling back and forth between North and South to visit relatives. They decided the traveling and the lack of commitment to their new community would drain them of their limited resources. Maggie explained,

> That's one of the reasons our people haven't accomplished any more than they have. We paid a part of it (our earnings) out to the railroad traveling back South. The fellows would work three months and run home, work three months and run home. And then they brought their wives and the wife had to go back home to see Mama. And if they got expecting a baby they had to go back home. They couldn't stay here because they was away from Mama or away from the South. (p. 51)

Whereas extended family living arrangements and exchanges testify to the tenacity and strong familial support available within all racial-ethnic groups, I should note that the experience of living in an extended family can produce stressful moments as well. For instance, although chain migration eases the cost and transition of each succeeding immigrant through the provision of residence, transportation, orientation, work referrals, and the diminishment of homesickness, these provisions can produce, at least temporarily, an inequality in the relationship. In laterally extended households, the "guest" family might feel they should avoid wearing out their welcome. Maura Toro-Morn (2002) interviewed Puerto Rican women who had immigrated in the 1950s, and were staying with their husbands' families in America for an interim period. She quotes one of her interviewees:

> My husband took us to my sister-in-law's house. There *pase la salsa y el guayacan* (a popular expression denoting a very hard time). We had four kids and no house of our own. Imagine? We had to wait to shower after everyone in the other family had taken their shower. If I had my little girl in the bathtub and one of her [sister-in-law's] children wanted to shower I had to hurry up and leave them use the shower. . . . I suffered a lot. I used to do everything for her. I cooked, I cleaned the house. (p. 233)

Similarly, remittances, money sent by immigrants to family members back in the home country, present a similar dilemma. Remittances often repay people who loaned money for passage, help other family members immigrate, or improve their standard of living in the home country. Therefore, those remittances may cause conflicts in the immigrant family, when one spouse feels the other is sending too much money back home to relatives. Sponsoring other family members' immigration to America can increase tension in the home as well.

Gender roles and family hierarchies add more layers to the dynamics. When a son and his wife go to live with his parents, the daughter-in-law often feels less power in that situation than does her husband and less power than would a daughter and husband who live with the daughter's parents. But in both cases, the women (the daughter or daughter-in-law) will do the bulk of work caring for the elders. Sonuga-Barke and Mistry's (2000) study of immigrant Pakistani multigenerational households in Britain found that although the grandparents and grandchildren of the household benefited from the extension, the mothers in extended households suffered from higher rates of depression and anxiety than mothers in non-extended households. The mothers, frequently caring for both an older and a younger family member, felt sandwiched between the two sets of competing needs. Similarly, a cross-cultural study by Warner, Gary, and Lee (1993) found that women in extended family structures were more supervised and had less influence in household decisions than women in nuclear families.

Despite these potential hurdles, quite a bit of evidence reveals that intensive extended family interaction produces positive outcomes for future generations. For instance, Weinick (1995) found that individuals who share a home with a grandparent (or other relatives) when growing up tend to provide more assistance to their own parents in later life. Similarly, Rossi and Rossi (1990) and King and Elder (1997) concluded from their research that adults reared in situations where grandparents and other extended family members were an integral part of family interactions are more likely to report stronger feelings of obligation to kin than those who lacked such ties. Silverstein and Parrott's (1997) research led them to conclude that early contact with grandparents led to positive attitudes toward the elderly and public policies that benefit the elderly. Finally, in their review of the literature, Cohen and MacCartney (2004) found that close extended family relations built resiliency in children and had positive effects on children's academic success and emotional well-being.

Nuclear Family Households

Also known as two-parent or married-couple families with children, nuclear family households contain two parents and their kids. Sometimes the term "intact" family is used synonymously, but that implies that a one-parent family is a "broken" family, an implication that many single-parent families would refute, particularly if they have always been single parents. Whereas the term "nuclear" is sometimes reserved for biological families, it usually refers to any family structure containing two married parents and children, which means that stepfamilies or adoptive families are also nuclear families. In census data, unmarried couples (gay or straight) without children are counted under nonfamily households. If they had children biologically or by adoption, their household would likely be counted as a single-parent (male- or female-headed) household.

Because of the high rates of divorce and nonmarital births, people assume the nuclear family is virtually extinct in the United States. Indeed, in 2000, less than one quarter (23.5 percent) of all U.S. households (35 percent of all U.S. family households) were nuclear. That percentage varies across racial groups, ranging from a high of 36 percent among Hispanics to a low of 16 percent among African Americans. Those percentages indicate that nuclear families do not represent the majority of American households. The growth of single-parent households, however, is not the only reason for the reduction in nuclear households.

The main reason for the reduction is the increase in the numbers of elderly and in the need for young people to postpone marriage. The proportion of these nonfamily households has tripled in the last 50 years. Also, as the population has aged, many married couples' children are now adults (18 or over); even if they continue to live in their parents' household, they are not counted under "married couples with children" households. Married couples without children account for 28.2 percent of U.S. households.

Although the 23.5 percent is a drop from earlier decades, the rate of decrease has been slowing. According to William Frey's (2003) study of several decades of census data, the share of married-couples-with-children families dropped 9.9 percent in the 1970s, 4.8 percent in the 1980s, and only 2.1 percent in the 1990s. To a large extent, the rate of decline has slowed because of immigration, particularly of Hispanic and Asian families. Immigrant families tend to be younger, are more likely to have children, and have lower rates of divorce.

Despite the relatively low percentage of nuclear households, the majority of American children currently live in two-parent, or nuclear family, households, and that percentage increased during the 1990s. As you can see in Figure 5.1, 69 percent of American children live in married-couple households. These include step- and adoptive families, but the majority involve biological parents. Once again these percentages vary by race and ethnicity: The percentage of children under 18 living in two-parent households in 2002 ranged from a high of 82 percent (Asians and Pacific Islanders) to a low of 38 percent (African Americans).

Research indicates that the main advantages two-parent households offer their children are higher education and potential for financial stability. Married men tend to make more money than single men, and if their wives work also, household income can substantially improve security and opportunities for children. Higher education and income are, in turn, associated with a lower likelihood of divorce and single parenting. Moreover, the children of educated parents have better health. Looking at Figure 5.2, you can see that across races, poverty is higher (two to six times higher) for single-mother families than it is for married-couple families.

In fact, family structure accounts for a significant proportion of the racial gap in median family income. Since female-headed households have a significantly lower household income, they reduce a group's overall median income. Lichter and Landale (1995), for instance, found that family structure accounted for 55 percent of the gap between Puerto Rican and White child poverty. Educational and occupational differences and discrimination also account for part of the difference.

Other social outcomes for children in two-parent households will be discussed in the next section, juxtaposed with those of single-mother families.

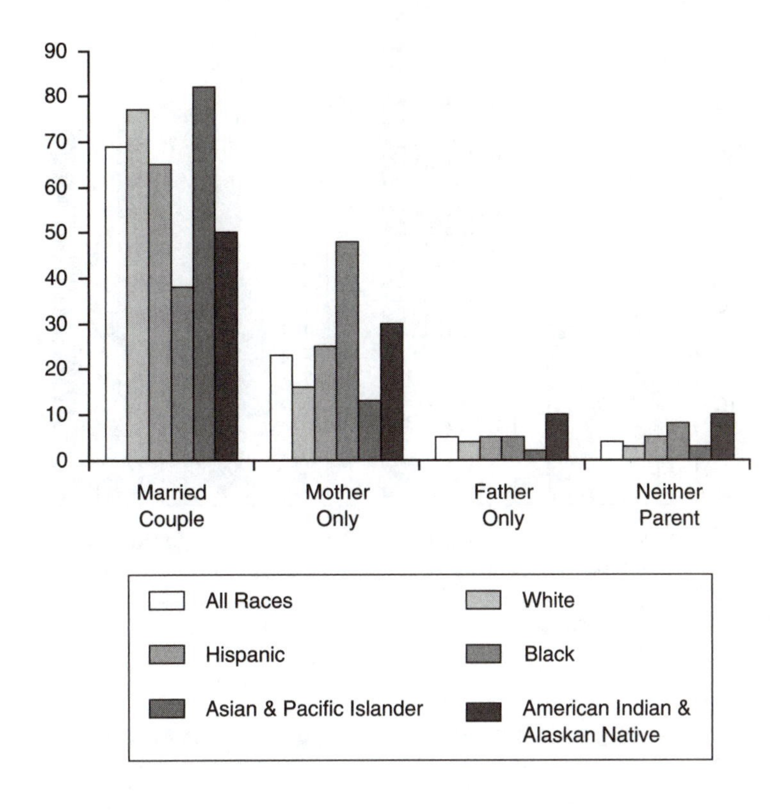

Figure 5.1 Living Arrangements of Children by Race, 2002 (in percentages)

SOURCE: Fields (2003), Table C2

a. The American Indian and Alaskan Native percentages are based on estimates from Lugaila & Overturf (2004), Table 6.

Single-Parent Families

As noted in Chapter 3, the modern era is not the first time American society has seen a relatively high proportion of single-parent families. In the colonial/agricultural era, high numbers of single-parent households existed due to high mortality and desertion rates. Today, because of improvements in health and life expectancy, mortality (or widowhood) accounts for only a small proportion of single parents. Now, the vast majority of cases stem from divorce and nonmarital births.

Divorce rates are highest for African Americans. According to the U.S. Department of Health and Human Services, 47 percent of Black marriages

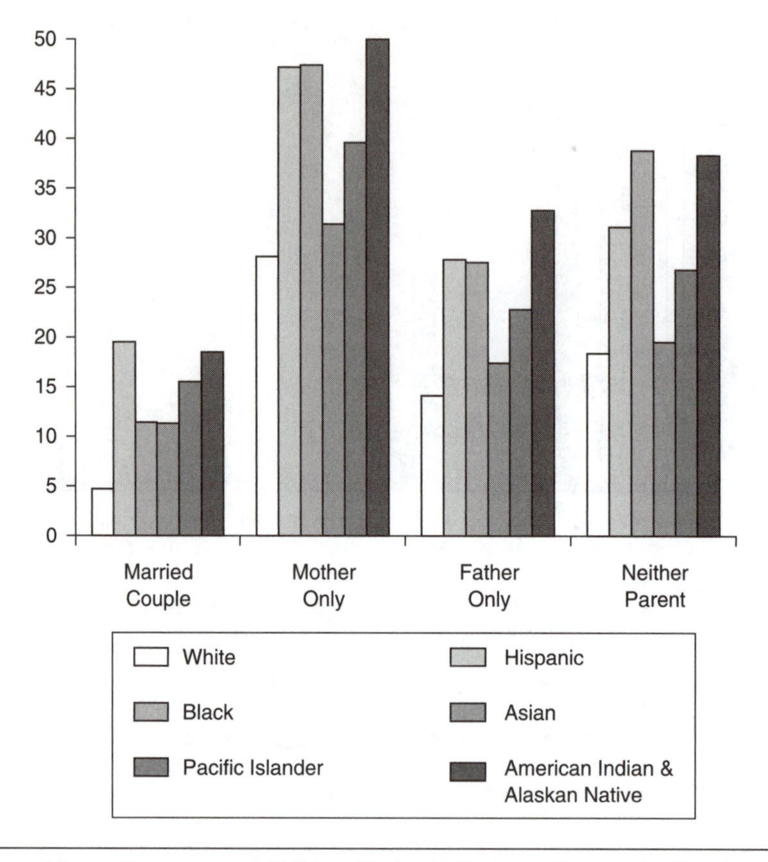

Figure 5.2 Percentage of Children Under 18 Living in Poverty by Family Structure and Race, 2000

SOURCE: Lugaila & Overturf (2004), Table 5

end within 10 years, compared with 34 percent of Hispanic marriages, 32 percent of non-Hispanic White marriages, and 20 percent of Asian marriages. Racial minorities also have lower remarriage rates than Whites. Within 5 years of divorce, 58 percent of non-Hispanic Whites remarry, compared with 44 percent of Hispanics, and 32 percent of Blacks (Bramlett & Mosher, 2001). Despite the higher divorce rates, nonmarital births account for the majority of single-parent households among African, Puerto Rican, and Native Americans, whereas divorce accounts for the majority of single-parent homes among Whites.

Female-Headed Households

A female-headed household is composed of a female with other related persons but no spouse present. Overall, in the United States in 2000, this type of household accounted for about 12 percent of all households, or 18 percent of all family households. A female-headed household is not synonymous with a single-mother household. A mother living with her adult child (18 years old or older) or with a sister or brother, or with her own elderly mother is also considered by the census to be a female-headed household. Therefore, the percentage of female-headed households with children under 18 is 7.2 percent of all households or 10.6 percent of family households. (Remember, these households may include cohabiting partners.)

Looking back at Table 5.1, you can see that African Americans have the highest proportion of female-headed households, with and without children, whereas Asians and non-Hispanic Whites have the lowest. This pattern is similarly reflected in Figure 5.1, which indicates that Black and Native American children have the highest proportions (48 percent and 30 percent, respectively) living with single moms, and Asian and non-Hispanic White children have the lowest proportions (13 percent and 16 percent, respectively).

Much controversy has attended the growth of female-headed households over the past few decades. In large part, the controversy has centered on their need for social services. In addition, most of the concern has focused on the role played by nonmarital births, particularly among teens and, to a lesser extent, among older women who chose to have nonmarital births. The former elicit controversy because of their vulnerability and need for social support; the latter because they appear to be flaunting traditional values.

Nonmarital Births

In 2002, nonmarital births accounted for 33.8 percent of all births (Fields, 2003), up from 18 percent in 1980 and 4 percent in 1940 (Martin & Hamilton, et al., 2003). The increased proportion reflects an actual increase in the birthrate of unmarried women, but it also reflects several other trends. First, marriage postponement has increased the number of unmarried women in the population. Second, pregnant women are not as likely to marry as in the past. Only about 10 percent of pregnant Black women marry before the birth, whereas 30 percent of non-Hispanic White, 28 percent of Hispanic, and 15 percent of other races do so (Bachu, 1999).

Finally, the birthrate among married women has declined. Birthrates among married women steadily declined from 1960 until 1995, whereas the birthrates among unmarried women increased until 1994, when the rate peaked at 46.9 per 1,000 unmarried women. Since then the birthrate for unmarried women has also declined slightly, but they continue to represent an increasing proportion of all births because of the substantial overall decline of marital births.

Nonmarital births vary by race and age. Table 5.2 shows that the nonmarital birthrate (the number of births for every 1,000 unmarried women of childbearing age in a given year) in 2002 was highest for Hispanic women (87.9 per 1,000 unmarried Hispanic women aged 15 to 44), followed by Black women (66.2), non-Hispanic White women (27.8), and finally Asian and Pacific Islanders (21.3). This represents an increase for Hispanic women and a steep decline for Black women; the rate for non-Hispanic White and Asian women has remained fairly stable over the past few years. In terms of the proportion of all births that unmarried births represent in each particular racial category, however, the rankings change somewhat. As enumerated in column six of Table 5.2, nonmarital births to African American women represent about 68 percent of all Black births, followed by Native American women at nearly 60 percent, then Hispanic (43.5 percent), White (23 percent) and Asian women (14.9 percent).

Teen Births

Today, when people discuss teen births, they frequently assume they are nonmarital births. It is true that the majority of teen pregnancies and births today are nonmarital (80 percent of teen births were nonmarital in 2002), but that wasn't always the case. Teen pregnancies and births were more common in the 1950s, but they were usually *married* teen pregnancies and births. Nonmarital teen births also were kept low by marriages that occurred during the 9 months between conception and birth.

Teen pregnancy rates and birthrates have been declining steadily since the 1960s; *nonmarital* teen pregnancies and births have been declining since the 1990s. As you can see from Table 5.2, they significantly declined in the 1990s for all racial-ethnic groups, though the greatest decline has been for Black teens. The decline has been greater among younger teens 15 to 17 than among older teens 18 to 19 (Martin et al., 2003). Today, teen births account for about 11 percent of all births, less than 30 percent of nonmarital births. Hence, the majority of nonmarital births are to women over 20 years old. The 1990s' drop in the nonmarital teen pregnancy rates and birthrates has been attributed to a small decline in sexual activity among teens and an increased use of condoms among the sexually active (Martin et al, 2003). The teen birthrate declined alongside a decline in the abortion rate as well.

Table 5.2 Teen and Nonmarital Birthrates by Race, 1991 and 2002

	1991 Teen Birthrates (per 1,000 girls ages 15–19)	*2002 Teen Birthrates (per 1,000 girls ages 15–19)*	*Percentage of Teen Births That Are Nonmarital*[a]	*2002 Nonmarital Birthrate (per 1,000 unmarried women ages 15–44)*	*2002 Nonmarital Births as a Percentage of All Births in Each Racial Group*
Non-Hispanic White	43.4	28.5	73	27.8	23.0
Hispanic	104.6	83.4	73	87.9	43.5
Black	118.2	68.3	96	66.2	68.4
Asian & Pacific Islander	27.3	18.3	71	21.3	14.9
American Indian & Alaskan Native	84.1	53.8	86	—[b]	59.7

SOURCE: Martin et al. (2003)

a. These percentages are based on 2000 figures from the U.S. Department of Health and Human Services (2004)

b. Because American Indians and Alaskan Natives are less than one percent of the U.S. population, certain rates frequently cannot be reliably computed for them.

Although teen pregnancies and births have been declining in the United States, they remain higher than in most other industrialized countries (although total U.S. nonmarital birthrates are lower than in many European countries). In a 37-country study, Forrest et al. (1993) found that teens in countries that have more openness about sex, more availability of sex education and contraceptives, and more generous health and welfare provisions have lower rates of adolescent pregnancy. Some have pointed to the high rate of births among Black American teens to explain intercountry differences, but the birthrates of White American teen girls are also higher than in any Western European country (Westoff, Calot, & Foster, 1983).

Explaining the Racial Gap in Nonmarital Births

Although nonmarital births occur among all races in the United States, scholars have focused almost entirely on Black and White teens to explain the racial gap. People often assume that the high rate of female-headed households in the Black community reflects a lack of interest in marriage, but a number of studies of Black women indicate that marriage is their preferred choice. For instance, Jarrett (1994) conducted focus group interviews with 82 low-income Black women and found that virtually all the women desired marriage, though many did not think that was a reachable goal.

Instead, a number of other factors appear to contribute to the racial gap. First and foremost is the difference in the rate of poverty between Whites and Blacks. Although teen nonmarital births can be found in all social classes, they are much more associated with poverty. Low-income teens may not perceive the need to postpone childbirth as would middle-class teens, because they feel their opportunities for higher education and careers are limited anyway (Astone & Upchurch, 1994; East, 1998). In particular, East found that girls' perceptions of their future goals varied by race. East surveyed 600 middle schoolgirls in suburban Southern California and found that Hispanic girls placed significantly less importance on achieving school and career goals and thought it less likely that they would actually achieve those goals than did Black, White, or Southeast Asian girls. This may explain why the Hispanic teen pregnancy rate has recently surpassed that of other racial groups. This rate differs significantly, however, between native-born Hispanic girls and immigrant Hispanic girls. Native-born Mexican American teen girls have a pregnancy rate that is two times higher than their foreign-born counterparts. Immigrant status, according to East, appears to work as a protective factor against early nonmarital births.

Likewise, Linda Burton's (1990) study of intergenerational teenaged childbearing in Black families concluded that early childbearing was a strategy used in part to compensate for lower life expectancies and poverty. In addition, the proximity of extended family members (potential caregivers) may have contributed to the perception that young single parenthood was feasible. The Black families in Burton's study accelerated the family timetable, with children taking on family responsibilities at earlier ages than common in America, and likewise having children earlier. Young grandmothers were available and willing to help rear the children.

Second, the racial gap in teen *pregnancy* rates is smaller than the gap in teen *birthrates*. Not all nonmarital pregnancies lead to nonmarital births. White teens, especially among the middle class, are more likely to choose abortion or to marry during the pregnancy, thus lowering their nonmarital birthrate. White teens also lower their single-parent rate because they are more likely to give their children up for adoption (although doing so has decreased among all groups; now only about 2 to 3 percent of unmarried mothers give their babies up for adoption [Benokraitis, 1999]).

Third, the window of opportunity to become pregnant while unmarried is wider for Black girls. Black girls reach puberty, on average, about a year earlier than White girls. Likewise, on average, Black girls start dating and sexual activity about a year earlier than White girls (East, 1998). In East's survey, Black middle schoolgirls expected the youngest age for first intercourse and the greatest likelihood of having a nonmarital birth. They were also twice as likely as Hispanic girls and six times as likely as White and Southeast Asian girls to already have experienced their first intercourse.

Of course, it takes more than girls to produce a pregnancy; it takes boys too. Research on Black, Hispanic, and White teen males indicate that Black and Hispanic teen males are more likely than White teen males to believe that pregnancy validates their masculinity and identity, gives them adult status, and carries on their family name (Pleck, Sonenstein, & Ku, 1993). Thus, it is possible that they may consciously pursue pregnancy as an outcome of their relationships. Also, from a practical perspective, research shows that Black and Hispanic teen males start sex earlier than both male and female White teens (Upchurch, Levy-Storms, Sucoff, & Aneshensel, 1998) and are less likely to use condoms (Rucibwa, Modeste, Montgomery, & Fox, 2003).

Moreover, when teens are exposed to single-parent households, have siblings who have had nonmarital pregnancies, or believe their peers are having sex, they are more likely to participate in nonmarital sex (Rucibwa et al., 2003). Hence, the higher rate may reproduce itself, as it appears normative to teens who observe early sex and pregnancy among their families and friends.

Outcomes for Female-Headed Households

Much research finds that the children of female-headed households fare less well than do those in two-parent households. A number of studies (for example, Ford, 1997; Kotchick, Dorsey, Miller, & Forehand, 1999) have concluded that high school students reared in two-parent homes were less likely than those reared in single-parent homes to engage in sexual intercourse and early childbearing. Other findings indicate that single parents don't monitor or supervise their children as well as do two parents (Astone & McLanahan, 1991).

Previous marital status, however, plays a distinguishing role in the outcomes. Never-married mothers tend to have fewer resources to offer their children, as never-married moms have more educational deficits, economic strain (less full employment, less child support, and lower income [Cohen & MacCartney, 2004]), and poor marital histories if they marry (Mott & Marsiglio, 1985; Zabin & Hayward, 1993). Divorced single parents, on the other hand, usually have better education and income and are more likely to remarry. White and Asian Americans have higher proportions of parents who are single by divorce or separation, whereas Black, Hispanic, and Native Americans have higher proportions of never-married parents. Nowadays, widowed marital status is one of the lowest proportions for all racial-ethnic groups.

Nevertheless, some factors mitigate the effects of single parenting. Furstenberg (1976) found that teen single moms and their children fared better if they remained in their parents' home (that is, in attenuated extended households). In line with this, some research has indicated that Black teen mothers have a higher rate of completing high school than do White teen moms, because they have more extended family support in caring for their children and they are less likely to marry the father. White teen moms have a higher rate of marriage, and when they marry, they are more likely to stay home with the children, foregoing their education, while the father works (Trent & Harlan, 1994).

Age and income of single mothers play a mediating role as well. When one compares young single moms to older single moms, research finds that the children of older single moms have fewer cognitive, social, and physical delays (Panzarine, 1988; Zabin & Hayward, 1993). Likewise, when comparing middle-class single-parent households to middle-class two-parent households, the gap in outcomes is narrower (but not fully closed [McLanahan & Sandefur, 1994]).

Male-Headed Households

Less common than female-headed households, male-headed households account for 4.2 percent of all American households. Again, not all of them have children under 18 years old; male-headed households with children under 18 account for only 2.1 percent of all households (or 3.1 percent of all families). Looking back at Table 5.1, you can see that 4 percent or less of children in each racial category except Native Americans live in male-headed households.

Most research on single-father families has been conducted on White fathers. A few conclusions can be drawn. Male-headed households tend to be better off financially. On average, fathers have higher rates of full-time employment and make more money than their female counterparts (Greif, 1990). Moreover, unemployed fathers frequently refrain from taking custody of their children, whereas unemployed mothers have less choice about if and when to take custody. Single fathers are less likely than single mothers to co-reside with extended family (Fields & Casper, 2001), but U.S. census data from 2002 indicate that single fathers are two-to-six times more likely to be cohabiting than are single mothers. Single dads, according to Greif, are also more likely to have custody of boys than girls.

Research on single minority full-time fathers is virtually nonexistent. My own limited research on single Black full-time fathers finds some similarities and some differences from the situations of their White counterparts. The small group of custodial fathers that I interviewed similarly had higher-than-average income for Black single men. More than 50 percent of them, however, were working one full-time job and supplementing that with one or two part-time jobs (Coles, 2003). Contrary to custom, the Black fathers in my respondent group had slightly more female custodial children, but they expressed more uncertainty and dissatisfaction with their parenting of female children than of male children (Coles, 2001c). Overall, these fathers were highly motivated to be custodial dads. The majority said they had not been close to their fathers and, in fact, some had seen their dads less than a handful of times during their childhood; so the main reason most of them cited for taking custody was to be the kind of father they had not experienced (Coles, 2002). In addition, although only one of them had been a teen father, many of them attested to the fact that if not for their children, they believed their lives would have taken a turn for the worse in terms of delinquency, unemployment, and so on. One father's statement was typical of most of the group:

> These two guys, they are the reason I live, you know. Because I feel without them ain't no telling what I'd be doing. . . . And I just think that if it weren't for those two, I probably wouldn't even be here myself. You know, I'd probably be in jail somewhere or probably dead, you know. So, they inspire me. But I'm just hanging strong because of those guys. . . . One is my heart, and one is my lungs. (Coles, 2001a, p. 78)

Noncustodial Parents

The term "absent father" is frequently, though incorrectly, used interchangeably with noncustodial father. Because of the high rate of single nonresident fathers in the Black community, some have even suggested that the phrase "Black father" has become an oxymoron in the American lexicon (Hanchard, 1997). In practice, however, noncustodial fathers' involvement actually runs the gamut, ranging anywhere from absent to very involved, so some scholars, such as Jennifer Hamer (2001), prefer to call them "live-away dads."

Most research on single noncustodial fathers indicates that over time their involvement with their children declines. Involvement is considerably hindered if either parent remarries, if the parent is geographically distant from the child, and/or if the ex-spouses do not get along. Several studies looking at Black nonresident fathers (Allen & Doherty, 1996; Hamer, 2001; Rivera, Sweeney, & Henderson, 1986; Seltzer, 1991) or comparing Black and White (and sometimes Hispanic) noncustodial fathers (Stier & Tienda, 1993) find that Black fathers have a slightly higher likelihood of remaining involved with their children through visitation and daily care (such as feeding, changing diapers, etc.), particularly in the first few years after birth. Lerman (1993) found that Black noncustodial dads are more likely than White fathers to pay some child support, but the amounts are less. In general, child support and visitation tend to be correlated; if a father is visiting his children, he's likely paying some support as well.

Nonfamily Households

Although this is a chapter on family structure, I should say a word here about nonfamily households. As mentioned in Chapter 3, in the last 30 to 40 years, the percentage of nonfamily households has tripled. In the 1990s, nonfamily households increased twice as fast as family households, so nonfamily households now represent about one third of all American households. The increase in proportion of nonfamily households has obviously led to a decrease in the proportion of family households.

The majority of nonfamily households consist of persons living alone, mostly at the beginning and end of adult life; 40 percent of those living alone are between the ages of 15 and 44, and 40 percent are 65 or older. Table 5.1 illustrates that Whites, Blacks, and Native Americans have the highest percentages of people living alone, because they have the highest percentages of native-born persons. Immigrants are less likely to live alone.

The other smaller category of nonfamily households includes those who have two or more unrelated people co-residing. These account for about 5.2 percent of all American households, but they range from 5.1 percent of Black households to 8 percent of Pacific Islander households. Although we don't know the exact relationship of the people in these households, the census categorizes them by two members of the same sex or two members of the opposite sex. In either case, they may just be roommates, but they are termed "cohabitors." Across all races, the vast majority (85 to 92 percent) of these two-person nonfamily households are opposite-sex.

Gay and lesbian families exist among all races, but it is difficult to know exactly how many exist because when children are present, the household is counted as a single-parent household (due to the same-sex marriage prohibition). It is estimated that between 6 and 14 million children are being reared by at least one gay parent (Kimmel, 2000). We can assume that a disproportionate share of these families have members of color because same-sex couples are more commonly interracial than are heterosexual couples, and adoption of minority and special needs children is increasing among homosexuals, as most states now allow single gays and lesbians to adopt.

The amount of research on gay and lesbian families is small; the amount on such families of color nearly nonexistent. The existing research indicates that on a number of measures, children of homosexual parents are well-adjusted and exhibit no more (and sometimes fewer) behavioral or emotional problems than children reared by heterosexual parents (Laird, 1993).

In conclusion, racial-ethnic minorities tend to have higher proportions of family households (though not necessarily nuclear), extended households, and fewer nonfamily households. Although all racial groups have witnessed a resurgence of single-parent homes, racial minorities, except Asians, have historically had higher levels.

Past family research frequently focused on White middle-class families, often overlooking the racial and structural variations of American families. The single-provider nuclear family became the benchmark, while other family forms were stigmatized, viewed as deficient, and in need of repair. In the last 40 to 50 years, however, White middle-class families are also more likely to be single-parent, childless, or stepfamilies. Therefore, some scholars (Dickson, 1993) have argued that as White families witnessed increases in divorce, nonmarital births, and single parenting, the discourse on family structure softened. Although labels such as "broken families" have not passed out of vogue, terms such as "family diversity" and "alternative families" have arisen to destigmatize these families.

Resources

Books and Articles

Amato, P. R. (1999). Diversity within single-parent families. In D. H. Demo, K. R. Allen, & M. A. Fine (Eds.), *Handbook of family diversity* (pp. 149–172). New York: Oxford University Press.

Barras, J. R. (2000). *Whatever happened to daddy's little girl?* New York: Random House.

Speaking in the first-person, Barras explores the impact of fatherlessness on Black women.

Datcher, M. (2001). *Raising fences: A Black man's love story.* New York: Penguin.

This is an autobiography of a man who grows up without a father and struggles to establish a family in which he is an integral part.

Entwisle, D. R., & Alexander, K. L. (1999). Diversity in family structure: Effects on schooling. In D. H. Demo, K. R. Allen, & M. A. Fine (Eds.), *Handbook of family diversity* (pp. 316–337). New York: Oxford University Press.

Videos

Diversity rules: The changing nature of families [Motion picture]. (2001). (Available from Insight Media Inc., 2162 Broadway, New York, NY 10024-0621, or at http://www.insight-media.com)

This 25-minute program explores why family structures have changed over time and looks at cultural differences.

Independent Television Service (Producer). (2000). *Baby love* [Motion picture]. (Available from Films Media Group, P.O. Box 2053, Princeton, NJ 08453-2053, or at http://www.films.com)

This hour-long video is a montage of interviews with teen moms from a number of races.

Symons, J. (Director/Producer). (2002). *Daddy & papa* [Motion picture]. (Available from New Day Films, 190 Route 17M, P.O. Box 1084, Harriman, NY 10926, or at http://www.daddyandpapa.com)

This award-winning documentary follows several gay couples through the process of interracially adopting and parenting.

Website

http://fatherfamilylink.gse.upenn.edu
This website links to research, organizations, and databases that focus on the father's role in the family.

CHAPTER 6

GENDER RELATIONS AND SEX RATIOS

As discussed in Chapter 4, most societies have a patriarchal social system to one degree or another. Women usually have less access to societal resources and power than do men. Still, within that framework of inequality, there exist myriad ways to define the roles of women and men within a family. Therefore, as with the concept of race, many social scientists agree that "gender" is a socially constructed, rather than a purely biologically determined, concept. How societies define the roles of men and women and what it means to be feminine and masculine varies over time and place.

In particular, societies with patrilineal and patrilocal family systems highly value males for their social and financial support in late life. In patrilineal cultures, daughters do not continue their family's descent line. The sons, on the other hand, are expected to inherit the land, provide for their parents, and carry on the family name. In traditional Chinese societies, for instance, the sons of concubines could inherit, but the daughters of the wife could not (Gonzales, 1998). In patrilocal societies, where the daughters leave their families to become members of their spouses' families' households, girls are seen as temporary members of their birth families. They will eventually marry into someone else's family and will no longer be seen as a benefit to their own families. Under these circumstances, the old Chinese expression, "raising a daughter is like watering another man's garden" (Stockard, 2002, p. 49), seems apropos.

Therefore, in some cultures, giving birth to a girl was seen as a sign of God's unhappiness with the parents (Ahmed, 1993). A party might be held if the newborn was a boy; if a girl, the birth might hardly be mentioned. In fact, traditionally in Korea, not only would a community celebration and naming rites be withheld if a daughter was born, but also the husband and mother-in-law might not speak to the mother for a month. The mother of a daughter would be required to return to her chores in a matter of days, whereas the mother of a son would be given a month to recover (Gonzales, 1998).

In worst cases, where higher male valuation combines with extreme poverty, such inequalities can have deadly repercussions. Women may not receive the same level of care—from nutrition to health care to education—that men do. For instance, in some cultures, men eat first and women and children eat what's left. In a poor setting, little food may remain. In least-developed countries, female infanticide may be practiced or girl babies might be abandoned or sold as workers or prostitutes, because they are seen as economic burdens to be avoided. The accumulation of these practices has resulted in a number of countries, such as Nepal and Bangladesh, exhibiting the unusual pattern of men outnumbering women in the general population. (I will discuss sex ratios later in this chapter.)

When women are so dependent on their husbands' status for sustenance and have little value of their own, they can be dispensed with easily. Recent archeological discoveries in Siberia have found that in the 7th century BC, the Scythians, a wealthy nomadic people, buried a man's wife and horse with him when he died. In that male-dominated society, women were sacrificed to guarantee the husband a robust afterlife (Edwards, 2003). Even today, in India women are still occasionally thrown or encouraged to jump onto their husband's funeral pyre, a practice called "sati" after the wife of a Hindu god. Buttressing this practice are the beliefs that a wife should not continue life without her husband, certainly not with another man, and if allowed to live, a husbandless wife would only be an economic drain on her or her husband's family (Bumiller, 1990).

Gender Stereotypes and Roles

Although many of these practices are declining worldwide due to economic and educational improvements, even in developed societies, many of the old stereotypes about femininity and masculinity persist. Such stereotypes indicate that women and men are viewed as opposites, each having characteristics that the other lacks. This dichotomous view of femininity and masculinity means that individuals who depart from these discrete categories are more likely considered deviant. Boys who have some "feminine" characteristics are called "sissies," "effeminate," or are assumed to be gay. Likewise, girls who exhibit some "masculine" characteristics are called "tomboys," "butch," or lesbian. Still, it is usually easier for women to adopt male behaviors than for men to adopt women's. For instance, it is more acceptable for a woman to be a tomboy, wear pants, or become an engineer than it is for a man to be a sissy, wear skirts, or become a secretary.

Historically, a few cultures escaped such polarized gender roles. That is, persons deemed abnormal by Westerners (transsexuals, transvestites, homosexuals) were seen in a number of other societies as just another gender on a continuum of gender possibilities. Such other genders, called "third gender" (for men) and "fourth gender" (for women) in today's social science literature, were common among some Native American nations. LaFromboise, Heyle, and Ozer (1990) estimate that at least 33 Native American tribes acknowledged some special role or power for cross-gendered persons. Cross-gendered American Indian women frequently were allowed to live their adult lives performing the duties of the male sex, dressing in male attire, becoming hunters, and taking wives (Blackwood, 1984). Sometimes cross-gendered individuals held an honorary status as a shaman or wise person. In *Lakota Woman*, Mary Crow Dog (1990) reports that it was considered good luck to have a *Winkte*, the Sioux name for a gay man, give one's newborn a secret name. The Sioux believed that *Winktes* lived long lives and that this extended life expectancy would transfer to the newborn. Roles for other genders have been found among other ethnic groups as well, such as the Asian Indian *Hijra* and the Omani *Xanith*. Because of Western influence, however, the acceptability of these alternate genders has diminished.

Research on homosexuality among other racial-ethnic minorities in the United States frequently indicates that homosexuality is seen as a White problem (Hetrick & Martin, 1987; Hidalgo & Christensen, 1976–1977). Hidalgo and Christensen found that homosexuals in minority communities experience more role conflicts, both because homosexuality is less acceptable in a number of ethnic groups and racial minority homosexuals must cope with discrimination on at least two fronts. Newman and Muzzonigro (1993) studied the "coming out" process for gay adolescents and found no race differences in the timing and manner in which gay teens came out. But the degree of the family's traditionality—which they measured by (1) the level of religiosity, (2) speaking a language other than English in the home, and (3) the degree of emphasis on marriage and children—was a pivotal factor in the ease with which gay adolescents felt they could reveal their sexual orientation to their families. Those from highly traditional families, which were more likely to be Hispanic and Asian, felt a greater sense of difference as children and greater need to hide their orientation. Moreover, Hidalgo and Christensen found that gay minority adolescents were more likely to lose their connections with family and community than were White gay adolescents.

These socially constructed gender expectations for girls and boys frequently translate into different experiences and roles throughout the life course. Generally, most cultures exhibit a higher expectation for obedience and duty from girls than from boys. For instance, Rindfuss, Liao, and Tsuya (1992) surveyed 2,500 Japanese men and women about what behavioral expectations they had for their children. Although several attributes were expected for both sons and daughters, the authors found that the adults were more than twice as likely to desire daughters to be "obedient" and "dutiful." Conversely, adults were more than twice as likely to desire sons to be "independent," "responsible," and "vital."

The expectation for obedience frequently focuses on girls' sexuality; sexually active girls are viewed more problematically than sexually active boys. Female chastity is given top priority in many countries, as a loss of virginity would hinder a family's search for a husband for their daughter (Ahmed, 1993). Because girls cannot hide their sexual activity as easily as boys (due to pregnancy), women's and girls' activities tend to be more stringently controlled. In America, that is particularly true among Hispanic, Asian, and Middle Eastern communities (Ting & Chiu, 2002). Girls tend to have earlier curfews, are prevented from dating until older ages than boys, or are restricted from unsupervised contact with boys (Bernal, 1984). Perez-Firmat (1995), a Cuban American, recounts in his memoirs that he enjoyed dating American-born girls more than the local Cuban American girls because the former would actually let the boys hold their hands and kiss them.

In some Asian, especially rural, cultures, girls marry at an early age (around puberty in some cases) to shorten the time period within which they might dishonor their families through premarital sex or nonmarital childbearing. (Child-marriage usually reduces the size of the dowry as well [Ahmed, 1993].) For instance, it remains common among the Hmong in America to marry off their daughters between the ages of 14 and 18. Hutchinson and McNall (1994) studied the Hmong community in St. Paul, Minnesota, and found that more than half of Hmong girls were married before they graduated from high school. According to Lee's (1997) interviews with Hmong college women, aside from fulfilling tradition, some Hmong American women choose to marry early to escape parental control or because they fear that Hmong men will find them too old to marry if they wait until college graduation.

In a number of countries, if unmarried girls have contact with a boy, they must marry that boy. If they get pregnant, even if by rape, the girl (and sometimes the boy) might be killed to save the honor of their family. These so-called "honor killings" can be punishment for premarital or extramarital sexual contact. A South Asian paper recently reported that more than 1,000 honor killings occurred in Pakistan's southern province in 2003 (Khan, 2004). While three fourths of the victims were female, nearly a fourth were male. These killings occurred despite the fact that Pakistan's highest court prohibited such practices in April 2003. Although rare, occasionally similar corporal incidents occur in the West. In the video documentary *Cambodians in America*, a Cambodian American police officer relates the story of a young, unmarried Cambodian American girl who was caught holding hands. The girl's family forced her to marry the boy. When she refused to consummate the marriage, her husband complained, and her family slashed her face.

Veiling, which is used by some Asian Indians and Muslims, is another method of protecting women's sexuality. Veiling actually comes in many forms, ranging from a simple scarf to a *hijab*, which shows the face, to a *furushiya*, a gown that only allows the eyes to show. The full-body cover is least common.

For many, veiling is the means to modesty, to fulfilling religious beliefs, although the Koran says nothing about covering the face and, in fact, advocates that Muslim men also dress modestly. (The traditional dress of Arab men is similar to the women's; they wear a gownlike dress and a head covering.) For others, the veil can be a practical necessity in dusty, arid climates or similar to a school uniform; one does not have to worry about the expense and social status of quickly passing fashion fads (although many middle-class women are wearing high fashion under the veil). Still others view the veil as a political statement, a way of maintaining their culture against what they see as encroaching Westernization.

In some conservative Middle Eastern communities, *purdah*, a system of rules designed to keep men and women separate, is practiced. In this case, women are more likely to remain indoors. Women can only be in public if accompanied by a husband or male relative. In social gatherings, a room may be partitioned for men and women. The practice of *purdah*, however, is rare among immigrants to the United States.

Other severe means of controlling female sexuality have included menstruation isolation, genital mutilation, and foot binding. Some cultures have viewed menstruation as having special—but usually negative—powers, such as causing crop failures. In her book on the Cree Indians, Regina Flannery (1995) said that traditionally Cree women moved to a separate tent during menstruation and were required to use separate utensils. It was believed that if a menstruating woman stepped over a man who was sitting on the ground, his hunting would be hindered. By the 1990s, Flannery no longer found evidence of this practice. Still the sense that women's menstruation is either polluting or dangerously powerful continues to pervade many cultures today.

Female genital mutilation, a practice generally involving the removal of the clitoris and sometimes closure of the labia, is still practiced. Although it currently is practiced mostly in Africa, evidence exists that at one time or another it has been practiced on all continents (Ebomoyi, 1987). The timing of the practice, whether performed on young girls or adult women, varies by ethnic group, but in either case it is frequently performed with little or no anesthesia and under non-hygienic conditions that can result in infection. The practice has had repercussions on America's legal system. In 1994, a teenage Togolese woman, Fauziya Kassindja, fleeing her country to escape genital mutilation, entered the United States on a false passport asking for protection. Instead, she was incarcerated in Immigration and Naturalization Service detention facilities for nearly a year and a half while she awaited a court decision. Finally, in 1996 Kassindja was awarded asylum, and her case established gender-based persecution as a basis for asylum.

Foot binding, practiced in China, was outlawed in the first half of the 1900s. You may, however, still come across mention of it in Chinese immigrant autobiographies. Foot binding was not directly aimed at sexuality, but it served to keep women under control. Binding required wrapping a child's feet tightly to prevent growth and frequently involved breakage of bones. This painful process resulted in deformed feet and lifelong discomfort. Because it limited women's mobility, it was rarely performed on lower-class women whose labor was essential. Middle-class women, however, were told that small feet were more beautiful, and their immobility signified an affluent life of leisure. In her memoir *Sweet Bamboo*, Louise Leung Larson (1989) wrote of her mother, who immigrated to the United States as an adult:

> Her feet were not unbound until after Lillie's [the author's sister's] birth. Mama was extremely sensitive on the subject of her bound feet. She was ashamed of them and didn't want to talk about the Chinese custom of lily feet. None of us ever saw her bare feet; she always wore white sox [sic] over them. Her bound feet were a lifelong burden, restricting her activities in every way. (p. 5)

Obedience constraints on girls seep into more mundane life experiences as well, such as chores around the home and educational opportunities. Parents often assign cooking and laundry to girls and outdoor activities, such as lawn mowing, to boys (Lamanna & Reidmann, 2003). Gager, Mooney, and Call (1999) examined data from ninth graders in St. Paul, Minnesota. They found that girls devote more time to household tasks than boys and that this gap increases during the high school years.

Although these patterns are manifested across racial-ethnic groups in America, most studies find gender differentiation in socialization to be sharper among Hispanic and Asian Americans (Bulcroft, Carmody, & Bulcroft, 1996) and less so among Black and Native Americans. According to Bernal (1984) and Min (1998), in Hispanic and Asian families it would not be uncommon that sisters wait on their brothers, whereas Hale-Benson (1986) found that in African American families both sons and daughters were socialized toward independence, employment, and child care. Flannery's (1995) study of the Cree Indians noted that children learned gendered skills through play—boys would be given bows and arrows and girls would be given cloth to make mini-tents. By adulthood, however, Flannery did not notice a sharp division of labor; both men and women could do the other's chores if necessary with no loss of face.

In families where resources and educational opportunities are scarce, parents are more likely to encourage boys to obtain whatever education is available, whereas the girls will be encouraged to marry and provide grandchildren (Rubin, 1993). When Asian or Hispanic American girls do attend college, they often are encouraged or required to study near or at home (Bernal, 1984; Ting & Chiu, 2002). According to Pidcock, Fischer, and Munsch's recent (2001) study of Hispanic and Anglo first-generation college students, Hispanic girls are particularly vulnerable to dropping out of college, especially to return home to help manage household affairs.

Illustrating this, sociologist Eshleman (2003) quotes a Mexican American girl:

> If my father had his way, I wouldn't be in college. My brother was encouraged to go so as to be able to support a family. But for me, he allows me to go just in case of a divorce or widowhood and not to be fully dependent on a man. In many ways, my brother was not overprotected like I was. He could go away to school but Dad won't allow me to live away from home. (pp. 165–166)

A couple of studies on Asian immigrant families found that daughters were encouraged to get a higher education to make them more marriageable to a higher-quality husband (Das Gupta, 1997; Zhou & Bankston, 1998). In Das Gupta's study of Asian Indian women, one daughter reported that she felt her parents wanted her to be a doctor or engineer so she would be a "lucrative investment" for another Indian family to consider for their son (p. 585).

In developing countries, these different educational experiences are manifested in higher rates of literacy and school enrollment for men. Here in America, among Hispanic, White, and Asian Americans 25 years or older, a higher proportion of men than women have college degrees. African Americans are the exception; African American women have a higher proportion of college graduates than do their male counterparts (Fields, 2003). White women will soon join Black women in having a higher proportion of college degrees than their male counterparts; for the last decade or so, White women have outnumbered White men in college. In addition, research indicates that Asian women will also catch up soon; many Asian women are motivated to do well in school to overcome gender inequality. In Lee's (1997) interviews of Hmong college women, one woman explained that a college education would give Hmong women the leverage they need to articulate their rights:

> We are in a patriarchal culture and men get the support, men get the respect, just, they get a lot more of things upon birth than the women. . . . And I think a lot of us have to speak up because if we don't speak up for ourselves, no one's gonna speak up for us. (p. 818)

Remember that within each racial group, much variation exists. Not every family abides by these ideologies, even if they themselves profess them.

Adult Roles

As seen in Chapter 3, gender roles in America have been changing throughout history, adapting to sweeping economic transformations. In America's colonial period, which was largely an agricultural economy, husbands and wives were co-providers, both performing economically valued labor for the benefit of the household. As the country industrialized, the gender roles separated, with women conducting most of the private, unpaid domestic labor, and men performing mostly the public, waged labor. Today, under pressure from a relatively low-paying service economy, more than 60 percent of married women have entered America's paid labor force. Unfortunately, they congregate in lower-paying occupations. Therefore, on average, women still make about 76 percent of what men make. Because men of color tend to make less money than White men, the gendered wage gap is narrower for Black and Hispanic women, who, respectively, make 85 percent and 88 percent of their male counterparts' income.

Despite an income gap, women's paid labor force participation generally benefits the family's overall financial status. Moreover, a higher percentage of women's income than their husband's goes directly to their children. Research on working women in America (Blumberg, 1991), India (Bumiller, 1990; Mencher, 1988), Mexico (Roldan, 1988), Cameroon (Guyer, 1984), and Ghana (Tripp, 1981) all found that across cultures women put more of their personal resources toward their children's nutrition and development, whereas men usually reserve a higher proportion of their income for personal activities.

Women's employment has also impacted the division of labor in the household, though not to the extent most women wish. Wives put in fewer hours of household labor than they did several decades ago, and husbands put in a few more. Still, on average, women perform about twice as much household labor (four times more if the focus is on core chores, such as cooking, cleaning, laundry, and ironing) than do men, even if the women are working full-time (Bianchi, Milkie, Sayer, & Robinson, 2000).

In general, American wives tend to perform the daily indoor household chores (cooking, laundry, cleaning up bathrooms and after meals, etc.), whereas husbands do the outdoor chores that are less frequently required and allow more flexibility in scheduling, such as mowing lawns, fixing dripping faucets, and changing car oil. Women tend to be held responsible for children's outcomes and household appearance, whereas men are seen as helpers. As "kinkeepers," women manage the children's schedules, social gatherings, and family rituals, and frequently mediate father-child relationships.

Not surprisingly, gender is significantly related to marital satisfaction. Most studies find that, regardless of race, women tend to be more dissatisfied in marriage than men. Most marriages experience some decline in satisfaction over time, but it takes a particular dip during the child-rearing years, again especially for women. Looking specifically at Mexican American families, Markides, Roberts-Jolly, Ray, Hoppe, and Rudkin (1999) found that while husbands' satisfaction rose again after the children left home, wives' satisfaction continued to decline, perhaps because the mother role has greater importance in parenting.

Sex Ratios

Every society has a sex ratio; that is, the number of men for every 100 women in the society, and then every subgroup within the society has its own ratio. The variability of these ratios across and within societies and over time is dependent both on genetics and environmental factors. As you can see from Table 6.1, the male-to-female ratio varies with age; usually it continues to decline throughout the life course, so that women far outnumber men in late life. At conception, the gender ratio is estimated to be about 125:100; about 125 male babies are conceived for every 100 female babies. But males, onward from conception, have higher mortality rates. Apparently, having two X chromosomes gives girls a better immune system; hence, by birth the sex ratio is down to about 105:100 (Renzetti & Curran, 2003).

Table 6.1 Sex Ratio (men per 100 women) by Age and Race in the United States, 2000

	Total U.S.	*Non-Hispanic White*	*Hispanic*	*Black*	*Asian*	*Native Hawaiian & Pacific Islander*	*American Indian & Alaskan Native*
Overall	96.3	95.7	105.9	90.4	93.5	102.4	97.6
< 18 Years	105.2	105.7	105.5	103.3	104.3	106.1	103.8
18–24 Years	104.6	102.6	111.9	96.2	100.6	105.8	103.3
25–44 Years	100.2	100.5	115.9	89.2	93.5	103.9	96.8
45–64 Years	94.8	96.7	94.5	83.9	86.5	98.0	93.6
> 65 Years	70.2	70.6	72.2	61.4	74.0	81.3	74.5

SOURCE: U.S. Department of Commerce (2000a), Matrices PCT3 and PCT4

But environmental factors intervene as well. As discussed earlier, girls are more constrained and protected; they are socialized to take fewer risks than boys, and they are not as expected to protect their country. Men are more likely to die of violence (criminal and military) than girls. Men hold more physically risky jobs. Men also have higher suicide rates than women. Men account for more than 70 percent of suicides each year, even though women attempt suicide more. As you can see from Figure 6.1, the rate of suicide varies by race; Native Americans have the highest overall rate, particularly during adolescence (37.5 per 100,000). Asians have the lowest overall rate. In the elder years, however, Asian women have the highest rate among women (8.1), whereas White men are highest among the elder males (37.5).

Consequently women's life expectancy is higher than men's across all racial groups. Currently, American women outlive men by about 5.5 years, which is a decrease from the 7.5-year gap in 1990, but up from the 2-year gap in 1920. As you can see from Figure 6.2, White Americans do not have

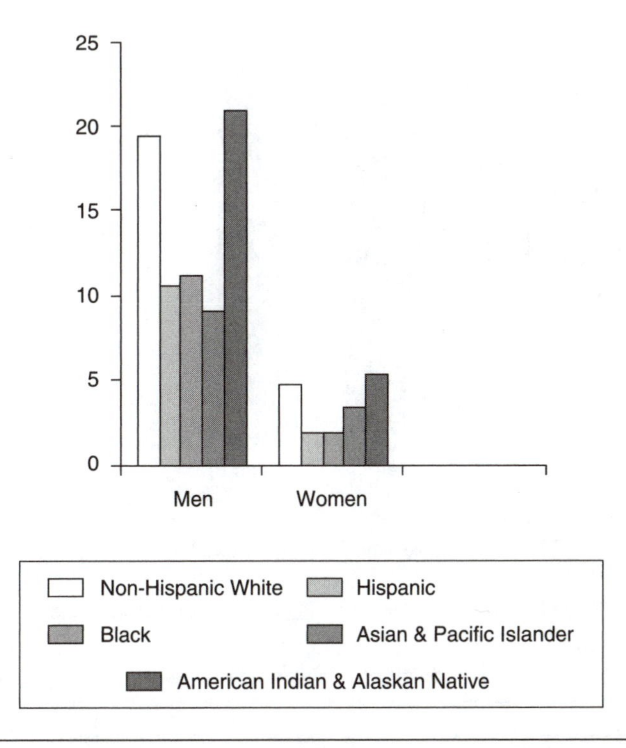

Figure 6.1 Suicide Rates per 100,000 by Race in the United States, 1996 to 1998

SOURCE: U.S. Department of Health and Human Services (n.d.)

the longest life expectancies. American Indian, Asian, and Hispanic women have longer life expectancies than White women, and Asian and Hispanic men have longer life expectancies than White men. African American men and women have the shortest life expectancies. The longer life expectancies among Asians and Hispanics are often explained by their high rate of immigration; as mentioned earlier, people who choose to come here are often healthier.

Table 6.1 also illustrates that the sex ratio in the United States differs by racial-ethnic group. Hispanic Americans and Pacific Islanders tend to have a higher male-to-female ratio, mostly due to immigration, and for Hispanic Americans, in particular, the ratio rises instead of declining until midlife, again because most immigrants tend to be of working age. Men are still more likely to immigrate than women, because women are often not allowed the freedom to attempt that adventure or because their family responsibilities hinder such travel. There are a few exceptions to this general pattern. For instance, among a number of Central American immigrant groups, such

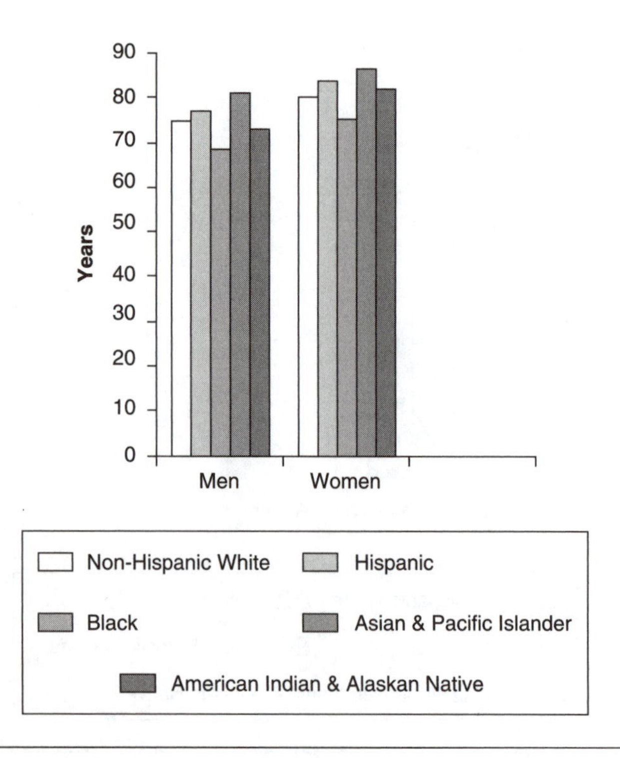

Figure 6.2 Life Expectancy by Race, 1999

SOURCE: U.S. Department of Commerce (2003b), Table C

as Salvadorans, women have dominated immigration to other countries. Push factors include political repression and violence, lack of paid work for women in rural areas, low marriage rates, high female-headed household rates, and men with multiple partners or loosely linked to several households. The pull factor is the availability of low-skill traditionally female jobs in the United States (Repak, 2002).

Sex ratios can affect mate selection and marriage rates for each ethnic group. As suggested in Chapter 4, an imbalanced sex ratio can lead to marriage forms other than monogamy. For instance, polyandry is more likely to occur when men outnumber women; polygyny when women outnumber men. A monogamous culture is not likely to switch to polygamy overnight, so in a monogamous culture a skewed sex ratio would more likely lead to fewer marriages, an increase in single people and parents, and/or outmarriage.

Because of differential histories, immigration trends, and sex ratios, some gender issues are more salient in one racial-ethnic group than another. Therefore, at this point I will focus briefly on each racial-ethnic group.

African American Gender Issues

Traditional stereotypes of women have never fully applied to Black women. Because of slavery, Black women in America were predominantly laborers. Even when laws didn't force them to work, their location in the social hierarchy didn't give them much choice; they frequently could not afford to stay home. Hence, Black American women have historically had higher labor force participation rates than White American women, and the recent feminist call to women to enter the paid labor force appeared as "old news" to many African American women.

In addition, research finds that Black girls are not as likely to experience the same pubescent fall in self-esteem that White girls do (Brown & Gilligan, 1992). Black girls may not relate to the media stereotypes and obsession with fulfilling a certain appearance and therefore don't buy into the same anxieties about not meeting those standards. Black women have higher educational aspirations than White women of the same social background and enter marriage with higher expectations and demands for gender equality and flexibility of roles (Dore & Dumois, 1990).

Studies on African American families have had mixed findings on the extent to which Black women are successful in actually achieving greater equality within marriage. In a review of the research, Taylor, Chatters, Tucker, and Lewis (1990) concluded that gender roles among Black married couples are more egalitarian than those among European American married couples. When researchers use women's paid labor force participation as a measure of equality in the home, they automatically find more equal gender relations in Black families because of Black women's higher rate of employment. Surveys also indicate, however, that both African American women and men are more likely than their White counterparts to view paid female employment as compatible with maternal and familial responsibilities (Herring & Wilson-Sadberry, 1993). Moreover, Blee and Tickamyer (1995) and Shelton and John (1993) found that Black men actually do more chores around the house than men of other racial groups (though still less than their wives).

On the other hand, a number of recent studies demonstrate that African American men hold stronger traditional gender role attitudes than do White men, except on the aspect of wives' employment (McLoyd, Cauce, Takeuchi, & Wilson, 2000). Tucker and Taylor (1989) found that African American men still see their own primary family role as provider, and Bulcroft and Bulcroft (1993) found that African American women also see Black men mainly as providers. Again, this only illustrates that people can hold certain values or attitudes but act contrary to them due to situational exigencies.

The sex ratio among African Americans is skewed toward women at an earlier age than for White women. Although this is not a new phenomenon—Black women have outnumbered Black men since 1850—it has worsened since 1920 (Dickson, 1993). Today, by the ripe old age of 18, Black women already outnumber Black men. The gender ratio is so skewed that Staples (1989) has suggested that Black men should be considered an endangered species. Moreover, with relatively high rates of unemployment and institutionalization (prison or mental institutions) among young Black men, and higher rates of college education among Black women, even the men who are available may not be viewed as desirable by Black women, thus further restricting the pool of marriageable men. Because Black women have been more financially self-sufficient than White women, historically, they have less to gain from marriage than White women (Schoen, 1995). This situation has contributed to the rise in single mothers, as pregnant women who estimate that the father will not be an asset to the family will choose to raise the child alone. In Jarrett's (1994) interviews with poor, never-married Black mothers, one mother explained: "I don't want to marry nobody that don't have nothing going for themselves. . . . I don't see no future. . . . I [can] do bad by myself" (p. 38).

Recent scholars suggest that this growing gap in availability and qualifications between Black women and men has also contributed to conflict between them. In order to marry, college-educated women frequently must marry men who have poorer educational levels and/or who have been married previously (Dickson, 1993). Being contrary to traditional expectations, this situation contributes to higher marital dissatisfaction and divorce rates (Broman, 1993).

Research attempting to decipher whether these Black family trends reflect attitudinal changes toward marriage finds a gender difference in desire for marriage. In a study of university women, 80 percent of Black respondents hoped to combine marriage with children and career in their futures (Bronzaft, 1991). But knowing ultimately that their desire for a suitable partner may go unfulfilled, some Black women decide to have children on their own without waiting for marriage (Lawson & Thompson, 2000; Staples, 1985). From the male perspective, South's (1993) study on desire for marriage found that among men, Blacks had the highest proportion of those not desiring marriage. Black men thought marriage would impede their social life without improving their sex life (whereas Hispanic and White men thought marriage would be a boon to their sex lives).

Black men's better market advantage gives them more leverage (i.e., less need to make a long-term commitment) in their relationships (Braithwaite, 1981; Dickson, 1993). Moreover, the combination of a highly skewed gender ratio, low marriage rate, and high rate of nonmarital births have led some to suggest that Black gender relations reflect a form of quasi-polygamy, as more men form relationships with and have children by several women (Scott, 1999).

Latina/o Gender Issues

The theme of gender pervades many Latina/o memoirs, suggesting that societal messages defining "good" or "bad" men and women are more overt in Latin society. For instance, in her autobiographical account *When I Was Puerto Rican*, Esmeralda Santiago (1993) recalls what she was taught about men and women:

> Men, I was learning, were *sinverguenzas*, which meant they had no shame and indulged in behavior that never failed to surprise women but caused them much suffering. Chief among the sins of men was the other woman, who was always a *puta*, a whore. (p. 29)

Gender studies of Hispanics have found a high degree of machismo among Latino males. Although male dominance is universal, the term machismo implies an exaggerated degree of dominance and has sometimes been explained as an attempt by Latinos to compensate for feelings of internalized inferiority (Baca Zinn, 1980). Machismo represents characteristics that could be considered positive or negative. Physical strength, vigor, courage, pride, a sense of competition, generosity, respect, the ability to control and provide for one's family are all part of machismo. Taken negatively, however, these could encourage

Latinos to prove their masculinity through exhibiting sexual prowess, oppressing women, or by participating in self-destructive or violent behavior.

The traditional feminine counterpart to machismo is *marianismo,* stemming from the image of the Virgin Mary. According to this conception, the Latina wife should defer to her husband's authority, be pure but produce many children, and be self-sacrificing for her family. In Sandra Cofer's (1990) memoir *Silent Dancing*, she writes that her grandmother, having no contraceptive options, gave birth to eight children (three of whom died). With each additional child, the grandfather built an additional room to their house. One day, Cofer's grandmother told her husband it was time to build another room. Assuming another child was on the way, he did just that. Upon completion, he told his wife the new room was ready to be occupied. The grandmother replied "Good, it's for you" (p. 28). Ousting the husband from her bedroom was her only means of gaining control over her body. These gender conceptions may explain why South (1993) found that Hispanic women had the highest proportion of respondents claiming no desire for marriage.

Consequently, most research on Latino families indicates a strong gendered division of labor. The Spanish expression "*mujeres en la casa, hombres en la calle*" (women in the house, men in the street) reflects a common tradition of separate spheres for women and men. Baer (1999) found that Mexican American husbands were willing to do household tasks if the chores were temporary and viewed as gestures of support for their wives.

Nonetheless, much research (Grasmuck & Pessar, 1991; Hondagneu-Sotelo, 1994; Pessar, 2002) indicates that the need for women's financial contribution to a household mitigates conventional gender beliefs. Upon immigration, couples frequently discover they need a dual income or that the wives can more easily obtain jobs in the new country. Frequently, the husbands must take lower-status jobs than those they held in their home country. Hondagneu-Sotelo and Messner (1994) found that Mexican American women did less housework than their counterparts in Mexico and had more influence over household decisions. Pessar, who interviewed immigrant couples from the Dominican Republic, found that husbands also made necessary adaptations. One husband said he never would have been found cooking in his home country; "*la cocina se respeta*" (the kitchen is the wife's domain), he explained (p. 68). But here his wife's employment required him to take on responsibilities, and the new environment meant he would receive fewer sanctions for doing so.

The change, however, can be stressful and some are unwilling to accommodate new gender roles. Repak (2002) interviewed Salvadoran women who had immigrated to Washington, D.C., and found that women who formed attachments to men after migration were more successful in getting them to participate in domestic work than those whose relationship predated immigration. Similarly, Margolis (1998) concluded in her study of Brazilian women immigrants in New York that couples who met in America were less likely to end up separated or divorced than couples who married before leaving Brazil. Apparently, if women were already employed when they met their future husbands, their work and economic clout were accepted from the start of the relationship.

Asian American Gender Issues

According to Espiritu (1997), Asian men have been stereotyped as asexual and weak, and consequently have been less attractive to American women than Asian women are to American men. Writing in his (1994) memoir *The Rice Room*, second-generation Fong-Torres writes that one of his first Chinese girlfriends, also second-generation American, didn't find many Chinese men desirable until she met Fong-Torres:

> In me, Michelle saw an Asian guy like none she'd encountered in her life. I wasn't headed into the straight life; I wasn't studying to become an accountant or a white-collar professional. My music wasn't confined to the violin. Before me, she'd never thought of Chinese boys as romantic figures. (p. 134)

Asian women, on the other hand, have traditionally been stereotyped as unusually mysterious, erotic, and deferential to men—the Geisha girls who enjoy attending to men's every need.

This latter stereotype may stem from the fact that most Asian countries are to one degree or another influenced by Confucianism, which clearly spells out a subordinate role for women. In youth, Asian women should be subordinate to their fathers, then to their husbands, then in widowhood to their sons again. Good women excel in their domestic duties; deviating from this role could cause disharmony in the social order. As one Korean proverb states, "If a hen crows, the household crumbles" (Jo, 2002, p. 78).

As with Latinas, however, immigration increases Asian women's paid labor-force participation. In Korea, for instance, in 1990 only about 25 percent of married women in urban areas were in the paid labor force. About 60 percent of Korean American married women work, however, again illustrating that necessity often overrules one's values. Min (1998) found that most of the Korean American women he interviewed thought they should be at home.

Increased employment of Korean women, according to a study of Korean American couples in Los Angeles by Kim and Hurh (1988), had only a small effect on the household division of labor: 78 percent of employed wives did the grocery shopping, 89 percent of them did the housekeeping, 87 percent washed the dishes, and 84 percent did the laundry. A later study indicated that employment reduced Korean women's hours of housework from 46 hours per week to 25 per week, but their husbands' only increased from 5.2 to 6.7 hours (Min, 1998). Moreover, one third of the wives were working for their husband. Tension at home increased as well. Min quoted one Korean husband to illustrate:

> My wife never talked back to me in Korea, but she began to talk back as soon as she assumed the economic role in this country. After seven years of paid work in this country, she now treats me, not as a household head, but as an equal. (p. 52)

Native American Gender Issues

Due to their low representation in the population, the diversity among the tribes, and their high intermarriage rate, few studies exist on Native Americans' gender relations in marriages. It appears that in most tribes, women were responsible for the children, small-game hunting and gathering, and food preparation (Gonzales, 1998). Although a few tribes allowed women a fair amount of sexual freedom (Coontz, 1997), men usually had more access to divorce, and unfaithful women could be beaten, gang raped, or mutilated (Gonzales, 1998).

As mentioned in Chapter 4, however, Native Americans are more likely than other ethnic groups to practice matrilineality, which tends to assign women more power. In matrilineal tribes, such as that of the Hopi, the husbands join their wives' households after marriage and support them economically, but they exercise more leadership and discipline in their natal home (over their sisters' children). Among the Pueblo Indians in the Southwest, traditionally matrilineal tribes, women built and owned the houses. Children frequently took their mothers' last names, and sons were part of their mothers' clans (Crow Dog, 1990).

Research on the Navajo, another matrilineal tribe, found that Navajo husbands reported higher rates of participation in child care and household labor than most studies show for the general population but still less than what Navajo wives were doing (Hossain, 2001). Interestingly, both Navajo wives and husbands reported equal amounts of time invested in maintenance activities, such as household repairs and lawn mowing, tasks husbands usually do more frequently than wives. Likewise, in Strodtbeck's (1951) study comparing

10 Texan, Mormon, and Navajo couples during decision-making incidents, the Navajo women prevailed in more of the decisions. Strodtbeck concluded their power derived from the Navajo's matrilineal system.

Even in non-matrilineal tribes, many mythical figures are female, which makes it appear that women have more power in that society. Writing of Sioux society, however, Crow Dog (1990) observed that there was a "curious tradition." Lip service is paid to women's position in the tribe, and rhetoric abounds about Grandmother Earth and the White Buffalo Woman, a religious figure, and other warrior women, but in daily life women do most of the work, are not taken seriously, and are frequently abused (pp. 65–67).

Domestic Violence

The data on rates of domestic abuse by race are difficult to assess. Some data seem to indicate no significant racial differences when comparing Blacks and Whites, whereas others indicate higher rates for Blacks. Hispanic Americans seem to have lower rates, but inconsistent data exist on Asian Americans and Native Americans (Wilt & Olson, 1996). U.S. Bureau of Justice statistics for 1993–1998, however, indicate that African Americans were victimized by intimate partners at significantly higher rates than persons of any other race (Rennison & Welchans, 2000). The Black female rate of intimate partner violence was 35 percent higher than the rate for White females and about 2.5 times higher than the rate for women of other races. The rate for Black male victims was 62 percent higher than it was for White males and about 2.5 times that of men of "other races" (the bureau combined Asians and American Indians). The rate for Hispanic females was slightly under the rate for White females, and the rate for Hispanic males was about the same as that of White males. The report also noted that part of the racial differential in victimization might be explained by the fact that among women, Black females had the highest rate of reporting their victimization.

One national survey of 8,000 women and 8,000 men conducted in 1995 and 1996 found that nearly 13 percent of Asian women reported physical assault by an intimate partner (Tjaden & Thoennes, 2000), lower than the rate for White women (21.3 percent), African American women (26.3 percent), and American Indians and Alaskan Natives (30.7 percent). Biu and Morash's (1999) study of Vietnamese American women suggests that Asian women may have lower rates of reporting the abuse.

As you can see, it is unclear how much of the difference in rates is due to an actual difference in occurrence or to a difference in reporting. For instance, Anderson (1997) found that cohabiting women and African American women are more likely to report their victimization. Other recent studies also suggest that Black female victims of domestic violence are more likely to report abuse, perhaps because they have fewer avenues to keep it private (Campbell, Masaki, & Torres, 1997).

In discussions of domestic violence, a question that usually arises is why abused wives or girlfriends refrain from reporting the abuse or why they remain in the household with their abusive partners. The question itself is problematic because most battered women do report the abuse and most leave, often several times, before the relationship ends. People pose the question to the victim, rather than asking why the abuser abuses. Perhaps people presume that men have violent tendencies, but men are abused by their partners as well. Although male victimization is less frequent (perhaps because their report rates are lower), men give many of the same reasons for enduring abuse as do women (Rennison & Welchans, 2000). Those reasons include

- I love him or her, and I was hoping she or he would change.
- I married for better or worse; this is the worse.
- I felt sorry for him or her, and I wanted to help change him or her or I was afraid she or he would commit suicide.
- I didn't know where to go; I didn't want to endanger family and friends.
- I was afraid I would lose or hurt the children.
- I didn't have money.
- I was afraid she or he would kill me if I left.

Although these reasons are common among all races, when specifically discussing why Black, Asian, Latino, or Native American women don't report or leave, additional factors enter the picture. In research on domestic violence among various racial groups, Rasche (1988) found that each racial-ethnic group cited factors peculiar to its situation. For instance, African, Native, and Latino Americans have experienced numerous incidents of police brutality and frequently have lower levels of trust for law enforcement than do European Americans. Manetta (1999) found that African American women, in particular, attempted to protect Black men from more discrimination. Also, because of residential segregation, many racial minorities live isolated from social services such as battered women shelters, and with higher levels of poverty, they may have fewer resources to rely on should they attempt to go it alone.

Immigrant women face additional barriers: unfamiliarity with the U.S. legal system, lack of support networks, and fear of deportation. Language barriers may also prove frustrating or result in the police using the abuser as an interpreter. Sometimes immigrant couples lack legal documentation of marriage, and an immigrant woman's legal status is usually contingent on her husband, although the Immigration Act of 1991 now allows immigrant women to self-petition for legal residency under certain conditions (Chow, 1994).

In addition, a number of ethnic groups have cultural beliefs—for example, "don't wash your dirty laundry in public"—that emphasize the privacy of family life (Campbell, Masaki, & Torres, 1997). Certain minority groups, such as the Hmong, believe that the elders in their communities are the appropriate mediators; others may have been socialized to believe that husbands have the right to discipline their wives. For instance, Hayslip (1989) recounted in her memoir of her life in Vietnam that it was usual behavior for Vietnamese husbands to hit their wives. Although her own father rarely did, Hayslip remembered one time vividly. Even her mother's attitude fed the cycle:

> [After an argument about giving food to some refugees,] I saw the glowing red mark on her cheek and asked if she was crying because it hurt. She said no. She said she was crying because her action had caused my father to lose face in front of strangers. She promised that if I ever did what she had done to a husband, I would have both cheeks glowing: one from his blow and one from hers. (p. 28)

Although domestic violence occurs among all types of people, much research indicates that it is greatly impacted by structural factors, such as age, cohabitation, unemployment, and socioeconomic status (DeKeseredy, 1995; Stets, 1991). Higher rates of domestic violence are visited upon women who are urban, poor, young, less educated, cohabiting (Gelles, 1993; Smith, 1990; Straus, Gelles, & Steinmetz, 1980), and unemployed (Liem & Liem, 1988). Kantor and Strauss (1987) found lower-class men condoned slapping their wives more than middle-class men and were more likely to admit hitting them. As you can see, many of these structural factors overlap with racial minorities, who frequently are younger and have lower income and less education. As awareness of domestic abuse has grown, more organizations, shelters, and education forums have opened to address the needs of specific racial-ethnic groups. (See websites in the resource list below.)

Resources

Books and Articles

Baluja, K. F. (2003). *Gender roles at home and abroad: The adaptation of Bangladeshi immigrants*. New York: LFB Scholarly Publishing.

This work studies how gender roles of Bangladeshi immigrants change after migration to New York.

Carroll, R. (1997). *Sugar in the raw: Voices of young Black girls in America.* New York: Crown.

Teen girls speak about identity, self-esteem, race, values, and the future.

Cole, J., & Guy-Sheftall, B. (2003). *Gender talk: The struggle for women's equality in African American communities.* New York: OneWorld/Ballantine.

The authors critique the state of relations between Black men and women.

DeBiaggi, S. D. D. (2002). *Changing gender roles: Brazilian immigrant families in the U.S.* New York: LFB Scholarly Publishing.

This book examines the effects of immigration on gender roles of Brazilian immigrants.

Espiritu, Y. L. (1997). *Asian American women and men: Labor, laws and love.* Thousand Oaks, CA: Sage.

Garcia, A. M. (2003). *Narratives of Mexican American women: Emergent identities of the second generation.* Walnut Creek, CA: Alta Mira Press.

This work relates stories from Chicana college students.

Hernandez-Avila, I. (Ed.). (2004). *Reading Native American women: Critical/creative representations.* Walnut Creek, CA: Alta Mira Press.

This is a collection of essays written by Native American women about identity, sovereignty, and community.

Malley-Morrison, K., & Hines, D. (2004). *Family violence in a cultural perspective: Defining, understanding, and combating abuse.* Thousand Oaks, CA: Pine Forge Press.

Read, J. G. (2004). *Culture, class, and work among Arab-American women.* New York: LFB Scholarly Publishing.

This book examines the intersections of race, class, and gender among first- and second-generation Arab American women.

Videos

The changing role of Hispanic women [Motion picture]. (1995). (Available from Films Media Group, P.O. Box 2053, Princeton, NJ 08453-2053, or at http://www.films.com)

This 44-minute video discusses how gender roles within the family and community are changing.

Hoe, H. (Director). (2000). *Who is Albert Woo? Defying the stereotypes of Asian men* [Motion picture]. (Available from Films Media Group, P.O. Box 2053, Princeton, NJ 08453-2053, or at http://www.films.com)

The makers of this 53-minute video interview Asian American men about how they are perceived in America.

Images and realities: African-American women [Motion picture]. (1993). (Available from Insight Media Inc., 2162 Broadway, New York, NY 10024-0621, or at http://www.insight-media.com)

This 60-minute video explores issues of love, work, and family among Black women through interviews with famous African American women.

Jeffrey, J. (Director). (1992). *Honoring our voices*. Elmonton, Alberta, Canada: Native Counselling Services of Alberta. (Available from Women Making Movies at http:// www.wmm.com)

This is a 33-minute video that shows Native American women talking about how they overcame family violence.

Wearing hijab: Uncovering the myths of Islam in the United States [Motion picture]. (2000). (Available from Films Media Group, P.O. Box 2053, Princeton, NJ 08453-2053, or at http://www.films.com)

This 34-minute video features six women from different ethnic backgrounds sharing their views on wearing the veil.

Websites

http://www.apiahf.org/apidvinstitute/default.htm
This website is the on-line portal for the Asian and Pacific Islander Institute on Domestic Violence based in San Francisco, California.

http://www.dvinstitute.org/
This is the home page for the Institute on Domestic Violence in the African American Community. The group is associated with the University of Minnesota School of Social Work in St. Paul.

CHAPTER 7

INTERGENERATIONAL RELATIONSHIPS: PARENT AND CHILD

Intergenerational relationships refer to relationships between two or more generations of people. In this chapter, I will discuss relations between parents and children. In the next, I will focus on the elderly, specifically the relationships between adult children and their parents and between grandparents and grandchildren.

The manner in which parents socialize their children obviously varies enormously within and between cultures. The behavioral goals that parents seek and the strategies they utilize to reach those goals are frequently affected by, among other things, cultural values, such as individual or communal orientation, family size, socioeconomic class, the constraints of the immediate environment, and, for racial-ethnic minorities, the need to prepare their children to function in a society where they do not represent the norm. In practice, these factors intersect with one another so that it is difficult to disarticulate cause and effect, but I will attempt to address them separately.

Individual and Communal Orientations

One of the ways in which non-Western societies have been compared with Western (or European-derived) societies has been on their degree of communalism (or collectivism) as opposed to individualism. When applied to family relations, communalism is often referred to as familism. Essentially, what these concepts capture is the extent to which people place the needs of their group (their community, ethnic group, country, family) above their own individual needs. If viewed on a continuum, Americans, particularly White or native-born Americans, lean toward individualism more than do Americans of color and/or the foreign-born.

Fuligni, Tseng, and Lam (1999) measured the attitudes of more than 800 American 10th and 12th graders from Asian, Hispanic, and White backgrounds. Specifically, they asked the students about their expectations for assisting family members in household chores, caring for siblings, spending time with family, respecting family members' advice, making sacrifices for the family, doing well for the sake of the family, and supporting family members in the future. The authors found dramatic racial-ethnic differences in attitudes, with Asian and Latino American youth having stronger familistic values than their European American counterparts.

More evidence of this difference in orientation is illustrated in the degree to which parents seek independent children. White Americans (and native-born parents generally) tend to value independence in their children more than do other racial-ethnic groups, particularly Asian, Hispanic, and Native

Americans (Bulcroft et al., 1996). Although the child's age is the most powerful predictor of independence, that is, older children tend to be given more independence, Griswold del Castillo (1984) found that Hispanic families extended dependency into adolescence, particularly for girls, more than did Black and White families.

Dependence of children on their parents and other siblings is reflected in the types of activities children and parents do jointly, from social activities to sleeping, and in the values and developmental skills parents encourage in their children. For instance, hiring babysitters so that parents can have a night out on the town is less common among racial-ethnic minorities in the United States than it is among White American families. This may be due to class differences as well as to, among certain groups, the more common use of extended family households, which have built-in babysitters. Immigrant parents, in particular, frequently invite grandparents to America to care for their grandchildren. Sometimes, young immigrant parents practice "transnational mothering," leaving their children with grandparents in the country of origin. Both practices allow the parents to devote themselves to work.

In many societies, infants and young children frequently sleep with the parents or with the mother, while the father sleeps separately (Werner, 1979). In part, this may be due to the family's economic status; they may have no choice but to share the same room. In her work among the Hmong in Wisconsin, Koltyk (1998) found that Hmong parents push their mattresses together so that the children and parents sleep in the same room. Koltyk said Hmong parents found it odd that most American parents put their children in separate rooms. American family sleeping arrangements prioritize the conjugal relationship. Middle-class American parents decorate a nursery for their new baby. Later, each child may have his or her own room, separate both from parents and from other siblings. When children sleep with their parents, American family experts express concerns about the potential negative effect on the marital relationship and the development of unhealthy attachments.

In other cultures, children's birthday parties are a mixture of adults and children. For instance, Perez-Firmat (1995) described Cuban *cumpleanos* (birthdays) as all-day communal feasts for the entire family. Guests congratulate the parents, not just the child. In contrast, in many middle-class White American homes, children's birthday parties likely consist of their peers with only a couple of adults present for supervision, signifying their independent social life.

Parental praise of offspring is another indication of valued individualism. American parents frequently praise their children for each accomplishment, attempting to build self-esteem, a sense of uniqueness, and agency in the child. In more communal cultures, less praise is lavished upon the child or it is given for different behaviors, as the emphasis is not on how special the child is but on how much she or he is a part of the family (Gonzalez-Mena, 1993). Praise then is bestowed more when children share with or care for others, less when they do something to call attention to their own talents. Modesty and humility are highly prized in many cultures. In fact, drawing attention to one's self can be unnerving to some American Indians. Lee's 1950s study noted that teachers reported that Hopi students would be very uncomfortable, sometimes breaking into tears, if they were singled out for praise (Lee, 1959).

American parents also stress happiness and individual fulfillment to their children more than do other racial-ethnic groups. "Whatever makes you happy," "Be true to yourself," and "Say what you think" are common American phrases. Many Asian cultures, however, stress social harmony, the ability to get along with and respect others, even if it means suppressing one's emotions or refraining from speaking one's mind (Kagan, 1984). Hence, the Asian versions of the American expression "The squeaky wheel gets the grease" are "The crab who crawls out of the bucket gets pulled back in" or "The nail that sticks out gets pounded back in" (Thrupkaew, 2002). The family or community comes first, and the individual may need to subordinate her or his individual expression to the needs of the larger unit.

American adolescence is viewed as a time developing children push for independence, reducing time spent with their families and increasingly associating with their peers. The adolescent stage, however, is relatively absent for a number of cultures, particularly some Asian and Middle Eastern cultures (Basit, 1997). Obviously, children don't literally skip those years, but the American way of framing the teen years as an extended transition into an independent lifestyle is unrecognized. Children continue to remain submissive to parents even after marriage; youth defers to age (Sue, 1981). In addition, where early marriage is prized, youth take on responsibilities of family life during adolescence. So when people from such societies arrive in America, where their children will more likely postpone marriage, parents may be unaccustomed to, and lack role models for, rearing teenagers (McInnis, 1991).

Some traditions that appear to be driven by familism may be affected by other factors, such as large family size or low income, but the outcome of the practices nevertheless is longer dependency of the child on the parents. Table 7.1 illustrates that White Americans have the lowest fertility and smallest family and household size relative to other racial-ethnic groups. Families with more children and/or more caregivers can encourage more interdependence between adults and children and between siblings.

In extended or large families, children often have numerous caregivers. Passed from mother, to aunt, to grandmother, to older cousin, and so on, their

Table 7.1 Fertility Rates and Family Size by Race

	2002 Total Fertility Rate (per woman)	*2000 Average Family Size (number of persons)*	*2000 Percentage of Households With 5 or More Persons*
Non-Hispanic White	1.83	2.97	7.9
Hispanic	2.72	3.93	28.6
Black	2.05	3.33	13.8
Asian	1.82	3.60	18.1
Pacific Islander	—[a]	4.07	28.3
American Indian & Alaskan Native	1.74	3.50	18.0

SOURCES: Martin et al. (2003), Tables 4 and 9; U.S. Department of Commerce (2000d), Quick Table-P10, Matrices PCT8, PCT17, PCT18, PCT26, PCT27, and PCT28

a. For the 2002 Total Fertility Rate, Pacific Islanders are subsumed in the Asian category.

emotional attachments are distributed among many people (Gonzalez-Mena, 1993). In addition, access to numerous family members provides built-in playmates, so parents may be less likely to encourage their children to develop friendships beyond the family. White American families, on the other hand, encourage a singular attachment to the mother and secondarily to the father in the earliest stages of life. In recent years, nonfamily day care providers are frequently used, but parents usually try to limit the number.

Likewise, babies reared in large families, or in societies where housing is crowded or of lower quality, may be carried around a lot. In America, many families place their babies on carpeted floors to explore and develop large motor skills. But for the former families, the floor is seen as dangerous, dirty, cold, or inappropriate for infants (Gonzalez-Mena, 1993).

Parents with several young children may toilet train the children earlier to avoid having too many tykes in diapers simultaneously. For instance, Boucke (2002) suggests a method whereby an at-home caretaker learns to read an infant's signals and dashes her or him off to the toilet. The stated goal may be a reduction in dirty diapers, but interdependence between parent and child is an outcome.

Larger families may delay teaching their children self-feeding in order to avoid the messes that children make feeding themselves. Some Hispanic families, for example, spoon-feed their children into the preschool years (Gonzalez-Mena, 1993). American child-rearing experts frequently advise parents to let children play with their food to develop motor skills, sensory experience, and eventually self-feeding. But in many other societies, particularly where food is costly or scarce, playing with food would be viewed as wasteful and nearly sacrilegious.

Parents with numerous children often require older children to assume more responsibilities at earlier ages. Therefore, older siblings care for younger siblings or do more housework, such as cooking or laundry. Peterson (1993) reports that in Filipino families, when the older siblings marry and have children, they in turn receive help from their younger siblings in child care.

Ultimately, the specific behavioral goals that parents from both individualistic and familistic cultures seek may be the same. But the cultural context supplies different interpretations of the same behavior. Osterweil and Nagano's (1991) study comparing Japanese and Israeli mothers found that when their children brushed their teeth and clothed themselves, Japanese mothers defined those behaviors in familistic terms, as signs of obedience to their parents, whereas Israeli mothers defined them in individualistic terms, as signs of the child's autonomy.

Aside from family size, most research on child well-being, parenting styles, and child socialization has focused on the effects of socioeconomic class. It is there that I turn now.

Effects of Socioeconomic Status on Children's Well-Being

Clearly, socioeconomic class forms the foundation on which the general well-being of children rests, both by directly affecting their health and by influencing parenting strategies. I have already mentioned that racial-ethnic minorities have higher proportions of their populations in the working class and in poverty, making them more vulnerable to ill health. For instance, infant mortality is higher among a number of racial-ethnic groups. Figure 7.1 displays the 2000 infant mortality rates by race. Although these rates are improvements over past decades, the rate for every racial-ethnic group, with the exception of Asian Americans, is higher than for Whites. If the Asian rate was itemized by ethnic subgroups, we would find the rate for Pacific Islanders to be higher as well. Higher mortality rates are produced by a higher incidence of low birth weight, sudden infant death syndrome (which is twice as high for infants of Black and American Indian mothers as it is for White mothers), and congenital malformations. Contributing maternal characteristics include young age, unmarried status, low education, smoking, and lack of prenatal care.

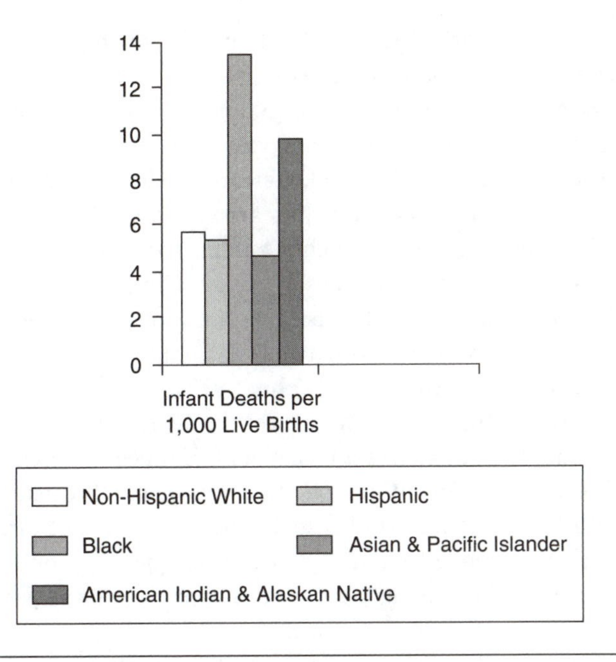

Figure 7.1 Infant Mortality Rates by Race, 2001

SOURCE: U.S. Department of Health and Human Services (2001)

Even though more children of all races are surviving into their youth and adolescence than in the past, severe racial gaps linger in health care, which in turn affect adult mortality rates and life expectancy. Although insurance coverage of children has improved since 1997, in 2002, 20.2 percent of Hispanic children and 8.8 percent of Black children, compared to 6.6 percent of White children, had no health coverage. The Hispanic rate is much higher because of the larger proportion of foreign-born in their population. Given the much higher rate of noninsurance among Hispanic Americans, one would expect that their infant mortality rate would be higher, but as mentioned earlier, immigrants tend to have better health and behave in ways that maintain their health. They have higher rates of two-parent families and are less likely to smoke, for instance.

Parenting Styles and Class

Many studies have concluded that socioeconomic class, more than culture, contributes to variation in parenting styles. Since most of the population falls within the working and middle classes, I will focus on differences between working- and middle-class parents.

Most parents, no matter their class status, have similar long-term goals for their children. They want them to have health, security, and the capacity to lead a successful life (Hill, 1999). Research indicates a class difference, however, in which behaviors and values are viewed as necessary to achieve those goals. For instance, working-class parents (or parents who themselves were reared in working-class families) place more importance on obedience, conformity, good manners, and respect for authority. Middle-class parents, on the other hand, are more likely to instill initiative, creativity, curiosity, and independence in their children (Kohn, 1977).

Likewise, socioeconomic class influences the tactics and disciplinary methods parents adopt to elicit certain behaviors from their children. All parents use a combination of commands, requests, coaxing, and threatening to obtain the desired behaviors. Commands usually involve the use of direct, explicit language, whereas requests and coaxing pose questions or use indirect, implicit language. Threatening incorporates appeals to intrinsic or extrinsic sanctions.

Research on American parents suggests that working-class parents use more commands or explicit language, such as "Brush your teeth" and "Go to bed." Middle-class parents more often use requests or indirect, implicit language, such as "Would you brush your teeth now?" or "It's time for bed." Moreover, middle-class parents use reason or give explanations for their commands and requests, whereas working-class parents frequently interpret this style as spoiling the child.

Most parents use threats of one sort or another to get children to control their behaviors. Working-class parents rely more on extrinsic appeals to reach their objectives. Extrinsic appeals refer to sources outside the person, such as authority figures or threats of punishment. Examples include "Wait 'til your dad gets home," "If you do this, they will put you in jail," or "If you do this one more time, I will spank you!" Lame Deer (Deer & Erdoes, 1993), a Lakota Sioux, reminisced about the external threats used by his grandmother to obtain his compliance.

> When I didn't want to go to sleep my grandma would try to scare me with the *ciciye*—a kind of bogeyman. "*Takoja, istima ye*—Go to sleep, sonny," she would say, "or the *ciciye* will come after you." Nobody knew what the *ciciye* was like, but he must have been something terrible. When the *ciciye* wouldn't work anymore, I was threatened with the *siyoko*—another kind of monster. Nobody knew what the *siyoko* was like, either, but he was ten times more terrible than the *ciciye*. (p. 139)

Intrinsic appeals, used more by middle-class parents, reference emotions or resources within the person or the potential damage to an important relationship. These might include "You should feel guilty if you do that," "Which choice do you think is the best one?" or "It disappoints me when you talk like that." When parents use intrinsic appeals, they frequently appeal to a sense of guilt or shame. Studies indicate that Americans, particularly White Americans, reference guilt more, whereas minority groups, especially Asians, Middle Easterners, and Native Americans, rely more on shame to achieve compliance. Shame includes a public element, emphasizing that others will become aware of the wrongdoing. The use of shame works best in communal cultures, where the individual's responsibility to the family unit is valued, and the individual's behavior has repercussions for the whole family's reputation within the community (Ng, 1998; M. G. Wong, 1998). Therefore, concerns with "losing face" or "dishonoring the family" accompany discipline that is shame-based (Agbayani-Siewart, 1994; Hattar-Pollara & Meleis, 2002).

Parenting Styles and Environment

Some family scholars (Baumrind, 1991; Maccoby & Martin, 1983) have classified these various strategies into four parenting styles—authoritative, permissive, uninvolved, and authoritarian. Authoritative parents set limits and expectations, but are also nurturing. They use reason and are responsive to their children's needs. Permissive parents are more responsive than demanding, frequently allowing the child considerable self-regulation. Uninvolved parents are neither responsive nor demanding. In extreme cases, they are neglectful. Authoritarian parents demand obedience, set many rules, and use coercion more than reason or love withdrawal (separation or time-outs).

Using this classification, some research has found that White parents fall more into the authoritative category, whereas parents of color disproportionately fall into the authoritarian mode. African American parenting style, in particular, has been described as leaning toward authoritarian (Hale-Benson, 1986). Similarly, a study of 1,200 Black, White, and Latino fathers (Toth & Xu, 2002) found that Black and Latino fathers were more likely than White fathers to monitor and supervise their children's activities, parenting strategies that would place them in the authoritarian category. Black fathers, however, were similar to White fathers in their degree of interaction and expression of affection, whereas Latino dads were higher than either Blacks or Whites on interaction. Few studies exist on Asian fathers, but those few indicate that Asian fathers maintain more authority and are more emotionally distant from their children (Ho, 1986; M. G. Wong, 1998). Some studies of Chinese parents, in particular, indicate that discipline is stricter than in the White community (Kelley & Tseng, 1992; Petersen, 1978).

Native American parents are the exception to this generalization. Traditionally, Native Americans were described as indulgent, relying more on persuasion, ridicule, shaming, and facial expression, or simply ignoring bad behavior rather than either yelling or corporal punishment (Ryan, 1981). In recent years, however, punitive methods are more evident among Native Americans.

Some have suggested that this parenting style classification privileges the White middle class (Hamner & Turner, 1990), and therefore should not be upheld as ideal. Research shows, however, that middle-class racial-ethnic minorities parent very similarly to middle-class White parents. Lareau (2002) compared Black and White middle-class parents and found that they were equally likely to enroll their children in organized activities that they believe transmit life skills and to rely on talking as the preferred mode of discipline. Likewise, Amato and Fowler (2002) compared interviews of African Americans, Hispanic, and White parents and found examples of authoritative parenting among all groups. Parental warmth and support, spending generous amounts of time with children, monitoring behavior, expecting children to follow rules, encouraging open communication, and reacting to misbehavior with discussion rather than harsh punishment, led to positive outcomes (i.e., higher grades, fewer behavioral problems, less substance abuse, better mental health, greater social competence, and more positive self-concept) among children of all races.

Reliance on authoritarian styles is frequently attributed to the harsher environment in which working-class and lower-income families (and hence many racial-ethnic minorities) find themselves. More rules, and strict enforcement of them, are perceived as necessary in harsh surroundings. Parental practices that appear overly restrictive in a middle-class environment may provide optimum supervision and support in a dangerous or impoverished neighborhood (Baldwin, Baldwin, & Cole, 1990). Others (Bell-Scott & McKenry, 1986; Comer & Poussaint, 1992) have argued that Black parents historically stressed obedience so their children did not violate any racial rules and, in so doing, bring difficulties to themselves or their families. Therefore, African American parents were more likely to use a language of control; that is, explicit commands such as "Get over here" or "Shut up." Even among more "permissive" Native American tribes, for instance, infants were strapped in cradleboards to make them easier to transport and to teach them restraint. If the infants cried, family members scraped a brushy stick across the baby's face or lips or pinched the child to teach it not to cry. Such tactics were necessary for safety in traveling through dangerous territory (Broker, 1993).

Similarly, families residing in lower-income neighborhoods may sense the need to teach their children the capacity to defend themselves. For instance, in *Life on the Color Line*, mixed-race author Greg Williams (1990) recounts his childhood in an African American Indiana neighborhood, where he and his brother were informally adopted and reared by an unrelated Black woman after his parents essentially abandoned them. One of his first encounters in the new neighborhood was getting beaten up by a neighborhood boy. Williams, about 10 at the time, ran home to get a knife. His "mother" said,

> You do hafta go back. If you don't, them boys is gonna think they can run over you whenever they want. But you can't take a knife. You liable to get kilt. . . . You got to go back up there with nothing but your own will. If he starts a fight, just do the best you can. (p. 133)

Likewise, some have suggested that the Cuban *choteo* humor and the African American game "playing the dozens," both of which involve teasing or insulting someone's family members or making light of a serious issue, are strategies to teach children coping or defense mechanisms. Psychologists Comer and Poussaint (1992), however, warn parents that although they might feel they should train their children to be more aggressive to deal with racism or with dangerous neighborhood streets, the victims of such aggression will likely be family and friends.

The environment has had contradictory effects for immigrants. Most native-born American parents, particularly White parents, feel they can rely on institutions, such as school, church, the workplace, and laws, to support their parenting and control children. Although some native-born American parents complain that schools teach material contrary to their values or that the media work against their family values, this is truer still for immigrant parents. For instance, in their interviews of Jordanian immigrant mothers, Hattar-Pollara and Meleis (2002) quote one mother:

> Life here is difficult; everything in this new environment works against us. Back home, life, in and outside the home, is the same. What we teach at home is reinforced by the society, but here we have too much responsibility to keep the family together. . . . So it [rests] upon me to raise children according to our customs. (p. 167)

Consequently, immigrant parents, who are unfamiliar with American ways and hold images of the high American crime rate in their minds, may hesitate to allow their children to participate in field trips or after-school activities, go to classmates' homes for group homework assignments, or attend social gatherings. People in many cultures have never heard of the American practice of sleepovers. For instance, Timm's (1992) study of Hmong children, found that parents refused to allow their children to visit non-Hmong homes after school for fear that their children would do something Americans would not understand and might be mistreated. They allowed after-school jobs, but thought athletics and other after-school activities were a waste of time. Groups of teens "chilling" in shopping malls or fast food restaurants were akin to gangs in their perceptions. As a counter-strategy, some immigrant families, Asian families in particular, form their own day care centers or after-school programs where they can teach their children their native languages and traditions. At older ages, they provide college-prep classes, called "cram schools" (Min, 1998).

On the other hand, immigrants from societies where collective socialization of children is a predominant style sometimes give children a lot of freedom; they assume other adults will step in to protect their children in the absence of the parents. According to Holtzman's (2000) ethnography of Sudanese immigrants in Minnesota, parents frequently let their children go outside without much supervision as they were accustomed to doing in their villages where everyone is a potential parent. Such a strategy can pose problems in American society, where this might appear as parental neglect.

Corporal Punishment and Child Abuse

Given the preceding discussion, it is not surprising that most research indicates that racial-ethnic minorities use corporal punishment at a higher rate than White Americans. Heffer and Kelley (1987) found that two thirds of both middle-class and lower-class African American mothers accepted spanking as a discipline technique, compared to one fourth of White women. In that study, lower-income African Americans rated the time-out option very low. White middle-class parents relied more on time-outs or attention withdrawal, essentially ignoring bad behavior. Similarly, McDade (1995) interviewed households in the State of Washington and found that 50 percent of the Black parents thought spanking was acceptable, compared with 10 percent of White parents. But only 7 percent of Asian parents and no Hispanic or Native American parents thought spanking was acceptable. Most surveys show, however, that the majority of American parents, regardless of race, use spanking at one time or another, even if the parents don't believe in corporal punishment (Day, Peterson, & McCracken, 1998).

In recent years, debates about the effectiveness of spanking have proliferated. But an overall review of the research indicates that spanking has no long-term negative consequences when (1) the purpose is to correct the child (rather than to vent the parent's anger), (2) accompanied by high levels of warmth and parental involvement, (3) part of consistent disciplinary warnings, and (4) absent verbal abuse or ridicule (Larzelere, 1996). Likewise, McLoyd and Smith (2002)—using data collected over 6 years on a sample of more than 1,000 White children, 550 African American children, and 400 Hispanic children from the National Longitudinal Survey of Youth—concluded that for all three groups spanking was associated with problem behavior in a context of low emotional support, but not in a context of high emotional support. Baumrind (1996) has suggested that socialization practices that are normative for a culture are generally well-accepted by children. Therefore, moderate corporal punishment may be less problematic among African Americans because it is more normative in the Black community (Deater-Deckard & Dodge, 1997).

Corporal punishment, spanking, is not equivalent to abuse. Physical child abuse appears to be correlated with low income and poverty (sexual abuse, which accounts for about 10 percent of child abuse incidents, is higher for middle-class families [Finkelhor, 1984]). Neglect, which accounts for about 60 percent of child abuse incidents, is highly associated with poverty (Giovannoni & Billingsley, 1970), and the most severe injuries occur in extreme poverty. Economic stress leads to depression and demoralization, which in turn lead to harsh, inconsistent, noninvolved parenting (Baumrind, 1994).

As you can see in Table 7.2, the rates of child abuse in 2002 are highest for Native Americans and African Americans, but some studies comparing Blacks and Whites find that when socioeconomic status is controlled, the Black rate appears the same or lower than the White (Cazenave & Straus, 1979). In addition to poverty, the higher likelihood of young unmarried motherhood makes Native and African American children more susceptible to abuse. Across racial groups, children under 3 have the highest rates of abuse, and mothers are twice as likely as fathers to be perpetrators.

As with spousal abuse, however, report rate or perception differences may account for some of the racial gap. Although Asians and Pacific Islanders and American Indians and Alaskan Natives represent lower percentages of abuse victims, they are 20 percent more likely than the other racial groups to be deemed victims when initial reports are investigated for substantiation (U.S. Department of Health and Human Services, 2004).

With the rates of abuse higher among Black and American Indian children, their representation in the foster care system is also disproportionate.

Table 7.2 Child Maltreatment Rates by Race, 2002

	Victimization Rate per 1,000 Population 17 and Under	*Percentage of Victim Population*
Non-Hispanic White	10.7	54.2
Hispanic	9.5	11.0
Black	20.2	26.1
Asian & Pacific Islander	3.7	1.8
American Indian & Alaskan Native	21.7	0.9

SOURCE: U.S. Department of Health and Human Services (2004)

Table 7.3 illustrates that Whites and Asians are the only racial-ethnic groups underrepresented in the foster care population. Unfortunately, a Wisconsin study (Courtney & Park, 1996) found that of all races African American children are the most likely (38 percent) to remain in foster care for 3 years or longer, followed by Hispanics (17 percent), Asians (10 percent), Whites (9 percent), and Native Americans (8 percent). As with the maltreatment figures, a few scholars have argued that their overrepresentation is due not only to a higher abuse incidence, but to the social service system's propensity to institutionalize children of color rather than work with the family or find another family member to care for them (Roberts, 2001).

Parenting Styles and the School System

Differences in parenting styles may explain perceived behavioral problems in other contexts, such as school. Children accustomed to stricter discipline and more authoritarian styles may not respond seriously to more permissive styles. Hale-Benson (1986) cautioned White teachers that Black children whose parents are more firm and physical in their discipline will "run all over" teachers who are practicing the techniques learned in college, and in turn those children will be labeled discipline problems.

Students reared with direct, explicit language might respond to indirect language literally. They may think that the request "Would you get in line now?" is a question to which "No" is an acceptable response. Writing in his 1995 autobiography, Gustavo Perez-Firmat, a Cuban American, recalled an elementary school experience. Every Monday morning, his teacher summarized the sermon she had heard the previous day in church.

Table 7.3 Foster Care Population by Race, 2000

	Percentage of Foster Care Population	*Percentage of U.S. Population Under 18*[a]
Non-Hispanic White	40.9	61.1
Hispanic	17.2	17.0
Black	35.3	14.8
Asian	1.1	3.4
Pacific Islander	0.3	0.2
American Indian & Alaskan Native	3.1	1.1

SOURCE: Lugaila & Overturf (2004)

a. These figures do not add up to 100 percent because they do not include those who identified themselves as "Some other race" or "Two or more races."

> [The teacher] once stopped in the middle of one of her warmed-over sermons to ask if anyone in the class would prefer not to listen to it. Understanding her question as an honest inquiry rather than a veiled threat, I was the only kid to raise his hand, and as a result spent the rest of the morning in the cafeteria. (p. 50)

Similarly, loud or disruptive behavior in school may mimic behavior necessary at home to garner attention from stressed parents in a setting where more family members and noise prevail. Racial-ethnic groups such as the Hmong and African Americans are known for high rates of television viewing (Ford, McDonald, Owens, & Robinson, 2002; Koltyk, 1998), suggesting that children of these racial-ethnic groups might require more stimulation in the academic setting. On the other hand, children taught to respect (or fear) authority and be quiet among adults ("Children should be seen and not heard," my working-class mother used to say) may have trouble participating in free-flowing classroom discussions. Similarly, American Indian children frequently are socialized to learn through observation with little verbal instruction, with the outcome that as adults they sense and anticipate what other family members expect (Miller & Moore, 1979; Swisher, 1991). Speaking from her or his own experience, Cheshire (2001) recalls that "Growing up, I was taught to listen and watch but not ask questions, because I would learn without having to ask questions, and what I would learn would have a deeper meaning to me" (p. 1533). In American classrooms, an inability or unwillingness to participate verbally may be viewed as diminished intelligence.

In Asian cultures, looking directly into the eyes of adults is a sign of disrespect. You can see how this might cause a problem in America, where adults often chastise young people to "Look at me when I speak to you." Whereas most societies consider prolonged staring to be rude, some cultures consider it downright dangerous. You may have heard of the "evil eye." In a number of societies, it is believed that someone can harm you by transmitting evil spirits, even unintentionally, through staring. (By the way, the traditional American bridal veil was originally designed to keep away evil spirits that might accompany all the staring the bride receives. The noisemaking and car decorating were also meant to scare away the evil spirits [Ingoldsby, 1995c]). I will return to the evil eye later in this chapter.

Perceptions of public displays of affection vary by culture as well. Public affection appears to be highest among Hispanic American families and lowest among Asian American families (M. G. Wong, 1998). In Asian cultures, hugging and touching may even be considered dangerous. For instance, in America patting children on the head, or even giving "nuggies," is a sign of affection, whereas in Vietnamese culture touching people on the head is thought to rob them of their spirit (Binh, 1975). Asian children may withdraw, therefore, from shows of affection from teachers or other adults.

The Asian and Native American focus on relational harmony may be reflected in smiling or agreeing at times that would seem odd to most native-born Americans. In her handbook for teachers, Binh (1975) related a teacher's complaint that her Vietnamese students smiled when being reprimanded. The teacher thought they were being insolent or stupid, but Binh explained that the students were indicating their acceptance of the reprimand. Similarly, Native Americans frequently choose to avoid confrontation to maintain harmony within themselves; but in a school setting parents who prefer to ignore a problem to maintain inner harmony might be seen by the staff as uninterested.

Racial Socialization

Racial-ethnic minorities must deal with what White Americans can generally avoid: teaching their children how to adapt to living in a culture where they are the numerical and cultural minority. As mentioned earlier, parents of color need to instill competencies to navigate within a sometimes hostile environment (Miller, 1999). Racial socialization involves the same tasks other parents must accomplish, plus the responsibility of raising healthy children within a society in which being of color has negative connotations. Thornton, Chatters, Taylor, and Allen (1990) point out that racial socialization aims to build personal and group identity, teach children how to cope with intergroup relations, and conveys messages about the individual's position in the social hierarchy. The critical message of such socialization is that race affects one's identity and what options and life chances are available to him or her.

Several studies indicate that most, but not all, minority parents engage in racial socialization (Bowman & Howard, 1985). In a study of African American adolescents, Sanders-Thompson (1994) found that nearly 80 percent of the respondents recalled having had race-related discussions with their parents, especially about racial barriers. Biafora et al. (1993) similarly found 73 percent of their sample of Black teens reported family discussions regarding race and prejudice.

The actual amount of racial socialization may to some degree be a matter of perception. The reports vary by whether the researcher interviewed the parents or the children. In Nagata and Cheng's (2003) study, parental reports indicated that 65 percent had discussed racial experiences with their children, but the children reported an absence of such communication. Similarly, Marshall (1995) noted in a study of racial socialization among African Americans that twice as many Black children as their parents said their parents had been silent on race. These findings only confirm that intergenerational communication gaps exist among all racial groups!

The few studies that have compared racial socialization across racial groups have concluded that the amount of racial socialization varies by race and by the type of socialization. Phinney and Chavira (1995) sampled Mexican American, African American, and Japanese American parents. They found that 94 percent of African American parents reported discussing racial bias and discrimination with their teens, whereas only 44.5 percent of Japanese American parents did so. The majority of each group, however, described efforts to instill cultural pride. Nagata and Cheng (2003) also found Japanese parents less inclined to engage in cultural socialization and preparation for bias communication.

Some have attributed the Japanese reticence to discuss race issues to the Asian values of self-restraint and relational harmony, but others have attributed it to their experience in World War II relocation camps. Specifically, Nagata and Cheng (2003; also Carr, 1993; Nagata, Trierweiler, & Talbort, 1999) looked at the experience of second-generation Japanese American parents and their third-generation children. They found that the parents consciously chose to socialize their children to blend into the dominant society, refrained from actively passing on language and culture, and preferred to avoid discussing their experiences in World War II relocation camps. The authors suggested that this strategy of avoiding racial issues might spare children from being hypersensitive to racial encounters and from being burdened by their parents' experiences.

Most research on racial socialization, however, has been conducted on Black families. Most studies conclude that African American parents validate ethnic identity and negate dominant cultural messages that might undermine their children's self-esteem and efficacy. Thornton et al. (1990), however, found that mothers, older people, married Black parents, and those who reside in the Northeast were more likely to report proactive racial socialization. (Nagata [1993] also found that Japanese mothers were more likely than fathers to engage in racial socialization.)

Jake Lamar's autobiography *Bourgeois Blues* (1991) illustrates the gender difference. Lamar's mom explained the civil rights movement, taught him about Martin Luther King, Jr., and Rosa Parks, and purchased African art for the house. His dad, on the other hand, "was indifferent to such gestures. Dad simply told me that if I worked hard and excelled in school, no one would care about my race" (p. 46).

Hughes and Johnson (2001) examined racial socialization processes among 94 African American parents of third, fourth, and fifth graders. They concluded that parents were more likely to discuss cultural socialization and pluralism (messages about ethnic history and cultural practices) but less likely to address the possibility of discrimination. Phinney and Chavira (1995) and Hughes and Chen (1997) found a similar pattern. Specifically, both studies found that cautions or warnings about interactions with other racial groups, particularly Whites, were reported by a minority (about 20 percent) of parents. The authors speculated that discussions about discrimination were more discomforting than discussions instilling ethnic pride, so parents refrained from initiating such discussions unless precipitated by a specific discriminatory incident. Thornton et al. (1990) found only 3 percent of their parent respondents instructed children to maintain social distance from Whites. When they did, it was usually precipitated by a child's report of unfair treatment by a peer.

Parents' communications to children are important determinants of children's race-related attitudes and their sense of efficacy in negotiating racial barriers and experiences (Bowman & Howard, 1985; Spencer, 1983). Those communications can prepare children to fail or succeed in mainstream endeavors (Hughes & Chen, 1999; Johnson, 2001). Most research indicates that racial socialization engenders a positive racial identity, facilitates the development of competence and academic achievement, and helps minorities handle stress and overcome negative stereotypes (McCreary, Slavin, & Berry, 1996; Oyserman, Kemmelmeier, Fryberg, Brosh, & Hart-Johnson, 2003; Peters, 1985; Stevenson, 1994).

Cultural Rituals That Contribute to Racial Socialization

Not all racial socialization occurs through direct conversation about racial issues and identity. Much of it occurs through observation, listening, and experience. The maintenance of cultural rituals helps develop positive racial identities and social competencies as well.

Socializing rituals can start immediately from birth. For instance, infant-naming ceremonies or birth celebrations are common among a number of racial-ethnic groups. Such traditions are most common when ancestor recognition is an important part of the culture or when higher infant mortality is prevalent (Ng, 1998).

Many Native American nations hold such ceremonies. The Hopi hold an infant-naming ceremony in which the paternal aunts name the child. The Ojibway celebrate a naming feast and ceremony 3 weeks after birth. A wise person is chosen from among tribal members to choose a name, as every person's spirit needs a name, a song, and an animal. The namer visits the child and then meditates on what the appropriate name should be. Ignatia Broker (1993, p. 89) said her grandmother was named Ni-Bo-Wi-Se-Gwe, which meant Night Flying Woman, because she had been born in the night.

Some Asian groups have similar traditions. Hmong infants are usually named and inducted into the world on the 3rd day of life. In Hindi tradition, a baby-naming ceremony occurs 10 days after birth. Chinese Americans traditionally celebrate a one-month birthday, originally only for boys, especially the first son, but recently celebrations are held for daughters too (Ng, 1998). In the traditional ceremony, performed before the family altar or at the temple, the grandmother shaves the infant's hair and eyebrows.

In many infant ceremonies, the navel cord plays a pivotal role, as it symbolizes the tie between mother and child. Some African tribes bury the cord by the house entrance to ensure that the child will always return home. In Vietnam, the cord is saved in a box to sustain the connection between child and mother, even when the two are far apart (Hayslip, 1989). The Sioux make two turtle or lizard amulets upon the birth of a child. The navel cord is placed inside one amulet, which is then hidden in the baby's cradleboard. The other amulet is displayed to deflect the evil spirits (Crow Dog, 1990). Because most births in America occur in hospital settings, it is more difficult for parents to access the navel cord, although more hospitals now ask parents if they want the cord.

Similarly, a number of Latino cultures purchase coral and onyx beads or *azabaches*, amulets made of black coral and blessed by a folk healer or priest, to keep away the *mal de ojo* (evil eye). In Turkey, parents pin gems or amulets on their babies to keep away the effects of the evil eye. In India, some families smudge black kohl under babies' eyes to ward off the evil spirits (Bumiller, 1990).

As the child enters puberty and adolescence, many cultures honor the ensuing bodily and developmental changes, recognizing them as transitions to adult responsibilities. Several Native American groups have ceremonies to mark puberty. The Ojibway hold an ear-piercing ceremony and feast for young girls. The Navajo celebrate the *kinaalda*, a 4-day initiation, and the Apache have a sunrise ceremony, both of which occur shortly after girls begin menstruating (Pleck, 2000). According to Crow Dog (1990), the Sioux used to announce the onset of a girl's menstruation to the whole village. Her family would hold a feast in honor of the event and give gifts to celebrate.

The Japanese celebrate 12th-year birthdays, whereas the Chinese mark 10th and 15th birthdays. Jews hold a bar mitzvah for 13-year-old boys and in recent years a bas mitzvah for girls. For Latinas, the *quinceanera,* a party celebrated near a girl's 15th birthday, is similar in purpose to a "sweet sixteen" party, a debutante ball, or cotillion. Sometimes accompanied by a Catholic mass, these parties can be quite lavish. Fifteen couples may perform a choreographed dance, and families might enlist the help of godparents to pay the costs of the gown, tiara, food, and religious medallions. The girl often dresses in white, to signify purity, as the celebration traditionally announced the girl's availability for courtship.

Holidays also serve as vehicles for cultural socialization. Because African Americans have been in America many generations and are largely Christian, they celebrate most of the same holidays and traditions as European Americans. The majority of Black families celebrate Christmas, but with the rise in "ethnic" toys, African American children's literature, Black-oriented greeting cards, Black Santa and nativity decorations (Jones, 1993), African Americans can now "tweak" Christmas celebrations to reflect Black culture.

A small segment of Black Americans have begun to celebrate Kwanzaa, a holiday created in the 1960s as a means for Blacks to forge an identity acknowledging their African roots (Pleck, 2000). The word Kwanzaa comes from the Swahili language and means "firsts," such as the first harvests of the year. Originally, Kwanzaa was intended to be a simple celebration, lighting a candle each of the 7 nights from December 26 through January 1. Families might gather for a southern-style dinner including mustard greens, corn bread, and black-eyed peas. Like other American holidays, over time Kwanzaa has become more commercialized with Kwanzaa cards and wrapping paper.

Hispanic Americans celebrate mostly Catholic holidays, such as saints' days (which originally substituted for children's birthday parties). In Mexico, a widely celebrated holiday is Day of the Dead (*El Día de los Muertos*), which originated in 9th-century Europe and is celebrated from October 31 to

November 2. It is believed that ancestors' souls return home for a joyful reunion during these days (Silva, 1995). Similar to Halloween, the streets are decorated with paper skeletons, coffins, death masks, and skulls. Sweets are made in these same shapes. In Guanajuato, Mexico, dead bodies are on public view. Music and dancing, as well as the maintenance of family gravesites, are part of this celebration.

The large number of Asian groups prevents me from describing holidays for each subgroup, but the main holiday for Chinese Americans, the largest Asian group in America, is the Chinese New Year, which is one of the world's oldest holidays and is celebrated for 2 weeks. As with most holidays, food plays a major role in the celebration. Chinese tea and pastries are abundant. Various foods carry symbolic meanings: candied melon (health), sugared coconut strips (togetherness), kumquat (prosperity), litchi nuts (strong family ties), red melon seeds (happiness), lotus seeds (many children), and lettuce (longevity). In China, red symbolizes happiness and luck, so adults give children red envelopes containing money for the New Year and on other occasions, including funerals (Fong-Torres, 1995). Parades with dragons and lions to ward off evil are common as well at the New Year's celebration.

Two of the most celebrated Muslim holidays are the Eid al Fitr and the Eid al Adha. The former celebrates the end of the month-long fast called Ramadan, and the latter commemorates Abraham's sacrifice of his son. Because Muslims reside in numerous countries, the style of celebration varies, but in most countries the celebration centers on food and families. Gifts are given to children, and elaborate henna tattoos decorate women's hands and feet. New clothes are purchased for the occasion, and some houses hang decorative lights. The dates of Muslim holidays change yearly because they follow the lunar calendar.

These traditions and rituals socialize children, bring extended families together, and bridge the generations. I turn now to the older generation.

Resources

Books and Articles

Gonzalez-Mena, J. (1993). *Multicultural issues in child care*. Mountain View, CA: Mayfield.

This short book provides examples of cross-cultural differences in child-rearing strategies among parents of preschoolers.

Gudykunst, W. B. (2004). Bridging differences: Effective intergroup communication (4th ed.). Thousand Oaks, CA: Sage.

This work provides an overview of cultural differences in interpersonal interaction and suggestions for avoiding misunderstandings.

LeVine, R. A. (2003). *Childhood socialization: Comparative studies of parenting, learning, and educational change*. Hong Kong: University of Hong Kong, Comparative Education Research Centre.

Here you will find articles on parenting practices in Africa, Japan, and Mexico.

Malley-Morrison, K., & Hines, D. (2004). Family violence in a cultural perspective: Defining, understanding and combating abuse. Thousand Oaks, CA: Pine Forge Press.

This book focuses on family violence among Native, African, Latino, and Asian Americans.

Pleck, E. H. (2000). Celebrating the family: Ethnicity, consumer culture, and family rituals. Cambridge, MA: Harvard University Press.

This work contains a historical account of various holidays and traditions among different racial groups in America.

Wright, M. A. (2000). *I'm chocolate, you're vanilla: Raising healthy Black and biracial children in a race-conscious world*. San Francisco: Jossey-Bass.

This readable book helps parents understand their children's racial identity development.

Videos

Carr, L. (Producer/Director). (2000). *Kinaalda: A Navajo rite of passage*. (Available from Women Making Movies, 462 Broadway, Suite 500, New York, NY 10013, or at http://www.wmm.com)

This one-hour documentary takes viewers inside a coming-of-age ceremony for young Navajo women.

Hammond, R. J. (Producer/Director). (1996). *Overcoming prejudice*. United States: Multimedia Creations Studio of Utah Valley State College. (Available from Insight Media Inc., 2162 Broadway, New York, NY 10024-0621, or at http://www.insight-media.com)

In this one-hour video, participants share stories illustrating important principles about overcoming prejudice. It includes a section on parenting issues.

Websites

http://ourworld.compuserve.com/homepages/hstein/parentin.htm
The website from the Alfred Adler Institutes gives a broad but brief overview of various parenting styles and their effects on children.

http://www.childrensdefense.org/
The Children's Defense Fund site has data, publications, and links to information about the state of America's children.

CHAPTER 8

INTERGENERATIONAL RELATIONSHIPS IN LATE LIFE: THE ELDERLY, THEIR ADULT CHILDREN AND GRANDCHILDREN

In most traditional societies, the elderly often occupy a special place in the family, assuming a position of authority and/or responsibility for the care and instruction of the youngest family members. Deference for the elderly may be signified in verbal or bodily language, such as using the Spanish *usted* for elderly and other people of authority and using *tu* for peers. In East Asian countries, young people are supposed to bow lower to elderly persons than to their peers. The elderly are served first at the family table. In Korea, a younger person should use both hands when giving something to an elder (Min, 1998). In Turkish culture, the young show respect to the elderly when they greet by kissing the hand of the elder and touching the hand to their foreheads.

The national policies of a number of countries honor the elderly. Japan has a national holiday for the elderly and a 1963 law stating that elders should be loved, respected, and guaranteed a wholesome, peaceful life. Many large Japanese corporations accommodate elderly employees with part-time work. Korea as well has a "Respect for the Elderly" week, during which prizes are awarded to individuals, particularly those of limited means, who made sacrifices to care for their elders (Sung, 1990). In a number of Asian countries, children traditionally organize a party for their parents' 60th birthdays, celebrating their longevity and the completion of a zodiac cycle (Tran, 1998). Although this celebration varies by class, it can be a very expensive enterprise.

Traditionally, Native American elderly were highly prized for their life experience and roles as cultural transmitters in the community. The Sioux, for instance, called a new child "little grandfather" or "little grandmother" to impress upon them the respect due an elderly person (Bahr, 1994). Under traditional indigenous governmental forms, elderly played a key role in shaping policy. That role eroded, however, as a result of federal initiatives that discarded traditional procedures, such as community consultation and informal consensus building, in favor of efficiency driven models (Baldridge, 2001).

Declining deference to the elderly has been widespread across cultures. The proportion of elderly has increased in most countries, rendering them more burdensome, and technology has displaced labor, reducing the value of experiential wisdom. In countries where rural-to-urban migration or immigration of young adults has been necessary to secure employment, the rural areas have become disproportionately elderly. Consequently, many elderly find themselves bereft of the family members they hoped would care for them (Coles, 2001b).

In response, governments are developing more extensive programs to accommodate their aging populations. Japan has introduced mandatory long-term care insurance, and Japan, Canada, and Australia have developed extensive hospital systems for the elderly. Nordic countries have expanded community care services, and Denmark has offered free home health care for the elderly (Angel & Angel, 2004).

Having a substantial proportion of elderly in any society is a fairly new phenomenon. In the United States, as life expectancy increased from 35 in the late 1700s to about 77 in 2000, the percentage of the population over 65 has also increased. Currently, nearly 13 percent of the population is over 65 (compared to about 4 percent in 1900). That percentage is expected to double over the next few decades as the Baby Boomers enter late life. Similar aging patterns are being replicated in much of the world. European countries have the oldest populations, but other countries in Asia, South America, and Africa, are also experiencing the aging of their populations (Tepperman & Wilson, 1993).

Minority elderly, however, are underrepresented in the American elderly population. As you see in Table 8.1, 14 percent of White Americans are over 65, whereas in all other racial groups the elderly account for less than 8 percent of their populations. For Hispanic and Asian Americans, the small numbers reflect their high proportion of younger immigrants. Lower life expectancies and higher mortality rates among Black and Native Americans play a strong role too (refer to Figure 6.2).

As the numbers of elderly have grown, more than tripling as a proportion of the population, the developmental stage of late life has increasingly

Table 8.1 Minority Elderly Population, 2000

	Percentage of Ethnic Group Over 65	*Minority Elderly as a Percentage of Total U.S. Elderly*[a]
Non-Hispanic White	14.0	83.6
Hispanic	5.3	5.0
Black	7.8	8.0
Asian & Pacific Islander	6.6	2.4
American Indian & Alaskan Native	7.3	0.4

SOURCES: U.S. Department of Commerce (2000b); U.S. Department of Commerce (2001b), Table 1

a. The percentages in this column do not add up to 100 because those who checked "Two or more races" or "Some other race" were not included.

become a focus of scholarship. Social scientists have begun exploring the relations between the elderly and their adult children and/or grandchildren. Such intergenerational interaction is frequently measured by the level of co-residence, amount of caregiving, exchange of various resources between the generations, and/or the amount of social interaction.

Intergenerational Interaction

Late life is replete with new adjustments, most commonly widowhood, learning to live alone again, and then disability. A network of support is essential to manage these transitions successfully. Demographic changes, however, have made support networks more tenuous. The aging of the population, the increase in the number of generations alive at one time, and the decrease in fertility rates have resulted in what scholars call a "verticalization" of the population (Mabry, Giarrusso, & Bengston, 2004). The younger generations have become narrower, and the older generations are "top heavy" in relation to the whole structure, potentially resulting in more care recipients than providers, particularly for elders who have only one or no children. Data indicate that 35 percent of elderly in their 90s are childless (either because they never had children or because they outlived their children), and 65 percent have also lost siblings. White elderly, in particular, are susceptible to this caretaker shortage due to their lower fertility rates, smaller family sizes, and fewer extended kin (Johnson & Barer, 1994).

Living Arrangements of the Elderly

As mentioned in Chapter 5, families of color are more likely than White Americans to live in multigenerational extended households. Using 1990 census data, Kamo (2000) found that racial-ethnic minority groups, particularly Asian Americans, were, on average, about four to five times more likely to have households containing adults 55 years old or older co-residing with grandchildren.

Many Asian families practice "filial piety," which in religious families includes ancestor worship. In Asian tradition, the oldest son is expected to care for his parents financially and to co-reside with them. His wife will do most of the daily care for his parents. A Chinese proverb illustrates this division of labor: "A son-in-law may perform half the duty of a son, but a daughter-in-law must do twice as much as a daughter" (Pleck, 2000). Consequently, sometimes eldest sons have more difficulty finding wives than do younger sons, as women anticipate their heavy workload (Min, 1998).

Despite the nod to patriarchal deference, upon immigration to America, Asian elderly are increasingly living with the daughter's family or independently. Also, research indicates that Asian American elderly increasingly prefer their freedom, acknowledging that co-residence in their adult child's household can lead to conflicts over food, bedtime, child rearing, and socializing (Min, 1998).

As mentioned in Chapter 5, although some of the high rate of multigenerational co-residence among racial-ethnic minorities arises from cultural values, some of it stems from situational exigencies. Research among Blacks and Whites indicates that if one controls for socioeconomic status, health, marital status, and kin availability, then the race differences in co-residence are minimal or nonexistent (Burr & Mutchler, 1999). For instance, the fact that African Americans have more unmarried elderly, with lower income and poorer health, and more adult children as potential caretakers, makes co-residence between Black adult children and elderly more common.

People often assume that multigenerational co-residence is motivated solely by the needs of the elderly; that is, that the elderly are being cared for in their adult child's home. Recent census data, however, indicate that in 65 percent of multigenerational households, the grandparent is the householder (Simmons & O'Neill, 2001). This pattern is particularly true for White and Black Americans and slightly less common among Hispanic Americans. For Asian Americans, a slight majority of multigenerational households are headed by the adult children (Kamo, 2000), probably indicating that in many cases adult children immigrate and then send for their parents.

The predominance of the older generation as household heads results from an increase in American young adults remaining or returning to their parents' household. Historically, American children have tended to leave home earlier than those in many other cultures, including some European ones. Leaving home has been viewed as a developmental step in the life of the young adult and a goal for many American parents who seek independent offspring. Now, because of marriage postponement, longer education, increased housing costs, repeal of the military draft, and government policy that has improved the financial security of older Americans, many young adults, 18 to 34 years old, remain with or return to their parents' home (Cohen & Casper, 2002). Figure 8.1 illustrates that increase and shows that young men are more likely than young women to reside with their parents.

These figures alone don't prove who is more dependent on whom, but it does bring under question the assumption of elder caregiving. In fact, several studies suggest that when adult children co-reside with parents under 75 years old, it is frequently the children who are the prime beneficiaries (Speare & Avery, 1993).

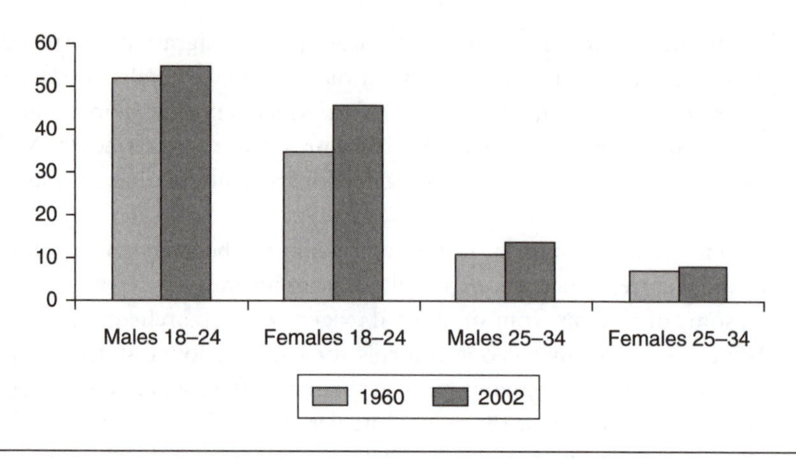

Figure 8.1 Percentage of Young Adults Living at Home, 1960 and 2002

SOURCE: U.S. Department of Commerce (2003d)

Caregiving for the Elderly

When elderly do face ill health, family members are the primary source of assistance for elderly among all races; but research on Hispanic, Black, and White Americans indicates that Black and White elderly rely on family, friends, and neighbors, whereas Hispanic elderly mostly rely on family only (Cantor, Brennan, & Sainz, 1994). Black Americans are more likely than White Americans to make use of adult day care (Wallace, Snyder, Walker, & Ingman, 1992) and home health care services (Cagney & Agree, 1999). Research on Asian Americans suggests that assistance from social service agencies and professionals is almost nonexistent (M. G. Wong, 1998).

Nursing Home Use

Families of color less frequently use nursing homes for their elderly members than do White Americans. In general, less than 5 percent of all American elderly reside in nursing homes at any point in time. The percentage of elderly of color in nursing homes is usually lower, about 2 to 3 percent. Of course, those percentages would increase if I were to estimate about how many elderly will ever spend some time in a nursing home.

Several factors account for lower nursing home usage among families of color. Quality nursing home care is costly, beyond the reach of a disproportionate share of minority families. For instance, 40 percent of African American nursing home residents (compared to 9 percent of White residents) live in low-tier facilities, which employ significantly fewer skilled staff and are more often cited for health deficiencies (Mor, Zinn, Angelelli, Teno, & Miller, 2004). Also, the higher rate of multigenerational co-residence among minorities prior to ill health makes co-residence after ill health more common. Finally, racial minorities, particularly immigrants, may anticipate parental discomfort in nursing homes where English is spoken, the food is different, cultural variations are not understood or appreciated, and discrimination may be present. Such a setting increases the opportunity for alienation and abuse.

Consequently, a number of ethnic groups have established nursing homes targeting elderly of their own ethnic group. Nursing homes and/or elderly day care centers have been developed by Latino social services, such as Casa Central in Chicago, to meet the special language and cultural needs of Latin elders (Suarez, 1998). Native Americans run about 12 nursing homes nationwide (Baldridge, 2001). Likewise, nursing facilities for Asians have opened on the West Coast in cities such as Sacramento and Seattle.

Informal Home Caregiving

If families of color use nursing homes less, it would seem logical to assume they are doing more in-home caregiving. The literature, however, is mixed. In part, contradictory results are often due to the way caregiving is measured (financial, daily activities, emotional, residence, etc.) and to class differences that researchers may overlook. Across races, middle-class families tend to assist with money and goods, whereas working-class families tend to assist through daily care support (Seelbach, 1981).

Other research indicates that elders of color have greater expectations and needs for caregiving. Several studies have found that older African and Hispanic Americans have greater expectations that adult children will personally care for them (Burr & Mutchler, 1999; Lee, Peek, & Coward, 1998). Burr and Mutchler found that when one controls for those expectations, the impact of race on the likelihood of caregiving and co-residence is insignificant. In addition, Black, Latino, and Native American elderly have lower life expectancies than White elderly and higher rates of nearly every major activity-limiting disease. They are more than twice as likely as White elderly to describe their health as fair to poor (Williams, Yu, Jackson, & Anderson, 1997). Black and Hispanic elderly see themselves as reaching old age more quickly than do Whites (Baldridge, 2001; Markides, 1985). Therefore, the opportunities for intergenerational caregiving are more frequent but perhaps of shorter duration in racial-ethnic minority groups with higher mortality and shorter lives.

Caregiver Stress

A number of studies have been conducted on caregiving across racial groups. Generally, daughters do more of the caregiving (bathing, feeding, and dressing) than sons, particularly when the elderly parent's needs are greater. Sons provide less-intensive care, such as transporting and shopping (Dwyer & Coward, 1991) and more intermittent care than daughters, and they tend to withdraw from care as parents become more disabled (Matthews & Rosner, 1988; Montgomery & Kamo, 1989; Stoller, 1990). But when one looks at helping *non-impaired* elderly, then sons help as frequently as daughters. Single sons and daughters contribute more care than married offspring (Laditka & Laditka, 2001).

Despite the greater need for caregiving, African American caregivers (mostly women) experience less stress in caregiving than do White caregivers. Hinrichsen and Ramirez (1992) studied people who were caring for elderly with dementia; Horwitz and Reinhard (1995) examined caregivers of severely mentally ill relatives; and Mui (1992) studied caregiving daughters of elderly. All found that Black caregivers expressed less burden and emotional strain. (Similar conclusions were found for those who studied caregivers of ill children as well [Carter, Urey, & Eid, 1992; Hill, 1994]). Black caregivers also experienced less conflict among their multiple roles of worker, parent, and elder caregiver. The researchers attributed the lower stress levels to African Americans' (1) stronger religious views (through which they interpret illness and caregiving as part of God's plan [Picot, 1995]); (2) idealization of the caregiving role (Hill, 1994); (3) greater acceptance of sickness as a normal part of life (Hill, 1994); and/or (4) having more relaxed caregiving strategies (Hinrichsen & Ramirez, 1992). Moreover, African Americans use more fictive kin in caregiving in late life (Taylor, Chatters, & Jackson, 1993), so the caregiving load may be more dispersed among Blacks than among Whites.

Studies on caregiving among other racial-ethnic groups have been few in number. Shomaker (1990) and Red Horse (1980) studied the Pueblo Indians; each found that intergenerational caregiving reflected the Pueblo communal culture and their ethos of interdependency and reciprocity. Hennessy and John (1995) and a later follow-up study (John, Hennessy, Dyeson, & Garrett, 2001) concluded that Pueblo caregivers, who were predominantly female kin, found substantial stress and guilt when outside responsibilities interfered with being a good caretaker. Purdy and Arguello (1992) found that Hispanic elderly exhibited more depression when they had to rely on informal familial support. Sotomayor and Curiel (1988) concluded that intergenerational caregiving among Hispanic families sometimes resulted in conflict because the elderly had greater expectations than the younger generation could live up to.

Elder Abuse

Few studies have been conducted on elder abuse generally, let alone across racial groups. It is well-known that victims' vulnerability enhances opportunity for abuse; when elders are dependent financially and physically on their children, especially when disability is severe or when the past relationship between elder and caregiver was strained, the opportunity for abuse increases.

Le (1997) conducted one small study of 20 Vietnamese elderly in San Jose, California, and found no evidence of physical abuse and only one case of financial abuse. Le, however, found fairly widespread incidence of emotional and verbal abuse. The Vietnamese elderly claimed that their daughters-in-law used them as free labor. Sometimes, they said, their children wouldn't let them leave the house or, to the contrary, threatened that they would kick them out of the house. The elders thought their daughters-in-law were jealous of the filial respect given to the parents by their husbands.

Brown (1989) conducted interviews among a sample of elderly Navajo and found that the most frequent type of abuse was neglect, followed by financial exploitation. Many Native American elderly fear abuse from increased violence, gang activity, and undisciplined kids on the reservation.

Social Interaction and Resource Exchange

Generally, most U.S. national surveys find that elderly family members have a high rate of interaction with the younger generation. About 60 percent of American elderly live within 10 minutes of one of their children (Lin & Rogerson, 1995), and 85 percent of American elderly report speaking to or seeing at least one of their children, particularly their daughters, weekly (U.S. Department of Health and Human Services, 1993). These findings are similar across racial groups (Chan, 1988; Mitchell & Register, 1984).

Most data on racial minorities show that African American and Hispanic elderly tend to live closer to family members than do White Americans (Burr & Mutchler, 1999). John (1991) studied a band of Potawatami Indians, a patrilineal nation in Kansas. Unlike nationwide findings, John found that Potawatami sons tended to live closer to parents, but daughters were more likely to have recently seen parents. Also contrary to most research on American elderly, John found that unmarried Potawatami elderly had more interaction with their adult children than did married elderly.

In terms of resource exchanges, middle generations tend to give more financial assistance to their adult children than to their elder parents (Logan & Spitze, 1996). But a few racial differences have been found in this respect. Black and Hispanic adult children tend to receive less money and social support from parents than do White adult children (Cox & Rank, 1992; Lee & Aytac, 1998; McGarry & Schoeni, 1995). In fact, when Lee and Aytac studied White, Black, and Hispanic families, they found that whereas White parents were more likely to assist their children financially than were Black and Hispanic parents, all three sets of parents gave more to their highly educated children. They also found that resource transfers to elderly parents from the middle generation were about the same in each racial group.

Grandparenting

Grandparenting on a noticeable basis is a 20th-century invention. In 1900, only 4 percent of the U.S. population was over 65 years old. Life expectancy was under 50 years old. So only a minority of families had grandparents around for a substantial period of their lives. Nowadays, life expectancy has increased while the median age at which people become grandparents has not risen dramatically (still in the late 40s). Therefore, a majority of young Americans have two or more grandparents alive. A minority of Americans even have one or more great grandparents alive as well. Moreover, people can now spend a substantial portion, maybe half, of their lives as grandparents. Consequently, the grandparent role has expanded. Most grandparents at least provide some degree of companionship to their grandchildren, and a growing percentage is very involved. In fact, some are primary caregivers to their grandchildren.

Most research looking at race and grandparenting has compared Black and White grandparents. Silverstein and Marenco (2001) found that African American parents are less involved in recreational activities with grandchildren but more involved in religious ceremonies and traditional events. Black grandparents are more likely to discipline their grandchildren and to live near or with them (also Cherlin & Furstenberg, 1986). Some research has found Black grandparents more frustrated in the role (Watson & Koblinsky, 1997), whereas others have found them to feel more proficient in the grandparent role than White grandparents (Silverstein & Marenco).

The recent increase in multigenerational households signifies that more grandchildren are residing with their grandparents. More significantly, more grandparents and grandchildren are co-residing without the presence of the middle generation (Lugaila, 1998). Table 8.2 illustrates the proportion of grandparents living with grandchildren, and the proportion of them who have primary responsibility for caring for their grandchildren. Pacific Islanders have the highest proportion of co-residing grandparents, but Native Americans and African Americans have the highest proportion of grandparents who are primary caregivers. These two groups have high rates of

Table 8.2 Grandparents Co-Resident With Grandchildren, as Primary Caregivers, and by Length of Time and Race, 2000

	Percentage of Population Age 30 and Over Residing With Grandchildren	*Percentage of Co-Resident Grandparents Responsible for Grandchildren*	*Percentage Who Have Been Responsible for 5 or More Years*
Non-Hispanic White	2.2	43.0	36.6
Hispanic	8.4	34.7	33.3
Black	8.2	51.7	45.2
Asian	6.4	20.0	32.7
Pacific Islander	10.0	38.7	43.3
American Indian & Alaskan Native	8.0	56.1	40.0

SOURCE: Simmons & Dye (2003), Table 1

nonmarital births and are concentrated in inner city areas or reservations where drug use, mortality rates, unemployment, and poverty are higher. All racial groups have a substantial minority of grandparent caregivers who have held that role for at least 5 years.

Because the primary caregiver role can be transitory, it is difficult to paint an exact profile of these grandparents. The majority are White, but African, Hispanic, and Native Americans (especially on reservations [John, 1998]), are overrepresented. The majority of primary caregivers are younger grandparents, under 65. About a quarter of them are in poverty, and a third have no health insurance. Most of these grandparents adopt this added responsibility due to substance abuse, homelessness, incarceration, teen pregnancy, or death among the middle generation. Most take on this role assuming it will be permanent (Woodworth, 1996).

Although this increased grandparent role signifies strong multigenerational ties, we shouldn't over-romanticize it; it can be difficult for grandparents to raise their grandchildren. Grandparents are more likely than parents to be older, have health concerns, and limited incomes. In their small qualitative study of 22 African American grandmothers who were taking care of their grandchildren, Rodgers-Farmer and Jones (1999) found that the grandparents reported that they became caregivers because they did not want to see their grandchildren go into foster care. They reported feeling rewarded by the companionship, meaning, and youthful activities that their grandchildren brought into their lives. But they also said they felt stressed by the experience. They encountered increased financial instability, lack of freedom, and sometimes resentment from their other children and grandchildren.

Acting as parents, grandparents may seek legal custody or guardianship to access state services and assistance. In many states, without this status, grandparents have difficulty enrolling their grandchildren in school or accessing medical care for them. A few states, such as Wisconsin, have developed Kin Care programs, which enable extended kin to qualify for monthly subsidies if they are caring for related children.

Illness and Death

Most elderly report being in good health and are able to continue family obligations and interactions, but illness and death do eventually occur. Although they can happen at any time, they usually happen in late life, so this is an appropriate place to discuss cultural differences in health- and death-related beliefs and practices.

Illness

Traditional folk beliefs about causes and treatments of illness remain prevalent to varying degrees in all racial-ethnic groups (Garner, Lipsky, & Turnbull, 1991; Seligman & Darling, 1997) and can usually coexist with modern medical beliefs. For instance, in one study, a researcher interviewed members of a four-generation Hispanic family, asking them to identify the possible causes of a baby born with disabilities. Whereas some members suggested substance abuse or lack of oxygen at birth as possible causes, others suggested an earthquake or punishment for the mother's ridiculing a disabled person (Salas-Provance, Erickson, & Reed, 2002).

Due to these different beliefs, several racial groups rely on their own forms of alternative medicine. The belief that illness is caused by an imbalance in hot and cold, yin and yang forces, or disharmony of spirits is common among Hispanic, Native, and Asian Americans. Therefore, these racial groups may seek the aid of traditional healers with foods or herbs that are considered hot or cold to correct the imbalance (Tanner, 1995). Native Americans use practices such as sweat lodges, the sacred circle, and ember, crystal, or star gazing for spiritual healing (Waller & Patterson, 2002). Others burn sage and fan the smoke with an eagle feather to purify the patient (Irish, 1993). Some Hispanic Americans practice a folk medical system called *curanderismo,* in which shamans perform various healing rituals and prepare herbal mixtures.

A number of ethnic groups in the United States seek medical treatment reluctantly because their cultural beliefs and practices regarding the body are opposed to Western conceptions. With regard to mental health, many ethnic groups, particularly those originating in societies with low levels of education, lack information on mental illness. Also, such illness is highly stigmatized, requiring secrecy or denial to avoid dishonoring the family. Therefore, some Asian Americans, particularly among the elderly, report somatic symptoms, such as headache, fatigue, or insomnia, instead of depression (Le, 1997).

Although a growing segment of Hmong have converted to Christianity, traditional Hmong practice a form of animism highly influenced by Buddhism. Hmong believe a spirit world coexists alongside the physical world. That spirit world is inhabited by ancestor spirits (especially the father's ancestors), house spirits, nature spirits, and evil spirits. Many of these spirits require appeasement, which is accomplished through animal sacrifice. Moreover, traditional Hmong believe that every human has 12 spirits or souls, each representing a body part. If those spirits wander and enter someone else's body, they can cause illness. Bliatout (1993) relates an incident occurring at the death of a Head Start teacher whose class contained a number of Hmong students. The teacher, a non-Hmong woman, previously had the children make Christmas ornaments with their photos on them. The family of the teacher decided to bury the ornaments with the teacher. The Hmong parents requested return of the photos, as they believed that burying photos of people who are still alive separates their spirits from their bodies, thereby making them susceptible to misfortune and early death.

Death

The way people treat a dead body or express their grief differs among societies. In some cultures, embalmment, autopsies, and cremation—standard American mortuary procedures—are unacceptable. Burial and funerals may take anywhere from one day to weeks. Grief may be expressed through laughter, crying, or self-inflicted injury. In Bali, for instance, emotional control is highly valued, as negative emotions are perceived as a threat to one's health. Therefore, people will help the bereaved to treat death lightly through humor or distraction (Wikan, 1988). In other cultures, such as Middle Eastern and African, wailing, pulling one's hair, and long-term depression is expected. In some cases, self-mutilation is acceptable. When people from more expressive cultures view American funerals, they think that Americans don't care about the people in their lives because funeral behavior is generally reserved.

African Americans

During slavery, funerals, if held at all, were held at night so as not to interfere with work. Immediate burial was necessary, so services frequently took place after the burial. Funerals might involve all-night vigils of song and prayer. Placing a piece of broken glass or pottery, lanterns, seashells, or other personal belongings on the grave, or throwing dirt into the grave were part of the ceremony and remain more common in southern funerals (Pleck, 2000). Flower girls dressed in white helping family members is also common in southern Black funerals.

Today, Black funerals, especially in the North, are more like White funerals, but they can be quite lavish. Music plays an important role. For African Americans who are members of Missionary or Southern Baptist, Church of God, or Pentecostal denominations, long emotional sermons, wailing, and sobbing are common (Perry, 1993). Henry Louis Gates (1994) recounts that when his mama died, they gave her a "modern Episcopal Milquetoast service," but he passionately wished that the funeral had been like the ones he grew up with, where

> The sermon was long and loud, demanding that you break down. . . . Oh, man, did those sermons feel *good,* sad-good, and hurting. And then they'd sing that killer song, people falling out all along. . . . At Mama's funeral, I wanted to fall out like that, too. . . . I wanted the Heavenly Gospel Choir to sing a lot of long, sad songs, and I wanted people to fall out. I wanted the church to be *hot,* with the windows closed. . . . I wanted starched collars to wilt and straightened hair to kink up and "go back," I wanted the kitchens [hair at the nape of the neck] crinkling up in that heat, crackling loud and long, before our very eyes. I wanted the whole world to know my mama's death and her glory while alive. (pp. 209–210)

Native Americans

Beliefs and rituals regarding death vary greatly among the many tribes. The Apache regard a dead person's body as an empty shell, whereas the Lakota speak to the body and understand it to be sacred. Although most American Indian nations don't believe in an afterlife, the Navajo and Lakota do (Brokenleg & Middleton, 1993). In the Lakota religion, the afterlife is called the "Spirit Land," where all dead humans and animals go, regardless of the kind of life they lived here on earth. Therefore, death is not feared much and is thought to be a natural part of the cycle of birth and death (LaFromboise & Bigfoot, 1988).

The Lakota believe they receive signs of an imminent death, such as the sighting of an owl or eagle, a blue light coming from the direction of the dead person's home, or a visit from the ghost of the person before hearing of the death. If a Lakota person knows that she or he is dying, she or he will gather possessions and distribute them to significant family members and friends (Brokenleg and Middleton, 1993).

In some cases, the deceased is buried within 24 hours. In most tribes, cremation and autopsies are commonly avoided, but there are few taboos about touching, kissing, or embracing the deceased's body. A Lakota wake may continue for 3 days, during which food and tobacco are served. Expressions of grief range from stoic to dramatic. Among the Lakota, loud wailing, mournful songs, the tearing of clothing, and wearing black may all be part of the mourning. Among the Paiute, cutting one's hair, braiding it, and laying it across the deceased's chest may also be accompanied by cutting long gashes in one's arms and legs and bleeding for several days. Paiute widows are supposed to wait until their hair returns to the pre-funeral length before they remarry; Paiute widowers, on the other hand, are immediately free to remarry (Hopkins, 1993).

Latino Americans

Predominantly Catholic, Latinos often administer last rites to the dying person, and novenas may be said during the 9-day period following the death (Lawson, 1990). Cremation is discouraged and burial is prompt; throwing dirt into the grave is common during burial. A wake will be held prior to the funeral, and expression of grief tends to be demonstrative. Traditionally, if a husband or child died, the wife or mother was often expected to dress in black for the remainder of her life (Pleck, 2000).

Some Puerto Ricans and other Caribbean peoples practice Santeria (or espiritism), a religious mixture of African, indigenous, and Catholic rituals. During such a ritual, a *santero* (similar to a shaman) may attempt to contact the spirits of the dead for advice (Younoszai, 1993).

Asian Americans

Asian beliefs and rituals about death are quite diverse, given the variety of ethnic groups encompassed by the racial label. Most Asian cultures, however, are highly influenced by Buddhism, a religion that teaches reincarnation. For Buddhists, the state of mind at the time of death is important; the more peaceful the state of mind, the better one's chances for a favorable rebirth (Truitner & Truitner, 1993). Therefore, family members may chant to calm the mind of a dying person. For this reason, it is considered unfortunate to die away from home.

Some Buddhist sects believe the body should remain untouched for at least 12 hours to allow the person's spirits to depart undisturbed; but other Buddhist sects place more importance on the karma of organ donation and so allow immediate intervention. After one's death, the body is wrapped in white cloth and placed in a casket. Unlike Confucianism and Taoism, which forbid cremation, Buddhism permits either burial or cremation. Tibetans, however, traditionally left the body exposed on a hill for eagles to dispose of (Yeung, 1995). Usually, a Buddhist funeral ceremony is short, and crying is not encouraged. The more influential Confucianism is in the family, however, the more likely there will be wailing, particularly by women.

Traditionally, after a death, Chinese men didn't shave and the women refrained from washing their hair for 60 days. Some funerals are accompanied by drums, music, and firecrackers. Burning fake money and food at the grave for the deceased's afterlife is also common. After the ceremony, chanting, lighting candles, and burning incense may continue for 49 days, which is considered the transitional period from one life to another. Family dinners are held on the 49th and 100th days after the death and then every year on the anniversary of the death (Truitner & Truitner, 1993). As in the Catholic religion, Buddhists also have an All Souls Day, but the Buddhist one is in August.

Among Southeast Asians, the Vietnamese and Hmong bury the dead and prohibit autopsy and embalming. Surgery, blood tests, and autopsies might release one's spirits or prevent a person from being reincarnated (McInnis, 1991). Cambodians and Laotians, on the other hand, allow cremation (Lawson, 1990), and the ashes are stored at a temple.

Funerals are given much attention in traditional Hmong life, because it is believed that proper burial and worship of ancestors directly influences the health, safety, and prosperity of the family. Every Hmong clan has its own elaborate rituals. The place of burial, direction of the casket and body, and the day of burial are important. A reed instrument is played to guide the deceased's spirit back to the world of the spirits. The funeral usually lasts 3 to 10 days, and post-funeral ceremonies continue at least 13 days.

In the Muslim religion, when a person is dying, his or her relatives should come to the bedside and pray and read the Koran to him or her. As soon as the person is dead, the body should be turned to face Mecca. Cremation and autopsy are also not practiced. The body's mouth and eyes should be closed and the face covered. Legs and arms should be straight. Then the body should be bathed three times by two people of the same sex as the deceased and wrapped in white cloth. Embalming is not practiced unless absolutely necessary, as ideally burial should occur within 24 hours. There is little concern about the funeral or how the body looks. Simplicity, a lack of materialism, is key. Traditionally, a casket would not be used. Music and singing is absent. Crying and wailing is expected and is presumed to help heal the survivors. Family members are expected to wear black for 40 days. Like Jews who sit "shivah" for 7 days after the funeral, Muslim friends and family will frequently remain at or visit the deceased's house for at least 7 days to pray, talk, and eat with the family. A special ceremony takes place on the 3rd day following burial, and people may visit the grave during those 7 days as well.

Even in their country of origin, practice of these traditions varies depending on the extent of religious belief in the family, the family's socioeconomic resources, and so on. In the United States, many racial-ethnic minorities have had to accommodate their practices to fit American lifestyle and legal regulations. Many elderly now die in hospitals and often undergo autopsies. Hmong Americans have been arrested for animal sacrifice, and so have had to curtail those aspects of the funeral ritual. Also, ethnic groups that practice lengthy ceremonies often have to squeeze several days of ritual into several hours at the local funeral home. Loud and lively ceremonies turn more subdued under the curious eyes of other Americans.

Resources

Books and Articles

Avila, E. (with Parker, J.). (1999). *Woman who glows in the dark: A curandera reveals ancient Mexican health secrets.* New York: Penguin.

This autobiography of a nurse who became a folk medicine healer explains the practices of curanderismo.

Detzner, D. F. (2004). *Elder voices: Southeast Asian families in the United States.* Walnut Creek, CA: Alta Mira Press.

This volume contains stories of loss and resilience among Southeast Asian refugee elders.

Fadiman, A. (1997). *The spirit catches you and you fall down: A Hmong child, her American doctors, and the collision of two cultures.* New York: Farrar, Straus & Giroux.

This is a true story of a Hmong girl with epilepsy who dies because of the communication gap between two medical cultures.

Kimbro, D. (2003). *What keeps me standing: Letters from Black grandmothers on peace, hope, and inspiration.* New York: Doubleday.

This is a collection of letters written by African American grandmothers to their children.

Nebelkopf, E., & Phillips, M. (Eds.). (2004). *Healing and mental health for Native Americans*. Walnut Creek, CA: Alta Mira Press.

These essays explore various health issues and promote healing through both traditional healers and Western medicine.

Olson, L. K. (Ed.). (2001). *Age through ethnic lenses: Caring for the elderly in a multicultural society*. Lanham, MD: Rowman & Littlefield.

This book discusses the needs of elderly among various ethnic groups and suggests possible programs and policies.

Video

Day of the dead. (1996). (Available from Films Media Group, P.O. Box 2053, Princeton, NJ 08453-2053, or at http://www.films.com)

This 52-minute video shows a celebration of this traditional holiday.

Websites

http://www.ethnicityonline.net/default.htm
This still developing website offers information about health and ethnicity, with special sections on various religious views on illness and death.

http://www.hhs.gov/specificpopulations/
The U.S. Department of Health and Human Services links to numerous sites containing information regarding minority health issues.

CHAPTER 9

AFRICAN AMERICAN FAMILIES

In 2002, the African American population of 36 million represented about 13 percent of the total U.S. population and resided in more than 12 million households. In numbers, the Black population has increased significantly since the first official census was taken in 1790, when they were only about 760,000 (92 percent were slaves). That, however, represented about 19.3 percent of the population.

The vast majority (about 96 percent) of African Americans are native-born, and most of their families have roots in America extending back at least 10 generations. English is now their native language and Christianity their main religion. Hence, African Americans are considered one of the most acculturated racial minorities in the United States. African Americans are generally homogenous in terms of ethnicity, because the years of slavery erased knowledge of their ethnic origins.

In other significant ways, African Americans are quite diverse. With recent immigrants coming from Africa, Haiti, Jamaica, Trinidad, and other West Indian or Caribbean countries, about 4 percent of Black Americans represent a wide variety of cultures. Economically, whereas a substantial minority of Black families remain below the poverty line, in recent decades others have experienced increased prosperity and education, expanding the Black middle and upper classes. African American families are also diverse in their distribution of family structures, with higher (than national) proportions of extended and single-parent families and a slightly higher proportion of people living alone. Although they are highly urbanized, substantial proportions reside in suburban (36 percent) and rural areas (13 percent).

Although African American families are studied much less than White American families, they are the most studied of the other minority groups, particularly in the last few decades. The earliest studies frequently characterized Black families as impoverished versions of White middle-class families in which the experiences of slavery, economic deprivation, and racial discrimination had induced pathological and dysfunctional features. This characterization precipitated a debate about the extent to which Black American families reflect the harsh conditions they have endured in America or manifest the cultural remnants of their African heritage (Ruggles, 1994). The dichotomous framing of the debate is problematic for a number of reasons.

First, in light of high rates of single-parent households, supporters of the former view frequently suggest that slavery destroyed the Black family. Although African American families have historically had a higher percentage of single-parent families than White families, until 1980 the majority of

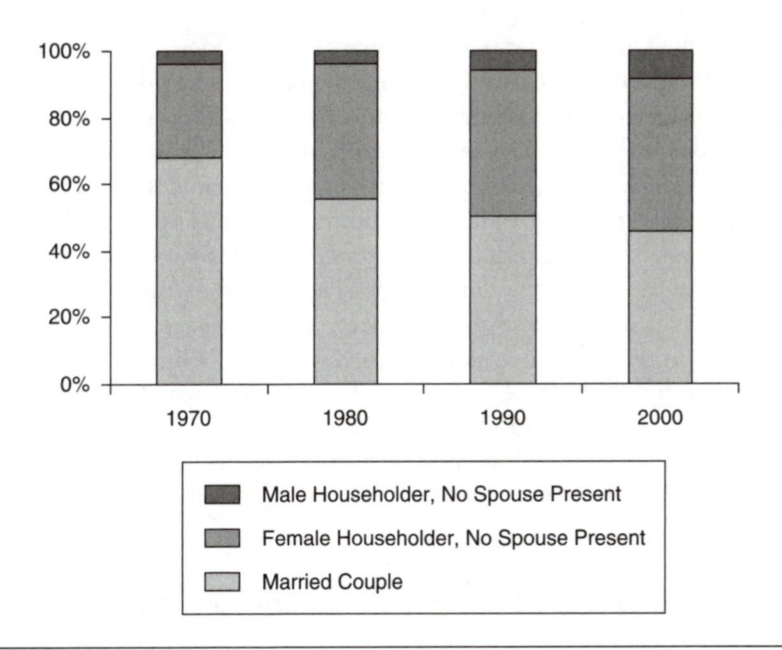

Figure 9.1 Composition of Black Families by Type and Year, 1970 to 2000

SOURCES: U.S. Department of Commerce (n.d.); U.S. Department of Commerce (2000d), Quick Table-P10

Black children lived in two-parent families (see Figure 9.1). The percentage of two-parent families has dropped for both Blacks and Whites over the past few decades, but the drop was significantly steeper for African Americans in the 1970s (Ruggles, 1994), indicating that some of the causes of increased single-parenthood are of more recent origin. Moreover, the contention that slavery destroyed the Black family presumes that if slavery had not occurred, African American families would be nuclear. In truth, if slavery had not occurred, the vast majority of African Americans would have remained in Africa and would have practiced the family forms that were prevalent there: extended, polygamous (though most are monogamous), non-co-residence of husband and wife, and so on. Most West African tribes were patriarchal and patrilineal, though a few, such as the Ashanti, were matrilineal. The point is that the nuclear family structure would not have predominated.

In response, those taking the Afrocentric view argue that the higher rate of extended and female-headed households and the lower rate of co-residence are remnants of African culture rather than merely a response to structural conditions. Proponents of this view, however, forget that even African cultural values and traditions are to some extent responses to the structural conditions in Africa. Polygamy, extended households, and so on are not peculiar to Africa; certain conditions present around the world tend to give rise to those types of family forms. Second, the Afrocentric advocates occasionally romanticize the conditions of today's Black families. Whereas many Black families are doing well, a significant number of Black children are reared in poverty, increasingly in inner-city neighborhoods where poverty has concentrated due to White flight. These neighborhoods have more environmental dangers and poorer quality school systems, with repercussions that shadow these children into adulthood. Whereas many Black parents are fortunate to be economically stable and/or able to draw upon the extensive kin network that characterizes much of African and Black American family life, a substantial minority of Black Americans are financially vulnerable, stressed, and failing their young members.

How Did Slavery Shape Black American Families?

The first Africans to settle in America arrived in 1619 in Jamestown, Virginia. At that point, slavery was not established in the colonies, and these new settlers spent years as indentured servants (as did many Whites), eventually buying their way out of servitude. So from the beginning, a small "free Black" population resided mostly in the North. Their numbers increased after Northern colonies passed manumission laws freeing slaves in the decades following the American Revolution. Made up of entrepreneurs, artisans, landowners, and laborers, free Blacks represented somewhere between 8 and 12 percent of the Black population.

The world slave trade was already well established, but slavery developed incrementally in the colonies. The first shipment of slaves arrived in 1638, and 3 years later, Massachusetts became the first colony to legally recognize slavery. Virginia followed in 1662, declaring slavery hereditary, according to the mother's status (which ran counter to the patriarchal conditions of the South). By 1700, slavery was firmly rooted in all 13 colonies.

Africans were captured from a number of Central and West African countries, mostly from the Ashanti, Ibo, Mossi, Yoruba, and Dohomean tribes, which had different languages, religions, and family and kin structures, though use of extended kin households was a commonality. Upon arrival, those Africans who managed to survive the horrendous trip were often auctioned to the highest bidders; the extent to which owners intentionally mixed slaves to hinder communication among them remains under debate (Burgess, 1995).

In the first 50 years of slave importation, American slave owners sought males for their physical labor. Eventually, it became apparent that if owners bought female slaves, who could also work in the fields or in the house, laborers could be reproduced rather than repeatedly purchased. This strategy became particularly important after 1807, when slave importation was prohibited. Moreover, theoretically, allowing male slaves to have families would keep males in check; their sexual needs would be met and the threat of separating families would deter rebellious behavior. Nevertheless, the sex ratio among Blacks did not reach parity until the 1840s, shortly before the Civil War.

Some slave owners viewed their slaves purely in terms of labor. In those cases, select male slaves might be used as studs, and the women as "breeders" (Hamer, 2001). Female slaves might be mated nonmaritally with several men over the course of their lives. Sexual relations between White slave owners and Black slave women were common as well. These relationships ranged from rape to rare cases in which the female slave was freed and made a legal wife. Occasionally, in White families where wives had no power, the husbands brought their slave mistresses into the household or provided them a small house nearby. Sometimes, slave mistresses and their mixed-race children were sold to new owners to avoid scandal or repeated harangues from the owners' wives. Biracial children often sold for more than black children and were more likely used as house slaves. Sometimes, the children of such unions were freed or educated. According to McAdoo (1998), some of the original historically Black colleges were founded for the purpose of educating these mixed-race children. By 1865, at the end of the Civil War, there were 4.4 million Black Americans, and 90 percent of them were slaves (Gonzales, 1998).

Slave women impregnated by husbands, breeders, or masters continued to work in the field until their delivery, which was aided by a midwife. Two or three days after delivery, the mother would return to the fields (Gonzales, 1998). By some accounts, most female slaves had one or two children by the age of 16 (others [Steckel, 1986] put the age a little higher, at 21), and might be grandmothers by age 30 (Green, 1975). In any case, early and frequent childbearing became a pattern because slave women were viewed as a means of producing more labor (Burgess, 1995). Nevertheless, it was not uncommon for slave women to induce abortion rather than bring another child into the slave world (Dill, 1988).

In the cases where slave marriages were allowed, their form and stability varied considerably by location, era, and historical account. In general, slave marriages had no legal standing; they existed purely at the owner's prerogative. In fact, one might say slave families had instability imposed upon them.

Slave parents had no legal rights to their children; all of them were property of the master and could be put to work or sold for a profit. One study estimated that 32 percent of all recorded slave marriages were disrupted by sale, 45 percent by death, 10 percent by choice, and 13 percent remained intact (Blassingame, 1972). A few states enacted laws that prohibited owners from selling children under 10 and separating them from their mothers, but apparently only Louisiana enforced the rule (Hamer, 2001).

The mode of marriage formation varied as well. Some slave owners gave their slaves a fair amount of freedom in choosing partners, and they were allowed to establish relatively stable families. Marrying someone from another plantation, called marrying "abroad," was common. In that case the father usually lived separately (Gutman, 1976) or on occasion would be sold to the other plantation to allow the family to reside together (Genovese, 1974). A study of George Washington's plantations indicated that 61 percent of the married slaves had "abroad" spouses, and 75 percent of the slave families with children did not have fathers present on a daily basis (Stevenson, 1995). Abroad marriages also appear to have been popular by choice as well, as it afforded slaves more freedom; abroad spouses were frequently allowed weekly travel passes to visit family. One former slave acknowledged that "Slaves always wanted to marry a gal on 'nother plantation 'cause dey could git a pass to go visit 'em on Saddy nights" (quoted in Stevenson, p. 52). Evidently, according to Stevenson, some slaves shrewdly married polygynously to obtain several passes.

Herbert Gutman's 1976 book *The Black Family in Slavery and Freedom* is considered a landmark book on the Black family during and after slavery. Gutman studied the birth registers, personal documents, census data, and marriage applications of six large plantations to recreate family and kinship structures among Blacks during and after slavery. He concluded that stable two-parent households predominated during slavery. More recent scholarship, however, has suggested that slave families were somewhat less stable than Gutman's portrayal. The skewed gender ratio, high mortality rates, separation by sale, abroad marriages, and importance of the mother's role in determining the status of the child resulted in high proportions of single male slaves, lack of co-residence among families, or disruption by sale or death.

Genovese (1974) analyzed plantation records and slave testimony and concluded that despite these severe constraints on their ability to enact and sustain normative family roles and functions, slaves created impressive family norms. Although carrying no legal import, some couples were allowed a Christian or African ceremony, such as jumping over a broom three times (Gutman, 1976). After childbirth, many slave women buried their infant's umbilical cord by the door to their hut, an African tradition thought to guarantee the child's return some day. Most historians document that extended kin played an active role in childbirth, child rearing, and household chores. Fosterage (informal adoption) and bestowing kin titles on elderly slaves were common (Gutman, 1976). Some slaveholders recognized bonds not only between parent and child, but also extended kin such as aunts and uncles.

Although the roles of Black men as husbands and fathers didn't begin to approach the degree of patriarchy rampant in the White South, some accounts indicate that Black fathers took an active role in child rearing, socialization, and supplementing the family diet through fishing and trapping. Boys were often named after their fathers. Because of the weakened status of slave men and the fact that slave wives worked, some have argued that the slave marriage approximated gender equality more than was possible for White families at the time. Nevertheless, recent studies of historical documents indicate that slave fathers were frequently not present to play a very involved role. In one account of interviews with former slaves, 82 percent mentioned their mothers' presence in their childhood, but only 42 percent recalled consistent contact with their father (Stevenson, 1995). Hence, the master, not the father, was frequently viewed as the provider of the family.

Originally, historians thought that the distinction between house slaves and field slaves played a pivotal role in the types of families that were formed during and after slavery. For instance, W. E. B. DuBois (1918) thought that the difference in treatment of and lifestyle between house and field slaves might have been the key factor giving rise to higher numbers of single-parent families among African Americans after slavery. House slaves were in constant contact with the owners and often cared for the owner's children, so they were more frequently allowed to develop families similar to those of their White owners. But field slaves were frequently viewed solely in terms of their labor. In these families, the father was a peripheral figure, and the mother-child unit might live in quarters separate from the father, or the family could be split by sale. Families whose members had been field slaves, it was therefore hypothesized, would have been more likely to break up before or after slavery, and house slaves would have been more likely to remain a nuclear family. But house slaves were fewer in number than field slaves, and nuclear families far outnumbered single-parent families post-slavery. What appears to have more value in explaining the two trends is whether slave families came from large or small plantations.

Large plantations had a number of advantages for slaves. Although all slaves were generally powerless, those on large plantations had relatively more protection by virtue of a slave community that could act as a buffer against White oppression (Burton, 1985). Housing on large plantations usually allowed more privacy. Wright (2000) found evidence that until the early 1800s, slaves were often permitted to build their own African-style housing. Later, slave families often were allotted small, individual windowless shacks with dirt floors (DuBois, 1918) or couples used clothes or quilts to partition shared shacks. They could cultivate a small garden and hunt for their own meat (Blassingame, 1972).

Small plantations or farms, on the other hand, were more susceptible to economic crises resulting in separation of slave families through sale or rental. Slaves on small holdings had very little leverage (Burton, 1985). Therefore, research indicates that the proportion of women who bore children was substantially lower on plantations with more than 100 slaves than on those with just a few. Childbearing at young ages, though high on most plantations, was higher on small than on large plantations (Steckel, 1986).

In terms of family structure, Kulikoff (1986) found that 47 percent of families on large plantations were nuclear, as opposed to only 18 percent on small plantations. Crawford (1980) reported that single-parent families were 50 percent more prevalent on plantations with 15 or fewer slaves. Available records also indicate that slave marriages on larger plantations lasted longer.

The probability of a slave child having a White father was also substantially higher on small plantations. For instance, an analysis of the 1860 census found that in general one tenth of all slave children were biracial. But if broken down by plantation size, the proportion was seven times higher on plantations of fewer than 10 slaves than it was on plantations of 75 or more (Steckel, 1986).

Since most slaves resided on large plantations, where their family life was less intruded upon, plantation size appears to be a better explanation of why African Americans had a majority of nuclear families, along with a higher rate of single-parent households, after slavery.

African American Families After Slavery

At the end of the Civil War, in which 14 percent of Black men served as soldiers, laborers, craftsmen, or servants (Hamer, 2001), the Thirteenth Amendment to the Constitution was passed, freeing the slaves. In 1867, the Reconstruction Act temporarily established martial law in the South, and the Freedman's Bureau was formed to assist slaves in their adjustment. During this temporary reprieve, Gutman (1976) found that many families who had been separated during slavery searched for their spouses and children through the Freedman's Bureau, which served as a registration center. According to Gutman's calculations on North Carolina records in 1866, 25 percent of the new registrants said they had already been married from 10 to 19 years, 20 percent said more than 20 years, and 10 percent said more than 30 years. Also, newly liberated slaves frequently adopted the name of their master so they could be identified by other family members. Although a few states proclaimed all marriages legal, in most cases former slave families paid fees, even if just a sweet potato, to legally register their marriages and have ceremonies performed at the nearest county seat. It is estimated that more than 75 percent of previously existing unions were formalized after emancipation (Franklin, 1997).

For the period from 1850 to 1930, Gutman (1976) concluded that Black families were as likely, or more likely, to be married-couple households than were native-born Whites. Looking at the period from 1880 to 1940, Ruggles's (1994) data also confirm that 70 to 72 percent of Black children lived in two-parent households. Like White American households of the time, extended households were the second most common household form, followed by single-parent and people living alone. Nevertheless, Black children were twice as likely as White children to live in single-parent households and three times as likely to live with no parents in 1880. Even among free Black children near the end of slavery, living with neither parent was common, either because their parents were still enslaved and/or because the children had been apprenticed out.

Other accounts, such as Manfra and Dykstra (1985), confirm high marriage rates existed alongside high numbers of female-headed households and nonmarital births. These could simultaneously coexist due to high rates of separation (without legal divorce) and remarriages among African Americans during and after slavery. Although these remarriages would have been considered illegal for Whites, the legal system didn't enforce these laws for Black couples.

Other family problems appeared after slavery. Black children were frequently seized to work as apprentices by former slave owners. Mothers sought help from the Freedman's Bureau, often to no avail (Franklin, 1997). In addition, White society bestowed some elements of patriarchy on Black men. The right to vote and run for office, though virtually retracted after Reconstruction, was given only to Black men. Like White women, Black women waited until 1919 to obtain suffrage. The Freedman's Bureau designated Black men as head of household and established their right to sign contracts for the labor of their entire family, a right about which many women complained. Wage scales were set to pay Black women less than Black men, and the bureau allotted less land to families without a male head (Franklin, 1997). The increased patriarchal role for Black men within their families appears to have contributed to a rise in reports of family violence as well.

With the South's economy in ruins, southern landowners transitioned to a sharecropping system, in which families planted and harvested the landowner's crop, retaining a portion for themselves. Although many Black families, particularly those that had been free, were headed by artisans, preachers, or house servants, the majority, whose main skill was agricultural work, became sharecroppers (Eshleman, 2003). In James Comer's (1988) account of his mother Maggie's childhood in the South, Maggie, whose African American family sharecropped, pointed out the irony that her dad "had more education than the white man he was working for. My father did all of his weighing of the cotton and taking care of his business because that white man could not read or write" (p. 3).

Initially, during Reconstruction, many Black women withdrew from field labor to concentrate on home life (Dill, 1988), but eventually most returned to the field to counteract poverty. Because sharecropping families, including children, worked together on the farm, women retained some flexibility to manage their home labor and their economic labor. Marriage of teenagers was discouraged because the family needed their labor, so even if a teen had a child, she was not encouraged to marry if it meant leaving the farm (Johnson, 1934). Children were valued for their labor, which prolonged the pattern of early and high fertility.

Many southerners could not reconcile themselves to freedom for Black Americans and believed they would not work (especially for Whites) without coercion. The Freedman's Bureau, which had been established by the northern Republicans to provide former slaves with wage labor, took the White planters' needs into consideration (Franklin, 1997). The bureau, which had claimed it would give each freed family 40 acres and a mule in reparations, instead relocated freed slaves to rural areas, where they could be more easily monitored, and arranged year-long contracts between sharecroppers and landowners, even though the work was seasonal. Since Black workers were now free, they had to purchase the inputs in the agricultural process and so frequently were in debt to the landowners. Although sharecropping usually involved a 50-50 split of the profits, deductions for housing, furnishings, and supplies meant that most sharecroppers remained dependent on their former slave owners. These factors, along with vagrancy laws that were used to arrest Black men who were traveling and northern laws that prohibited migrants from the South, meant that the vast majority of African Americans remained in the South.

The situation for African Americans in the South deteriorated after the end of Reconstruction in the 1880s. At that point southern states quickly implemented Jim Crow laws that segregated public facilities, such as schools, transportation, businesses, and employment, and hindered Black political participation; the use of lynching increased as a mechanism of control.

As World War I approached, European immigration was reduced, American men went off to war, and northern labor shortages ensued, serving as pull factors for southern Blacks. In the South, flooding, drought, and economic problems began to push Black labor out. Together, these factors gave birth to the "Great Migration," the period from World War I to 1970, during which more than 5 million African Americans moved north.

In northern cities, life was different. Many single Black men migrated, forming groups to find work. If unsuccessful, sometimes they wandered homeless and aimless. Until World War II, Black men exhibited higher labor force participation than White men, but they were employed in low-paying, unstable jobs with few benefits. Black women who moved to northern urban areas, like many immigrant women today, could more easily find jobs in domestic work than could men. Their jobs were frequently more secure as well, since domestic jobs were not weather dependent, and working in a White household sometimes gave Black women access to resources and support that Black men did not have (Franklin, 1997). Once again, this led to the lack of a productive role for Black men in the family. At the same time, Black women's long hours as maids or nannies meant that they spent little time in their own homes, with their children (some were only allowed to come home on the weekends). This situation may have given Black women more control over household resources, but also increased domestic conflict and desertion rates. On the other hand, these circumstances quite likely gave rise to the more flexible gender roles that are frequently found among married Black couples today (see Chapter 6).

The cost of living was higher in northern cities than in the southern rural economy, where the availability of extended kin networks made joblessness, ill health, or nonmarital births more manageable. In the North, homeless men, women, and children became dependent on public aid.

In the 1930s, to mitigate the effects of the Great Depression, President Franklin Roosevelt passed New Deal reforms (social security, unemployment insurance, public aid, work and wage regulations), but most of these did not apply to agricultural or domestic workers. This left two thirds of employed Black Americans with no protection for old age or unemployment (Franklin, 1997). In fact, public aid (welfare) was monitored to keep payments low so that it would not compete with the needs of planters to find cheap labor. In some states, African Americans were excluded from receiving unemployment or public aid during harvest period so that they would have to work for planters. State public aid programs also allotted lower payments to African American recipients than to European Americans. These policies continued into the 1950s. Eventually, widowed women or children of deceased wage earners were transferred from the Aid to Dependent Children (ADC) program to the social security program (which is neither means-tested nor stigmatized), whereas abandoned wives, never-married mothers, or widows of nonworking husbands were left on ADC. Because Black families were more likely to fall into those latter categories, higher proportions of Black children were on ADC and higher proportions of White children were on social security benefits. In recent decades, welfare payments have decreased in size, while social security payments to children have increased (Baca Zinn & Eitzen, 2002).

Northern urban housing was overcrowded. A 1917 survey in Pittsburgh found that 80 percent of Black migrants from the South had boarders living with them. In 1930, more than 40 percent of Black families in Harlem had from one to four lodgers living with them (Franklin, 1997). Moreover, as Blacks continued to move to the cities, Whites moved outward, particularly after World War II, when the economic boom funneled millions of dollars into building a highway system, and the Federal Housing Association subsidized the purchase of homes in new suburban developments for White families. Housing segregation and the deterioration of central cities skyrocketed over the next few decades. The "Happy Days" of the 1950s were mostly a White experience, as Black Americans still lived a highly segregated and limited life.

World War II played a pivotal role in both the women's movement and the civil rights movement. As men went off to war, Black and White women went to work in traditionally male industries. Though Black women usually were assigned the more physically demanding and lower-paying jobs, they accepted these jobs in such high numbers that 50 percent of White housewives who employed Black domestics lost their services. As one Black woman remarked at the time: "Lincoln freed the Negroes from cotton picking and Hitler . . . got us out of the White folks' kitchen" (quoted in Franklin, 1997, pp. 104–105). Marriage and divorce rates for Blacks and Whites went up during and after the war. Whereas the White divorce rate decreased during the 1950s, the Black divorce rate remained high.

Moreover, the irony of thousands of Black men going off to sacrifice their lives for a country that still segregated them was too much to bear for the Black community. During and after the war, many painful civil rights actions eventually triumphed, culminating in the 1960s with passage of the Civil Rights Act and the Voting Rights Act, which overturned Jim Crow laws and voting restrictions on African Americans and other people of color. Enforcement of these new laws eventually enabled more African Americans to improve their educational attainment levels and access jobs previously closed to them. At the same time, the recession of the 1970s and 1980s, the loss of industrial jobs to globalization, and the invasion of relatively cheap crack cocaine into inner-city areas took a toll on African American families. Although the 1990s bolstered the economy, the recession of the 2000s has once again hit Black families disproportionately due to the continued decline of industrial, working-class jobs. Since the 1970s, a slight remigration of Black families to the South has occurred. Consequently, as you can see in Figure 9.2, a slight majority live in the southern states.

African American Families Today

In the 20th century, many indicators for African American families improved. Life expectancy increased for all ethnic groups, but it increased by 30 years for Blacks and 20 years for Whites. Infant and adult mortality rates decreased for African Americans, though they still remain higher than for Whites. Substandard housing and poverty decreased, but those too remain at higher levels for Black than for White families.

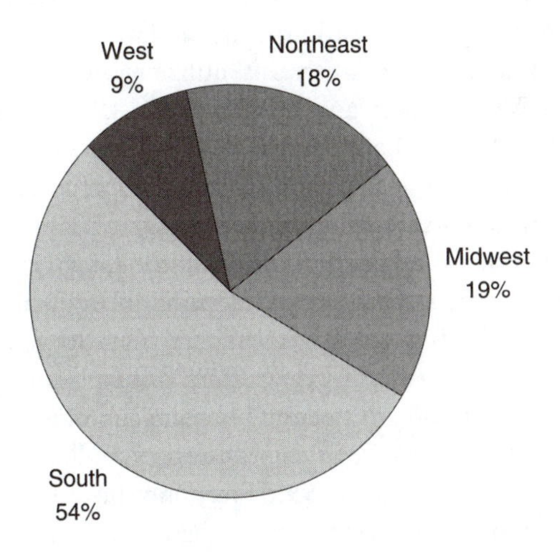

Figure 9.2 Regional Distribution of the African American Population, 2000

SOURCE: McKinnon (2003)

Despite these overall improvements, the class structure of today's Black families, unfortunately, leans too heavily toward the lower end. A small African American upper class does exist, consisting of old wealth having its ancestral roots among free Blacks or mixed-race former slaves and new wealth accumulating among recent celebrities, corporate executives, or entrepreneurs. The middle and working classes contain the majority of Black families who have been able to take advantage of increased opportunities for education and professional jobs or have been able to hang on to the few remaining blue-collar jobs. This middle class has expanded, but relative to the White middle class, it remains less stable due to lack of wealth (see Chapter 2) and higher dependence on two or more household wages. Unfortunately, however, a significant minority of Black families are either struggling to keep afloat or have succumbed under the weight of long-term poverty. Consequently, in 2002 about 32 percent of Black children remained in poverty (compared to about 9 percent of White children).

The obvious strength of Black families has been their resiliency under policies and conditions intended to weaken them. The main strategy that African Americans have utilized is a strong sense of communalism reflected in extensive and fluid kin and fictive kin networks noted for their ability to expand and contract, absorbing others into households as necessity demands (Fine, Schwebel, & James-Myers, 1987). Most studies indicate that Black family members live in proximity, in part an outcome of segregated communities. These close-knit communities helped to produce strong fictive kin relations with neighbors and fellow church members, which in turn provided support in the face of discrimination from the larger society. A number of studies indicate that African Americans utilize fictive kin at a somewhat higher rate than White Americans. Stack's book *All Our Kin* (1974) illustrated the high level of exchange in Black communities, and other studies indicate that African Americans, more than other racial groups, use fictive kin for intergenerational caregiving (Coke & Twaite, 1995; Perry, 1999).

Informal adoption, the taking in of children for caregiving, is estimated to be about 10 times greater than formal adoption in the Black community, a strategy that stems the flow of Black children into the foster care system. "Other mothering"—the use of grandmothers, sisters, aunts, cousins, and so on as co-mothers—and "other fathering" is quite common in the Black community (Lempert, 1999; Troester, 1984). Gregory Williams, in his autobiography *Life on the Color Line* (1995), recounts how he and his younger brother were abandoned by their White mother, and their biracial father was an alcoholic. Fortunately, a Black neighbor woman took them in and reared them to adulthood. Although the proportion of nonresident fathers is high, studies show that frequently other adult men, such as uncles, grandfathers, or fictive kin share parenting responsibilities and provide a role model for young children. Children are loved and welcomed regardless of parents' marital status.

Black churches (or for Black Muslims, mosques) have played a strong role in the lives of African Americans individually and communally. African Americans have high levels of religious belief and church attendance; only 10 percent of African Americans claim to have no religion. About 50 percent are Baptist, 12 percent Methodist, and 6 percent Catholic. About 25 percent of American Muslims are Black (McAdoo, 1998). As one of the few organizations under their own control, the church has provided opportunities for Black individuals to develop leadership skills. In addition, African Americans tend to look to the church not just as a site of worship but for support and assistance as well. Black churches and mosques are known for their prophetic quality of providing social services and taking initiative in social issues (Billingsley, 1992).

For the most part, these multiple and intricate ties provide support and satisfaction to African Americans. According to a survey of 2,000 African Americans (Hachett & Jackson, 1993), more than 90 percent feel emotionally close to their families, interact frequently with family members (even distant relatives, as yearly reunions are common), live fairly close to immediate family, and have a high degree of affection associated with family life. These ties compensate for some of the increasing problems African American families have faced in recent decades.

Some, however, have speculated that the multiple ties and roles may make some aspects of family life more tenuous. Perhaps the multiple responsibilities leave less time for maintenance of conjugal ties. For instance, Black couples have children earlier in their marriages than do White couples (Littlejohn-Blake & Anderson-Darling, 1993). Divorce is almost twice as high in the Black community as in the White community (regardless of income, age, education, and occupation). Black remarriage rates are lower than for other racial groups, and the divorce rates of their remarriages are higher. Therefore, Black women can expect to spend about 16 years of their 73-year life with a husband, whereas White women can expect to spend about 33 years of a 77-year life with a husband. Although most surveys indicate that married Blacks are happier than unmarried, studies (Kitson & Holmes, 1992) also find that African Americans adjust to divorce more easily than do Whites. This may be due to the extended support systems or because there is greater acceptance of alternative child-rearing structures (Fine, McKenry, & Chung, 1992). (See Chapters 5 and 8 for more details on single parenting and parenting by grandparents.)

Postponement of marriage has occurred among all racial groups, but significantly more so among African Americans. In 1975, 94 percent of Whites and

87 percent of Blacks in their early 30s had married. By 1990, the percentages had dropped to 86 percent of Whites and 61 percent of Blacks. It appears that in the future, three fourths of all Black Americans (compared to 90 percent of Whites) will marry (Norton & Miller, 1992).

Because the fertility rate of married Black couples dropped nearly 50 percent between 1970 and 1996 (nearly twice the decline for White married couples [Eshleman, 2003]), nonmarital births now account for the majority of all births in the Black community. Although nonmarital births are highly correlated with lower income, even at higher income levels Black women have more nonmarital births than do White women. For instance, in the 1990s, among Black women with incomes of more than $75,000, 22 percent had a nonmarital birth, a rate 10 times higher than White women of the same income. Among poor Black women, 65 percent had a nonmarital birth, a rate twice as high as for poor White women (McAdoo, 1998).

Between the increasing tendency for marriage postponement and the higher incidence of divorce and nonmarital births, consanguineal ties appear to be stronger than conjugal ties in the Black community. Consanguineal ties have the advantage of providing a web of support and diffusing resources and emotional fulfillment over multiple sources. But clearly, the skewed gender ratio, rising unemployment among Black men, a growing gap in college attendance rates between Black men and women, and generally higher poverty rates hinder the formation and/or maintenance of stable families—extended, nuclear, or single-parent—in the African American community and pose concerns in and of themselves.

Resources

Books and Articles

Campbell, B. M. (1989). *Sweet summer.* New York: Putnam.

This is Campbell's account of growing up in a single-mother family.

Comer, J. (1988). *Maggie's American dream: The life and times of a Black family.* New York: Penguin.

Comer, a medical doctor, retells his mother's life story, which spans from her childhood as part of sharecropping family in the South to the establishment of her own family in the North.

Dash, L. (1996). *Rosa Lee: A mother and her family in urban America.* New York: Basic Books.

Based on a series of Pulitzer Prize–winning articles, Dash recounts the true story of a low-income Black family.

Dunaway, W. A. (2003). *The African-American family in slavery and emancipation.* New York: Cambridge University Press.

This author contends that past studies of the American slave family neglected small plantations and other profit-maximizing strategies that were used to disrupt slave families.

Franklin, D. (1997). *Ensuring inequality: The structural transformation of the African American family.* New York: Oxford University Press.

Donna Franklin provides one of the most complete accounts of African American families from slavery to the present.

Fulwood, S., III. (1996). *Waking from the dream: My life in the Black middle class.* New York: Anchor.

This is a memoir that confirms that although race and class intersect, race continues to have a defining effect on the lives of middle-class African Americans.

Haight, W. L. (2001). *African American children at church.* New York: Cambridge University Press.

Wendy Haight provides a look at the socialization beliefs and practices of Black adults and children within a religious community.

Hill, R. B. (2003). *The strengths of African American families* (2nd ed.). Lanham, MD: University Press of America.

This edition includes a special section that examines the impact of social forces and policies on the status of African American families.

McAdoo, H. P. (1996). *Black families.* Thousand Oaks, CA: Sage.

This volume explores the experiences of Black families, ranging from the African continent through historical accounts to current essential issues.

Moody, A. (1968). *Coming of age in Mississippi.* New York: Random House.

This is the autobiography of a Black girl growing up in the rural South.

Taylor, R. L. (Ed.). (2002). *Minority families in the United States: A multicultural perspective* (3rd ed.). Upper Saddle River, NJ: Prentice Hall.

This book covers a number of racial groups, but it especially has two good chapters on Haitian and West Indian families in the United States.

Thornton, Y. S. (as told to Coudert, J.). (1995). *Ditchdigger's daughters: A Black family's astonishing success story.* New York: Penguin.

This is a memoir of a Black working-class family struggling to achieve the American Dream.

Toliver, S. D. (1998). *Black families in corporate America.* Thousand Oaks, CA: Sage.

Willie, C. V., & Reddick, R. J. (2003). *A new look at Black families* (5th ed.). Lanham, MD: Alta Mira Press.

The authors take an in-depth look at the variety of family experiences among African Americans.

Videos

Bagwell, O. (Director). (1998). *Africans in America.* United States: Public Broadcasting Service. (Available from Shop PBS for Teachers at http://teacher.shop.pbs.org/product/index.jsp?productId=1406321)

Although not specifically on Black families, this four-volume set chronicles the history of Africans in America through the 1800s.

Dworkin, J. (Director). (2002). *Love & Diane.* (Available from Women Making Movies, 462 Broadway, Suite 500, New York, NY 10013, or at http://www.wmm.com)

This award-winning 155-minute video follows three generations of one family in New York City as they struggle with poverty, welfare, and drug rehabilitation.

Gurievitch, G. (Producer). (n.d.). *Kicking high . . . in the golden years.* (Available from New Day Films, 190 Route 17M, P.O. Box 1084, Harriman, NY 10926, or at http://www.newday.com/films/Kicking_High_Golden_Years.html)

This hour-long video shows a positive view of aging in the African American community.

Website

http://www.blackrefer.com/family.html
This website has links to sites dealing with African American genealogy, racial socialization, adoption, and many other topics.

CHAPTER 10

NATIVE AMERICAN FAMILIES

Although their numbers have been increasing in recent decades, Native Americans are the smallest of the racial-ethnic groups discussed in this text. Their relatively small population of about 2.5 million represents less than one percent of the U.S. population. (Another 1.6 million Americans, however, reported being Native American and some other race.) This small number, combined with the variety of tribes (more than 300 different tribes and between 150 and 200 Native languages), makes research difficult, and it is virtually impossible to generalize about their traditional norms and values and changes in those over time. These conditions, along with the high rate of interracial marriage among Native Americans, render them almost invisible. Consequently, as you may have noticed throughout the text, less reliable data exist on Native Americans to facilitate rich descriptions or comparisons.

Although Native Americans are indigenous to the Americas in the sense that they resided in North and South America for centuries before the Europeans arrived, anthropological evidence indicates that they originally migrated to the Americas from Asia thousands of years ago when a land bridge joined what is now Asia and Alaska. Many migrated into South America, where they developed large and complex civilizations, known as the Mayan, Aztec, and Incan civilizations. Native American peoples still survive throughout Central and South America.

Other Native Americans settled in North America, where the pattern of settlement was more dispersed. Consequently, hundreds of tribes, each with their own languages, religions, governmental forms, means of livelihood, and family systems, developed. According to John (1998), virtually all the cross-cultural variations in family forms and mate selection (mentioned in Chapter 4), such as bride price, dowry, arranged marriage, social marriage, bride abduction, polygamy, patrilineality, matrilineality, and bilineality, could at one time be found among Native Americans. Assimilation and the decline in their population have reduced such variation. The number of indigenous languages alone has been reduced by half.

Since no census was taken until 1790, we have only estimates of how many American Indians existed at the time the first European settlers arrived in what would later become the United States. The estimates range anywhere from one million to 18 million (John, 1998). What is clear is that by 1890, only 250,000 indigenous people remained (Stuart, 1987). Exposure to new diseases (smallpox, measles, influenza, and diphtheria), forced labor, massacre, removal from their land, and destruction of their food sources had decimated their numbers (Gonzales, 1998).

Since World War II, the Native American population has experienced a dramatic increase. In 1950, they numbered about 377,000; so over the past 50 years the Native American population has experienced more than a six-fold increase. This explosion in the Native American population resulted from higher-than-average fertility rates and, more recently, to nonreservation American Indians declaring their ethnicity on census documents. Since 1960, the census has allowed individuals to self-identify, and with more racial tolerance and revival of interest in ethnicity, more Native Americans have claimed their identity. Others have argued as well that the increase in gambling revenues has provided an incentive to declare one's tribal affiliation. (In reality, however, only a small portion of the tribes who use gaming are actually profiting from it.) Tribal membership is usually determined by proof of blood quantum. The federal standard requires one fourth American Indian heritage to be legally considered Native American (Brokenleg & Middleton, 1993), but tribal governments may go as low as one sixteenth (Lamanna & Riedmann, 2003).

Table 10.1 lists the 10 largest American Indian tribes today. The top six account for about 40 percent of all Native Americans who listed one race only on the 2000 census; many tribes only have a few dozen members remaining. About three quarters of Native Americans live either in western or southern states (see Figure 10.1).

Table 10.1 Ten Largest American Indian Tribal Groups, 2000

Tribe	*Population in Numbers (American Indian Alone)*	*Population in Numbers of Those Who Identified as American Indian and Some Other Race*
Cherokee	729,533	281,069
Navajo	298,197	269,202
Latin American Indian	180,940	104,354
Choctaw	158,774	87,349
Sioux	153,360	108,272
Chippewa	149,669	105,907
Apache	96,833	57,060
Blackfoot	85,750	27,104
Iroquois	80,822	45,212
Pueblo	74,085	59,533

SOURCE: Ogunwole (2002)

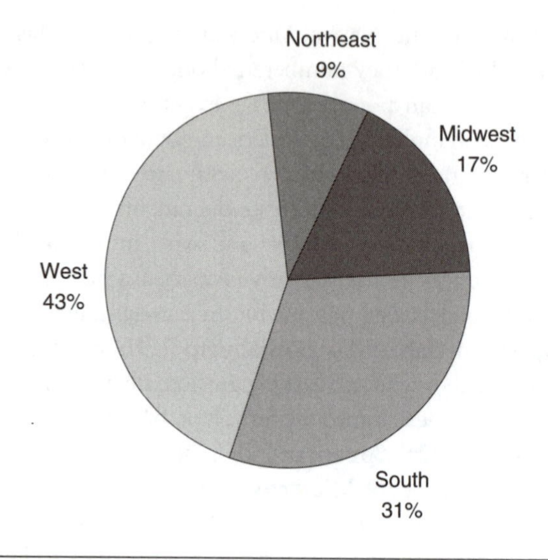

Figure 10.1 Regional Distribution of Native Americans, 2000

SOURCE: Ogunwole (2002)

Looking Back in History

Like African Americans, Native Americans were involuntarily incorporated into the United States. Thus, they experienced more severe and longer-lasting discrimination than later-arriving racial minorities, the effects of which are still reflected in their current social status. Although it is estimated that about 5 to 10 percent of American Indians were enslaved, the Native American experience under European settlement was more one of war, genocide, and forced acculturation.

Prior to the American Revolution, official policy of the British government was to recognize each indigenous tribe as a sovereign nation. Colonists who wanted to obtain more land or trade agreements with Native Americans were supposed to negotiate treaties in public with a representative of the king present. This proclamation, however, was nearly impossible to enforce. The new White settlers' enormous appetite for land and resources far outweighed the royal army and American Indians. Nevertheless, more than 600 treaties were signed by the colonial government and leaders of various American Indian tribes (sometimes under compulsion). Although most of the treaties disadvantaged Native Americans by reducing their land holdings, and eventually most were broken, many treaties established some rights for the tribes, such as access to the natural resources or indefinite payments in return for the loss of land.

After the United States won independence from Britain, official policy changed from treaties to forced removal and/or assimilation. The United

States government no longer viewed American Indian nations as sovereign; rather, each Native American individual was considered a "ward of the state." The two most infamous policies that reflected these changes were the 1830 Indian Removal Act and the 1887 Dawes Act.

Removal and Reservations

In 1830, the Indian Removal Act initiated a process that eventually led to the creation of the reservation system. This act called for the expulsion of all Native Americans east of the Mississippi River to territory west of the river. Prior to passage of the act, the Cherokee nation had sued the State of Georgia, which had annexed Cherokee land for its growing cotton industry. The Georgia Supreme Court ruled in favor of the Cherokee, but President Andrew Jackson, newly reelected and supported by Congress, forged ahead on removal.

Five main tribes were targeted. These tribes—the Creek, Cherokee, Choctaw, Chickasaw, and Seminole—were referred to as the "civilized" tribes because they had made many adaptations to accommodate the European settlers. The Cherokee, in particular, had converted their economy to an agricultural one and modified their political system to include a written constitution, a code of laws, a legislature, and a judiciary. They created a written language and established churches, schools, sawmills, and newspapers. By most Western definitions, the Cherokee were prospering. Nevertheless they lived on land coveted by European settlers.

So starting in 1830 and continuing for nearly two decades, four of the five tribes made the tragic journey that later came to be called the "Trail of Tears." The Choctaw of Mississippi were first to be relocated. In the 6-month trip that took them to Oklahoma, 5,000 of their 20,000 members died from famine or disease. The Creek in Alabama were moved next; 2,000 of their 17,000 members died en route and another 3,500 died shortly after arrival. About 1,000 Chickasaw from Mississippi died as well. Following a lengthy battle in the legal system and Congress, the Cherokee were also removed. About 4,000 of their 13,000 members died (Parrillo, 2003). The Seminole in Florida was the only tribe to successfully (but only temporarily) fight off removal in a 7-year guerrilla war that killed 2,000 soldiers and cost the U. S. Army $20 million (Josephy, 1991). Nevertheless, by 1858 only 3,000 Seminole remained in the Florida Everglades; like the others, most had been moved west of the Mississippi.

Although these were the main tribes moved in the Southeast, eventually the Delaware, Kickapoos, Miamis, Ottawas, Peorias, Potawatomis, Sacs, Foxes, Shawnees, and Wyandots were moved to so-called "Indian territory." The only tribe to substantially remain in the Northeast was the Iroquois League. In all, about 100,000 Native Americans were moved west of the Mississippi River, where there were already a number of Indian nations, such as the Comanche, Osage, and Pawnee, who were not particularly enthused by the influx of refugees into their hunting territory. Although the U.S. government had promised that it would protect the refugees from other tribes and from the increasing influx of White settlers into the western half of the continent, help was inconsistent (McLemore, Romo, & Baker, 2001).

Following the removal period, the U.S. government moved to a policy of segregation and isolation, allotting poor quality (or at least what appeared at that time to be useless) land to tribes as reservations. For instance, the Pine Ridge Sioux reservation in South Dakota is located in the "Badlands," a name indicative of its soil quality. Most of today's more than 300 reservations were established between 1850 and 1880 with the help of an 1871 appropriations bill that ended federal recognition of the tribes as sovereign nations. Instead, that law designated Native Americans "wards of the state" and made the welfare of the indigenous tribes dependent on the government. Food rations and other supplies were issued (though they didn't always arrive), and most aspects of Indian life came under supervision of the Bureau of Indian Affairs (BIA).

Let's take a moment to consider the impact of such relocation on a tribe's social organization. When European settlers first arrived, Native American tribes were scattered across North America. Depending on the climate and topography of their location, each tribe relied on a specific form of livelihood. For instance, those on the coasts were often fishers. Others were nomadic tribes that hunted and gathered. The plains tribes relied heavily on buffalo and big-game hunting. Some were herders, and some farmers. When a tribe's way of life is defined primarily by one mode of livelihood, usually everyone's role in the tribe is defined by his or her relation to that process. For instance, in a fishing village, gender roles would be constructed around fishing and the processing of fish. Perhaps fathers taught their sons how to build boats and fishing instruments; mothers taught their daughters how to build traps and process various water animals for food or how to recognize edible plants in and along the waterways. The elders' years of experience instilled them with sought-after knowledge about when and where fish were more easily caught. People earned their status in the tribe according to their accomplishments in fishing. So what happens to these roles and statuses once the community is relocated to a setting where there are no bodies of water, no fishing? The skills of the adults must be abandoned and new ones learned. The wisdom of the elderly becomes worthless. The parents can no longer teach their children useful skills. The new location often fails to support the tribe's social organization. Uprooting a people from a territory very likely entailed major transformations not only in the skills needed to provide for the sustenance of the tribe but also in their collective and individual identity and self-worth. As we shall see later, whereas some Native Americans made the adjustment, many did not.

As if the relocation were not enough, in 1887 the Dawes Act (sometimes called the General Allotment Act) was passed. This act had as its goal the breakup of the communal ownership of reservation land. Teddy Roosevelt described the law as "a great pulverizing engine, designed to break up the tribal mass" (quoted in Baldridge, 2001, p. 1518). Native Americans were allotted 80- to 160-acre parcels of land for agricultural purposes. Because many American Indians knew nothing about agriculture, and most had no money to purchase the necessary inputs, over time much of the land ended up owned or leased by White Americans. By the time this policy was repealed in the 1930s, Native American land holdings had been reduced from 138 million to 56 million acres (Parrillo, 2003). Through these combined land policies, Native Americans essentially lost control of their lives and livelihoods. Any esteem, meaning, and identity they reaped from self-government and provision was obliterated.

Assimilating Native Americans

Hand in hand with reducing Indian land holdings and decimating the population was a policy of assimilation. On the surface, juxtaposed to the horrors of genocide, assimilation appeared to be a fairly benevolent policy. In 1819, the U.S. Congress passed an act to supply education "for the purpose of providing against further decline and final extinction of the Indian tribes . . . to instruct them in the mode of agriculture suited to their situation and for teaching their children in reading, writing, and arithmetic" (Tyler, 1973, p. 45). Congress initially authorized $1,000 for this so-called "civilization fund," but by 1842, $214,000 in federal funds were directed to missionary organizations to maintain 37 schools, employing 85 teachers for nearly 1,300 students. These schools were usually day schools located near Indian communities (Lomawaima, 1994). In the late 1800s, President Ulysses Grant gave certain Indian reservations to churches with the mandate to strip them of their religious ceremonies (such as the Sun Dance and the Ghost Dance).

Few studies of these missionary schools exist. Clemmons's (2000) study of Protestant missionary schools in Minnesota before the Civil War found that many missionaries schooled Dakota children in missionary homes.

Dakota parents and children had more control over the curriculum and regulations than did most parents and students at the off-reservation boarding schools that later followed. Nevertheless, Clemmons concluded that European American society rarely accepted the graduates.

Eventually, the U.S. government became more directly involved in the school system. In 1879, the BIA authorized a former army officer to convert an abandoned military barracks in Pennsylvania into an off-reservation boarding school. Boarding school behavioral rules were generally modeled on a military format, and the curriculum was designed to replace Indian heritage with the vocational skills and culture of European American society, though, in fact, most of the schools prepared students for employment in Indian schools, not in mainstream society.

The schools' living conditions were designed to separate them from their tribal surroundings and expose them to White society. It was thought that if schools were too close to the reservation or Indian community, they would be less successful in assimilation. Therefore, boarding schools were opened farther away in Oregon, Oklahoma, New Mexico, Kansas, and Nebraska. In addition, many schools had a policy of "outing," in which Indian students would live with White families year-round or in the summers; sometimes outing continued for up to 3 years after graduation.

By 1899, 24 off-reservation schools held over 6,200 students. During the Great Depression, 29 percent of Indian children were in boarding schools; 15 percent were in off-reservation boarding schools (Lomawaima, 1994). Off-reservation boarding schools, in place until the 1970s, have been depicted as harsh, repressive institutions where abuse was common. Certainly, the intent of the BIA school system, on- or off-reservation, was to force Native Americans to assimilate to European culture, so children in these schools were usually not allowed to speak their language, practice their religion, or don their native dress. Contact with home was restricted, and letters to family were read by teachers. Punishment was solitary confinement in the "dark room."

Simon Ortiz (1993), an Acoma Indian from New Mexico, remembers in his childhood:

> The language we all spoke was Acoma, and it was a struggle to maintain it against the outright threats of corporal punishment, ostracism, and the invocation that it would impede our progress towards Americanization. Children in [BIA day] school were punished and looked upon with disdain if they did not speak and learn English quickly and smoothly. (p. 30)

Nevertheless, according to some reports (Lomawaima, 1994), many Native American families sent their children to these schools by choice, hoping that their children would be advantaged in society from the experience. Lomawaima concludes that

> Boarding-school students had the resilience of children, and in many cases, they found happiness in their surroundings. Some people hated and endured their boarding-school years; others hated and did not endure: they ran away. Some count their years away at school among the happiest and most carefree of their lives. (p. xiv)

These happier accounts appear to be more the exception than the rule. In the early 1920s, the schools were investigated, and the findings were published in the 1924 Meriam Report, which criticized off-reservation schools for severe malnutrition, poor health care, overcrowding, unsanitary living conditions, restrictive discipline, low-quality teaching staff, and inordinate dependence on student labor. Specifically, it was found that the schools were feeding the children on 11 cents a day when the recognized standard was 35 cents. The number of boarding schools, especially off-reservation, dropped from 76 to 65 by 1933 (Lomawaima, 1994).

After World War II, as public awareness grew and families refused to send their children away, boarding schools increasingly served troubled students. A handful of boarding schools were still in operation in the 1990s, but most of those have been turned over to tribal control. The structure and curriculum of the schools now reflect more Indian history and culture, and only about 10 percent of Native American children attend these schools.

Increased Tribal Sovereignty

Since the early 1930s, particularly under pressure from the American Indian Movement of the 1960s and 1970s, the U.S. government has softened its approach to Native Americans. With some notable exceptions, most of the laws that have been passed in regard to Native Americans have restored tribal status and given American Indians more self-control over their activities. That is not to say the relationship has been fully resolved, but improvements have been made.

Some of the major laws increasing tribal control include the following:

- The 1975 Indian Self-Determination and Education Assistance Act expanded Indian control over reservation programs and provided funding for more schools on or near reservations.
- The 1978 Education Amendments Act gave tribes substantial control over local education programs.

- The 1978 Indian Child Welfare Act gave tribal courts jurisdiction to place Native American children in Native American homes for adoption or foster care.
- The 1978 American Indian Religious Freedom Act protected the religious rights of Native Americans, including their use of peyote.

Native Americans are now dual citizens, both of the United States, since 1924, and of their tribes. Some carry passports from each. For the most part, tribes are regulated by federal, not state, law. As it turned out, some of the useless reservation land has been found to hold some of the richest resources, such as coal, oil, gas, uranium, and forests. Control over these and other resources, such as water and food, remains under continuous negotiation. Several tribes now run very successful industries. For instance, the Cherokee run a military parts industry, whereas the Choctaw run auto parts and greeting card businesses. Moreover, about 200 tribes now run gaming industries of one sort or another, generating about $6 billion per year (still far short of the revenues generated by Las Vegas, Reno, and Atlantic City). Although some of this revenue is donated or turned over to state governments, much has become an important source of education, jobs, and social services for a few tribes (Holmstrom, 1994).

The State of American Indians and Their Families Today

As stated earlier, it is a risky enterprise to generalize about Native American families, but for the sake of facilitating some learning, I'm about to take that risk. Several researchers (Miller & Moore, 1979; Red Horse, 1988) have attempted to form a typology of Native American families ranging from traditional to acculturated, based on a number of criteria: language (whether they speak the tribal language or English), religious beliefs (tribal, pan-Indian, or Christian), family structure (extended or nuclear), health practices (traditional healing or Western), and attitude toward land (sacred or utilitarian). One of the main factors contributing to where Native American families fall on the continuum is their relationship to the reservation.

On or Off the Reservation

The United States contains more than 300 reservations. Currently, it is estimated that about 22 percent of American Indians live on reservations; another 15 percent or so live near reservations or in tribal areas (John,

1998), making Native Americans one of the most rural racial-ethnic groups in America.

As noted above, reservations originally were not residences of choice for Native Americans. By default, however, they now serve as the locus of Indian culture and tradition for those who want to maintain some semblance of their heritage. Therefore, American Indian families who reside full-time on reservations tend to be those who are tied to their particular tribe, as opposed to a pan-Indian identity. They tend to practice the religious traditions and rituals peculiar to their tribe or to the Native American Church, a 20th century pan-Indian religion combining Christian beliefs with traditional practices. Whereas off-reservation family experiences range widely from alienation to economic success, reservation families tend to have higher-than-average poverty, unemployment, domestic violence, fertility, and extended household rates (Baca Zinn & Eitzen, 2002; John, 1998). For many Native Americans, then, it sometimes seems that one has to choose between maintaining one's heritage or surviving financially. Some choose to do both by living and working off reservation but visiting family periodically on reservation.

Tribal Structure

Each tribe is united by a common language and governing structure. Though these structures vary, they frequently consist of several bands or clans, such as the seven clans of the Cherokee Nation, which are usually composed of extended kin with mutual economic interests. Each band or clan is often headed by a senior male who represents the clan at the tribal level. Traditionally, some of these representatives (chiefs) inherited their position by virtue of their ancestral line, whereas others were selected or elected by a council of elders based on their personal characteristics. A number of studies indicate that Native Americans define leadership skills differently from European Americans. Whereas most Americans would look for experience, education, and authority when choosing a leader, Native Americans are more likely to seek wisdom, bravery, humility, and intuition (Hoebel, 1978). In recent years more tribes have moved to leadership by selection or election.

The chief usually rules with a council of elders (usually male, but occasionally female, as in the Iroquois Nation) and with shamans or religious leaders, persons who are perceived as having special powers or understanding of the universe. Following the council of elders and religious leaders are the warriors and braves, usually young men and boys who have proven themselves capable of providing security for the tribe. Stereotypes usually associate warriors with fighting, but security involved more than intertribal relations. Anna Lee Walters (1993, p. 46), a Pawnee, explains that in her tribe it was customary that warriors always bring food, preferably meat, when visiting friends or family. The food would then be prepared by the host and served to the warrior and the rest of the family. Nevertheless, Native American men do have a history of serving disproportionately in the U.S. armed services (as do many other racial minorities) and holding regular ceremonies honoring veterans. Some have suggested that this military commitment has served as a substitute for the loss of such opportunities within the tribe.

Cultural Values

Although Native American cultural values can be found on and off the reservation, they are more easily maintained and socialized in succeeding generations on the reservation where the context and structure support such values. Again, values vary by tribe and individual, but some observers have noted the following commonalities.

Cooperation, more than competition, is encouraged. In the two-part documentary *Winds of Change* (Cotter, Iverson, & Lucas, 1990), the filmmakers interview a young White man who coaches a Native American football team. He complains that it is difficult to get his Native American team to exhibit enough competitive spirit to continue to play hard against the other team; winning by one point is enough.

The collective is valued over the individual. Unlike most of America, where guests are expected to bring gifts to birthday and graduation parties, in a number of Native American tribes, the host gives gifts at his or her celebration. Personal achievements are viewed as the result of a family enterprise, and giving gifts is the individual's way of acknowledging all the people who helped along the way. As noted earlier when discussing U.S. laws regarding American Indian land, many tribes had no concept of private property. Land either couldn't be owned or was owned communally. Similarly, food obtained through fishing or hunting would be shared by the extended family, not just by those who caught it. Flannery (1995) describes the traditional Cree practice of winter hunting groups gathering in spring near a good fishing area. They would build a trap and all would share in the catch. If men hunted together, they would divide the caribou equitably regardless of who shot it.

Harmony between spirit, mind, and body is desired. As mentioned in the chapter on parent-child relationships, like many Asians, Native Americans try to avoid conflict and confrontation to maintain harmony both within oneself and among relationships. For instance, Flannery's (1995) study of the Cree confirmed that Cree individuals tend to avoid direct criticism of, or intervention in, matters involving people outside the family. Writing of the Ojibwa, Shkilnyk (1985) also noted that when relational norms were transgressed, the Ojibwa seldom engaged in open expressions of anger or face-to-face confrontation; instead, they retaliated by covert means, namely by the use of sorcery and magic to punish those who violated social norms.

Current Family Trends

As with African American families, Native American families have been known for their reliance on extended family members as systems of support and for their fluid household boundaries. The use of other family and nonfamily members as co-parents is common and is sometimes reflected in tribal languages that refer to anyone who does parenting as "mother" or "father" even when they are not the biological parents. For instance, among the Hopi, the mother's sister is also called Mother and her children are called brother and sister. Among the Omaha, any female of the mother's clan is referred to as mother (Stanton, 1995).

Fluid household borders also accommodate cyclical migration between reservation and city. For instance, Lobo (2002) describes one American Indian household in the San Francisco area that had accommodated the comings and goings of at least 38 people during the course of one month. Yet, according to some recent estimates, the use of extended family households is declining among Native Americans (Yellowbird & Snipp, 1994).

Throughout the text I have pointed out that matrilineality is most commonly found in the United States among Native Americans, particularly among eastern tribes, such as the Creek, Choctaw, and Seminole, and among the southwestern Pueblo tribes, such as the Hopi, Acoma, Zuni, and Laguna. Nevertheless, most American Indian tribes are patriarchal and patrilineal. Traditionally, girls were married quite young (usually to older boys), and this may account for the current pattern of early marriage and childbirth.

The young age distribution among Native Americans (which results in fewer elderly living alone), combined with high rates of nonmarital childbearing, results in a higher percentage of family households (as opposed to nonfamily households) than that found among Black or White Americans (Refer to Table 5.1). In the past, among some tribes, the Micmac for instance (Guillemin, 1975), nonmarital births did not diminish a woman's marital prospects, but this pattern has declined, creating an increased proportion of female-headed households (now second to African Americans).

High rates of divorce also contribute to the increased proportion of single-parent households. Historically, divorce was easily obtained, particularly by men, and less stigmatized among Native Americans, a practice that irked many Jesuit missionaries (Schwartz & Scott, 2003). For instance, according to Bates and Fratkin (2003), among the Navajo, people traditionally married and divorced four or five times, not expecting that marriage should last forever. What differs today is that the divorces are less likely followed by remarriage (John, 1998). Consequently, according to Lamanna and Reidman (2003), Native Americans have higher proportions of their population divorced than do other racial-ethnic groups.

As discussed in Chapter 7, Native American parenting styles were traditionally viewed as permissive and indulgent. Very little corporal punishment was used. Children were given quite a bit of latitude in making behavioral choices, and socialization was widely dispersed among clan members. The boarding school policy that separated generations of parents and children, however, contributed to a loss of parenting skills and traditions, and the generations of students who grew up in boarding schools frequently adopted the more authoritarian discipline methods of the schools. Today, Native Americans have higher rates of child abuse, foster care, and grandparent care than other groups (see Chapters 7 and 8). Since the 1978 Indian Child Welfare Act was passed, more than 80 percent of tribes adopted juvenile codes and courts to deal with child welfare issues and specifically to reduce the number of Indian children in foster care, particularly non-Indian foster care, but it has met with little success.

Like African Americans, Native Americans have made great strides in education, occupation, and income in recent decades. For instance, in 1940 only 2.2 percent of Native Americans held professional jobs (Gonzales, 1998); now nearly 20 percent do. Nevertheless, inequities in those areas linger, and severe social repercussions following relocation remain for a substantial minority. The rates of alcoholism, violence, and suicide reached frightening proportions in some Native communities in the last century. Though an extreme case, Anastasia M. Shkilnyk tells of the effects of such relocation in her 1985 book *A Poison Stronger than Love: The Destruction of an Ojibwa Community.* Shkilnyk describes the transformation of the traditional Ojibwa extended family system, which was guided by codes of respect and tolerance for each other, elaborate rituals of puberty and transition, strong taboos against incest, promiscuity, and marriage within bloodlines. Many of these traditions apparently were destroyed after relocation and were followed by an exponential increase in alcohol and drug use, which in turn gave rise to high rates of gang rape, child neglect, and self-destruction.

Although the majority of Native Americans are not alcoholics, the rate of alcoholism is higher among Native Americans than among any other racial group. Not traditionally part of the Native American way of life, alcohol was introduced by European Americans to the indigenous population, frequently as a way of lubricating treaty negotiations. Today, Native Americans, like many American college students, are known for binge drinking, drinking until highly inebriated or unconscious (Shkilnyk, 1985). Some have speculated that because most reservations have laws prohibiting alcohol on the reservation, Native Americans are more likely to binge when and where they can get alcohol.

Consequently, health issues among Native Americans remain prominent. Diabetes is four times higher than the national average. In some communities, for instance the Pima in Arizona, more than 50 percent of the elderly have diabetes (Baldridge, 2001). Mortality from alcohol-related illnesses, accidents, and homicides is above average as well. Fetal alcohol syndrome is highest among Native American babies (Schwartz & Scott, 2003).

In particular, Native American teens have the highest drug and alcohol use rates of all racial-ethnic groups. Youth gang activity has increased exponentially on reservations (Youth Gangs, 1997), and adolescent suicide rates are four times higher than the national average for that age group. Some have suggested a cultural explanation for the high suicide pattern, because in some tribes death is approached as part of the natural circle of life (LaFromboise & Bigfoot, 1988). Poverty, substance abuse, and limited educational and economic opportunities, however, would be sufficient reason as well.

Some tribes have chosen to address these problems through economic development, with revenues and employment garnered from gaming, tourist, timber, and other industries, or with the development of tribal colleges, which now number about 30 (Conover, 1997; Serwer, 1993). Many attribute these problems, however, to the erosion of Native American culture and traditions. Consequently, in recent years, many tribes have instituted programs to overturn these trends through a revival of cultural practices, such as the sweat lodge or the Sioux Sun Dance, and renewal of spiritual values (Holmstrom, 1997). Although these tradition renewal efforts continue, the overwhelming trend is toward marital assimilation (see Chapter 13), which will make it difficult for Native Americans as a whole, let alone as particular tribes, to maintain unique cultural boundaries.

Resources

Books and Articles

Caduto, M. J., & Bruchac, J. (1992). *Native American animal stories.* Golden, CO: Fulcrum.

This is a children's book.

Crow Dog, M. (with Erdoes, R.). (1990). *Lakota woman.* New York: HarperCollins.

This is an autobiographical account of a Lakota Sioux woman coming of age during the height of the American Indian Movement.

Lomawaima, K. T. (1994). *They called it prairie light: The story of Chilocco Indian School.* Lincoln: University of Nebraska Press.

A researched account of the off-reservation boarding school system, this volume uses one school as a case study.

Marshall, J. M., III. (2002). *The Lakota way: Stories and lessons for living: Native American wisdom on ethics and character.* New York: Penguin.

These stories capture the values and beliefs of the Lakota people.

McCubbin, H., Thompson, E. A., Thompson, A. I., and Fromer, J. E. (Eds.). (1998). *Resiliency in Native American and immigrant families.* Thousand Oaks, CA: Sage.

Part II of this collection of studies addresses cultural resiliency and its effects on Native American youth.

Riley, P. (Ed.). (1993). *Growing up Native American.* New York: Avon.

Patricia Riley collected essays from Native Americans of various tribes writing about their childhood.

Videos

Cotter, C., Iverson, D., & Lucas, P. (Producers). (1990). *Winds of change: A matter of promises* [Video recording]. Alexandria, VA: PBS Video. (Available from Wisconsin Public Television at https://secure.uwex.edu/wpt/videos/)

This 2-part, one-hour each, documentary explores Indian families on and off the reservation.

Native Americans: Celebrating traditions. (2001). (Available from Films Media Group, P.O. Box 2053, Princeton, NJ 08453-2053, or at http://www.films.com)

By presenting the experiences of Native Americans from a wide array of fields including artisans, performers, and teachers, this 30-minute video shows how many tribes are returning to the traditions and spirituality of their ancestors.

Obomsawin, A. (Producer). (1977). *Mother of many children.* Canada: National Film Board of Canada. (Available from Women Making Movies, 462 Broadway, Suite 500, New York, NY 10013, or at http://www.wmm.com)

This 58-minute film examines matrilineal Indian culture.

Sacred spirit: The Lakota Sioux, past and present. (1999). (Available from Films Media Group, P.O. Box 2053, Princeton, NJ 08453-2053, or at http://www.films.com)

This 51-minute video reviews the history and culture of the Oglala Sioux.

Teaching Indians to be White. (1993). (Available from Films Media Group, P.O. Box 2053, Princeton, NJ 08453-2053, or at http://www.films.com)

This 28-minute video looks at several tribal reactions to the different school systems developed for Native American children.

Websites

http://www.cherokee.org
The Cherokee Nation has its own web page. Many other Indian Nations have their own informational websites as well.

http://www.indiancountry.com
This is the on-line version of the pan-Indian newspaper *Indian Country Today.*

http://www.indianeduresearch.net
This website, affiliated with ERIC Digests, gives abstracts of research on Native Americans.

http://www.nativetelecom.org
This is a good collection of available media resources about Native Americans.

http://www.nativeweb.org
This website contains information about indigenous people around the world.

CHAPTER 11

LATINO AMERICAN FAMILIES

Latino Americans recently became the largest racial-ethnic minority group in the United States. The three main Latino ethnicities that have had historical importance in the United States are Mexican, Puerto Rican, and Cuban. Table 11.1 shows that in 2002 Mexican Americans accounted for the majority of Hispanic Americans, followed by Puerto Ricans, and then Cubans. Many other Hispanic nationalities, mostly from Central and South America, have arrived in greater numbers in recent decades, so that they now represent about 21 percent of the Hispanic American population (see Table 11.1). As individual ethnic groups, however, they remain small percentages and few studies have been conducted on their families. Hence, here I will focus on Mexican, Puerto Rican, and Cuban history and family trends.

Although ethnically diverse, these three groups have many cultural commonalities because these countries were all colonized by Spain in the late 1400s and early 1500s. The Spanish instituted a system of slavery in these countries to extract the plentiful minerals (e.g., gold and silver) and cultivate tobacco, coffee, and sugar plantations. As in the United States, the indigenous populations (the Taino Indians in Puerto Rico, the Aztecs in Mexico, and the Cubanacan Indians in Cuba) were nearly eradicated by disease, massacre, and forced labor, so the Spanish turned to importing slaves from Africa to replace the rapidly dwindling indigenous peoples. The working conditions and type of work (mining) was difficult and more dangerous in many of the Spanish colonies than in the United States. Therefore, slave turnover was high, and more slaves were shipped to these locations than to the United States overall. Legally, however, the Spanish slave system was less harsh than the slave system in the United States. Due largely to the influence of the Catholic church, the Spanish slave system usually allowed slaves to purchase their freedom. The church eventually required that one third of all imported slaves be female so that slaves could marry. The church recognized these marriages and required baptism of slaves. The church also

Table 11.1 Latino Population by Ethnicity, 2002

Ethnicity	*Percentage of Hispanic Population*	*Percentage Foreign-Born*[a]
Mexican	66.9	42
Puerto Rican	8.6	1
Cuban	3.7	68
Other Hispanic	20.8	76

SOURCE: Ramirez & de la Cruz (2003)

a. These percentages came from Fields (2003).

allowed Spanish invaders, who were virtually all men, to marry indigenous people and slaves (Black or Indian), particularly if a pregnancy had occurred (Gonzales, 1998). Although these countries continue to have a social hierarchy based on race (for instance, until the 1960s in Cuba, non-Whites frequently were excluded from vacation resorts, beaches, and private schools [Suarez, 1998]), this intermixing resulted in a highly mixed population, called "mestizo," which led to a concept of race that is more of a continuum than the dichotomous concept of Black or White in the United States.

Under the Spanish, the family system was largely patriarchal, patrilineal, and patrilocal, as had been the indigenous family systems before them. Women married at early ages and had few rights and little power. The Aztec Indians in Mexico had allowed polygamy for the nobility, but marriage was considered a lifelong commitment, though divorce was allowed. Infidelity was not tolerated; perpetrators were punished by strangulation or having their head crushed with a stone. The Catholic church allowed neither polygamy nor divorce, but after Mexican independence the church agreed to recognize both religious and civil-ceremony marriages. Also, the governments of these countries recognized *union libre,* common law marriages, which were most prevalent in rural areas, as it was the cheapest form of marriage. Such unions carried over into the Southwest United States after the annexation of half of Mexico, as it was estimated that about 6 to 7 percent of Mexican American families were the result of common-law marriages in Los Angeles in the late 1880s (Griswold del Castillo, 1979). Puerto Ricans continue to have a high rate of common-law marriages.

Manner and Timing of Entry

Although Mexican, Puerto Rican, and Cuban Americans have a common cultural heritage due to Spanish colonization, they differ in the manner and timing of how their members were introduced into the United States, and these differences impact the current social status of their families.

Mexico

In 1821, Mexico won a war of independence from Spain. Over the following years, a dispute developed between Mexico and the United States over control of Texas, which had seceded from Mexico and existed as an independent republic from 1836 to 1845. In 1845, the United States and Mexico went to war. The United States won the Mexican-American War, and under the 1848 Treaty of Guadalupe Hidalgo the United States annexed about one half of Mexico (what is now California, New Mexico, Nevada, Colorado, Arizona, and Utah) in exchange for $15 million. The treaty also assured Mexican nationals living in this territory that they could maintain their language, culture, and traditions, while also obtaining American citizenship (Gonzales, 1998). Most of the 75,000 to 100,000 Mexicans in the annexed territory at that time were small landowners (farmers); a few were large landowners. According to the treaty, they were supposed to be able to keep their land, but many did not have proof of ownership and when they did, the deeds were often in Spanish. Eventually, much of their land was confiscated by White Americans.

In addition, the discovery of gold in California attracted thousands of new European American settlers who competed with indigenous Mexicans for mining jobs. Mexican Americans found most employment in agriculture and railroad construction. With no restrictions on Mexican immigration until the 1920s, the Mexican American population increased exponentially. As the transcontinental railroad was completed and the Gold Rush dwindled, more Mexican American workers were funneled into agriculture. Many men came north, often on a seasonal basis, to do agricultural work. During some seasons, especially early summer, entire families migrated for work, often in chain-like fashion. When whole families were incorporated into the labor process, it was usually on a gendered basis. Men worked in agriculture, ranching, mining, and railroads and as common laborers in industry. Women worked as domestics and in canning and packinghouses, the textile industry, and agriculture.

The Mexican Revolution of the early 1920s pushed, and the World War I labor shortage pulled, more Mexicans into the United States. By 1929, more than 3 million Mexicans resided in the United States (Gonzales, 1998). Then the stock market crashed, and native-born Americans began looking for scapegoats. To reduce relief rolls and competition for jobs, from 1929 to 1935, the United States instituted its first repatriation of Mexican Americans. More than 415,000 Mexicans (many of whom were American citizens) were expelled; tens of thousands more left voluntarily. In all, about 40 percent of the Mexican American population returned to Mexico.

World War II soon followed. More than 400,000 Mexican Americans served in the military, and Mexicans were also recruited back into the United States to fill labor shortages at home. In 1942, the United States and Mexico agreed to create the bracero program, a farmworker program that brought laborers into the United States with the agreement that their working conditions would be monitored. The program was intended as a temporary wartime measure, but U.S. agricultural growers lobbied for extension and expansion of the program through the 1950s and into the 1960s. By the time the bracero program ended in 1964, due to opposition by organized labor, more than 4 million workers had come and gone (Becerra, 1998). The net effect, however, was a doubling of the Mexican American population from 1940 to 1970 so that they constituted nearly 3 percent of the population. This exponential growth has continued through both legal and illegal immigration. Thus, although a portion of Mexican Americans currently in the United States are descendants of the originally annexed population, a larger proportion is foreign-born or only the second or third generation.

One of the historical factors distinguishing Mexican Americans from Puerto Rican and Cuban Americans is that Mexican Americans resided in the United States in substantial numbers prior to the civil rights movement and experienced more legal discrimination, such as antimiscegenation laws, differential pay scales, and so on, than did later Hispanic groups. In fact, Mexican Americans (Chicanos) developed a viable political movement in the 1960s that focused on land recovery, political rights, and migrant farming conditions. Although their countries became affiliated with the United States at the turn of the 20th century, Puerto Ricans did not arrive on the mainland in substantial numbers until the 1940s and 1950s and Cubans not until the 1960s.

Puerto Rico and Cuba

In 1898, the Spanish still controlled a number of islands, including Puerto Rico and Cuba. That year, the U.S.S. *Maine* was sunk in the Havana harbor, killing 260 U.S. sailors. The United States declared war on Spain and, very shortly, the United States had control of Cuba, Puerto Rico, the Philippines, Samoa, and Guam. The United States took a different strategy in Puerto Rico than in Cuba, however.

Puerto Rico

The United States took possession of Puerto Rico. An American military general served as governor of the island. The Foraker Act of 1900 stated that all Puerto Rican legislative acts had to be approved by the governor and that the U.S. Congress could nullify any Puerto Rican law. Puerto Rico became integrated into the U.S. economy through the establishment of free trade, the inclusion of Puerto Rican production under the U.S. tariff system, and incorporation of the island into the American monetary system. The 1917 Jones Act gave U.S. citizenship to Puerto Ricans, making the men eligible for the World War I draft. In 1947, Puerto Rico was allowed to hold popular elections, and the people elected their first native-born governor. In 1950, the United States granted the country the right to draft its own constitution, and

Puerto Rico became known as a commonwealth, which means it is neither a U.S. state nor independent. Though Puerto Ricans have U.S. citizenship, it is not full citizenship, except for those born on the mainland. Islanders are not required to pay federal taxes, they cannot vote in presidential elections, and Puerto Rico has only a nonvoting representative in Congress. As you can see in Table 11.1, because of this legal status only one percent of the Puerto Rican American population is considered foreign-born. Pertinent to our discussion as well, citizenship means they are not subject to immigration laws. Money notwithstanding, Puerto Ricans can travel to and from the mainland as they please. Since 1965, it is estimated that about three million travel back and forth from the United States to Puerto Rico annually. Of late, many of those 55 and older retire to Puerto Rico (Sanchez-Ayendez, 1991). Such continuous contact between island and mainland facilitates maintenance of Puerto Ricans' ethnic identity (see Chapter 13 for a discussion on acculturation).

In the first 40 years of control, the United States transformed Puerto Rican agriculture, particularly sugar production, from subsistence to export. U.S. corporations took over more land in Puerto Rico, and a depression hit the sugar industry. Unemployment more than doubled and so did the island's mostly rural population. Many Puerto Ricans turned their eyes toward the mainland.

By World War II, about 70,000 Puerto Ricans lived on the mainland. Most were unskilled peasants who spoke little English. They arrived in search of employment opportunities and most found them in lower-status blue-collar work. Unlike most immigrants, Puerto Rican women frequently made the trip, as it was known that women could find jobs in the garment industry or domestic work (Gonzales, 1998).

The 20-year period after the war is known as the "Great Migration" for Puerto Ricans. A total of 640,000 came during that period. This migration was primarily facilitated by the development of a direct commercial air flight from San Juan to New York City, which was much cheaper and quicker than the previous 5-day boat trip (Gonzales, 1998). The vast majority of those who came settled in the urban Northeast, mostly New York and New Jersey (Sanchez-Ayendez, 1998). In recent decades, especially with the decline in industrial jobs, Puerto Ricans have moved to other northeastern states, as well as to Florida, California, and Illinois. In the last 25 years, more young professionals have also immigrated.

Cuba

After the Spanish-American War, the United States militarily occupied Cuba and assumed control for a few years, finally granting Cuba home rule in 1902. Although Cuba was technically independent, the United States wielded considerable influence in Cuba politically and economically for the next 50 years. U.S. corporations and a small group of corrupt Cuban politicians benefited from these relations. The last of these politicians was Fulgencio Batista, who was overthrown by Fidel Castro in 1959.

By this time, there were already about 50,000 Cubans in the United States, mostly concentrated in Key West and Tampa, Florida, many running cigar businesses (Suarez, 1998). The largest waves of Cuban immigrants, however, were about to start. With the overthrow of Batista, it is estimated that 10 percent of Cuba's population came to the United States between 1959 and 1980 (Gonzales, 1998). As political refugees, Cubans had a very different immigrant experience than did Mexicans or Puerto Ricans. The types of people who came, the timing of their entrance, and their status as political exiles greatly enhanced their life in America.

Cuba's short distance from the United States and its well established ties to the U.S. economy made America the logical destination for most Cuban exiles, who arrived in America in essentially five waves of immigration. The 215,000 exiles who arrived from January 1959 to October 1962 constitute the first wave (Portes & Bach, 1985). Nicknamed the "golden exiles," they were the social, economic, and political elites of Cuba. Many had been banking and industrial executives, firm owners, big merchants, sugar mill owners, manufacturers, cattlemen, or former government officials. They had the most to lose by remaining in Cuba under Castro. Following a communist ideology, Castro nationalized Cuban industry, instituted agrarian reform, and severed economic ties with the United States. Castro prohibited the exiles from taking their financial assets out of the country, but they arrived with other assets—their families, education, business skills, and the English language. Ninety percent of this first wave would be considered racially white and middle to upper class. The majority brought most of their family members, though some families were split up, and about 14,000 children were smuggled out and placed in American foster homes (Gonzales, 1991). In addition, the first wave was politically conservative and viewed themselves largely as temporary exiles planning to return to Cuba as soon as Castro could be ousted.

Their attempts to bring that scenario to fruition were foiled during the Bay of Pigs invasion in 1961, when the United States failed to deliver promised air cover to Cuban "freedom fighters" who attempted to liberate Cuba. Perez-Firmat (1995) remembered how his Cuban Miami community prepared for the invasion:

> For months rumors of a military action against Fidel had been circulating. Young men kept disappearing from the streets, and it was an open secret that they were going to Central America for military training. So when the day of the invasion arrived, exiles were ready with their shortwave radios and their

> Cuban passports. . . . That afternoon . . . the Brigada 2506 seemed to be on the verge of defeat (how could this be?), but there was still the possibility, indeed the likelihood, that President Kennedy would take action—provide air cover, send reinforcements, invade the island. But within a matter of days it became clear that the expedition had failed miserably and that, regardless of what had been planned or promised, no help from the United States was forthcoming. (pp. 59–60)

For the next 3 years, Cuban immigration was greatly reduced. Only a relatively small number (74,000) were able to escape through clandestine means (Suarez, 1998). Mostly, this wave was a middle-class cohort of merchants, landlords, mid-level professionals, and skilled workers.

In late 1965, the United States and Cuba agreed to allow two daily "freedom flights" out of Cuba. These flights continued until 1973, transporting between 275,000 and 340,000 refugees to the United States. Most of them arrived as intact families as did the first wave. This wave was largely working-class employees, independent craftsmen, small merchants, and semiskilled workers, because the Cuban government had begun barring the migration of young men of military age and professional, technical, and skilled workers to mitigate the deleterious effect the emigration of the most-skilled population was having on Cuba. Forty percent of this group were students, women, or children uniting with relatives (Bean & Tienda, 1987). After the end of the freedom flights in 1973, a smaller number of refugees (about 38,000) managed to arrive on their own until 1980.

Early in 1980, more than 125,000 immigrants left Cuba in a perilous boatlift, through a Cuban port known as Mariel, and arrived on the shores of Florida in the spring and summer of 1980. Unlike previous waves, this one was greeted warmly by neither the general American public nor the Cuban American community. The *marielitos* arrived on the tail end of a recession in the United States, and their lack of resources indicated that they would be less self-sufficient than had been the previous waves. About 16 percent of the *marielitos* had been political prisoners or petty thieves. Eighty-five percent were single men with no relatives in the United States, and the vast majority were blue-collar workers. They were also darker skinned than the previous waves; about 40 percent would be considered racially black in America.

From 1985 to 1992, nearly 6,000 Cubans survived hazardous trips over the seas from Cuba to Florida. The numbers of people arriving as *balseros* (named after the type of raft they rode on) increased, keeping the U.S. Coast Guard busy rescuing them at sea. In the mid-1990s, the United States signed an agreement that future *balseros* would be returned to the island. Since then, at least 500 have been turned back, although the U.S. government continues to accept about 20,000 immigrant visas from Cuba each year (Suarez, 1998).

Because of their status as refugees from a communist government, Cuban exiles, particularly those of the first three waves, received a more generous welcome than other immigrants. The U.S. Cuban Refugee Program spent more than $1.5 billion on settling 486,000 Cubans during the first 20 years of migration. Another federal program provided special scholarships for Cuban college students. Until 1995, any Cuban who came, legally or not, was automatically granted permanent legal status (Suro, 1998).

Because more than 60 percent of the Cuban exiles settled in the Miami area, particularly in Dade County, a number of state or local programs were set up to facilitate retraining and settlement. The University of Miami created a course to prepare Cuban doctors for licensing exams and provided loans while they studied. Dade County public schools launched a program to recertify Cubans who had teaching experience. Between 1968 and 1980, 46 percent of Small Business Administration loans in Dade County went to Cuban- and Latino-owned businesses (Suro, 1998).

Shortly before the arrival of the *marielitos*, however, the U.S. Congress passed the Refugee Act of 1980, which declared that immigrants from Cuba had to prove political or religious persecution before they would be given refugee status and access to benefits. Therefore, the *marielitos* were ineligible for assistance.

These varying immigration histories of Mexican, Puerto Rican, and Cuban Americans have contributed to major educational, occupational, and economic differences among the three Hispanic subgroups. On average, Cubans are better off on these three measurements than either Puerto Ricans, who have the highest poverty rates, or Mexican Americans. The better socioeconomic status of Cubans largely results from the fact that the majority of Cuban immigrants arrived here as political refugees; they were the elites of Cuba, and they received government assistance upon arrival. On the other hand, Puerto Rican, and in particular Mexican, immigrants are largely economic immigrants, attracted or recruited to America for its economic opportunities. Their lower educational levels are reflected in their lower occupational status (see Table 11.2). Puerto Ricans, who had congregated in decent-paying factory work, were recently hard hit by deindustrialization, and now have high levels of unemployment and poverty. Although the proportion of Mexican Americans in farming has greatly declined over the decades (replaced by Central Americans), a high proportion remains in low-paid service and blue-collar jobs.

Moreover, many Cubans arrived in America with their entire families. Not only did that give them added emotional support, but also their population now has a higher proportion of middle-aged and older adults, who are employed and established economically. Note in Table 11.2 that Cubans have

Table 11.2 Select Social Characteristics by Latino Ethnicity, 2000

	Mexican	*Puerto Rican*	*Cuban*
Education			
< 9th Grade	34.0%	16.0%	19.0%
High School or Higher	45.8%	63.3%	62.9%
BA or Higher	7.5%	12.5%	21.2%
Occupational Distribution			
Professional/Managerial	15.0%	24.0%	32.0%
Sales/Office	21.0%	30.0%	29.0%
Service	22.0%	20.0%	14.0%
Farming/Fishing/Forestry	4.0%	< 1.0%	< 1.0%
Construction/Maintenance	15.0%	8.0%	10.0%
Production/Transportation	23.0%	18.0%	15.0%
Income			
Median Family Income (1999)	$31,123	$30,129	$38,312
Families in Poverty	20.4%	24.2%	13.1%
Age Distribution			
< 15 Years	32.2%	25.8%	16.4%
65 and Over	4.0%	6.6%	22.6%
Median Age (years)	24.0	25.4	40.4
Fertility Rate (per woman)	3.3	2.6	1.9
Sex Ratio (men per 100 women)	112.6	95.0	99.6

SOURCES: Elliott & Umberson (2004); U.S. Department of Commerce (2000c), Table 1; U. S Department of Commerce (2003c), Tables 46 and 47

the oldest median age. This also means that certain family trends, such as fertility, marriage, and divorce are lower because a good portion of the Cuban population is in or nearing the developmental stage where those behaviors are least likely to occur. The older age structure, however, also portends a higher proportion of elderly who will eventually need to be supported.

Similarities Among Hispanic Families

In the aggregate, Hispanic families have been characterized by observers as having a high level of familism (similar to communalism, discussed in Chapter 7, but often excluding non-kin). Familism emphasizes collective family welfare and requires individuals to defer to family goals and behave according to their role or status within the family (Ting & Chiu, 2002). It can be described in normative, behavioral, and demographic terms.

Normatively, a few studies have concluded that Latinos have stronger familistic values (such as deference to elders, desiring to be with their families, etc.) than do White Americans (Vega, 1995). Other Hispanic norms that indicate high valuation of interpersonal and interdependent relationships, particularly those of family, include *personalismo* and *dignidad*. The former reflects a person-oriented approach to social relations. Latinos favor face-to-face interactions, preferring to deal with others in a network of relationships rather than through organizations. People, especially family members, are expected to perform favors, such as finding jobs for or loaning money to one another. Cash payment for services would be considered an insult, but eventual repayment with another favor is expected.

Dignidad involves recognition of the inherent value and dignity of the human being and therefore requires a generalized deference in all social interactions, but especially those involving men and older family members. Esmeralda Santiago (1993) remembers what *dignidad* meant in her Puerto Rican family:

> It meant you never swore at people, never showed anger in front of strangers, never stared, never stood too close to people you'd just met, never addressed people by the familiar *tu* until they gave you permission. . . . It meant, if you were a child, you did not speak until spoken to, did not look an adult in the eye, did not raise your voice nor enter or leave a room without permission. It meant adults were always right, especially if they were old. It meant men could look at women any way they liked but women could never look at men directly, only sidelong glances, unless they were *putas* [prostitutes]. . . . It meant men could say things to women as they walked down the street, but women could not say anything to men, not even to tell them to go jump in the harbor and leave them alone. (p. 30)

Behaviorally, studies indicate that Hispanic families tend to live near or with extended relatives, have frequent interaction with family members, and exchange a wide range of goods and services (Muller & Espenshade, 1985). (In terms of emotional and instrumental exchanges of support and assistance, I should note that in a study comparing Black, White, and Hispanic families, Roschelle [1997] found them equally familistic.) I discussed the greater incidence of extended families, both multigenerationally and laterally, among Hispanic families in Chapter 5. Table 5.1 also indicates that of the main racial-ethnic groups, Hispanic Americans have the largest proportion of family households.

The common practice of godparenting (*compadrazgo*) among Hispanic families is another indicator of their strong family ties. Godparents are viewed as spiritual mentors and potential parents for the child should anything happen to the child's parents. Sometimes godparents function as mentors for a new young couple, if they choose an older more experienced couple. In the United States, many Hispanic families use family members as godparents, unless they don't have family in the United States (Lopez, 1999). Traditionally, however, in some Latin American communities, non-kin were used as a way of building a network of obligations in a community. Today, one set of godparents is usually appointed for a child at the infant's baptism, but traditionally some communities chose different sets of godparents at the child's first Holy Communion, confirmation, and marriage as well. Hence, the potential network of obligations would have been quite extensive (Alvarez, 1987).

In demographic terms, researchers have pointed to the following trends among Hispanic Americans as evidence of familism: earlier age at marriage, higher fertility rates, lower divorce rates, and larger family size (than national averages). You can see some of these demographic trends in Tables 11.2 and 11.3; they are most pronounced among Mexican Americans.

Many have pointed to the predominance of Catholicism as the main explanation for these trends, particularly the high fertility and low divorce rates. More than 70 percent of Latino Americans identify as Catholic; more than 20 percent identify as Protestant (Schick & Schick, 1991). In general, the Hispanic form of Catholicism places greater emphasis on the worship of particular saints than does American Catholicism. Many Hispanic families have an altar to honor a special family saint, who it is believed will protect them (Gonzales, 1998). Whereas most Latinos are Christian, one can find some who practice Santeria, a type of voodoo having its roots in African blood rites. Spiritual leaders of Santeria are called *santeros*, and their services may be sought for healing. Another common religion is *Espiritismo*, which flourished in Europe in the late 1800s and involves communication with the spirit world. Believers seek the help of clairvoyants (called *facultades*) to help predict their future (Cofer, 1990). Santeria and *Espiritismo* are found more commonly among lower-income Hispanic Americans (Suarez, 1998).

Divergent Trends Among Latino Ethnic Groups

Although Hispanic Americans do express strong familistic attitudes, when one disaggregates Hispanic families and looks at them by ethnic group, we find that the behaviors and demographic statistics used as evidence (and

Table 11.3 Household and Family Structure by Latino Ethnicity, 2000 (as a percentage of all households within each ethnicity)

	Mexican	*Puerto Rican*	*Cuban*
Nonfamily Households	17.3	26.1	28.0
Family Households	82.7	73.9	72.0
Married Couple	58.3	41.2	53.8
Married Couple With Children	55.6	23.8	23.8
Female-Headed Household	15.2	26.5	13.0
Female-Headed Household With Children	10.1	18.4	5.8
Male-Headed Household	9.2	6.2	5.3
Male-Headed Household With Children	4.3	3.5	2.0
Households With 5 or More People	34.3	17.1	12.7
Average Family Size (number of members)	4.16	3.45	3.22

SOURCE: U.S. Department of Commerce (2000d), Quick Table-P10

sometimes as stereotypes) do not always hold across groups. If you look at Table 11.3, you will note that Cubans and Puerto Ricans have nearly the same proportion of nonfamily households as the general American population (compare to Table 5.1). Whereas single young adult Hispanic family members are still more likely to remain at home during college and/or until marriage than are White young adults, living alone at all ages is increasing. Cohabitation as well is increasing among all the groups, but cohabitation is generally more practiced and accepted among Puerto Ricans, and the childbearing rates among Puerto Rican cohabitors are similar to married couples (Landale & Fennelly, 1992).

Although married-couple households account for the majority of households among Mexican and Cuban Americans, single-parent households have been increasing among all Hispanic groups (as among the American population in general). They are particularly high among Puerto Ricans, due to a high rate of nonmarital births and to a high divorce rate. In 1999, about 60 percent of all Puerto Rican births were nonmarital, compared to 40 percent of Mexican and 26 percent of Cuban American births. Whereas Mexican Americans, particularly the foreign-born, have a higher teen birthrate than Puerto Ricans, Mexican American teens are more likely to be married.

The aggregate divorce rate among Hispanic Americans is lower than that of White Americans, though the rate is somewhat misleading because Hispanic Americans have a higher separation rate, which doesn't get figured into the divorce rate (Bramlett & Mosher, 2001). When we look at the groups separately, however, Puerto Ricans have the highest divorce rate of the three ethnic groups and Mexican Americans have the lowest. Again, many point to religion as a cultural explanation, but all three groups are predominantly Catholic. What more likely explains the variation is that Puerto Ricans have the highest poverty rate, which induces marital stress.

Cuban Americans, who have an intermediate divorce rate, have the lowest poverty rate, which would make one think their divorce rate should be lowest. But among Hispanic American women, young Cuban women are the most educated and employed. Educated, working women feel they can afford to leave an unhappy marriage. Because Cuban American women marry later and have fewer children, when they do divorce, it less frequently produces a single-parent family.

On the other hand, Mexican American women marry and bear children early, resulting in dependency of women on men. With their lower levels of education and paid employment, Mexican American women may feel they have no choice but to stay in an unhappy marriage to provide for the children. The high proportion of foreign-born, who are less likely to divorce, and the presence of extended family members, who may exert pressure on married couples to stay together, also suppress the Mexican American divorce rate.

Family size varies among the three ethnic groups as well (see Table 11.3). Although they all have larger-than-average families, Mexican Americans have the largest average family size and certainly have the highest proportion of households with five or more members. This is of concern because these larger families, particularly ones with very young or elderly members, have to be supported on smaller incomes (see the median family incomes in Table 11.2). Among all three groups, the greater use of multigenerational and laterally extended families (the latter particularly true among Mexican Americans) plays a role in the larger family sizes. If these extended family members are also economic contributors, family size is not problematic.

Among Mexican Americans, however, higher fertility also accounts for the larger families (shown in Table 11.2). As mentioned earlier, many point to Catholicism (and sometimes to gender ideology, see Chapter 6) as cultural sources of high fertility; but structural factors play a role as well. Mexican American women, who have the lowest level of education, marry earlier and have a higher rate of having children within the first year of marriage, which means they have a longer window of opportunity in which to have children (Bean & Tienda, 1987). Poverty, the younger age distribution of Mexican Americans (that is, more of their population in the childbearing years), and the high proportion of foreign-born (see Table 11.1), who tend to give birth to more children than do native-born, will continue to sustain high fertility rates and family size among Mexican Americans for the near future.

You will note that despite similar levels of Catholicism and similar gender ideology, Cubans have the lowest fertility rate of the three groups, lower than that of White Americans. This lower fertility rate results from the fact that Cuban women have more education than Mexican and Puerto Rican American women. Therefore, Cuban women tend to marry at later ages and delay childbearing, resulting in a narrower window of opportunity to have children. In addition, as a group, Cubans have lower poverty and relatively high median family income as compared to Puerto Rican and Mexican Americans, both factors that tend to reduce birth rates. Although Cubans have the highest proportion of foreign-born, that factor is outweighed by the older age distribution, which means that many Cubans are beyond the childbearing years.

In sum, Hispanic families cannot easily be lumped together. Their commonalities, though plentiful, are counterbalanced by distinct immigration and demographic histories. Most Hispanic families, particularly Mexican Americans, culturally benefit from the constant influx of new immigrants. In addition, many Hispanic Americans, particularly Puerto Ricans, have the opportunity to travel back and forth between the mainland and their country of origin, and Cubans have the cultural resources of the Miami enclave to draw upon. This continuous cultural input enables Hispanic American families to maintain their values and close familial ties while making a new life and identity in America.

Resources

Books and Articles

Artico, C. I. (2003). *Latino families broken by immigration.* New York: LFB Scholarly Publishing.

The author explores how piecemeal immigration affects Latino adolescents and their relations to their parents after a prolonged separation.

Boswell, T., & Curtis, J. (1983). *The Cuban-American experience: Culture, images, and perspectives.* Totowa, NJ: Rowman & Allanheld.

This book provides an overall historical and cultural view of the Cuban community.

Garza, E., Reyes, P., &, Trueba, E. T. (2004). *Resiliency and success: Migrant children in the U.S.* Boulder, CO: Paradigm.

This volume contains case studies of the life journeys of academically successful migrant children.

Lopez, A. (Ed.). (1980). *The Puerto Ricans: Their history, culture, and society.* Cambridge, MA: Schenkman.

Margolis, M. L. (1998). *An invisible minority: Brazilians in New York City*. Boston: Allyn & Bacon.

Perez-Firmat, G. (1995). *Next year in Cuba: A Cubano's coming-of-age in America*. New York: Anchor.

This is Gustavo Perez-Firmat's memoir of growing up in an exiled Cuban family.

Santiago, E. (1993). *When I was Puerto Rican*. New York: Random House.

In this memoir and in the sequel *Almost a Woman* (1999), the author chronicles her life before and after immigration to the mainland.

Strachwitz, C., & Nicolopulos, J. (1993). *Lydia Mendoza: A family autobiography*. Houston, TX: Arte Publico.

This is the story of singer Lydia Mendoza's family, who fled the Mexican Revolution and settled in the United States.

Trujillo, N. (2004). *In search of Naunny's grave: Age, class, gender and ethnicity in an American family*. Walnut Creek, CA: Alta Mira Press.

Using his grandmother's life as the focal point, Trujillo traces how family members use stories to create a collective view of family relationships and responsibilities.

Valle, I. (1994). *Fields of toil: A migrant family's journey*. Pullman: Washington State University Press.

A reporter who lived and worked with a migrant family for a year describes the life of the Martinez family as they move through six states in search of work.

Villasenor, V. (1991). *Rain of gold*. Houston, TX: Arte Publico.

This autobiography, which has been called the Hispanic "*Roots*," chronicles the poverty, immigration, struggles, and success of the author's family.

Williams, N. (1990). *The Mexican American family: Tradition and change*. Dix Hills, NY: General Hall.

Norma Williams provides a historical and cultural sketch of Mexican families in the United States.

Videos

Americano as apple pie: Latino experience in America [Motion picture]. (2001). (Available from Films Media Group, P.O. Box 2053, Princeton, NJ 08453-2053, or at http://www.films.com)

This two-part, 30-minute each video traces the history and identity of Hispanic groups in America.

CBS News (Producer). (1995). *Legacy of shame* [Motion picture]. (Available from Films Media Group, P.O. Box 2053, Princeton, NJ 08453-2053, or at http://www.films.com)

This hour-long video is an update of a 1960 film that looked at the conditions of migrant farm workers by following one main family.

Frankenstein, E. (Producer). (1987). *Miles from the border: Portrait of Mexican American families* [Motion picture]. (Available from New Day Films, 190 Route 17M, P.O. Box 1084, Harriman, NY 10926, or at http://www.newday.com)

This 15-minute video gives a brief view of immigrant families.

Growing up Hispanic: Children in crisis. (2003). (Available from Films Media Group, P.O. Box 2053, Princeton, NJ 08453-2053, or at http://www.films.com)

This 58-minute video focuses on health problems and academic performance of Hispanic children.

Websites

http://ohioline.osu.edu/hyg-fact/5000/5237.html
This site gives a brief overview of some common Hispanic etiquette behaviors.

http://www.nclr.org/
The National Council of La Raza site has publications and other information regarding various aspects of Hispanic life in America.

CHAPTER 12

ASIAN AMERICAN FAMILIES

A myriad of nationalities and ethnicities fall under the geographical umbrella of "Asian." Table 12.1 shows the geographical categories of a number of Asian countries. Some of the ethnicities that are geographically Asian are considered racially White. For instance, most Central and West Asians are classified as White, even though they may be quite dark in skin tone. The West Asian countries are usually classified as Middle Eastern and are combined with North African countries because of their cultural similarities (primarily Arabic language and Islam). Space constraints prevent me from addressing each ethnic subgroup. Also, since many of the subgroups represent relatively small populations in the United States, little research has been conducted on them. Until recently, East Asians have had the largest populations and longest histories in the United States. After the Vietnam War, Southeast Asians began arriving as refugees in significant numbers. Therefore, these two broader groups will constitute the main focus of this chapter.

In 2000, as you can see in Table 12.2, the Chinese formed the largest Asian ethnic group in the United States, followed by Filipinos, Asian Indians, Vietnamese, and Koreans. Historically, until 1980 the Chinese and Japanese were the two largest Asian groups represented in the United States, but after

Table 12.1 Asian Countries by Region

South Asia	*East Asia*	*Southeast Asia*	*Central Asia*	*West Asia*
Afghanistan	China (including Hong Kong and Taiwan)	Cambodia	Armenia	Bahrain
Bangladesh	Japan	Indonesia	Azerbaijan	Cyprus
Bhutan	Mongolia	Laos	Belarus	Iran
Burma	North Korea	Malaysia	Estonia	Iraq
India	South Korea	Papua New Guinea	Georgia	Israel
Nepal		Philippines	Kazakhstan	Jordan
Pakistan		Singapore	Kyrgyzstan	Kuwait
Sri Lanka		Thailand	Latvia	Lebanon
		Vietnam	Lithuania	Oman
			Moldova	Qatar
			Russia	Saudi Arabia
			Tajikistan	Syria
			Turkmenistan	Turkey
			Ukraine	United Arab Emirates
			Uzbekistan	Yemen

Table 12.2 Population of Select Asian Ethnic Groups in the United States, 2000

Ethnicity	*Population*	*Percentage Foreign-Born*
Asian Indian	1,678,765	75.4
Cambodian	171,937	65.8
Chinese	2,314,537	70.9
Filipino	1,850,314	67.7
Hmong	169,428	55.6
Japanese	769,700	39.5
Korean	1,076,872	77.7
Laotian	168,707	68.1
Native Hawaiian & Pacific Islander	398,835	19.9
Thai	112,989	77.8
Vietnamese	1,122,528	76.1

SOURCES: U.S. Department of Commerce (2000g), (2000i)

World War II, as Japan's economy grew in strength, fewer Japanese immigrated to the United States. Changes in U.S. immigration law in 1965 opened the doors for other Asian groups to come in increasing numbers. Today, Asian Americans are the second-fastest growing racial group, following Hispanic Americans.

Over the past few decades, Asian Americans have been characterized as a "model minority." Despite discrimination, by traditional aggregate measures of success (education, income, family stability), Asian Americans are doing quite well. I will address the accuracy and causes of this characterization later, but for now, let's turn to history to see that Asians weren't always portrayed so positively in America.

East Asians in America

East Asian groups—Chinese, Japanese, Korean—and later Asian Indians and Filipinos had similar experiences in America. Each of these ethnic subgroups arrived, one after the other; as one group was restricted, another replaced them. Originally, most of the early East Asian immigrants were recruited first to the Hawaiian sugar plantations, but as the Gold Rush and then settlement percolated on the West Coast, Asian immigration spilled into that region as well. Like the immigration history of Mexican Americans, the ebb and flow of East Asian immigration resulted from battles between American corporations recruiting their labor and American workers resenting their competition.

Unlike the European immigrants who entered through Ellis Island on the East Coast, many Asian immigrants sailed across the Pacific and were processed at Angel Island in San Francisco Bay. Asian immigrants would be detained at the island's dormitories for weeks for examination and interrogation. Men, women, and children were segregated from one another. Bathrooms contained a couple of sinks and a row of open toilets. According to Fong-Torres (1995), some women resorted to placing a sack over their heads so that they couldn't see themselves being observed. A few, who were detained for months or who had failed the examination, committed suicide. Most, however, remained undeterred. It's their story I turn to now.

Chinese Americans

Although Chinese immigrants had resided in the United States as early as 1785, their numbers were negligible (M. G. Wong, 1998). The first significant wave of Chinese immigrants arrived in the 1840s and 1850s. China had been disrupted by two wars—the Opium War (1839–1842) with the British and the Taiping Rebellion (1850–1865), a civil war resulting in 25 million deaths. In addition, these years also witnessed a number of natural disasters, such as droughts and plagues, which dislodged millions of Chinese (Gonzales, 1998). The discovery of gold in America in 1848 pulled uprooted Chinese to the West Coast. These largely uneducated, rural southern Chinese were portrayed in American newspapers as dirty opium addicts who were invading the country.

When the Chinese first arrived on the West Coast, the shortage of European Americans enabled them to secure work in a variety of occupations. With the Gold Rush, however, there was an influx of European Americans, and they soon found ways to limit Chinese and other racial minorities to low-status menial labor (Chan, 1991). In 1850, California passed the Foreign Miner's Tax, which required Chinese gold miners to pay higher taxes. Chinese businesses and products were boycotted, and unions barred Chinese membership, hindering their access to licensed occupations. In the 1860s, Chinese labor was recruited by Union Pacific railroad to help build the western half of the first transcontinental railroad (Irish immigrants were building the eastern half). Nearly 10,000 Chinese men were employed, often in the most dangerous positions. At the railroad's completion in 1869, the Chinese workers were not invited to the celebration, nor were they given a lift on the train back to California. Many walked back or found new jobs where they were (Chan, 1991).

Resistance to the Chinese presence on the West Coast continued to grow. In 1870, California passed the Sidewalk Ordinance, which outlawed the Chinese method of peddling vegetables and carrying laundry on poles across their backs and fined them $15 for not using a horse. Other ordinances were passed against the firecrackers and gongs associated with Chinese festivals. In 1871, the Cubic Air Ordinance was passed in San Francisco; aimed at Chinese cramped living quarters, the law required that each adult have at least 500 cubic feet of living space. The 1873 Queue Ordinance in San Francisco required Chinese men to cut their braids (called queues). Although the law was not strictly enforced, gangs of boys attacked Chinese men, cut off their braids and displayed them as trophies on belts and caps (M. G. Wong, 1998). Numerous laws barred the Chinese from working in government, the fishing industry, or public schools and from purchasing property outside of San Francisco's Chinatown (M. G. Wong, 1998). California and several other states passed laws excluding Chinese children from attending integrated schools. These laws varied locally, so Chinese children either attended White schools, segregated Black schools, or were not allowed in any school. Violence in the form of burning and hanging occurred as well (Chan, 1991).

In 1882, under pressure from labor groups, the U.S. Congress passed the Chinese Exclusion Act. This act, the first immigration restriction targeting nationality, prohibited entry of Chinese laborers and their relatives, but Chinese officials, students, tourists, merchants, and their relatives were exempt. Any Chinese American who had obtained citizenship through birth or naturalization (a small number) was also exempt. The exclusion was followed shortly thereafter by the 1888 Scott Act, which barred reentry of laborers if they left. Between 1890 and 1920, the effect of such restrictions was to reduce the Chinese American population from 107,488 to 61,630 (M. G. Wong, 1998). In 1924, the U.S. passed immigration acts that instituted a quota system based on nationality and simultaneously excluded all Asian immigration, even wives of merchants. Although a few subsequent laws provided exceptions, by and large these restrictions remained in place until 1965.

In response to these state and national restrictions, many Chinese Americans moved to cities and formed ethnic enclaves, where they opened small businesses, such as restaurants, grocery stores, laundries, and gift stores. By 1940, a couple dozen Chinatowns had formed throughout the United States. Basically, these enclaves served as bachelor communities, where men could eat Chinese food, play mah-jongg, and form social and political associations based on dialect and clan. These associations, often sponsored by local merchants, governed Chinatowns, mediated conflicts, provided private police protection, and collected refuse. Some were involved in organized crime and battled for allegiance and territory within Chinatowns.

The vast majority of the early Chinese immigrants were men, because Chinese familial tradition (patriarchal, patrilineal, and patrilocal) prevented most women from accompanying their husbands (M. G. Wong, 1998). In China, marriages were arranged with little to no input from the marriage partners. Frequently, the first time the couple would have met was when the bride arrived at the groom's home transported in a red-curtained chair (red is a symbol of joy in China). Traditionally, Chinese men were also allowed to practice polygyny or to take concubines, which are similar to mistresses but have some legal recognition (not as much as a wife). In general, secondary wives held less status and usually came from lower socioeconomic standing than the first wife. In fact, they were often chosen by the husband himself rather than arranged by the parents (Stockard, 2002).

Therefore, Chinese brides usually remained in the husband's family's home while he sojourned to America for work. Keeping the wife at home was often the family's way of guaranteeing the husband's remittances and eventual return. It also allowed the family to safeguard the wife's chastity, thus protecting the family's reputation, and use her labor within the household. In China, these wives were often called "gold mountain" wives, in reference to the gold mines in which they hoped their husbands would find good fortune.

In these "split-household" families, the sojourning husbands often waited until their new wives were pregnant before they left for the United States. The husband would reside in America for years with only occasional trips back to China, during which time he attempted to produce more children. Often sojourning continued intergenerationally; when the father retired, he would return to China and the eldest son would replace him. As you can imagine, the conjugal relationship was unimportant in this situation, and father-child relationships were distant.

Due to these practices, of the 11,800 Chinese in California in 1852, only 7 were women. By 1870, the Chinese population in the United States had risen to 63,199, of which only 7 percent were women, and many of these women had been sold into prostitution by poor families in China. Therefore, from 1860 through 1910, the gender ratio for Chinese Americans ranged from 1,284 to 2,679 men for every 100 women (Gonzales, 1998). In 1850, California passed an antimiscegenation law that prohibited Chinese from marrying European Americans; 15 other states also passed laws prohibiting interracial marriage, thus hindering Chinese men from taking non-Chinese wives. In 1875, Congress approved the Page Act, which required that would-be immigrant Chinese women prove to American consuls in Hong Kong that they were not prostitutes before they could enter. And, in 1922, the U.S. Congress passed the Cable Act, which said that any American woman who married a person ineligible for citizenship would forfeit her own. Nevertheless, some Chinese men entered into common-law marriages with White women or married Anglo women in Mexico and returned to the United States (Pleck, 2000).

By the turn of the 20th century, Chinese women in the United States were mainly wives of Chinese merchants. Conditions for merchant wives were sometimes harder in the United States than they had been in China. They were usually confined to their houses, often with bound feet (see Chapter 6). When they did venture out, they often rode in covered carriages lest they be considered prostitutes or be kidnapped by rival Chinese political associations or White gangs (Pleck, 2000). Social isolation in the United States and separation from their families gave rise to a suicide rate in San Francisco's Chinatown four times higher than that of the city as a whole. The victims were mostly women.

Because merchant families were relatively few in number, they had only a small and slow effect on the number of children in the Chinese American community. In 1900, children under age 14 accounted for less than 4 percent of the Chinese American population (whereas that age group accounted for 37 percent of the White population). By 1930, however, the ratio of men to women had fallen to four to one and the percentage of children had risen to 20.4 percent (M. G. Wong, 1998).

Meanwhile, some Chinese sojourners accumulated enough money to open small businesses, thereby changing their status from laborer to merchant and enabling them to bring wives to the United States before the 1924 restrictions. In this small-producer family, all family members contributed to the management of the business. Chinese women in these families had slightly more power due to the need for their labor and the absence of in-laws (Pleck, 2000). In addition, between the offspring of these families and of merchant families, a small second generation of Chinese was forming. By 1930, about half of Chinese married couples had at least one native-born spouse.

Chinese American men, native- or foreign-born, frequently returned to China for a wife, as native-born Chinese American women were viewed as less compliant than their foreign-born counterparts. In turn, the relatively few native-born Chinese American women often sought Chinese American men living in rural America (where male authority patterns were not as strong) or wealthy Chinese American merchants as marriage partners.

In 1943, as World War II cemented China's relationship with the United States, the Chinese Exclusion Act was repealed, making Chinese immigrants eligible for citizenship. Chinese men could send for wives, but the United States gave China an immigration quota of only 105. After World War II, immigration recommenced with the War Brides Act and the GI Fiancées Act, which enabled Chinese women who had married American soldiers to enter. In 1948, California declared its antimiscegenation law unconstitutional, and in 1952 the McCarran-Walter Act, which eliminated race as a bar to immigration and gave preferences to relatives, was passed. Therefore, from 1943 to 1965 Chinese immigration was largely female; so by 1960 the sex ratio (the number of men for every 100 women) was 140:100, and by 1990 it had normalized at 99:100 (M. G. Wong, 1998).

In 1965, immigration quotas and the restrictions on Asian immigration were repealed. That change, along with China's recent economic reform and open door policy, has resulted in more educated and professional Chinese immigrants entering the United States. Many Chinese have left Chinatowns for the suburbs and have since purchased a lot of residential and commercial property in New York, Los Angeles, and San Francisco. At least 30 Chinese-owned banks have opened in California. Nevertheless, a significant minority of poorer Chinese Americans remain in service sector occupations.

The Japanese American Experience

After immigration restrictions of the 1880s reduced the number of Chinese who entered the United States, Japanese immigration increased. In many aspects, the Japanese experience mimics that of the Chinese, as Americans made little distinction between the two, and many of the laws implemented to hinder the Chinese were subsequently applied to other Asian groups. Nevertheless, in several aspects, the Japanese experience was also unique.

Japan was a fairly isolated country until the late 1860s when its new emperor increased trade and encouraged greater contact with the West (Kitano & Kitano, 1998). By 1890, 12,000 Japanese resided in Hawaii and 3,000 lived on the mainland, mostly in California. By 1930, their numbers had grown to nearly 140,000 (98,000 in California). Although they constituted less than one percent of the nation's population, they were still viewed as a threat, a "Yellow Peril" (Kitano & Kitano, 1998).

Like the early Chinese immigrants, most of the Japanese immigrants were men of agricultural background who came as sojourners to earn money and return to their country. Railroad building and gold mining opportunities had declined by the time of their arrival, so many Japanese immigrants entered tenant farming and eventually purchased land. Like the Chinese, the Japanese formed organizations based on ken (province) for social and occupational opportunities. Their organizations and success in agriculture threatened the

European American working population, which formed the Asiatic Exclusion League. The league advised Americans that assimilation of Asiatics would harm America. Arguing against Japanese citizenship and intermarriage, members of the league feared that giving freedoms to the Japanese might lead to repeal of the Chinese exclusion (Kitano & Kitano, 1998).

Consequently, in 1907 the governments of the United States and Japan came to a "gentleman's agreement," which, similar to the Chinese Exclusion Act, prohibited the entry of laborers. Unlike the Chinese Exclusion Act, the agreement did not prohibit laborers from sending for wives. When the agreement went into effect, Japanese laborers knew they should move fast before more restrictions went into place. Between 1909 and 1924, before all Asian immigration was prohibited, the "picture bride" era ensued. Japanese American laborers had their families arrange marriages for them through the exchange of photos.

Men who sought picture brides had to demonstrate their ability to support a wife, submit proof of steady employment, and have at least $1,000 in savings (required by the Japanese government) to obtain approval for sponsoring a wife (Gonzales, 1998). Some of the tens of thousands of women who arrived were disappointed to discover their husbands were older or poorer than they had been told. It was not unusual to find advertisements placed by husbands searching for their runaway wives (Ichioka, 1988). Nevertheless, most Japanese American couples quickly got to work doing the family thing, and by 1930 almost half of Japanese Americans were native-born.

Because Japanese immigration occurred in fairly distinct waves, it is common to speak of distinct generations within the Japanese American community. The first generation of immigrants arrived between 1890 and 1920, and they are commonly referred to as the Issei. Life for the Issei generation consisted of long days of farming or running small businesses. Issei parents, particularly fathers, were known for their strictness and emotional and verbal restraint. Most Issei marriages were arranged marriages, illustrating the priority of consanguineal relations over conjugal, and they exhibited a rigid division of labor between husband and wife (Yanagisako, 1985).

The second-generation Nisei, those born in America between 1915 and 1945, grew up with English as their primary language, which sometimes became a source of tension in the household (Gonzales, 1998). Some Issei sent their children to live with extended family in Japan for education and socialization. Unlike their parents, most Nisei entered romance-based marriages. By 1940, the Nisei represented two thirds of the Japanese American population.

After the bombing of Pearl Harbor (December 1941), President Franklin Roosevelt passed an executive order declaring much of the West Coast a military-sensitive area. On short notice, more than 110,000 Japanese

Americans (two thirds of them native-born citizens) were removed from their homes and placed in army-style relocation camps located outside of the area. Many camp families lost their businesses and farms, along with their community reputations.

To some extent, camp residents were allowed to govern themselves and arrange activities within the camp. Due to their language skills, the Nisei were often given more authority in the camps by the American administration, resulting in a shift in authority from parent to child (Knaefler, 1991). The camps eventually offered a release program for Nisei to attend college and relocate to the Midwest and East Coast. After signing a loyalty oath, some Nisei entered the U.S. military and were able to take advantage of the GI Bill for education.

The relocation camps closed in 1946, but many of the Japanese feared returning to the old communities. Initially, many scattered to the Midwest and the East Coast, but eventually the majority returned to California, where the economy was booming, anti-Japanese prejudice had diminished, and new targets (Blacks and Hispanics) were arriving (Kitano & Kitano, 1998). In 1988, the U.S. government awarded $20,000 in reparations to each remaining survivor of the internment camps.

As frequently happens with the second generation, the Nisei attained higher education and occupational levels than did the Issei. Though many civil service positions and other professional jobs remained closed to them, the Nisei were a high-achieving group that benefited from a leap in real estate values in California. Nisei families adapted to American mores, reflected in greater acceptance of romantic love as a basis for marriage and more flexibility in gender roles (Kitano & Kitano, 1998). Nisei families were smaller than the Issei's, and their children, the third generation Sansei, were born between 1940 and 1960. Most Sansei were reared in middle-class homes and resided in integrated or predominantly White neighborhoods. Consequently, the Sansei have high intermarriage rates. The fourth-generation Yonsei, born after 1960, are so assimilated, structurally and maritally, that some have wondered whether we can continue to speak of Japanese Americans as an ethnic group.

Asian Indian, Filipino, and Korean Americans

Less is recorded of the histories of these three groups in America, only one of which is East Asian, but these were the main Asian groups recruited as labor sources to supplement restricted Chinese and Japanese labor around the turn of the 20th century. Each group faced discrimination and exclusion, as had the Chinese and Japanese before them.

Between 1900 and 1920, about 7,300 Asian Indians, mostly Sikhs, were recruited into the United States (Segal, 1998). To exclude Asian Indians, their racial status first had to be determined. At the time, anthropologists classified Asian Indians as "Aryan," which was considered racially White. Then, in 1923, just in time for a 1924 immigration act that prohibited all Asian immigration, the U.S. Supreme Court declared Asian Indians non-White.

Shortly before the "gentleman's agreement" that restricted Japanese laborers, about 7,000 Koreans were recruited to Hawaii to work on sugar plantations. About a thousand arrived on the mainland before the Korean government, pressured by Japan, stopped sending laborers to Hawaii (Chan, 1991). From that point until 1924, Korean Americans, like Japanese Americans, experienced a picture-bride era.

The Philippines, a Spanish colony for more than 300 years, had been taken by the United States from Spain after the Spanish-American War, as had Puerto Rico and Cuba (see Chapter 11). Filipinos were thus considered nationals of the United States and were not subject to immigration law. Initially, a small number of Filipino students of elite families arrived; then between 1907 and 1924, 57,700 farm workers were recruited to Hawaiian sugar and pineapple plantations. After 1924, when Asian immigration (except Filipinos) was totally barred, another 64,000 arrived (Chan, 1991). To mollify political pressure for restrictions on Filipino immigration, the U.S. government changed the status of the Philippines. In 1934, the U.S. Congress passed the Tydings-McDuffie Act, which initiated a process for Filipino independence and simultaneously assigned the Philippines an annual quota of 50 persons (Chan, 1991). The following year, Congress passed a repatriation act that offered free passage to any Filipinos who agreed to permanently return to their homeland. Less than 5 percent accepted (Gonzales, 1998).

As occurred with other racial-ethnic groups, World War II provided the impetus to chip away at racial exclusions. In 1940, the United States passed the Alien Registration Act, which made noncitizen residents eligible for the draft. Many Asians joined the military, as one reward was the opportunity to apply for citizenship after 3 months of active duty. As did African Americans, Asian Americans served in segregated units. After the war, several immigration restrictions were loosened to allow soldiers to bring home Asian wives and allow Chinese, Filipino, and Japanese Americans to obtain citizenship.

As the Chinese and Japanese before them, the Korean, Filipino, and Asian Indian populations were largely male. In the case of Filipinos, the male-heavy sex ratio reflected American recruiters' desire for male labor, rather than Filipino cultural traditions, which reflected several centuries of Spanish colonization. Only about 10 percent of Filipino men brought wives and children with them. As with the Chinese and Japanese, not until the 1940s did their second generation match or exceed their foreign-born portion (Chan, 1991).

Whereas East Asians are known for transmitting their cultural heritage to the second generation, this was less true for early Filipino and Asian Indian immigrants, as many of them outmarried. For instance, a substantial minority of Asian Indian men married Mexican women. Thus, the second generation's upbringing and identity was highly influenced by their non-Asian mothers (Leonard, 1982; Posadas, 1981).

The immigration flows of all Asian groups ebbed until the Korean War in the 1950s and the passage of the 1965 immigration act. Korea became independent of Japan in 1945, and 5 years later the Korean civil war, in which the United States was a protagonist, began. Between 1950 and 1975, 28,000 Korean women arrived in the United States as brides of American soldiers, and 35,000 orphaned Korean children were adopted by American families (Shin, 1987). The war bride family was highly unstable, as the marriages often originated in Korea as a result of the loneliness of military men and the strong desire of Korean women to escape poverty in their homeland. When the couple transferred to the United States, serious adjustment problems, precipitated by in-law rejection, general prejudice and discrimination, and a feeling of alienation, led to a high divorce rate (Shin, 1987).

As mentioned earlier, the 1965 immigration act overturned the national origins quota system and lifted the restrictions on Asian immigration. That act guaranteed a yearly quota of 20,000 for every nation, regardless of race or ethnicity, and gave preference to the immigration of family members of current residents, highly skilled and educated workers, and victims of natural disasters or political upheavals. Logically, this act accelerated immigration, particularly of Latinos and Asians. Over the ensuing decades, Filipinos, Koreans, and Asian Indians have overtaken Japanese in immigration.

Southeast Asians in America

The growing Southeast Asian presence in America stems from the Vietnam War. Vietnam, Cambodia, and Laos, referred to collectively as Indochina, were colonized by China for more than 1,000 years, by the French until World War II, and then briefly by Japan. At the end of World War II, France attempted to retake Vietnam but met domestic resistance. In 1953, Laos and Cambodia gained independence, but in 1954 the United Nations partitioned Vietnam. Vietnam entered a civil war, and the mostly rural population became caught in the crossfire of the battling ideologies of North and South, the French, and the United States.

Over a 20-year period, the United States became increasingly invested in the war. Eventually, 500,000 U.S. troops were in Vietnam, and $2 billion a month was going to the war. As the war spread to Cambodia and Laos, the United States bombed guerrillas in those two countries while simultaneously securing the backing of Laotian militia and recruiting the Hmong, a Chinese ethnic minority residing mostly in the mountains of Laos, for intelligence and military work. Those combined forces failed against the will of the northern Viet Cong. With the chance for military success receding, the United States began withdrawal in 1973, and South Vietnam fell to the North in 1975.

Shortly thereafter, the communist government of Vietnam invaded Cambodia, starting another war and creating more refugees. The communist Khmer Rouge regime took over Cambodia in the late 1970s. This fanatical regime confiscated children, land, and other property and relocated hundreds of thousands of people into concentration camps. By the time the regime ended, more than 20 percent of the Cambodian population had died by murder or starvation. Eventually, Vietnam overtook the Khmer Rouge, and its leader Pol Pot escaped into the countryside, where he and his followers continued a civil war until he died in 1998. Between the civil war, the ensuing famine, and drought, millions attempted to escape Vietnam and Cambodia through mass exodus. Hundreds of thousands ended up in refugee camps where they remained for 10 or more years before they could be relocated.

Many of those who succeeded in escaping the "killing fields" of Indochina came to the United States, despite opposition from the American public (Tran, 1998). Arriving in three main waves, the Vietnamese refugees followed a pattern similar to Cuban refugees. The first wave, about 160,000 people from 1975 to 1978, was largely composed of the elite of Vietnam and Laos, those who had been associated in some capacity with Western business, government, or education. Leaving to avoid persecution from the new regime, many arrived with their whole families. Mostly urban, skilled, and educated, about two thirds of them spoke English, and about 50 percent were Christian. As refugees they received 3 years of assistance and sponsorship in the United States, and they spent little or no time in refugee camps.

The second wave, consisting of about half a million refugees from 1978 to 1982, had a decidedly more difficult time arriving in the United States. Some walked through jungles; others escaped by way of makeshift boats to find shelter in Thailand, Malaysia, Singapore, and Japan. It is estimated that about 10 to 15 percent died of starvation, illness, or drowning. Many were robbed, and many women were raped. This wave had a large population of ethnic Chinese, who were persecuted in Vietnam. Many of the Hmong came during this period as well. Unlike their predecessors, this wave was less urbanized, Westernized, monied, skilled, and educated. Fewer elderly, women, and families came in this wave.

The third wave of refugees came after 1985, mostly through an orderly departure that gave priority to spouses, children, parents, and siblings of refugees who had already entered the United States. The approval process required 5 to 10 years in some cases. Through this program, more elderly arrived. Also, often abandoned Amerasian children, created by liaisons between American soldiers and Southeast Asian women, were allowed in (Tran, 1998). This wave received less assistance than the first two waves, as the U.S. government reduced assistance from 3 years to 18 months in 1982, and then to 12 months in 1988. Hmong refugees, in particular, are still arriving in the United States. Another 15,000 arrived after 2004.

Although other groups, such as Cubans, have arrived in the United States as refugees, Southeast Asians are the only group in recent years to have spent a number of years in refugee camps before arriving in the United States. This experience imposed extraordinary stressors for immigrants. Many Southeast Asians endured or witnessed torture and deprivation in their home countries prior to beginning a harrowing trip to a refugee camp. Those who survived the journey still had to cope with deep feelings of loss and grief for family members. Moreover, refugees who remain in camps for extended periods frequently are exposed to undesirable social behavior, as refugees with addictions, criminal histories, and/or mental problems are less likely to be approved for relocation. Female refugees are sometimes subject to sexual abuse and abduction or to hastily arranged marriages in order to escape such conditions (Williams, 1993).

Given these experiences, it is no wonder that U.S. health officials found that 45 percent of one sample of Cambodian adults had post-traumatic stress disorder and 51 percent suffered from depression (Thrupkaew, 2002). Moreover, medical officials discovered an unusual pattern of death among Laotian and Hmong refugees, mostly men, which they called "sudden unexpected nocturnal death syndrome," because the men died during their sleep. Although the deaths were associated with panic dreams, the exact cause was never determined, but many speculated that they were related to the stress of immigration (Adler, 1991; Munger, 1987).

Collectively, Southeast Asians in America now number about 1.6 million. Like most other Asian groups (except Japanese and Pacific Islanders), a large majority of their population is foreign-born (see Table 12.2). Their histories and immigrant status greatly affect their social status in the United States today.

Asian American Families Today

As you can see from the historical review above, several Asian ethnic groups experienced multiple forms of discrimination in America. Once thought of as morally dangerous to America, Asian Americans were segregated and restricted. Such experiences usually have lingering consequences for the victimized ethnic group. Yet, in the aggregate, in measurable terms, Asian American families appear to be doing well in America. As a group, their median family income and college education levels are higher than those of the White American majority (see Table 2.1 and Figure 2.1 as reminders). The Asian American family poverty level is only slightly higher than that of Whites and significantly lower than other racial-ethnic minorities.

Moreover, by traditional measures of family success, Asian Americans have high percentages of family households, particularly high rates of married-couple families, and low rates of single-parent families (see Table 12.3). In addition, as mentioned in Chapter 5, they commonly use multigenerational extended households, and they have low divorce rates. We can't assume, however, that intact marriages are necessarily happy. Some have suggested that the low rates of divorce have been sublimated into a higher suicide rate among women (Sung, 1967). Divorce has increased among the younger generation (M. G. Wong, 1998), and Japanese Americans, who are the most assimilated, have the highest divorce rates.

Asian American educational achievement is often explained solely by cultural values, such as their spiritual beliefs and filial piety that encourage obedience and respect for education. Such values, no doubt, are influential; many Asian parents supplement their children's schooling, private or public, with attendance at Chinese language schools, math tutors, and other extracurricular academic activities.

Others have attributed their high levels of education to an inherently strong aptitude for science and math. Immigrant Asian Americans, however, concentrate in science and engineering frequently because those disciplines don't require extensive writing and language facility, and these majors have the potential to offer high salaries in the future. Immigrant parents often feel they sacrificed to come to the United States, and they want their children to prove the sacrifice worthwhile. This can cause conflicts when the student prefers to study a liberal arts subject. Min (1998) quotes one young man's experience:

> So I decided to pursue history but I still had to tell my parents. Over the years my dad and I communicated less and less so telling him was almost a perfunctory

(Text continues on page 225)

Table 12.3 Selected Social Characteristics of Asian American Groups, 2000

	Asian Indian	*Chinese*	*Filipino*	*Korean*	*Japanese*	*Cambodian*	*Hmong*	*Laotian*	*Vietnamese*	*Pacific Islander*
Education	Percentage of population 25 years and older									
< Ninth Grade	5.6	14.1	7.2	6.9	3.6	37.3	50.7	32.6	18.0	7.5
High School Degree	10.3	13.2	14.9	21.6	22.2	18.8	16.1	24.4	19.1	33.7
BA or More	63.9	48.1	43.8	43.8	41.9	9.2	7.5	7.7	19.4	13.8
Occupational Distribution	Percentage of workers in occupational category									
Management/ Professional	59.9	52.3	38.2	38.7	50.7	17.8	17.1	13.4	26.9	23.3
Sales/Office	21.4	20.8	28.1	30.2	26.9	23.5	20.6	19.1	18.6	28.8
Service	7.0	13.9	17.5	14.8	11.9	15.9	15.6	14.5	19.3	20.8
Farming/ Fishing/ Forestry	.2	.1	.5	.2	.4	.5	.4	.5	.6	.9
Construction/ Maintenance	2.1	2.6	4.1	3.9	4.3	5.5	4.5	5.8	5.9	9.6
Production/ Transportation	9.4	10.4	11.5	12.2	5.9	36.8	41.7	46.6	28.8	16.5
Economic Indicators										
Median Family Income (dollars per annum)	$70,708	$60,058	$65,189	$47,624	$70,849	$35,621	$32,384	$43,542	$47,103	$45,915

	Asian Indian	*Chinese*	*Filipino*	*Korean*	*Japanese*	*Cambodian*	*Hmong*	*Laotian*	*Vietnamese*	*Pacific Islander*
Per Capita Income (dollars per annum)	$27,514	$23,756	$21,267	$18,805	$30,075	$10,366	$6,600	$11,830	$15,655	$15,054
Percentage Family Poverty	6.7	10.3	4.7	13.2	4.2	26.6	34.8	16.6	14.2	14.6
Demographic	Percentage of population within this age group									
< 18 yrs	25.0	21.3	22.3	24.3	12.7	39.0	56.0	34.5	27.1	31.9
> 65 yrs	4.0	9.7	8.9	6.4	20.2	3.8	2.8	3.6	5.2	5.2
Median Age (years)	30.0	35.3	35.2	32.4	42.4	23.4	16.1	25.6	30.2	27.5
Sex Ratio (men per 100 women)	113.7	93.7	82.0	80.5	78.7	94.9	104.0	103.9	102.3	103.3
Family Structure	Percentage of all households									
Nonfamily Household	23.3	27.1	20.4	28.7	41.1	10.3	6.6	11.5	16.5	22.5
Living Alone	16.0	20.0	14.0	21.7	34.0	6.6	4.4	6.8	11.1	15.0
Family Household	76.7	72.9	79.6	71.3	58.9	89.7	93.4	88.5	83.5	77.5

(Continued)

Table 12.3 (Continued)

	Asian Indian	*Chinese*	*Filipino*	*Korean*	*Japanese*	*Cambodian*	*Hmong*	*Laotian*	*Vietnamese*	*Pacific Islander*
Married Couple	68.8	60.6	60.7	58.2	48.0	60.5	75.3	66.1	62.7	53.8
Married Couple With Children	41.3	32.5	34.1	31.6	19.2	47.7	67.2	46.7	40.9	33.4
Female-Headed Household	4.1	7.9	13.9	9.4	8.0	20.8	11.9	12.7	12.2	16.1
Female-Headed Household With Children	2.1	3.1	6.4	4.4	2.5	15.3	9.5	8.5	6.1	9.8
Male-Headed Household	3.8	4.4	5.0	3.7	2.9	8.4	6.2	9.7	8.6	7.6
Male-Headed Household With Children	1.0	1.0	1.8	0.9	0.6	4.3	3.6	5.1	2.4	3.8
Average Family Size (number of persons)	3.52	3.43	3.78	3.3	2.94	4.66	6.51	4.53	4.05	4.05

SOURCES: U.S. Department of Commerce, (2000a), Quick Table-P1; U.S. Department of Commerce (2000g), (2000h), (2000i)

> exercise. For my mom the news that I was majoring in history was the intellectual equivalent of coming out of the closet. She was initially shocked and upset. Then she tried to convince me that I was wrong. And finally she struggled to understand why it had happened. (p. 72)

The pressure to succeed is enormous for many Asian immigrants, as achievement honors one's family and renders immigration not in vain (B. Wong, 1998). Nevertheless, we need to look at structural explanatory factors as well.

Because the majority of Asian Americans are foreign-born, only a small percentage are descendants of the people who experienced the discrimination described earlier. That is not to say that Asian Americans today are not exposed to discrimination and stereotypes, but since the majority of those who are here arrived after the civil rights movement, they have not had to experience legal or severe discrimination in America (though many experienced it elsewhere). Remember also that foreign-born tend to have better health, lower mortality, fewer divorces, and nonmarital births than native-born populations.

In addition, due to the types of discrimination (mostly immigration restrictions and antimiscegenation laws) the early immigrants experienced in the late 1800s and early 1900s, relatively few Asian American families existed until the 1940s. Consequently, during those decades a high adult-to-child ratio existed in the Asian American community. This helped the older generation maintain more control and influence over children and made it possible to invest relatively large amounts of financial and educational resources into a small number of second- and third-generation children.

Moreover, unlike many Mexican American foreign-born, who arrive with low levels of education and money, a high proportion of Asian immigrants are the "cream of the crop" in many of their home countries. Although China and India have extraordinary levels of poverty, by and large, it is not the poor Chinese and Asian Indians who immigrate to the United States. Instead, many of the immigrants arriving under the provisions of the 1965 and 1991 immigration acts are skilled professionals. Therefore, whereas only about 5 percent of Chinese adults in China have a college education, more than 48 percent of Chinese Americans have a college degree. Only 14 percent of Koreans in Korea have a college degree (Min, 1998), but 44 percent of Korean Americans have at least a college degree (see Table 12.3). In fact, many Asians arrive in the United States with a college degree (for instance, 60 percent of Filipinos come with a degree [Gonzales, 1998]) and come specifically to obtain a postgraduate degree. After obtaining the degree, many decide to put it to use in America.

In fact, given that Asian Americans have such a high rate of college education, one would expect their median income to be even higher. Per capita income (essentially individual income) for Koreans and Filipinos, for instance, is lower than the per capita income for the nation ($21,587), even though their education levels are substantially higher (see Table 12.3). This incongruity between education and income is due to language barriers, a high rate of employment in family-owned businesses (especially Koreans), the fact that the diplomas and credentials from their home countries are not often recognized here, and racial stereotypes that inhibit promotions to management or executive positions (Gonzales, 1998).

Remember that median family income reflects family structure and size, not just the skills and education of the family members. Many Asian Americans have lower rates of single-parent households, which bolster their family or household income relative to racial-ethnic groups with high rates of single-parent households. Having a family household with more working adults increases family income as well. As with many Hispanic families, Asian American young adults are known for remaining at home until marriage. Also, except for Cambodian, Hmong, and Japanese, Asian American women work in the paid labor force at close to the same rate as the national average (57.5 percent). A number of Asian groups (Chinese, Filipino, and Japanese in Table 12.3) also have an older age structure, indicated by their median age, which raises income levels. Finally, Asian Americans reside predominantly on the West and East coasts and in Hawaii, all of which have high costs of living and, therefore, their salaries appear greater than their actual purchasing power.

To understand the actual state, rather than a stereotype, of Asian families, we need to disaggregate, that is, to separate, the Asian American subgroups to explain this phenomenon better. Space limitations prevent coverage of each group, but comparing East Asians and Southeast Asians will illustrate that the data used to support the "model minority" image does not hold for every Asian American group.

Asian Indians and East Asians exhibit most of the characteristics (the higher education and income, lower poverty and single-parenting rates) associated with the model minority. Table 12.3 is set up to contrast Asian Indians and East Asians in columns on the left and Southeast Asians and Pacific Islanders on the right. As you can see, Asian Indians and East Asians constitute the brain drain of their countries. Also East Asian groups, compared to Southeast Asians, have older age structures, which is associated with higher group income. Their higher education levels contribute to delayed marriage and lower fertility, which in turn give them more income stability and provide more opportunities for their children. Because East

Asians numerically dominate in the Asian American population, their statistics mask the case of Pacific Islanders and Southeast Asians, and some East Asians who are not doing as well.

Southeast Asians, who were pushed out of their countries, do not exhibit the same degree of self-selection. Whereas the elites came in the first wave of immigrants following the Vietnam War, later waves were mostly working-class and less-educated people. If dissatisfied or unsuccessful here, they lack the option of returning. With less education and higher poverty and mortality rates, we find higher fertility, larger families, younger age distribution, more single parenting, earlier marriage for young women, and a proliferation of youth gangs (Emery, 2003)

As with Hispanic Americans, the high ongoing rate of immigration will continue to sustain Asian American cultural traditions. Moreover, the predominance of highly skilled and educated East Asian immigrants will continue to shape the social and economic patterns among Asian Americans for some time to come. As Southeast Asians catch up in education and skills in the United States, the divide between those two subgroups will lessen.

Resources

Books and Articles

Chong, D. (1994). *The concubine's children: The story of a Chinese family living on both sides of the globe.* New York: Penguin.

This is Denise Chong's family biography mixed with social history.

Fong-Torres, B. (1995). *The rice room: Growing up Chinese-American from number two son to rock 'n' roll.* New York: Plume.

This is an autobiography of an American journalist.

Hayslip, L. L. (with Wurts, J.). (1989). *When heaven and earth changed places: A Vietnamese woman's journey from war to peace.* New York: Plume.

Hayslip's memoir recounts her childhood in warring Vietnam to her escape to America.

Keown-Bomar, J. (2004). *Kinship networks among Hmong-American refugees.* New York: LFB Scholarly Publishing.

This volume explores how Hmong kinship patterns and beliefs help and hinder Hmong in their immigration experience.

Koltyk, J. (1998). *New pioneers in the heartland: Hmong life in Wisconsin.* Boston: Allyn & Bacon.

Koltyk describes the Hmong community in Wausau, Wisconsin.

Lai, H. M. (2004). *Becoming Chinese American: A history of communities and institutions.* Walnut Creek, CA: Alta Mira Press.

Lai discusses the historical and cultural development of Chinese American life in the 1900s.

Larson, L. L. (1989). *Sweet bamboo: A saga of a Chinese American family.* Berkeley, CA: University of California Press.

The author details her immigrant family's life in America in the first half of the 20th century.

Lee, H. (2002). *In the absence of the sun: A Korean American woman's promise to reunite three lost generations of her family.* New York: Harmony.

The author's story of her mission to rescue a long-lost uncle from within North Korea.

Videos

Asian Americans [Motion picture]. (1993). (Available from Insight Media Inc., 2162 Broadway, New York, NY 10024-0621, or at http://www.insight-media.com)

This 3-volume set of 30-minute videos looks at the cultural heritage of Chinese, Japanese, and Korean Americans and probes how cultural identity differs among each generation.

Between two worlds [Motion picture]. (2003). (Available from Films Media Group, P.O. Box 2053, Princeton, NJ 08453-2053, or at http://www.films.com)

The second in a 3-volume set, this 89-minute video examines the exclusion years (1882–1943) through stories of Chinese American families.

From a different shore: The Japanese-American experience [Motion picture]. (1994). (Available from Films Media Group, P.O. Box 2053, Princeton, NJ 08453-2053, or at http://www.films.com)

This 50-minute video compares three generations of three different families.

Levine, K., & Levine, I. W. (n.d.). *Becoming American* [Motion picture]. (Available from New Day Films, 190 Route 17M, P.O. Box 1084, Harriman, NY 10926, or at http://www.newday.com)

This 58-minute video also comes with a study guide; it traces a Hmong family's transition from a Thai refugee camp to resettlement in the United States.

Mass, H. (Producer). (2000). *The new generation: Vietnamese Americans today* [Motion picture]. (2000). (Available from Films Media Group, P.O. Box 2053, Princeton, NJ 08453-2053, or at http://www.films.com)

In this 35-minute video, the filmmakers interview first- and second-generation Vietnamese American family members.

Ohama, L. (Producer). (2001). *Obachan's garden: A Japanese immigrant's memoir* [Motion picture]. (Available from Films Media Group, P.O. Box 2053, Princeton, NJ 08453-2053, or at http://www.films.com)

This 95-minute video traces one family's experience settling in Canada in the early 1900s.

Websites

http://erc.msh.org/mainpage.cfm?file=5.0a.htm&module=provider&language=English
This website, the Providers Guide to Quality and Culture, has links to several ethnic groups, but it is one of the few that looks specifically at Pacific Islanders.

http://www.hmongstudies.org
This website, the Hmong Studies Internet Resource Center, is produced by the Hmong Cultural Center in St. Paul, Minnesota.

CHAPTER 13

ACCULTURATION AND MULTIRACIAL FAMILY ISSUES

When two or more ethnicities come into contact with one another, several conflicts frequently ensue. One is an inner conflict, described by J. W. Berry (1986) as a state of dissonance between one's former culture and the new one. Individuals or groups must find a way to make the two cultures consonant for themselves; doing so usually involves some degree of acculturation. At the societal level, a debate ensues over the degree to which to accommodate the unfamiliar and frequently results in laws regulating immigration, access to resources, and intergroup relations, such as marriage and adoption.

In this chapter, I will explore the acculturation process and its effect on family and conclude with a historical overview of the laws and trends associated with interracial dating, marriage, and adoption.

Acculturation

As stated above, exposure to a new culture frequently precipitates a sense of dissonance and an exploration of individual and/or group identity. Over time, it may result in the adoption of new behaviors and identity. Throughout the past century, social scientists have studied how immigration changes people. Which aspects of their lives change first? How does the first generation negotiate the differences between cultures? What does that generation pass on to subsequent generations? How much of one's original culture can be maintained in a new setting?

Early theories on immigrant adaptation assumed that over time immigrants assimilate; inevitably and incrementally they adapt their attitudes and behaviors until they imperceptibly blend with the institutions, culture, and identity of the new society. Theorist Milton Gordon (1964) distinguished between *cultural assimilation (acculturation),* adopting the language, religion, dress, and values of a society; *structural assimilation,* becoming integrated into the social institutions, such as education, employment, residence, and politics; and *marital assimilation,* widespread intermarriage with members of the majority. These distinctions later allowed theorists to acknowledge that immigrants might acculturate, but not structurally assimilate or vice versa. Assimilation, we were discovering, was neither inevitable nor unidirectional. According to Berry (1997), most research now indicates that the adaptive experience most immigrants encounter can be characterized as a "complex pattern of continuity and change" (p. 6).

Between the two monocultural responses of either losing one's culture entirely and adopting the new or, vice versa, maintaining one's culture and rejecting the new one entirely lies a strategy of biculturalism, in which individuals maintain some of the old and adopt some of the new. Research on immigrant groups in the United States indicates that wittingly or not, immigrants—at least those in the first 2 to 3 generations—frequently straddle the two cultures. Moreover, this bicultural response appears to be consistently predictive of positive outcomes (Berry, 1997). A bicultural approach mitigates the stress accompanying adaptations required by the demands of a new environment and improves well-being among adults and children (Greenfield, 1994; Pyke, 2004; Szapocznik, Kurtines, & Fernandez, 1980). For instance, Bankston and Zhou's (1995) research on Vietnamese immigrants finds that maintaining their native language abilities while learning the new language leads to greater overall scholastic achievement.

Despite these findings, the road to a bicultural identity can be an ambiguous experience. On the positive side, bicultural individuals are skilled in two or more languages, a rarity in the United States. Hence, some ethnic groups have coined comical terms, such as Spanglish or Turklish, to describe the mid-sentence verbal leaps they make between two languages. Having experience within two or more cultures can endow a person with a deeper understanding of human nature, an appreciation of difference, and the ability to maneuver successfully in both cultures.

On the negative side, a bicultural person can feel untethered, torn between two cultures (Berry, Kim, Minde, & Mok, 1987; Mena, Padilla, & Maldonado, 1987). Trying to make sense of her bicultural experience, Arab American Joanna Kadi wrote in her 1994 book *Food for our Grandmothers,*

> Do transplants ever find home? Are we weakened by the ever-present feeling of not belonging in the west or the east, of having a foot in both worlds but no solid roots in either? Or are we stronger, more innovative and creative, able to make home in odd sites, able to survive in small, hard places, plants growing out of rocks? Perhaps this is our advantage, perhaps this is what we bring to the world. Find home wherever you can make it. Make home so you can find it wherever. (p. xv)

Seeing one's self or loved ones change can be a frightening experience, because many immigrants have tarnished views of American family life and may not want to admit that they are becoming like Americans. Perez-Firmat recalls (1995, p. 169) that his Cuban immigrant mother had to confront family problems that she regarded as American—separations, loneliness, divorces, and family strife. With one of her sons in jail, she was convinced that had they remained in Cuba she never would have had troubled children. In *The Rice Room,* journalist Ben Fong-Torres (1994) recounts that his first-generation mother viewed Americans negatively, using them as examples of how not to be:

> We were not to talk back. If we dared to say anything about friends at school being able to go more places or do more things than we did, our mother would admonish us about Americans.
>
> "They don't care about family," she said, meaning that no race cared about family the way the Chinese did. In China, she said, grandparents were members of the household—and honored ones, too. "Chinese take care of one another," she said. "Americans take care of themselves." (p. 60)

These perceptions of American life, combined with the difficulties of transitions and the fear of losing oneself, often engender a strategy of resistance. Furthermore, other intervening factors facilitate or hinder the acculturation process.

Factors Hindering and Helping Acculturation

Group-level and individual factors can enhance or hinder acculturation. At the group level, the reason for the ethnic group's immigration—that is, push or pull factors—impacts their intent to stay and desire to acculturate. On the other side of the coin, the degree of acceptance or discrimination from the receiving country can facilitate or place obstacles in the path of acculturation. The immigrants' residence pattern and degree of continuing contact with the original culture also affects their desire and ability to interact with the new culture.

As discussed in Chapter 2, people who arrived by force or who were exiled from their country frequently resist acculturation. In some cases, they may hope their time in the United States is only a temporary diversion, necessary to earn money or until turmoil subsides at home. In his memoir, Perez-Firmat (1995) describes this psychological gap between an immigrant and an exile:

> The exile and the immigrant go through life at different speeds. The immigrant is in a rush about everything—in a rush to get a job, learn the language, set down roots, become a citizen. He lives in the fast lane. . . . Not so with the exile, whose life creeps forward an inch at a time. If the immigrant rushes, the exile waits. He waits to embark on a new career, to learn the language, to give up his homeland. He waits, perhaps indefinitely, to start a new life. If immigration is an accelerated birth, exile is a state of suspended animation that looks every bit like a slow death. For the exile, every day is delay, every day is deferral. (pp. 121–122)

The other side of immigrant desire is the reception. Resistance from the American community to the immigrant's presence makes acculturation more difficult and less desirable. History has shown that resistance from the U.S.

community is heightened when the newcomers are darker skinned or culturally identifiable, arrive in large numbers, settle densely, and/or are of economically lower status and are perceived to be a drain on the community (Aguirre & Turner, 2004; Berry, 1997; Espin, 1987).

If newcomers live in segregated communities, surrounded by other members of their ethnic group, the original culture remains a strong influence. To avoid being the targets of community gossip, families adhere to old cultural practices when they are around their compatriots, though they may deviate from such practices when absent their presence. One Arab American high schoolgirl acknowledged that she dressed more conservatively when she was in the Arab American community, but when "we're away, and there are no Arabic people there, it's different. It depends on who's there to see you" (Eisenlohr, 1996, p. 256).

Moreover, the availability of a strong support network reduces the need to seek contact with the mainstream community. Min (1998) reports that a high proportion of the Korean American workforce is involved in a Korean ethnic economy. This segregation facilitates Korean maintenance of cultural traditions and social interaction with co-ethnics. If they hired outside their group, Korean businesses were more likely to hire Latinos, which also served to reinforce their gender values, since Latinos are similarly patriarchal.

Likewise, if a high level of immigration persists, such that more people from the same ethnic group continue entering the community, bringing with them the ways and values of the original culture, those former traditions will hamper acculturation. As illustrated in Table 13.1, large portions of the Asian and Latino American populations are foreign-born. This makes it easier for those groups to maintain their ethnic identities and traditions. Or, if immigrants frequently visit their original culture, a pattern called "cyclical migration," acculturation is prolonged.

Table 13.1 Foreign-Born by Race, 2000 and 2002

	Percentage of Race That Is Foreign-Born	*Percentage of Total U.S. Foreign-Born*[a]
Non-Hispanic White	3.5	14
Hispanic	40.2	52
Black	6.1	8
Asian & Pacific Islander	68.9	26
American Indian & Alaskan Native	5.4	< 1

SOURCES: Malone, Baluja, Costanzo, & Davis (2003); Martin & Midgley (2003)

a. These percentages are based on 2002 figures.

Individual factors influencing acculturation include generation and gender. In an immigrant family, the members who arrive first are referred to as the first generation. Their children who are born in the new country are second generation. When young children arrive with the first generation, they are sometimes called the 1.5 generation. Perez-Firmat (1995) writes in his autobiography that as a 1.5-generation person, he was "born in Cuba, made in the USA" (p. 1). Even if the first generation of immigrants minimally acculturates, the subsequent generations acculturate more rapidly, frequently becoming bicultural. Typical of a bicultural lifestyle is this description from one second-generation Japanese American:

> [I] sat down to American breakfasts and Japanese lunches. My palate developed a fondness for rice along with corned beef and cabbage. I became equally adept with knife and fork and chopsticks. I said grace at meal times in Japanese and recited the Lord's Prayer at night in English. I hung my stocking over the fireplace at Christmas and toasted "mochi" at Japanese New Year. (Daniels, 1962, p. 14)

Most studies indicate that acculturation varies by gender as well, with women acculturating at a slower rate than men (Berry, 1997), except in regard to gender roles (Thomas, 1995). A study of Iranian immigrants, for instance, found Iranian American men more likely than Iranian American women to view premarital sex, marriage, and family from a traditional standpoint (Hojat et al., 2000). The Iranian American men also were more likely than the women to send home for a spouse.

Several studies indicate that second-generation Latino immigrants, regardless of gender, desire more egalitarian marital relations. Jimenez-Vasquez (1995) reports that second-generation Cuban couples moved away from the traditional gender roles of their parents and toward egalitarian relationships, whereas more Cuban women were pursuing careers. Cooney, Rogler, Hurrell, and Ortiz (1982) found foreign-born Puerto Ricans were patriarchal in their belief system, but second-generation Puerto Ricans were more flexible in their gender role conceptions.

To a large extent, gender differences in acculturation probably depend on immigrant women's level of integration in society. If the women remain home, isolated from social networks, while their husbands work and interact in public life, the women more strongly desire to return to their country of origin. In a 1999 study of adolescent Arab Americans in Dearborn, Michigan, Ajrouch (1999) concluded that many Arab families restricted their daughter's ability to acculturate while giving more freedom to their sons to participate in mainstream society. Ajrouch proposed that "these immigrant families hold onto their Arab ethnicity through their daughters and strive to attain the American dream through their sons" (p. 138). In any case, girls' and women's roles in the family as kinkeepers, upholders of family honor, and bridges between generations mean that they often get caught in the middle of the cultural conflict.

Effects of Acculturation on Family Life

A number of other indicators illustrate that a degree of acculturation occurs with each generation. Fertility and divorce rates, attitudinal change, and language facility are impacted by acculturation.

Fertility rates often decline with each generation (Bachu & O'Connell, 2000). For instance, Min (1998) found that foreign-born Korean American women had a fertility rate of 1.78 in 1990, compared to 3.10 for women in Korea. Research on Hispanic Americans also confirms that second- and third-generation families have lower fertility rates than the first generation (Gurak, 1980).

The divorce rate, on the other hand, usually increases among immigrants compared to their compatriots in the home country. For instance, Hojat et al. (2000) found that the divorce rate among Iranian Americans was much higher than in Iran (66 percent versus 10 percent). Similarly, Min (1998) found that the divorce rate was three times higher among Korean American men and five times higher among Korean American women than their counterparts in Korea.

Attitudinal changes occur as well. A survey conducted of Vietnamese Americans found that first-generation immigrants ranked much higher on family values (measured by affirming statements such as "A person should talk over important life decisions with family members before taking action" or "If possible, married children should live close to their parents") than did their second-generation children (Tran, 1998). Likewise, Zsembik and Bonilla (2000) found that attitudes supporting a sense of filial obligation decreased among second-generation Puerto Ricans. In a study of 100 Puerto Rican families in New York, Colleran (1984) found that first- and second-generation Puerto Ricans regretted the loss of family unity and closeness. They perceived mainland Puerto Ricans to be less generous, more disrespectful, and less concerned about family members than those still in Puerto Rico.

Finally, language acculturation necessarily occurs in subsequent generations. Obviously, second-generation Americans speak English more than the first-generation and, therefore, use English-language media and interact socially with other English speakers. These behaviors, in turn, socialize them toward American culture and may distance them from their first-generation family members. In his memoir, *The Rice Room*, Fong-Torres (1995) says his first-generation parents spoke very little English, whereas he and his siblings spoke English with a patchwork of Cantonese, thus creating a rift between him and his parents:

> What we have here is a language barrier as formidable, to my mind, as the Great Wall of China.
>
> The barrier has stood tall, rugged, and insurmountable between my parents and all five of their children, and it has stood through countless moments when we needed to talk with each other, about the things parents and children usually discuss: jobs and careers; marriage and divorce, health and finances; history, the present, and the future.
>
> This is one of the great sadnesses of my life. How ironic, I would think. We're all well educated, thanks in part to our parents' hard work and determination; I'm a journalist and a broadcaster—my *job* is to communicate—and I can't with the two people with whom I want to most. (p. 5)

These generational differences in language, attitudes, and behavior illustrate that the acculturation process can be quite stressful on the family. Because children acculturate more rapidly than their parents, they gain some power over their parents in the new context. In an ethnography of Haitians in South Florida, Stepick (1998, p. 24) said that stories abound in the Haitian community about students who receive an "F" on their report card and tell their first-generation parents that it means "Fine." Tseng and Fuligni (2000) interviewed families of Asian and Latino adolescents whose parents had immigrated to the United States and didn't speak much English. The researchers found that teens who shared a common language with their parents had the closest relationship to their parents and were more likely to discuss present and future concerns with their parents. Second-generation teens were more likely to use English and exhibited higher levels of conflict with and embarrassment of their parents. In turn, the parents felt they had less authority over their children and expressed less appreciation for their children's viewpoints.

In her autobiography, *When I Was Puerto Rican,* Santiago (1993) delights in the powerful position she acquired upon arrival in America as a young girl. The New York City school wanted to place her in seventh grade, though she would have been in the eighth in Puerto Rico. She disagreed with the principal, and her mother, who was at her side, warned her in Spanish that those were the rules and she shouldn't argue. But Santiago persisted and convinced the principal to let her try the eighth grade. She recalls her victory:

> I was so proud of myself, I almost burst. In Puerto Rico if I had been that pushy, I would have been called *mal educada* by the [principal] and sent home with a note to my mother. But here it was my teacher who was getting the note, I got what I wanted, and my mother was sent home. (p. 227)

This reversal of authority can be unsettling to parents, who now have to rely on the child for aid in translation, filling out forms, and navigating their new surroundings. The parents also feel competition in the socialization of their children, and they don't always win. Consequently, some parents resort to control and rigidity, more than if they were in their home country. On a daily basis, parents may institute new rules about when, where, and with whom their children can associate. One Jordanian mother's statement reflects the increased monitoring:

> When it comes to the behavior of my children, I am tough. I have to be tough and make sure they know that we are different because, if I do not, who will? The environment of schools, the parties, and the daily interaction between boys and girls, especially teenagers, may influence our kids in ways that go against our culture. I and my husband always keep an eye on them. We take and bring them from school. I also go to school always to find out what kind of friends they have and what the teachers think of them. (Hattar-Pollara & Meleis, 2002, p. 165)

In her study of Asian Indian women, Das Gupta (2002) found that young Asian Indian women reported that they were monitored by their parents, had strictly imposed curfews, and had their friends screened. Whereas some of this is the cultural norm for the rearing of Asian Indian daughters, Das Gupta reported that the daughters felt their parents had become more Indian than Indians in India. The parents portrayed American culture as degenerate and Indian culture as superior, but the daughters argued that the parents' image of Indian culture did not account for changes that had also occurred in India. Das Gupta (p. 87) called this the "museumization" of selected practices. By participating in this polar portrayal of the two societies and the maintenance of traditions that were actually disappearing in India, parents could attempt to stifle the acculturation of their daughters and their own loss of influence.

I shouldn't overstate the effect of immigration on intergenerational conflicts, however. While the requisite transitions of immigration exacerbate such conflicts, all families, native-born and foreign-born, experience intergenerational conflicts. Each new generation differentiates itself from the former generation and accommodates modern technology and knowledge.

Multiracial Issues

Biculturalism engenders less resistance from members of both the sending and receiving cultures than do multiracial issues. The former results from fairly subtle changes in behavior and attitudes over a period of time, whereas multiracial identity results from a high degree of intimacy in intergroup relations. Consequently, societies debate and monitor these intergroup interactions more. In the following sections, I will discuss interracial dating and marriage, interracial or transracial adoptions, and bi- or multiracial identity.

Interracial Dating and Marriage

Interracial dating and marriage have frequently been viewed as a barometer of race relations and a measure of acculturation. Higher levels of interracial relationships are seen as indicative of improved race relations, whereas endogamy, marrying within one's group, is viewed as a strategy to maintain ethnic boundaries and "purity." The majority of interracial marriages in America result from pairings between racial-ethnic minorities and the White majority. A smaller number of marriages occur between racial minority groups, such as between Blacks and Asians, or within racial groups ("interethnic" marriages), such as between Puerto Ricans and Mexicans or Koreans and Chinese. The U.S. census treats Latinos as an ethnic (not a racial) group, so any intermarriage involving a Latino and a non-Latino is counted as an interethnic marriage as well.

Dating and Cohabitation

Interracial dating is more prevalent than interracial marriage. Compared to marriage, dating is less stigmatized, more experimental, and easier to extricate one's self from. Few studies have focused on interracial dating, but those few find that the biggest factor determining the likelihood of interracial dating is propinquity; individuals in settings where they naturally meet people of other races (especially integrated schools) are more likely to date interracially than those who are not in diverse settings (Yancey, 2002). That sounds obvious, but it reveals that people rarely go out of their way to date interracially.

Interracial dating patterns vary by gender and race. In nearly every racial group, except Asian Americans, men are more likely than women to indicate a willingness to date interracially (Gardyn, 2002), although when it comes to making the marriage commitment women are as or more likely to intermarry. In terms of racial variation, a survey of 1,300 respondents found Whites least likely to have dated interracially (36 percent), whereas more than 50 percent of Black, Hispanic, and Asian Americans had dated interracially (Yancey, 2002). The proportion of each group that actually intermarries is much lower.

Similarly, cohabitation is more interracial than marriage. Census 2000 data reveal that interracial or interethnic relationships are twice as common among cohabitors than among married couples, and that pattern persists whether the cohabitors are gay or straight. Among married couples, 7.4 percent are interracial or interethnic, but 15 percent of heterosexual cohabitors, 15.3 percent of same-sex male cohabitors, and 12.6 percent of same-sex female cohabitors are interracial or interethnic. Traditionally, social stigma and legal restrictions against interracial marriage led these "unpopular" couples to cohabit rather than marry. Although the legal restrictions are gone, some social stigma and uncertainty remain.

Interracial Marriage

In the early colonial years, informal sexual relations among Black and White indentured servants and Black slaves were fairly common (Williamson, 1995). Slavery was still not fully institutionalized in all the colonies, and the laws governing interactions between people of different races were still in their nascence. With the expansion of slavery, all slave states prohibited marriage among slaves; laws governing free Blacks varied.

Maryland and Virginia were the first colonies in the early 1660s to pass antimiscegenation laws. Other states followed, but it was not until after slavery that a majority of states passed stringent laws against interracial marriage. Until the mid-1800s, most antimiscegenation laws targeted Black-White relations (secondarily American Indian–White relations, which were more acceptable). Whipping, jail sentences, and public penance were punishments meted out for interracial relations, although the laws were rarely enforced against relations between White men and Black women. With influxes of Latinos and Asians, some states, mostly in the West, added or amended laws to include them.

Antimiscegenation laws in California were aimed primarily at Asians. Enforcement varied, however. Filipinos in California could often meet White women at local dance halls, and though prohibited from seeing them outside this context, many did so anyway. If couples couldn't find a California judge who would look the other way, they crossed the border to Mexico or Arizona, which had no antimiscegenation laws (Posadas, 1981). Many Asian Indian men, mostly Sikhs, in California married local Mexican American women, whom they worked with in agriculture. A few marriages occurred between Asian Indians and Whites or Blacks. A shortage of White women in Southwest cities, however, particularly in Texas and New Mexico, in the late 1800s also led to marriages between White men and Mexican women in California (Griswold del Castillo, 1979). Despite the growing restrictions, determined couples found places to marry. Consequently, interracial marriages rose after emancipation, peaked around 1900, and then declined until 1940 (Foeman & Nance, 2002).

In 1948, the California Supreme Court ruled that the state's antimiscegenation law was unconstitutional (Gonzales, 1998), but most states' antimiscegenation laws remained in place until the late 1960s, when *Loving v. Virginia* came before the U.S. Supreme Court. In 1958, the Lovings, a White husband and Black wife, married and moved to Virginia, a state prohibiting interracial marriage. Virginia authorities arrested the Lovings and sentenced them to one year in jail. At that time, 29 states maintained legal restrictions against such marriages. In 1967, the U.S. Supreme Court ruled that such restrictions were unconstitutional.

Within a few years, most antimiscegenation laws were overturned, although Alabama didn't repeal its ban until 2000. Since the Supreme Court's decision, the number of interracial marriages has increased more than eightfold. Since they were nearly nonexistent to begin with, however, interracial marriages still only constituted 5.7 percent of all U.S. marriages in 2000. The proportion varies by region; it is lowest in the Midwest (3.5 percent) and highest in the West (10.6 percent; Simmons & O'Connell, 2003).

As you might guess by now, not all people are equally likely to intermarry. Of course, personal values and dispositions play a role, but certain structural factors—race, gender, generation, and population distribution—impact the trend as well. One would expect a racial group's sex ratio to play a strong role, but apparently it is outweighed by gender ideology and societal norms of attractiveness.

Race and Gender Influences on Interracial Marriage Rates

Interracial marriage rates vary by race, generally with groups of color having higher rates than Whites. According to 1998 data (Suro, 1999), interracial marriages accounted for 3 percent of White American marriages, nearly 17 percent of Hispanic American marriages, 15 percent of Asian American marriages, and 5 percent of Black American marriages. Suro's data did not include American Indians, who have the highest rate of intermarriage. In terms of gender, Black and White men outmarry more than do women, and Asian and Hispanic women outmarry more than their male counterparts.

Despite White Americans' low rate of outmarriage, because they are the majority, most interracial marriages involve a White person. As you can see in Table 13.2, the majority of outmarriages for all racial minority groups involve a White partner. Most White interracial (interethnic) marriages are to Hispanic Americans, followed by Asian and Pacific Islanders, and

Table 13.2 Percentage of Interracial Marriages by Race of Spouses, 1990

	White	*Hispanic*	*Black*	*Asian*	*Native American*
Non-Hispanic White	—	54	5	27	14
Hispanic	90	—	4	4	2
Black	65	19	—	12	4
Asian	81	15	3	—	1
Native American	90	6	3	2	—

SOURCE: Adapted from Lee & Fernandez (1998)

NOTE: These data do not include interethnic marriages.

American Indians. Black-White marriages accounted for only 5 percent of White interracial marriages. According to Suro, White men outmarry slightly more than women (3.3 percent versus 2.7 percent).

African Americans have the second-lowest rate of intermarriage. One would think that the skewed sex ratio among African Americans would lead Black women to outmarry more than Black men, but, according to Suro (1999), Black men are about twice as likely as Black women to outmarry (6.6 percent versus 3.4 percent). In terms of Black-White marriages, in 2000, 73 percent of Black-White interracial marriages were Black husband and White wife (Sailer, 2003). Only recently are Black women portrayed as fulfilling America's beauty norms (Blackwell, 1991), and Black women historically have been seen as stronger, more assertive women, which may reduce their desirability among men of all races.

Hispanic Americans have the second-highest rate of outmarriage. By ethnic group, Cuban Americans have the highest intermarriage rate, followed by Puerto Ricans, and then Mexican Americans. Despite an aggregate sex ratio that favors men, Suro (1999) found that Hispanic American women outmarry slightly more than men (17.8 percent versus 15.6 percent). Most observers have pointed to gender ideology as an explanation for this pattern, assuming that Hispanic women may seek non-Hispanic men in hopes of attaining an egalitarian marriage. The sex ratio favors men only among Mexican Americans, however; Cuban women outnumber Cuban men, and Cuban women outmarry at a high rate.

Asian Americans have the third-highest interracial marriage rate, but the rate varies significantly by ethnicity. Japanese Americans have the highest outmarriage rates of any Asian ethnic group; more than 25 percent were outmarried in 1990 (Lee & Fernandez, 1998). Vietnamese and Koreans have the lowest rates, 8 percent and 7 percent, respectively (Lee & Fernandez, 1998). In addition, Lee and Fernandez found that Asian American outmarriage decreased from 25 percent in 1980 to 15 percent in 1990 as a proportion of all Asian marriages, although Asian interethnic marriages increased.

Again, despite the fact that in the aggregate Asian American men outnumber women, Suro (1999) reported that Asian American women outmarry twice as often as Asian American men (20 percent versus 9.2 percent). Some have suggested that, like Hispanic women, Asian American women are dissatisfied with Asian male attitudes toward women (Huang & Uba, 1992) and seek more liberated men. Lee and Yamanaka (1990) conducted 60 interviews of Asian young adults and concluded that Asian American men are more concerned than Asian American women about purity of family lineage. The stem family tradition (see Chapter 5) gives Asian men more responsibility for their elderly parents, so Asian men may be more responsive to their parents' wishes. But other reasons may account for the higher female rate too. Many Asian interracial marriages were formed when American military men were stationed in other countries and brought home Asian wives. Also, as mentioned in Chapter 6, Asian American men have not been portrayed by American media in traditionally masculine roles and so may be less attractive to women. Asian women, on the other hand, have been portrayed as "exotic" and "erotic." Starting in the 1980s, a number of Internet sites offered to locate foreign wives for American men, particularly those men who feel that American women are too liberated. Asian women were the "wives of choice" in the 1980s (Kitano & Daniels, 1988); in the last decade, Russian and Ukrainian women have become more popular.

The Native American intermarriage rate is the highest of all racial-ethnic groups; in 1990 about 60 percent of American Indians were married to non-Indians, and about 50 percent of Native Alaskan Eskimos were interracially married (Yellowbird & Snipp, 1994). In some regions, the American Indian rate is as high as 75 to 80 percent (Eshleman, 2003). The vast majority of those intermarriages involve White American spouses. Little data on American Indian interracial marriages exist, but gender differences in the propensity to intermarry appear negligible.

The extremely high rate of outmarriage among American Indians leads many to ponder what the long-term consequences will be for the viability of the group's ethnic identity and political power. Even American Indian interethnic marriages pose a problem, as over a couple of generations, the children of both interracial and interethnic marriages lose their legal status as Native Americans or as tribal members if they lack sufficient ancestry of any one tribe to qualify for membership.

Generation, Education, and Residence as Influences on Interracial Marriage

Interracial marriages increase with later generations. This is only logical, because older generations were restricted by antimiscegenation laws. Also, second or later generations are the most acculturated and have more opportunity than the first generation to meet people of other races. Moreover, many adult first-generation immigrants are already married when they arrive.

In addition to generational effects, higher education usually is associated with increased interracial marriage, though this doesn't hold across all groups. For instance, Suro (1999) found that Hispanic Americans with a college degree intermarry at a rate five times higher than Hispanic Americans with less than a high school degree. For Whites, however, the rate of outmarriage remains about the same no matter the level of education. For Asian Americans, education plays a reverse role; the highest levels of education have lower rates of intermarriage (Qian, 1999).

Interracial marriage also is highly impacted by settlement patterns. When a racial-ethnic minority group resides in an area densely populated with others of their own group, they are less likely to outmarry, though White Americans in the region are more likely to outmarry (Suro, 1999). Therefore, Hispanic and Asian Americans have lower rates of outmarriage in the Southwest, where the majority of them reside, and African Americans have higher rates of intermarriage on the West Coast than in the South, where the majority of them reside (Tucker & Mitchell-Kernan, 1990). As expected, Native Americans who live on reservations have lower intermarriage rates than those residing off reservation (Lee & Fernandez, 1998).

These patterns reflect opportunity. When members from one group are exposed to more people of another group, through acculturation, higher education, or residence, the chances are higher that they will marry someone from that group. Also, when fewer people of the same cultural group are nearby, the family's control over the decision and the social pressure to marry endogamously are reduced.

Why Marry Interracially?

The motivations precipitating interracial marriages are more scrutinized than same-race marriages. People assume that those who resist marriage norms must be compelled by ulterior motives or unmet psychological needs. Most of the scrutiny has targeted Black-White couples. Over the years, observers argued that Black men desired White women as "forbidden fruit."

Lamar's (1991) description of his African American father's interracial relationship with a White woman reflects this suspicion:

> Watching my father and Ruth chatting on the couch together, I couldn't help but feel that the affection between them was deep, genuine. But, at the same time, I sensed that Dad saw Ruth as some sort of prize, one more mark of his success, one more thing denied him in his youth that he had grown up to obtain. (pp. 90–91)

Others have suggested psychological weaknesses, such as rebellion, guilt, or low self-esteem, especially on the part of White women (Davidson, 1992). More blatantly, according to Foeman and Nance (2002), some interracial couples have said that they were called "wiggers" (Whites who want to be Black) or "oreos" (Blacks who want to be White).

Sociologists have proffered status exchange theory, the idea that spouses are trading racial status for income, as a possible explanation. For instance, Fu and Heaton's (2000) research on intermarriage in Hawaii concluded that intermarriage most frequently occurred between higher-income/higher-educated Native Hawaiians or Filipinos, who have lower social status in Hawaiian society, and less educated Japanese or Caucasians, who have higher social status. Most studies indicate, however, that mate seekers of all races gravitate to, and marry, people similar to themselves in education and class (Davidson, 1992).

Social Acceptance and Outcomes of Interracial Marriage

Interviews of interracially married couples indicate that although most families support the couple, the level of approval is lower than for same-race marriages and the level of support varies by race. Lewis and Yancey (1995) interviewed interracial (Black-White and Mexican-White) couples and found that more than 50 percent of them felt their families accepted their marriages. Yet, where acceptance was lacking, White families were more disapproving, especially of Black-White marriages. Black families were most supportive, and Mexican American families took an intermediary position.

Because marriages are social arrangements as well as personal decisions, the lack of social acceptance and the degree of social stigma that attend interracial marriages may render them less viable (Davidson, 1992). Foeman and Nance (2002) found that Black spouses were more attuned to, and therefore more cautious about, public reactions; White spouses often were oblivious to reactions. Such differences in perception contribute to marital conflicts. In addition, cultural differences—over religious beliefs, dress codes, food tastes and preparation, political and economic beliefs—contribute to lower satisfaction and higher divorce rates (Martin & Bumpass, 1989). Bahr (1981) found that interfaith marriages had higher and quicker divorce rates, and Fu, Tora, and Kendall (2001) found that marriages that had both racial and cultural differences had the lowest levels of happiness.

Not all studies have found higher instability, however. For instance, Negy and Snyder's (2000) study comparing Mexican-White intermarriages and White-White marriages found comparable levels of conflict. According to Segal (1998), the divorce rate among recent second-generation Asian Indian intermarriages did not appear to be higher than the divorce rate among Asian Indian same-race marriages.

Several qualitative studies have interviewed interracially married couples about strategies they develop to cope with public reactions. Foeman and Nance (2002) concluded that Black-White couples used strategies of insulation, such as not attending family reunions, or of negotiation, such as discussing how to respond to criticism. Killian (2001) described one Black-White couple that would sit separately on public transportation when they passed through White or Black neighborhoods to avoid hostility. In addition, some couples likened the process of informing new friends about their interracial marriage to "coming out." Hence, they display family photos on their desk or mention their spouse's ethnic name in order to indirectly introduce acquaintances to the situation.

Historically, one of the impediments to the acceptance of interracial marriages was their likelihood of producing mixed-race children. The increased rates of interracial dating, cohabitation, and marriage have indeed swelled the number of biracial or multiracial children (and adults) in the United States.

Bi- or Multiracial Identity

In 1977, less than 2 percent of births were babies born to parents of different races. By the end of the 1990s, this number rose to 5 percent of all births (Sado & Bayer, 2001). In 2000, the first time the census allowed respondents to choose more than one race for their identity, nearly 7 million people (about 2 percent of the population) claimed bi- or multiracial identity.

Until the 1930s, social thought regarding mixed-race people combined religious ideology with so-called scientific theories, leading to opposition based on biological explanations. One widespread biological theory was called "hybrid degeneracy," which held that people of multiracial heritage were genetically inferior to pure races, regardless of whether the race was socially dominant or subordinate. Sex and/or marriage between two races was viewed as unnatural. Hence, the product of such relations was assumed to be physically, morally, and mentally weaker (Zack, 1993). Mixed-race people, it was presumed, would have shorter life expectancies and would produce inferior children, if they could reproduce at all. Novels and movies depicted mixed-race people as psychologically dysfunctional or desirous of hiding their minority heritage.

Because of these beliefs of physical and psychological inferiority, mixed-race people were frequently subjected to differential treatment. They were given labels to distinguish them from "pure" race people. Biracial Black-White people were called "mulatto," a term derived from the Spanish word for mule. Other terms (quadroon, octaroon, mustee, mustefino, sambo) were used for people who were less than 50 percent Black or who were mixtures of Black and non-White races (Haizlip, 1994). Although many mulattoes were free, they frequently could not vote, hold office, testify in court, marry Whites, and had to pay special taxes. In some states, however, particularly South Carolina and Louisiana, free mixed-race people were fairly prosperous, formed an elite population, and a few even owned slaves (Williamson, 1995).

In most southern states, the treatment of multiracial people depended on the race of their parents. As mentioned earlier, throughout U.S. history most mixed-race children were products of relations, frequently forced, between White southern men and Black women. Even where interracial and extra-marital relationships were illegal, such practices were often tolerated because the male landowners in a southern patriarchy had power to do as they pleased. A woman in colonial America described the situation:

> Our men live all in one house with their wives and their concubines, and the mulattoes one sees in every family exactly resemble the white children—and every lady tells you who is the father of all the mulatto children in everybody's household, but those in her own she seems to think drop from the clouds, or pretends to think so. (quoted in Haizlip, 1994, p. 39)

Contrary to the patriarchal protocols of the time, the children of these relations usually inherited the slave status of their mother rather than the status of their fathers (Williamson, 1995). In some cases, however, White men freed their biracial offspring or took them into their house and educated them or "promoted" them to house slaves. The majority, however, remained slaves.

In the less common instances when the mixed-race children were of White mothers, state laws often required the mother to be bound into indentured servanthood for up to 5 years and children up to 30 years. In addition, the mother could be banished and/or fined (Williamson, 1995).

Despite intermarriage punishments, by the time of the American Revolution (1776), it is estimated that between 60,000 and 120,000 mixed Black-White people resided in the colonies. By 1850, they represented about 11 percent of the Negro population (2.5 percent of the total population), and about half were free (Williamson, 1995). Near the end of slavery, the mulatto slave population had increased by 67 percent, whereas the Black slave population had increased by only 19 percent. So as slavery became Whiter, and calls to abolish slavery increased, the laws defining who was Negro became broader, going from anyone with one quarter to "one-drop" Negro ancestry. Even today, multiracial people are most often categorized with the group of color (the subordinate group) than with their White ancestry, a pattern called "hypodescendancy." Scientists estimate that perhaps up to 75 percent of African Americans have White ancestry.

Variations in skin tone play a covert but important role in social status. By the end of slavery, large mixed-race populations lived among free Blacks in the North, and they usually had a higher social status. Mixed-race females were often sought after as partners (not necessarily marriage partners) by well-to-do men at "quadroon balls" (Zack, 1993). Writing of her childhood in the 1940s, Thornton (1995) recalled a teacher who addressed a new light-skinned classmate as "little Miss Sunshine" and called on her for all the answers. Thornton's mother Tass told her that the girl's "high yella" skin color accounted for the teacher's favoritism. When her father heard about the favoritism, he lectured his daughters:

> Being black doesn't necessarily guarantee you entrance to a black affair; at the door you lay your hand on a brown paper bag and if your skin is darker than the bag, you're turned away. "White, you're all right; black, step back; brown, stick around," was how it went, he said. . . .
>
> "That's why I'm telling you, you got to get smart," he said. "When you're grown, this society is gonna look at you as an ugly black female—not just white people but black people, too, are gonna see you that way—and the only thing that's gonna get you above that is if you're educated. Light-skinned people generally have everything given to them. They don't have to bother 'bout learnin'. But you are not light, so studyin' is the only way I can see you gettin' ahead of this." (p. 34)

Even today, this favoritism for lighter skin can be found among many ethnic groups. Recent studies indicate that wealthier African Americans tend to be lighter skinned (Hill, 2000). Among Native Americans, Mary Crow Dog (1990) asserted in her autobiography that "half-breeds" were seen as pawns of the White bureaucracy, "Uncle Tomahawks" who betrayed full-blooded Indians for special privileges (p. 114). Writing of her encounters in India in the 1990s, MacDonald (2002) recounted that she was repeatedly told how lucky she was to have pale skin. Some Asian Indians were shocked to hear she used tanning lotions, as they were using skin-bleaching creams.

Because of the growth in diversity generally and in the multiracial population specifically, a multiracial movement has advocated moving away from the traditional racial categories. More government forms now provide an "other" category or allow people to self-identify and claim as many racial-ethnic identities as they want or Nevertheless, many people of color worry that such changes will diminish their political power (Tilles, 1995).

Trans- or Interracial Adoption

When we discuss interracial adoptions, we are nearly always talking about White families adopting children of color. For several reasons, only about 2 percent of all adoptions are non-White families adopting White children (National Adoption Information Clearinghouse, 2004). White families are better recruited by adoption agencies and are more likely to meet the criteria set by adoption agencies. Families of color frequently adopt informally, and children of color are disproportionately represented among the children available for adoption.

Interracial adoption was fairly common until the 1960s, when in the wake of the civil rights movement, a number of racial minority groups argued that interracial adoption resulted in the loss of culture and racial identity among adopted minority children. In a worst-case scenario, they argued it was a conscious strategy to reduce minority numbers. Black social workers worked diligently to recruit more African American families, and Native Americans succeeded in persuading Congress to pass the 1978 Indian Child Welfare Act, which gave Native Americans jurisdiction over the placement of foster and adoptive Native American children.

Consequently, the number of transracial adoptions decreased for several decades. Then in 1994, under concern that children were lingering in foster care unnecessarily or remaining in abusive homes, the Multiethnic Placement Act (MEPA) was passed. This law, strengthened 2 years later, said that agencies receiving federal funds could not deny or delay placement of an adoptive or foster child based on the parents' or the child's race. It did not, however, overturn the Indian Child Welfare Act, which does allow placement on the basis of race, allowing Native American tribes to attempt to place American Indian children with American Indian families. The number of transracial adoptions has increased since then, in part due to the growing popularity of international adoptions.

International adoption started largely as a response to various wars. The first wave of international adoptions began after World War II, when nearly 6,000 children—European and Japanese orphans—were adopted by American parents (Hollingsworth, 2003). The 1950s Korean War led to a wave of adoptions of Korean children, at first mostly war orphans, then later of unwanted female infants or children born to unwed Korean mothers (because of patrilineality ancestry requirements, these children cannot be incorporated into the father's family registry [Wilkinson, 1995]). The Vietnam War produced another wave of international adoptions. These were frequently Amerasians, biracial children created by American soldiers and Vietnamese women and largely stigmatized in Vietnam. The fall of communism in Central and Eastern Europe created yet another wave in the late 1980s and early 1990s. The most recent wave from China has stemmed from China's one-child policy. Since most Chinese families want boys to carry on the family line, most of the adopted children are girls. Currently, Russia and China are the largest suppliers of children.

Although other countries also adopt, U.S. families account for almost 50 percent of all international adoptions. In 1991, 7,093 children were adopted into the United States, but by 2001 that number had increased to 19,237 (Volkman, 2003). According to 2000 census data, international adoptions represent about 13 percent of all adoptions. They tend to be higher in the Northeast and specifically in Minnesota, where they represent about 20 percent of all adoptions (Kreider, 2003).

Although the pros and cons of transracial adoption have been hotly debated, most studies indicate that children adopted interracially fare no worse nor better than kids with same-race parents. For instance, Simon (1995) repeatedly interviewed 206 White families (204 parents and 366 children) who had adopted non-White children (mostly Black, but also Korean and Native American) over a 20-year period. In general, she found the children to be comfortable with their racial identity. In a later interview, Simon asked the children (now young adults) whether they agreed with the policy discouraging transracial adoption. Eighty percent of the adoptees disagreed with the position opposing interracial adoption.

All indications appear to signal that we can expect the United States to become more diverse over the next few decades. Controversies over language and cultural policy will continue, but continued increases in interracial marriage and adoption and in the multiracial population will redefine the boundaries of debate about race relations and equality in America. Finally, the extent to which both new and native Americans are willing to accommodate one another will impact the country's viability.

Resources

Books and Articles

Alumbkal, A. W. (2003). *Asian American evangelical churches: Race, ethnicity, and assimilation in the second generation.* New York: LFB Scholarly Publishing.

While the church serves to uphold ethnic identity, second-generation Chinese and Korean American evangelicals have religious beliefs similar to White Americans.

Arana, M. (2001). *American Chica: Two worlds, one childhood.* New York: Random House.

This is the autobiography of a Mexican American woman.

Canniff, J. G. (2001). *Cambodian refugees' pathways to success: Developing a bi-cultural identity.* New York: LFB Scholarly Publishing.

This volume explores how Cambodians have both retained and adapted their ethnic identity to make their way successfully in the United States.

Crane, K. R. (2003). *Latino churches: Faith, family, and ethnicity in the second generation.* New York: LFB Scholarly Publishing.

Crane reveals that second-generation Latinos in the Midwest have used the church to help retain their ethnic identity.

Delman, C. (2002). *Burnt bread and chutney: Growing up between cultures: A memoir of an Indian Jewish girl.* New York: Random House.

Fogg-Davis, H. (2002). *The ethics of transracial adoption.* Ithaca, NY: Cornell University Press.

Fogg-Davis analyzes arguments on both sides of the debate.

Kennedy, R. (2003). *Interracial intimacies: Sex, marriage, identity, and adoption.* New York: Pantheon.

This book takes a historical view as well as offering a vision for the future.

Mori, K. (1997). *Polite lies: On being a woman caught between cultures.* New York: Ballantine.

The author's autobiography explores the conflicts between her lives and societal expectations in Japan and in the American Midwest.

Reddy, M. T. (1994). *Crossing the color line: Race, parenting and culture.* New Brunswick, NJ: Rutgers University Press.

Written by a White woman married to a Black man with a Black daughter, Reddy explores how her relationships with her husband and daughter have impacted her experience with Whiteness.

Rockquemore, K. A., & Brunsma, D. L. (2002). *Beyond Black: Biracial identity in America*. Thousand Oaks, CA: Sage.

The authors interviewed biracial college students about their racial identity and what social factors influence their identity choices.

Rojewski, J. W., & Rojewski, J. L. (2001). *Intercountry adoption from China: Examining cultural heritage and other postadoption issues*. Westport, CT: Bergen & Garvey.

This book explores the process of transracial adoption and postadoption adjustment issues.

Williams, G. (1995). *Life on the color line: The true story of a White boy who discovered he was Black*. New York: Penguin.

This work is the autobiography of the son of an interracial couple.

Videos

ABC News. (1999). *Chinese Americans: Living in two worlds* [Videorecording]. (Available from Films Media Group, P.O. Box 2053, Princeton, NJ 08453-2053, or at http://www.films.com)

This 22-minute ABC News video traces the bicultural experience of a Chinese American woman, her siblings, and parents.

Crumbley, J. (Producer). (1998). *The impact of transracial adoption on the adopted child and the adopted family*. [Motion picture]. (Available from Insight Media Inc., 2162 Broadway, New York, NY 10024-0621, or at http://www.insight-media.com)

This 58-minute video examines parent-child and family-community interactions in transracial adoptions.

Jajeh, J., & Byrd, N. (Producers/Directors). (2001). *In my own skin: The complexity of living as an Arab in America* [Motion picture]. (Available from Insight Media Inc., 2162 Broadway, New York, NY 10024-0621, or at http://www.insight-media.com)

This 15-minute video, made shortly after 9/11, portrays five young Arab American women and how they create their bicultural identities.

Mass, H. (Producer). (2000). *The new generation: Vietnamese-Americans today* [Motion picture]. (Available from Films Media Group, P.O. Box 2053, Princeton, NJ 08453-2053, or at http://www.films.com)

This 33-minute video contains interviews with first- and second-generation Vietnamese Americans, documenting the process of assimilation.

Perin, M. G. (Producer/Director). (1995). *Hispanic Americans: The second generation* [Motion Picture]. (Available from Films Media Group, P.O. Box 2053, Princeton, NJ 08453-2053, or at http://www.films.com/id/9951)

This 44-minute video, hosted by actor Jimmy Smits, examines how second-generation Hispanics are adapting to American society.

Websites

http://www.diversitydtg.com
This site has information on interracial families.

http://www.parenting-child-development.com
This site has information and other links on raising biracial children.

http://www.pollywannacracka.com
A website for interracial relationships has links to articles, statistics, chatlines, and more.

REFERENCES

Adler, S. R. (1991). Sudden unexpected nocturnal death syndrome among Hmong immigrants: Examining the role of the "nightmare." *Journal of American Folklore, 104,* 54–71.

Agbayani-Siewart, P. (1994). Filipino American culture and family: Guidelines for practitioners. *Families in Society: The Journal of Contemporary Human Services, 75*(5), 429–438.

Aguirre, A., Jr., & Turner, J. H. (2004). *American ethnicity: The dynamics and consequences of discrimination* (4th ed.). Boston: McGraw-Hill.

Ahmed, A. U. (1993). Marriage and its transition in Bangladesh. In L. Tepperman & S. J. Wilson (Eds.), *Next of kin: An international reader on changing families* (pp. 74–83). Englewood Cliffs, NJ: Prentice Hall.

Ajrouch, K. (1999). Family and ethnic identity in an Arab-American community. In M. W. Suleiman (Ed.), *Arabs in America: Building a new future* (pp. 129–139). Philadelphia: Temple University Press.

Allen, W. D., & Doherty, W. J. (1996). The responsibilities of fatherhood as perceived by African American teenage fathers. *Families in Society: The Journal of Contemporary Human Services* 77(3), 142–155.

Alvarez, R. R., Jr. (1987). *Familia: Migration and adaptation in Baja and Alta California, 1800–1975.* Berkeley: University of California Press.

Amato, P. R., & Fowler, F. (2002). Parenting practices, child adjustment, and family diversity. *Journal of Marriage and Family, 64*(3), 703–717.

AmeriStat. (2000). *Occupational segregation* [Electronic version]. Available from the Population Reference Bureau at http://www.prb.org/AmeristatTemplate.cfm?Section=RaceandEthnicity&template=/ContentManagement/ContentDisplay.cfm&ContentID=7896

AmeriStat. (2003a). *Having children later or not at all* [Electronic version]. Retrieved from the Population Reference Bureau at http://www.prb.org/Template.cfm?Section=PRB&template=/ContentManagement/ContentDisplay.cfm&ContentID=7964

AmeriStat. (2003b). *U.S. fertility rates higher among minorities* [Electronic version]. Retrieved from the Population Reference Bureau at http://www.prb.org/Template.cfm? Section=PRB&template=/ContentManagement/ContentDisplay.cfm&ContentID=7981

Anderson, K. L. (1997). Gender, status, and domestic violence: An integration of feminist and family violence approaches. *Journal of Marriage and Family, 59*(3), 655–669.

Angel, R. J., & Angel, J. L. (2004). Family, the state, and health care: Changing roles in the new century. In J. Scott, J. Treas, & M. Richards (Eds.), *The Blackwell companion to the sociology of families* (pp. 233–252). Carlton, VIC, Australia: Blackwell.

Angel, R. J., Angel, J. L., Lee, G. Y., & Markides, K. S. (1999). Age at migration and family dependency among older Mexican immigrants: Recent evidence from the Mexican American. *The Gerontologist, 39*(1), 59–65.

Aquilino, W. S. (1990). The likelihood of parent-adult-child coresidence: Effects of family structure and characteristics. *Journal of Marriage and Family, 52*(2), 405–419.

Astone, N. M., & McLanahan, S. S. (1991). Family structure, parental practices and high school completion. *American Sociological Review, 56,* 309–320.

Astone, N. M., & Upchurch, D. M. (1994). Forming a family, leaving school early and earning a GED: A racial and cohort comparison. *Journal of Marriage and Family, 56*(3), 759–771.

Baca Zinn, M. (1980). Gender and ethnic identity among Chicanos. *Frontiers, V*(2), 18–24.

Baca Zinn, M., & Eitzen, D. S. (2002). *Diversity in families* (6th ed.). Boston: Allyn & Bacon.

Bachu, A. (1999). Trends in premarital childbearing: 1930–1994: Special studies. *Current Populations Reports* [Electronic version]. Retrieved from the U.S. Department of Commerce, U.S. Census Bureau at http://www.census.gov/prod/99pubs/p23-197.pdf

Bachu, A., & O'Connell, M. (2000). Fertility of American women: June 1998. *Current Population Reports* [Electronic version]. Retrieved from the U.S. Department of Commerce, U.S. Census Bureau at http://www.census.gov/prod/2000pubs/p20-526.pdf

Baer, J. (1999). Family relationships, parenting behavior, and adolescent deviance in three ethnic groups. *Families in Society: The Journal of Contemporary Human Services, 80*(3), 279–285.

Bahr, H. M. (1981). Religious intermarriage and divorce in Utah and the Mountain States. *Journal for the Scientific Study of Religion, 20*(3), 251–261.

Bahr, K. S. (1994). The strengths of Apache grandmothers: Observations on commitment, culture and caretaking. *Journal of Comparative Family Studies, 25*(2), 233–248.

Bains, T. S., & Johnston, H. (1995). *The four quarters of the night: The life-journey of an emigrant Sikh.* Montreal, QC, Canada: McGill-Queen's University Press.

Baldridge, D. (2001). Indian elders: Family traditions in crisis. *The American Behavioral Scientist, 44*(9), 1515–1527.

Baldwin, A. L., Baldwin, C., & Cole, R. E. (1990). Stress-resistant families and stress-resistant children. In J. Rolf, A. Masten, D. Cicchetti, K. Neuchtherlin, &

S. Weintraub (Eds.), *Risk and protective factors in the development of psychopathology* (pp. 257–280). New York: Cambridge University Press.

Bankston, C. L., & Zhou, M. (1995). Religious participation, ethnic identification, and adaptation of Vietnamese adolescents in an immigrant community. *The Sociological Quarterly, 36*(3), 501–512.

Basit, T. N. (1997). "I want more freedom, but not too much": British Muslim girls and the dynamism of family values. *Gender and Education, 9*(4), 425–439.

Bates, D. G., & Fratkin, E. M. (2003). *Cultural anthropology* (3rd ed.). Boston: Allyn & Bacon.

Baumrind, D. (1991). The influence of parenting style on adolescent competence and substance abuse. *Journal of Early Adolescence, 11*(1), 56–95.

Baumrind, D. (1994). The social context of child maltreatment. *Family Relations, 43*(October), 360–368.

Baumrind, D. (1996). The discipline controversy revisited. *Family Relations, 45*(October), 405–414.

Bean, F. D., & Tienda, M. (1987). *The Hispanic population of the United States.* New York: Russell Sage.

Becerra, R. M. (1998). The Mexican-American family. In C. H. Mindel, R. W. Haberstein, & R. Wright, Jr. (Eds.), *Ethnic families in America: Patterns and variations* (pp. 153–171). Upper Saddle River, NJ: Prentice Hall.

Bell-Scott, P., & McKenry, P. C. (1986). Black adolescents and their families. In G. K. Leigh & G. W. Peterson (Eds.), *Adolescents in families* (pp. 410–432). Cincinnati, OH: South-Western.

Bengtson, V. L., & Harooytan, R. A. (1994). Generational linkages and implications for public policy. In V. L. Bengtson & R. A. Harootyan (Eds.), *Intergenerational linkages: Hidden connections in American society* (pp. 210–233). New York: Springer.

Benokraitis, N. V. (1999). *Marriages and families: Chances, choices, and constraints* (3rd ed.). Upper Saddle River, NJ: Prentice Hall.

Bernal, G. (1984). Cuban families. In M. McGoldrick, J. K. Pearce, & J. Giordano (Eds.), *Ethnicity and family therapy* (pp. 186–207). New York: Guilford.

Berry, J. W. (1986). The acculturation process and refugee behavior. In C. L. Williams & J. Westermeyer (Eds.). *Refugee mental health in resettlement countries* (pp. 25–37). Washington, DC: Hemisphere.

Berry, J. W. (1997). Immigration, acculturation, and adaptation. *Applied Psychology: An International Review, 46*(1), 5–68.

Berry, J. W., Kim, U., Minde, T., & Mok, D. (1987). Comparative studies of acculturative stress. *International Migration Review, 21*(3), 491–511.

Biafora, F. A., Warheit, G. J., Zimmerman, R. S., Gil, A. G., Apospori, E., Taylor, D., et al. (1993). Racial mistrust and deviant behaviors among ethnically diverse Black adolescent boys. *Journal of Applied Social Psychology, 23,* 891–910.

Bianchi, S. M., Milkie, M., Sayer, L., & Robinson, J. (2000). Is anyone doing the housework? *Social Forces, 79,*191–228.

Billingsley, A. (1992). *Climbing Jacob's ladder.* New York: Simon & Schuster.

Binh, D. T. (1975). *A handbook for teachers of Vietnamese students: Hints for dealing with cultural differences in schools.* Arlington, VA: Center for Applied Linguistics.

Biu, H. N., & Morash, M. (1999). Domestic violence in the Vietnamese immigrant community: An exploratory study. *Violence Against Women, 5*(7), 769–795.

Blackwell, J. E. (1991). *The Black community: Diversity and unity* (3rd ed.). New York: Harper & Row.

Blackwood, E. (1984). Sexuality and gender in certain Native American tribes: The case of cross-gender females. *Signs, 10*(1), 27–42.

Blassingame, J. W. (1972). *The slave community: Plantation life in the antebellum South.* New York: Oxford University Press.

Blauner, R. (1994). Colonized and immigrant minorities. In R. Takaki (Ed.), *From different shores: Perspectives on race and ethnicity in America* (2nd ed., pp. 149–160). New York: Oxford University Press.

Blee, D. M., & Tickamyer, A. R. (1995). Racial differences in men's attitudes about women's gender roles. *Journal of Marriage and Family, 57,* 21–30.

Bliatout, B. T. (1993). Hmong death customs: Traditional and acculturated. In D. P. Irish, K. F. Lundquist, & V. J. Nelsen (Eds.), *Ethnic variations in dying, death, and grief: Diversity in universality* (pp. 79–100). Washington, DC: Taylor & Francis.

Blumberg, R. L. (Ed.). (1991). *Gender, family, and economy: The triple overlap.* Newbury Park, CA: Sage.

Borjas, G. J., & Bratsberg, B. (1996). Who leaves? The outmigration of the foreign-born. *The Review of Economics and Statistics, 78*(10), 165–176.

Boucke, L. (2002). *Infant potty training: A gentle and primeval method adapted to modern living* (2nd ed.). Lafayette, CO: Boucke-White.

Bowman, P. J., & Howard, C. (1985). Race-related socialization, motivation, and academic achievement: A study of Black youth in three-generation families. *Journal of the American Academy of Child Psychiatry, 24*(2), 134–141.

Braithwaite, R. I. (1981). Interpersonal relations between Black males and Black females. In L. E. Gary (Ed.), *Black men* (pp. 83–97). Beverly Hills, CA: Sage.

Bramlett, M. D., & Mosher, W. D. (2001). *First marriage dissolution, divorce, and remarriage: United States* (Advance Data 323) [Electronic version]. Retrieved from the Department of Health & Human Services, Centers for Disease Control and Prevention, National Center for Health Statistics at http://www.census.gov/nchs/data/ad/ad323.pdf

Brokenleg, M., & Middleton, D. (1993). Native Americans: Adapting, yet retaining. In D. P. Irish, K. F. Lundquist, & V. J. Nelsen (Eds.), *Ethnic variations in dying, death, and grief: Diversity in universality* (pp. 101–112). Washington, DC: Taylor & Francis.

Broker, I. (1993). Ni-Bo-Wi-Se-Gwe. In P. Riley (Ed.), *Growing up Native American* (pp. 87–95). New York: Avon.

Broman, C. L. (1993). Race differences in marital well-being. *Journal of Marriage and Family, 55*(August), 724–732.

Bronzaft, A. L. (1991). Career, marriage, and family aspirations of young Black college women. *Journal of Negro Education, 60,* 110–118.

Brown, A. S. (1989). A survey on elder abuse at one Native American tribe. *Journal of Elder Abuse and Neglect, 1*(2), 17–37.

Brown, L., & Gilligan, C. (1992). *Meeting at the crossroads: Women's psychology and girls' development.* New York: Ballantine.

Bulcroft, R. A., & Bulcroft, K. A. (1993). Race differences in attitudinal and motivational factors in the decision to marry. *Journal of Marriage and Family, 55,* 338–356.

Bulcroft, R. A., Carmody, D. C., & Bulcroft, K. A. (1996). Patterns of parental independence giving to adolescents: Variations by race, age, and gender of child. *Journal of Marriage and Family, 58*(November), 866–883.

Bumiller, E. (1990). *May you be the mother of a hundred sons: A journey among the women of India.* New York: Fawcett Columbine.

Burgess, N. J. (1995). Looking back, looking forward: African American families in sociohistorical perspective. In B. B. Ingoldsby & S. Smith (Eds.), *Families in multicultural perspective* (pp. 321–334). New York: Guilford.

Burr, J. A., & Mutchler, J. E. (1999). Race and ethnic variation in norms of filial responsibility among older persons. *Journal of Marriage and Family, 61*(August), 674–687.

Burton, L. M. (1990). Teenage childbearing as an alternative life-course strategy in multigenerational Black families. *Human Nature, 1*(2), 123–143.

Burton, O. V. (1985). *In my father's house are many mansions: Family and community in Edgefield, South Carolina.* Chapel Hill: University of North Carolina Press.

Cagney, K. A., & Agree, E. M. (1999). Racial differences in skilled nursing care and home health use: The mediating effects of family structure and social class. *Journals of Gerontology, Series B: Psychological Sciences and Social Sciences, 54B*(4), S223–S236.

Campbell, D. W., Masaki, B., & Torres, S. (1997). Water on rock: Changing domestic violence perceptions in the African American, Asian American, and Latino communities. In E. Klein, J. Campbell, E. Soler, & M. Ghez (Eds.), *Ending domestic violence: Changing public perceptions/halting the epidemic* (pp. 64–87). Thousand Oaks, CA: Sage.

Cantor, M. H., Brennan, M., & Sainz, A. (1994). The importance of ethnicity in social support systems of older New Yorkers: A longitudinal perspective (1970 to 1990). *Journal of Gerontological Social Work, 22*(3/4), 95–128.

Carr, L. (1993). *The Japanese-American internment: The transmission of trauma to the offspring of the internees.* Unpublished doctoral dissertation, Columbia University.

Carter, B. D., Urey, J. R., & Eid, N. S. (1992). The chronically ill child and family stress: Family development perspectives on cystic fibrosis. *Psychsomatics, 33*(4), 397–403.

Cazenave, N., & Straus, M. (1979). Race, class, network embeddedness and family violence: A search for potent support systems. *Journal of Comparative Family Studies, 10,* 281–300.

Chan, F. (1988). To be old and Asian: An unsettling life in America. *Aging, 358,* 14–15.

Chan, S. (1991). *Asian Americans: An interpretive history.* Boston: Twayne.

Chase-Lansdale, P. L., Brooks-Gunn, J., & Zamsky, E. S. (1994). Young African-American multigenerational families in poverty: Quality of mothering and grandmothering. *Child Development, 65*(2), 373–393.

Cheeseman Day, J. (with Jamieson, A.). (2003). *School enrollment: 2000* [Electronic version]. Retrieved from the U.S. Department of Commerce, U.S. Census Bureau at http://www.census.gov/prod/2003pubs/c2kbr-26.pdf

Cherlin, A. J., & Furstenberg, F. F., Jr. (1986). *The new American grandparent: A place in the family, a life apart.* New York: Basic Books.

Cheshire, T. C. (2001). Cultural transmission in urban American Indian families. *The American Behavioral Scientist, 44*(9), 1528–1536.

Chow, E. N.-L. (1994). The feminist movement: Where are all the Asian American women? In R. Takaki (Ed.). *From different shores: Perspectives on race and ethnicity in America* (pp. 184–191). New York: Oxford University Press.

Clarke, S. C. (1995). Advance report of final divorce statistics: 1989 and 1990 [Electronic version]. *Monthly Vital Statistics Report, 43*(9, Suppl.). Available from the U.S. Department of Health and Human Services, Centers for Disease Control and Prevention, National Center for Health Statistics at http://www.cdc.gov/nchs/

Clemmons, L. (2000). We find it a difficult work. *American Indian Quarterly, 24*(4), 570–601.

Cofer, S. (1990). *Silent dancing: A partial remembrance of a Puerto Rican childhood.* Houston, TX: Arte Publico.

Cohen, P. N., & Casper, L. M. (2002). In whose home? Multigenerational families in the United States, 1998–2000. *Sociological Perspectives, 45*(1), 1–20.

Cohen, P. N., & MacCartney, D. (2004). Inequality and the family. In J. Scott, J. Treas, & M. Richards (Eds.), *The Blackwell companion to the sociology of families* (pp. 181–192). Carlton, VIC, Australia: Blackwell.

Coke, M. M., & Twaite, J. A. (1995). *The Black elderly: Satisfaction and quality of later life.* New York: Haworth.

Coles, R. L. (2001a). African American single full-time fathers: How are they doing? *Journal of African American Men, 6*(2), 63–82.

Coles, R. L. (2001b). Elderly narrative reflections on the contradictions in Turkish village family life after migration of adult children. *Journal of Aging Studies, 15,* 383–406.

Coles, R. L. (2001c). The parenting roles and goals of single Black full-time fathers. *The Western Journal of Black Studies, 25*(2), 101–116.

Coles, R. L. (2002). Black single fathers: Choosing to parent full-time. *Journal of Contemporary Ethnography, 31*(4), 411–439.

Coles, R. L. (2003). Black single custodial fathers: Factors influencing the decision to parent. *Families in Society: The Journal of Contemporary Human Services, 84*(2), 247–258.

Colleran, K. (1984). Acculturation in Puerto Rican families in New York City. *Research Bulletin,* Hispanic Research Center, 7, 2–7.

Comer, J. P. (1988). *Maggie's American dream: The life and times of a Black family.* New York: Penguin.

Comer, J. P., & Poussaint, A. F. (1992). *Raising Black children.* New York: Plume.

Conover, K. A. (1997, May 21). Tribal colleges: Gains for "underfunded miracles." *Christian Science Monitor,* p. 12.

Cooley, M. L., & Unger, D. G. (1991). The role of family support in determining developmental outcomes in children of teen mothers. *Child Psychiatry and Human Development, 21*(3), 217–234.

Cooney, R. S., Rogler, L. H., Hurrell, R. M., & Ortiz, V. (1982). Decision making in intergenerational Puerto Rican families. *Journal of Marriage and Family, 44,* 621–631.

Coontz, S. (1992). *The way we never were: American families and the nostalgia trap.* New York: Basic Books.

Coontz, S. (1997). *The way we really are: Coming to terms with America's changing families.* New York: Basic Books.

Cotter, C., Iverson, D., & Lucas, P. (Producers). (1990). *Winds of change: A matter of promises* [Videorecording]. Alexandria, VA: PBS Video. Available from Wisconsin Public Television at https://secure.uwex.edu/wpt/videos/

Courtney, M. E., & Park, L. (1996). *Children in out-of-home care in Wisconsin: 1988 through 1994.* Madison: Wisconsin Department of Health and Social Services.

Cox, D., & Rank, M. (1992). Inter-vivos transfers and intergenerational exchange. *The Review of Economics and Statistics, 74*(2), 305–314.

Crawford, S. C. (1980). *Quantified memory: A study of the WPA and Fish University slave narrative collections.* Unpublished doctoral dissertation, University of Chicago.

Crimmins, E., & Ingegneri, D. (1990). Interaction and living arrangements of older parents and their children: Past trends, present determinants, future implications. *Research on Aging, 12*(1), 3–35.

Crow Dog, M. (with Erdoes, R.). (1990). *Lakota woman.* New York: Harper.

Dalla, L., & Gamble, W. C. (1997). Exploring factors related to parenting competence among Navajo teenage mothers: Dual techniques of inquiry. *Family Relations, 46*(2), 113–122.

Daniels, R. (1962). *The politics of prejudice.* Berkeley: University of California Press.

Darrett, B., & Rutman, A. H. (1979). New wives and sons-in-law: Parental death in seventeenth century Virginia Country. In T. W. Tote & D. L. Ammerman (Eds.), *The Chesapeake in the seventeenth century* (pp. 153–183). Chapel Hill: University of North Carolina Press.

Das Gupta, M. (1997). What is Indian about you? A gendered transnational approach to ethnicity. *Gender & Society, 11*(October), 572–596.

Das Gupta, M. (2002). To be an Asian Indian woman in America. In N. V. Benokraitis (Ed.), *Contemporary ethnic families in the United States:*

Characteristics, variations, and dynamics (pp. 83–91). Upper Saddle River, NJ: Prentice Hall.

Davidson, J. R. (1992). Theories about Black-White interracial marriage: A clinical perspective. *Journal of Multicultural Counseling & Development, 20*(4), 150–157.

Day, R. D., Peterson, G. W., & McCracken, C. (1998). Predicting spanking of younger and older children by mothers and fathers. *Journal of Marriage and Family, 60,* 79–94.

Deater-Deckard, K., & Dodge, K. A. (1997). Externalizing behavior problems and discipline revisited: Nonlinear effects and variation by culture, context, and gender. *Psychological Inquiry, 8,* 161–175.

Deer, L., & Erdoes, R. (1993). From Lame Deer: Seeker of visions. In P. Riley (Ed.), *Growing up Native American* (pp. 135–149). New York: Avon.

DeKeseredy, W. S. (1995). Enhancing the quality of survey data on woman abuse: Examples from a national Canadian study. *Violence Against Women, 1*(2), 158–173.

Demos, J. (1970). *A little commonwealth: Family life in Plymouth Colony.* New York: Oxford University Press.

DeNavas-Walt, C., & Cleveland, R. (2002). Money income in the United States: 2001. *Current Population Reports* [Electronic version]. Retrieved from the U.S. Department of Commerce, U.S. Census Bureau at http://www.census.gov/prod/2002pubs/p60-218.pdf

Dickson, L. (1993). The future of marriage and family in Black America. *Journal of Black Studies, 23*(4), 472–491.

Dill, B. T. (1988). Our mothers' grief: Racial ethnic women and the maintenance of families. In M. Anderson & P. Hill-Collins (Eds.), *Race, class and gender: An anthology* (pp. 215–238). Belmont, CA: Wadsworth.

Dore, M. M., & Dumois, A. O. (1990). Cultural differences in the meaning of adolescent pregnancy. *Families in Society: The Journal of Contemporary Human Services, 71,* 93–101.

DuBois, W. E. B. (1918). *American Negro slavery.* New York: Appleton.

Dworkin, A. G., & Dworkin, R. J. (1999). *The minority report: An introduction to racial, ethnic, and gender relations* (3rd ed.). Orlando, FL: Harcourt Brace.

Dwyer, J. W., & Coward, R. T. (1991). A multivariate comparison of the involvement of adult sons versus daughters in the care of impaired parents. *Journals of Gerontology: Series B: Psychological Sciences and Social Sciences, 46B*(5), S259–S269.

East, P. L. (1998). Racial and ethnic differences in girls' sexual, marital, and birth expectations. *Journal of Marriage and Family, 60*(1), 150–162.

Ebomoyi, E. (1987). Prevalence of female circumcision in two Nigerian communities. *Sex Roles, 17,* 139–150.

Edwards, M. (2003). Siberia's Scythians: Masters of gold. *National Geographic, 203*(6), 112–129.

Eisenberg, A. R. (1988). Grandchildren's perspectives on relationships with grandparents: The influence of gender across generations. *Sex Roles, 19,* 205–217.

Eisenlohr, C. J. (1996). Adolescent Arab girls in an American high school. In B. C. Aswad & B. Bilge (Eds.), *Family and gender among American Muslims: Issues facing Middle Eastern immigrants and their descendants* (pp. 250–270). Philadelphia: Temple University Press.

Elliott, S., & Umberson, D. (2004). Recent demographic trends in the U.S. and implications for well-being. In J. Scott, J. Treas, & M. Richards (Eds.), *The Blackwell companion to the sociology of families* (pp. 34–53). Carlton, VIC, Australia: Blackwell. **[Need page nos.]**

Emery, J. (2003, March 20). Defiant youth, weak leaders hurt Hmong [Electronic version]. Available from FresnoBee.com

Eshleman, J. R. (2003). *The family* (10th ed.). Boston: Allyn & Bacon.

Espin, O. M. (1987). Psychological impact of migration on Latinas. *Psychology of Women Quarterly, 11,* 489–503.

Espiritu, Y. L. (1997). *Asian American women and men: Labor, laws and love.* Thousand Oaks, CA: Sage.

Fielding, W. (1942). *Strange customs of courtship and marriage.* New York: New Home Library.

Fields, J. (2004). *Current population reports* [Electronic version]. Retrieved from the U.S. Department of Commerce, U.S. Census Bureau at http://www.census.gov/prod/2004pubs/p20-553.pdf

Fields, J., & Casper, L. M. (2001). America's families and living arrangements: Population characteristics. *Current Population Reports* [Electronic version]. Retrieved from the U.S. Department of Commerce, U.S. Census Bureau at 222.census.gov/prod/2001pubs/p20-537.pdf

Fine, M., McKenry, P. A., & Chung, H. (1992). Post-divorce adjustment of Black and White single parents. *Journal of Divorce and Remarriage, 17,* 121–134.

Fine, M., Schwebel, A. I., & James-Myers, L. (1987). Family stability in Black families: Values underlying three different perspectives. *Journal of Comparative Studies, 18*(1), 1–23.

Finkelhor, D. (1984). *Child sexual abuse: New theory and research.* New York: Free Press.

Flannery, R. (1995). *Ellen Smallboy: Glimpses of a Cree woman's life.* Montreal, QC, Canada: McGill-Queen's University Press.

Foeman, A., & Nance, T. (2002). Building new cultures, reframing old images: Success strategies of interracial couples. *The Howard Journal of Communications, 13,* 237–249.

Fong-Torres, B. (1995). *The rice room: Growing up Chinese-American from number two son to rock 'n' roll.* New York: Plume.

Ford, B. S., McDonald, T. E., Owens, A. S., & Robinson, T. N. (2002). Primary care interventions to reduce television viewing in African-American children. *American Journal of Preventive Medicine, 22*(2), 106–109.

Ford, G. M. (1997). Family strengths, motivation, and resources as predictors of health promotion behavior in single-parent and two-parent families. *Research in Nursing and Health, 20*(3), 205–217.

Forrest, J. D., Goldman, N., Henshaw, S., Lincoln, R., Rosoff, J. I., Westoff, C. F., et al. (1993). Teenage pregnancy in industrial countries. In L. Tepperman & S. J. Wilson (Eds.), *Next of kin: An international reader on changing families* (pp. 135–139). Englewood Cliffs, NJ: Prentice Hall.

Foster, G. (2000). The capacity of the extended family safety net for orphans in Africa. *Psychology, Health and Medicine, 5*(1), 55–62.

Franklin, D. L. (1997). *Ensuring inequality: The structural transformation of the African-American family.* New York: Oxford University Press.

Frey, W. H. (2003). Married with children. *American Demographics, 25*(2), 17–19.

Fu, X., & Heaton, T. B. (2000). Status exchange in intermarriage among Hawaiians, Japanese, Filipinos and Caucasians in Hawaii: 1983–1994. *Journal of Comparative Family Studies, 31*(1), 45–61.

Fu, X., Tora, J., & Kendall, H. (2001). Marital happiness and inter-racial marriage: A study in a multi-ethnic community in Hawaii. *Journal of Comparative Family Studies, 32*(1), 47–60.

Fuligni, A. J., Tseng, V., & Lam, M. (1999). Attitudes toward family obligations among American adolescents with Asian, Latin American, and European backgrounds. *Child Development, 70*(4), 1030–1044.

Furstenberg, F. F. (1976). *Unplanned parenthood: The social consequences of teenage childbearing.* New York: Macmillan.

Gager, C. T., Mooney, T. M., & Call, K. T. (1999). The effects of family characteristics and time use on teenagers' household labor. *The Journal of Marriage and Family, 61,* 982–994.

Gardyn, R. (2002). The mating game. *American Demographics, 24*(7), 33–37.

Garner, A., Lipsky, D. K., & Turnbull, A. P. (1991). *Supporting families with a child with a disability: An international outlook.* Baltimore: University Park Press.

Gates, H. L., Jr. (1994). *Colored people.* New York: Knopf.

Gelles, R. J. (1993). Through a sociological lens, social structure and family violence. In R. J. Gelles & D. R. Loseke (Eds.), *Current controversies on family violence* (pp. 31–45). Newbury Park, CA: Sage.

Genovese, E. (1974). *Roll Jordon roll.* New York: Vintage.

Giovannoni, I., & Billingsley, A. (1970). Child neglect among the poor: A study of parental adequacy in families of three ethnic groups. *Child Welfare, 49,* 196–204.

Glick, J. E. (1999). Economic support from and to extended kin: A comparison of Mexican Americans and Mexican immigrants. *International Migration Review, 33*(3), 745–766.

Glick, J. E., Bean, F. D., & Van Hook, J. V. W. (1997). Immigration and changing patterns of extended family household structure in the United States: 1970–1990. *Journal of Marriage and Family, 59*(1), 177–191.

Gonzales, J. L., Jr. (1991). *The lives of ethnic Americans.* Dubuque, IA: Kendall/Hunt.

Gonzales, J. L., Jr. (1998). *Racial and ethnic families in America* (3rd ed.). Dubuque, IA: Kendall/Hunt.

Gonzalez-Mena, J. (1993). *Multicultural issues in child care.* Mountain View, CA: Mayfield.

Goode, W. (1963). *World revolution and family patterns.* Glencoe, IL: Free Press.

Gordon, M. M. (1964). *Assimilation in American life.* New York: Oxford University Press.

Grasmuck, S., & Pessar, P. R. (1991). *Between two islands: Dominican international migration.* Berkeley: University of California Press.

Green, M. A. (1975). Impact of slavery on the Black family: Social, political and economic. *Journal of Afro-American Issues, 3*(3/4), 343–356.

Greenfield, P. M. (1994). Independence and interdependence as developmental scripts: Implications for theory, research, and practice. In P. M. Greenfield & R. R. Cocking (Eds.), *Cross-cultural roots of minority child development* (pp. 1-37). Hillsdale, NJ: Lawrence Erlbaum.

Greif, G. L. (1990). *The daddy track and the single father.* Lexington, MA: Lexington Books.

Griswold del Castillo, R. (1979). *The Los Angeles barrio, 1850–1890: A social history.* Berkeley: University of California Press.

Griswold del Castillo, R. (1984). *La familia.* South Bend, IN: Notre Dame University Press.

Guillemin, J. (1975). *Urban renegades: The cultural strategy of American Indians.* New York: Columbia University Press.

Gurak, D. T. (1980). Assimilation and fertility: A comparison of Mexican American and Japanese American women. *Hispanic Journal of Behavioral Sciences, 2*(3), 219–239.

Gutman, H. G. (1976). *The Black family in slavery and freedom, 1750–1925.* New York: Pantheon.

Guyer, J. (1984). *Family and farm in southern Cameroon.* (Boston University African Research Studies No. 15). Boston: Boston University, African Studies Center.

Haizlip, S. T. (1994). *The sweeter the juice: A family memoir in Black and White.* New York: Simon & Schuster.

Hale-Benson, J. E. (1986). *Black children: Their roots, culture and learning styles.* Baltimore: Johns Hopkins University Press.

Hamer, J. (2001). *What it means to be daddy.* New York: Columbia University Press.

Hamner, T. J., & Turner, P. H. (1990). *Parenting in contemporary society.* Englewood Cliffs, NJ: Prentice Hall.

Hanchard, M. C. (1997). On "good" Black fathers. In A. C. Willis (Ed.), *Faith of our fathers: African-American men reflect on fatherhood* (pp. 74–89). New York: Penguin.

Harden, B. (2001, May 21). Bible belt couples "put asunder" more, despite new efforts. *The New York Times*, p. A1.

Hatchett, S., & Jackson, J. (1993). African American extended kin systems. In H. McAdoo (Ed.), *Family ethnicity: Strength in diversity* (pp. 90–108). Newbury Park, CA: Sage.

Hattar-Pollara, M., & Meleis, A. I. (2002). Parenting and the stress of immigration among Jordanian mothers. In N. V. Benokraitis (Ed.), *Contemporary ethnic families in the United States: Characteristics, variations, and dynamics* (pp. 162–169). Upper Saddle River, NJ: Prentice Hall.

Hawkins, A. J., Nock, S. L., Wilson, J. C., Sanchez, L., & Wright, J. (2002). Attitudes about covenant marriage and divorce: Policy implications from a three-state comparison. *Family Relations, 51,* 166–175.

Hayslip, L. L. (with Wurts, J.). (1989). *When heaven and earth changed places: A Vietnamese woman's journey from war to peace.* New York: Plume.

Heffer, R. W., & Kelley, M. L. (1987). Mothers' acceptance of behavioral interventions for children: The influence of parent race and income. *Behavior Therapy, 2,* 153–163.

Hennessy, C. H., & John, R. (1995). The interpretation of burden among Pueblo Indian caregivers. *Journal of Aging Studies, 9*(3), 215–229.

Herring, C., & Wilson-Sadberry, K. R. (1993). Preference or necessity? Changing work roles of Black and White women. *Journal of Marriage and Family, 55,* 314–325.

Hetherington, P. (2001). Generational changes in marriage patterns in central province of Kenya, 1930–1990. *Journal of Asian and African Studies, 36*(May), 157–180.

Hetrick, E. S., & Martin, A. D. (1987). Developmental issues and their resolution for gay and lesbian adolescents. *Journal of Homosexuality,* 2(1/2), 25–43.

Hidalgo, H. A., & Christensen, E. H. (1976–1977). The Puerto Rican lesbian and the Puerto Rican community. *Journal of Homosexuality,* 2(2), 109–121.

Hill, M. E. (2000). Color differences in the socioeconomic status of African American men: Results of a longitudinal study. *Social Forces, 78*(June), 1437–1460.

Hill, S. A. (1994). Motherhood and obfuscation of medical knowledge. *Gender & Society, 8*(1), 29–47.

Hill, S. A. (1999). *African American children: Socialization and development in families.* Thousand Oaks, CA: Sage.

Hinrichsen, G. A., & Ramirez, M. (1992). Black and White dementia caregivers: A comparison of their adaptation, adjustment, and service utilization. *The Gerontologist, 32,* 375–381.

Ho, D. Y. F. (1986). Chinese patterns of socialization: A critical review. In M. H. Bond (Ed.), *The psychology of the Chinese people* (pp. 1–37). Hong Kong: Oxford University Press.

Hoebel, E. A. (1978). *The Cheyennes: Indians of the Great Plains* (2nd ed.). New York: Holt, Rinehart & Winston.

Hojat, M., Shapurian, R., Foroughi, D., Nayerahmadi, H., Farzaneh, M., Shafieyan, M., et al. (2000). Gender differences in traditional attitudes toward marriage and the family: An empirical study of Iranian immigrants in the United States. *Journal of Family Issues, 21*(May), 419–434.

Hollingsworth, L. (2003). International adoption among families in the United States: Considerations of social justice. *Social Work, 48,* 209–217.

Holmstrom, D. (1994, July 8). Gambling ventures reverse poverty for only some Indians. *Christian Science Monitor,* p. 3.

Holmstrom, D. (1997, July 14). Indian traditions help "drunk town" shed its image. *Christian Science Monitor,* pp. 10–11.

Holtzman, J. D. (2000). *Nuer journeys and Nuer lives.* Boston: Allyn & Bacon.

Hondagneu-Sotelo, P. (1994). Overcoming patriarchal constraints: The reconstruction of gender relations among Mexican immigrant women and men. *Gender & Society,* *6*(September), 393–415.

Hondagneu-Sotelo, P., & Messner, M. (1994). Gender displays and men's power: The "new man" and the Mexican immigrant man. In H. Brod & M. Kaufman (Eds.), *Theorizing masculinities* (pp. 200–218). Thousand Oaks, CA: Sage.

Hopkins, S. W. (1993). From "Life among the Piutes." In P. Riley (Ed.), *Growing up Native American* (pp. 73–85). New York: Avon.

Hortacsu, N. (2003). Marriage in Turkey. In R. R. Hamon & B. B. Ingoldsby (Eds.), *Mate selection across cultures* (pp. 155–171). Thousand Oaks, CA: Sage.

Horwitz, A. V., & Reinhard, S. C. (1995). Ethnic differences in caregiving duties and burdens among parents and siblings of persons with severe mental illnesses. *Journal of Health and Social Behavior, 36,* 138–150.

Hossain, Z. (2001). Division of household labor and family functioning in off-reservation Navajo Indian families. *Family Relations, 50*(3), 255–261.

Huang, K., & Uba, L. (1992). Premarital sexual behavior among Chinese college students in the United States. *Archives of Sexual Behavio*r, *21*(3), 227–240.

Hughes, D. L., & Chen, L. A. (1997). When and what parents tell children about race: An examination of race-related socialization among African American families. *Applied Developmental Science, 1,* 198–212.

Hughes, D. L., & Chen, L. A. (1999). The nature of parents' race-related communications to children: A developmental perspective. In L. Balter & C. S. Tamis-Lemonda (Eds.), *Child psychology: A handbook of contemporary issues* (pp. 467–490). Philadelphia: Psychology Press.

Hughes, D. L., & Johnson, D. (2001). Correlates in children's experiences of parents' racial socialization behaviors. *Journal of Marriage and Family, 63*(4), 981–986.

Human Rights Campaign. (2004). *Equality in the states: Gay, lesbian, bisexual and transgender Americans and state laws and legislation in 2004* [Electronic version]. Retrieved from http://www.hrc.org/content/ContentGroups/News_Releases/20042/leg_report032004.pdf

Hurst, C. E. (2004). *Social inequality: Forms, causes, and consequences* (5th ed.). Boston: Allyn & Bacon.

Hutchinson, R., & McNall, M. (1994). Early marriage in a Hmong cohort. *Journal of Marriage and Family 56*(August), 579–590.

Ichioka, Y. (1988). The Issei: The world of the first generation Japanese immigrants, 1885–1924. *Pacific Historical Review, 49*(2), 339–357.

Ingoldsby, B. B. (1995a). Family origin and universality. In B. B. Ingoldsby & S. Smith (Eds.), *Families in multicultural perspective* (pp. 83–96). New York: Guilford.

Ingoldsby, B. B. (1995b). Marital structure. In B. B. Ingoldsby & S. Smith (Eds.), *Families in multicultural perspective* (pp. 117–142). New York: Guilford.

Ingoldsby, B. B. (1995c). Mate selection and marriage. In B. B. Ingoldsby & S. Smith (Eds.), *Families in multicultural perspective* (pp. 143–160). New York: Guilford.

Ingoldsby, B. B. (2003). The mate selection process in the United States. In R. R. Hamon & B. B. Ingoldsby (Eds.), *Mate selection across cultures* (pp. 3–18). Thousand Oaks, CA: Sage.

Irish, D. P. (1993). Multiculturalism and the majority population. In D. P. Irish, K. F. Lundquist, & V. J. Nelsen (Eds.), *Ethnic variations in dying, death, and grief: Diversity in universality* (pp. 1–10). Washington, DC: Taylor & Francis.

Jarrett, R. L. (1994). Living poor: Family life among single-parent African-American women. *Social Problems, 41*(1), 30–49.

Jimenez-Vazquez, R. (1995). Hispanics: Cubans. *Encyclopedia of social work* (19th ed.). Washington, DC: NASW Press.

Jo, M. H. (2002). Coping with gender role strains in Korean American families. In N. V. Benokraitis (Ed.), *Contemporary ethnic families in the United States: Characteristics, variations, and dynamics* (pp. 78–83). Upper Saddle River, NJ: Prentice Hall.

John, R. (1991). Family support networks among elders in a Native American community: Contact with children and siblings among the Prairie Band Potawatomi. *Journal of Aging Studies, 5*(1), 45–59.

John, R. (1998). Native American families. In C. H. Mindel, R. W. Haberstein, & R. Wright, Jr. (Eds.), *Ethnic families in America: Patterns and variations* (pp. 382–420). Upper Saddle River, NJ: Prentice Hall.

John, R., Hennessy, C. H., Dyeson, T. B., & Garrett, M. D. (2001). Toward the conceptualization and measurement of caregiver burden among Pueblo Indian family caregivers. *The Gerontologist, 41*(2), 210–219.

Johnson, C. L., & Barer, B. (1994). Childlessness and kinship organization: Comparisons of very old Whites and Blacks. *Journal of Cross-Cultural Gerontology, 10,* 289–306.

Johnson, C. S. (1934). *Shadow of the plantation.* Chicago: University of Chicago Press.

Johnson, D. J. (2001). Parental characteristics, racial stress, and racial socialization processes as predictors of racial coping in middle childhood. In A. Neal-Barnett (Ed.), *Forging links: Clinical/developmental perspective of African American children* (pp. 57–74). Westport, CT: Greenwood.

Jones, L. C. (1993). Dreaming of a Black Christmas. *Ebony, 49*(2), 94–97.

Josephy, A. M., Jr. (1991). *The Indian heritage of America* (Rev. ed.). Boston: Houghton Mifflin.

Joyce, T., Kaestner, R., Korenman, S., & Henshaw, S. (2004). *Family cap provisions and changes in births and abortions* (National Bureau of Economic Research Working Paper No. w10214) [Electronic version]. Abstract retrieved from http://papers.nber.org/papers/W10214

Kadi, J. (Ed.). (1994). *Food for our grandmothers: Writings by Arab-American and Arab-Canadian feminists*. Boston: South End Press.

Kagan, J. (1984). *The nature of the child*. New York: Basic Books.

Kamo, Y. (2000). Racial and ethnic differences in extended family households. *Sociological Perspectives, 43*(2), 211–229.

Kamo, Y., & Zhou, M. (1994). Living arrangements of elderly Chinese and Japanese in the United States. *Journal of Marriage and Family, 56*, 544–558.

Kantor, G. K., & Straus, M. A. (1987). The "drunken bum" theory of wife beating. *Social Problems, 34*(3), 213–230.

Kelley, M. L., & Tseng, H. (1992). Cultural differences in child rearing: A comparison of immigrant Chinese and Caucasian American mothers. *Journal of Cross-Cultural Psychology, 23*(4), 444–455.

Khan, A. N. (2004). New law fails to curb honor killings in Pakistan. *OneWorld SouthAsia* [Electronic version]. Retrieved May 14, 2004, from http://southasia.oneworld.net/article/view/86057/1/

Kiernan, K. (2004). Changing European families: Trends and issues. In J. Scott, J. Treas, & M. Richards (Eds.), *The Blackwell companion to the sociology of families* (pp. 17–33). Carlton, VIC, Australia: Blackwell.

Killian, K. D. (2001). Reconstituting racial histories and identities: The narratives of interracial couples. *Journal of Marital and Family Therapy, 27*(1), 27–42.

Kim, K. C., & Hurh, W. M. (1988). The burden of double roles: Korean wives in the U.S.A. *Ethnic and Racial Studies, 11*(2), 151–167.

Kimmel, M. (2000). *The gendered society*. New York: Oxford University Press.

King, V., & Elder, G. H., Jr. (1995). American children view their grandparents: Linked lives across three rural generations. *Journal of Marriage and Family, 57*(1), 165–178.

King, V., & Elder, G. H., Jr. (1997). The legacy of grandparenting: Childhood experiences with grandparents and current involvement with grandchildren. *Journal of Marriage and Family, 59*(4), 848–859.

Kitano, H. H. L., & Daniels, R. (1988). *Asian Americans: Emerging minorities*. Englewood Cliffs, NJ: Prentice Hall.

Kitano, K. J., & Kitano, H. H. L. (1998). The Japanese-American family. In C. H. Mindel, R. W. Haberstein, & R. Wright, Jr. (Eds.), *Ethnic families in America: Patterns and variations* (pp. 311–330). Upper Saddle River, NJ: Prentice Hall.

Kitson, G. C., & Holmes, R. (1992). *Portrait of divorce: Adjustment to marital breakdown*. New York: Guilford.

Knaefler, T. K. (1991). *Our house divided: Seven Japanese American families in World War II*. Honolulu: University of Hawai'i Press.

Koebel, C. T., & Murray, M. S. (1999). Extended families and their housing in the U.S. *Housing Studies, 14*(2), 125–143.

Kohn, M. (1977). *Class and conformity: A study in values* (2nd ed.). Chicago: University of Chicago Press.

Koltyk, J. A. (1998). *New pioneers in the heartland: Hmong life in Wisconsin*. Boston: Allyn & Bacon.

Korson, H. J. (1979). Endogamous marriage in a traditional Muslim society: West Pakistan: A study in intergenerational change. In G. Kurian (Ed.), *Cross-cultural perspectives of mate selection and marriage* (pp. 180–190). Westport, CT: Greenwood.

Kotchick, B. A., Dorsey, S., Miller, K. S., & Forehand, R. (1999). Adolescent sexual risk taking behavior in single-parent ethnic minority families. *Journal of Family Psychology, 13*(1), 93–102.

Krieder, R. M. (2003). *Adopted children and stepchildren: 2000* (Table 3) [Electronic version]. Retrieved from Census 2000 Special Reports, U.S. Department of Commerce, U.S. Census Bureau at http://www.census.gov/prod/2003pubs/censr-6.pdf

Kreider, R. M., & Simmons, T. (2003). *Marital status: 2000* [Electronic version]. Retrieved from Census 2000 Brief, U.S. Department of Commerce, U.S. Census Bureau at www.census.gov/prod/2003pubs/c2kbr-30.pdf

Kulikoff, A. (1986). *Tobacco and slaves: The development of southern cultures in the Chesapeake, 1680–1800.* Chapel Hill: University of North Carolina Press.

Laditka, J. N., & Laditka, S. B. (2001). Adult children helping older parents. *Research on Aging, 23*(4), 429–456.

LaFromboise, T. D., & Bigfoot, D. S. (1988). Cultural and cognitive considerations in the prevention of American Indian adolescent suicide. *Journal of Adolescence, 11,* 139–153.

LaFromboise, T. D., Heyle, A. M., & Ozer, E. J. (1990). Changing and diverse roles of women in American Indian cultures. *Sex Roles, 22*(7/8), 455–476.

Laird, J. (1993). Lesbian and gay families. In F. Walsh (Ed.), *Normal family process* (2nd ed., pp. 282–330). New York: Guilford.

Lamanna, M. A., & Riedmann, A. (2003). *Marriages and families: Making choices in a diverse society* (8th ed.). Belmont, CA: Thomson Wadsworth.

Lamar, J. (1991). *Bourgeois blues: An American memoir.* New York: Penguin.

Landale, N. S., & Fennelly, K. (1992). Informal unions among mainland Puerto Ricans: Cohabitation or an alternative to legal marriage? *Journal of Marriage and Family, 58*(May), 269–280.

Landrine, H. (1985). Race and class stereotypes of women. *Sex Roles, 13*(1/2), 65–75.

Lareau, A. (2002). Invisible inequality: Social class and childrearing in Black families and White families. *American Sociological Review, 67,* 747–776.

Larson, L. L. (1989). *Sweet bamboo: A saga of a Chinese American family.* Los Angeles: Chinese Historical Society of Southern California.

Larzelere, R. E. (1996). A review of the outcomes of parental use of nonabusive or customary physical punishment. *Pediatrics, 93,* 824–831.

Laslett, P. (1971). *The world we have lost* (2nd ed.). New York: Scribner.

Lawson, E. J., & Thompson, A. (2000). *Black men and divorce.* Thousand Oaks, CA: Corwin Press.

Lawson, L. V. (1990). Culturally sensitive support for grieving parents. *MCN: The American Journal of Maternal Child Nursing, 15*(March/April), 76–79.

Le, Q. K. (1997). Mistreatment of Vietnamese elderly by their families in the United States. *Journal of Elder Abuse and Neglect, 9*(1), 51–62.

Lee, D. (1959). *Freedom and culture.* Englewood Cliffs, NJ: Prentice Hall.

Lee, G. (1982). *Family structure and interaction: A comparative analysis.* Minneapolis: University of Minneapolis Press.

Lee, G., Peek, C. W., & Coward, R. T. (1998). Race differences in filial responsibility expectations among older parents. *Journal of Marriage and Family, 60,* 404–412.

Lee, S. J. (1997). The road to college: Hmong American women's pursuit of higher education. *Harvard Educational Review, 67*(4), 803–827.

Lee, S. M., & Fernandez, M. (1998). Trends in Asian American racial/ethnic intermarriage: A comparison of 1980 and 1990 census data. *Sociological Perspectives, 41*(2), 323–342.

Lee, S. M., & Yamanaka, K. (1990). Patterns of Asian American intermarriage and marital assimilation. *Journal of Comparative Family Studies, XXI*(2), 287–303.

Lee, Y., & Aytac, I. A. (1998). Intergenerational financial support among Whites, African Americans and Latinos. *Journal of Marriage and Family, 60*(2), 426–441.

Lempert, L. B. (1999). Other fathers: An alternative perspective on African American community caring. In R. Staples (Ed.), *The Black family: Essays and studies* (pp. 189–201). Belmont, CA: Wadsworth.

Leonard, K. (1982). Marriage and family life among early Asian Indian immigrants. *Population Review, 25,* 67–75.

Lerman, R. I. (1993). Employment patterns of unwed fathers and public policy. In R. I. Lerman & T. J. Ooms (Eds.), *Young unwed fathers: Changing roles and emerging policies* (pp. 316–334). Philadelphia: Temple University Press.

Lessinger, J. (1995). *From the Ganges to the Hudson: Indian immigrants in New York City.* Boston: Allyn & Bacon.

Lewis, R., Jr., & Yancey, G. (1995). Biracial marriages in the United States: An analysis of variation in family member support. *Sociological Spectrum, 15*(4), 443–462.

Lichter, D. T., & Landale, N. S. (1995). Parental work, family structure, and poverty among Latino children. *Journal of Marriage and Family 57*(2), 346–354.

Liem, R., & Liem, J. H. (1988). Psychological effects of unemployment on workers and their families. *Journal of Social Issues, 44*(4), 87–105.

Lin, G., & Rogerson, P. A. (1995). Elderly parents and the geographic availability of their adult children. *Research on Aging, 17*(3), 303–331.

Littlejohn-Blake, S. M., & Anderson-Darling, C. (1993). Understanding the strengths of African American families. *Journal of Black Studies, 23*(4), 460–471.

Lobo, S. (2002). *Census-taking and the invisibility of urban–American Indians* [Electronic version]. Retrieved from the Population Reference Bureau at http://www.prb.org/Template.cfm?Section=PRB&template=/ContentManagemen/ContentDisplay.cfm&ContentID=5678

Logan, J. R., & Spitze, G. (1996). *Family ties: Enduring relations between parents and their adult children.* Philadelphia: Temple University Press.

Lomawaima, K. T. (1994). *They called it prairie light: The story of Chilocco Indian school.* Lincoln: University of Nebraska Press.

Lopez, R. A. (1999). *Las Comadres* as a parenting support system. *Affilia, 14*(Spring), 24–41.

Lugaila, T. (1998). *Marital status and living arrangements: March 1997 update* [Electronic version]. Retrieved from Current Population Reports, U.S. Department of Commerce, U.S. Census Bureau at http://www.census.gov/prod/3/98pubs/p20-506.pdf

Lugaila, T., & Overturf, J. (2004). *Children and the households they live in 2000* (U.S. Department of Commerce, U.S. Census Bureau 2000 Special Report). Washington, DC: Government Printing Office.

Mabry, J. B., Giarrusso, R., & Bengston, V. L. (2004). Generations, the life course, and family change. In J. Scott, J. Treas, & M. Richards (Eds.), *The Blackwell companion to the sociology of families* (pp. 87–108). Carlton, VIC, Australia: Blackwell.

Maccoby, E. E., & Martin, J. A. (1983). Socialization in the context of the family: Parent–child interaction. In P. H. Mussen (Series Ed.) & E. M. Hetherington (Vol. Ed.), *Handbook of child psychology: Vol. 4. Socialization, personality, and social development* (4th ed., pp. 1–101). New York: John Wiley.

MacDonald, S. (2002). *Holy cow: An Indian adventure.* New York: Broadway Books.

Malone, N., Baluja, K. F., Costanzo, J. M., & Davis, C. J. (2003). *The foreign-born population: 2000* [Electronic version]. Retrieved from U.S. Department of Commerce, U.S. Census Bureau, Census 2000 Brief at http://www.census.gov/prod/2003pubs/c2kbr-34.pdf

Manetta, A. A. (1999). Interpersonal violence and suicidal behavior in midlife African American women. *Journal of Black Studies, 29*(4), 510–522.

Manfra, J. A., & Dykstra, R. P. (1985). Serial marriage and the origins of the Black stepfamily: The Rowanty evidence. *Journal of American History, 72*(1), 18–44.

Margolis, M. L. (1998). *An invisible minority: Brazilians in New York City.* Boston: Allyn & Bacon.

Markides, K. S. (1985). Minority aging. In B. B. Hess & E. W. Markson (Eds.), *Growing old in America* (3rd ed., pp. 113–135). New Brunswick, NJ: Transaction.

Markides, K. S., Roberts-Jolly, J., Ray, L. A., Hoppe, S. K., & Rudkin, L. (1999). Changes in marital satisfaction in three generations of Mexican Americans. *Research on Aging, 21*(January), 36–45.

Marshall, S. (1995). Ethnic socialization of African American children: Implications for parenting, identity development, and academic achievement. *Journal of Youth and Adolescence, 24,* 377–396.

Martin, J. A., Hamilton, B. E., Sutton, P. D., Ventura, S. J., Menacker, F., & Munson, M. L. (2003). Births: Final data for 2002. *National Vital Statistics Reports, 52*(10). Washington, DC: Government Printing Office.

Martin, P., & Midgley, E. (2003). Number of foreign-born reaches all-time high in U.S. [Electronic version]. Excerpt retrieved from the Population Reference Bureau's upcoming Population Bulletin, *Immigration: Shaping and Reshaping America* at http://www.prb.org/Template.cfm?Section=PRB&template=/ContentManagement/ContentDisplay.cfm&ContentID=8733

Martin, T. C., & Bumpass, L. (1989). Recent trends in marital disruption. *Demography, 26,* 37–51.

Matthews, S. H., & Rosner, T. T. (1988). Shared filial responsibility: The family as the primary caregiver. *Journal of Marriage and Family, 50,* 185–195.

McAdoo, H. P. (1998). African-American families. In C. H. Mindel, R. W. Haberstein, & R. Wright, Jr. (Eds.), *Ethnic families in America: Patterns and variations* (pp. 361–381). Upper Saddle River, NJ: Prentice Hall.

McCreary, M. L., Slavin, L. A., & Berry, E. J. (1996). Predicting problem behavior and self-esteem among African American adolescents. *Journal of Adolescent Research, 11*(2), 216–234.

McDade, K. (1995). How we parent: Race and ethnic differences. In C. K. Jacobson (Ed.), *American families: Issues in race and ethnicity* (pp. 283–300). New York: Garland.

McGarry, K., & Schoeni, R. F. (1995). Transfer behavior in the health and retirement study: Measurement and the redistribution of resources within the family. *Journal of Human Resources, 30*(5), S184–S226.

McInnis, K. (1991). Ethnic-sensitive work with Hmong refugee children. *Child Welfare, 70*(5), 571–580.

McKinnon, J. (2003). The Black population in the United States: March 2002. *Current Population Reports* [Electronic version]. Retrieved from the U.S. Department of Commerce, U.S. Census Bureau at http://www.census.gov/prod/2003pubs/p20-541.pdf

McLanahan, S., & Sandefur, G. (1994). *Growing up with a single parent: What hurts, what helps.* Cambridge, MA: Harvard University Press.

McLemore, S. D., Romo, H. D., & Baker, S. G. (2001). *Racial and ethnic relations in America* (6th ed.). Boston: Allyn & Bacon.

McLoyd, V. C., Cauce, A. M., Takeuchi, D., & Wilson, L. (2000). Marital processes and parental socialization in families of color: A decade review of research. *Journal of Marriage and Family, 62,* 1070–1093.

McLoyd, V. C., & Smith, J. (2002). Physical discipline and behavior problems in African American, European American, and Hispanic Children: Emotional support as a moderator. *Journal of Marriage and Family, 64*(1), 40–54.

Medora, N. P. (2003). Mate selection in contemporary India. In R. R. Hamon & B. B. Ingoldsby (Eds.), *Mate selection across cultures* (pp. 209–230). Thousand Oaks, CA: Sage.

Meekers, D. (1995). Freedom of partner choice in Togo. *Journal of Comparative Family Studies, 26,* 163–179.

Mena, F. J., Padilla, A. M., & Maldonado, M. (1987). Acculturative stress and specific coping strategies among immigrant and later generation college students. *Hispanic Journal of Behavioral Sciences, 9*(2), 207–225.

Mencher, J. (1988). Women's work and poverty: Women's contribution to household maintenance in South India. In D. Dwyer & J. Bruce (Eds.), *A home divided: Women and income in the third world.* Palo Alto, CA: Stanford University Press.

Miller, D. B. (1999). Racial socialization and racial identity: Can they promote resiliency for African American adolescents? *Adolescence, 34*(135), 493–501.

Miller, D. L., & Moore, C. D. (1979). The Native American family: The urban way. In E. Corfman (Ed.), *Families today: A research sampler on families and children* (pp. 441–484). Washington, DC: Government Printing Office.

Min, P. G. (1998). *Changes and conflicts: Korean immigrant families in New York.* Boston: Allyn & Bacon.

Mintz, S., & Kellogg, S. (1988). *Domestic relations: A social history of American family life.* New York: Free Press.

Mitchell, J., & Register, J. C. (1984). An exploration of family interaction with elderly by race, socioeconomic status and residence. *The Gerontologist, 24,* 48–54.

Montgomery, R. J. V., & Kamo, Y. (1989). Parent care by sons and daughters. In J. A. Mancini (Ed.), *Aging parents and adult children* (pp. 213–230). Lexington, MA: Lexington Books.

Mor, V., Zinn, J., Angelelli, J., Teno, J. M., & Miller, S. C. (2004). Driven to tiers: Socioeconomic and racial disparities in the quality of nursing home care [Electronic version]. *The Milbank Quarterly, 82*(2). Retrieved from http://www.milbank.org/quarterly/8202feat.html

Morrill, D. (2003). Marriage enrichment programs: How to save a marriage. *Wisconsin Women, 6*(3), 16–17.

Mott, F. L., & Marsiglio, W. (1985). Early childbearing and completion of high school. *Family Planning Perspectives, 17,* 234–237.

Mui, A. C. (1992). Caregiver strain among Black and White daughter caregivers: A role theory perspective. *The Gerontologist, 32,* 203–212.

Muller, T., & Espenshade, T. (1985). *The fourth wave: California's newest immigrants.* Washington, DC: Urban Institute Press.

Munger, R. G. (1987). Sudden death in sleep of Laotian-Hmong refugees in Thailand: A case-control study. *American Journal of Public Health, 77*(9), 1187–1190.

Murdock, G. P. (1949). *Social structure.* New York: Macmillan.

Murdock, G. P. (1967). Ethnographic atlas: A summary. *Ethnology, 6*(April), 109–236.

Murray, C. I., & Kimura, N. (2003). Multiplicity of paths to couple formation in Japan. In R. R. Hamon & B. B. Ingoldsby (Eds.), *Mate selection across cultures* (pp. 247–268). Thousand Oaks, CA: Sage.

Nagata, D. K., & Cheng, W. J. Y. (2003). Intergenerational communication of race-related trauma by Japanese American former internees. *American Journal of Orthopsychiatry, 73*(3), 266–278.

Nagata, D. K., Trierweiler, S. J., & Talbort, R. (1999). Long-term effects of internment during early childhood on third-generation Japanese Americans. *American Journal of Orthopsychiatry, 69,* 19–29.

National Adoption Information Clearinghouse. (2004). *Statistics on transracial adoption* [Electronic version]. Retrieved from http://statistics.adoption.com/transracial_adoption.php

Negy, C., & Snyder, D. K. (2000). Relationship satisfaction of Mexican American and non-Hispanic White American interethnic couples: Issues of acculturation and clinical intervention. *Journal of Marital and Family Therapy, 26*(3), 293–304.

Newman, B. S., & Muzzonigro, P. G. (1993). The effects of traditional family values on the coming out process of gay male adolescents. *Adolescence, 28*(109), 213–226.

Newman, D. M. (2002). *Exploring the architecture of everyday life* (4th ed.). Thousand Oaks, CA: Pine Forge Press.

New York Academy of Medicine. (2003). *Involuntary sterilization the focus of the academy's Lilianna Sauter lecture* [Electronic press release]. Retrieved May 18, 2004, from http://www.nyam.org/news/1141.html

Ng, F. (1998). *The Taiwanese Americans.* Westport, CT: Greenwood.

Norton, A. J., & Miller, L. F. (1992). *Marriage, divorce, and remarriage in the 1990's* [Electronic version]. Retrieved from the U.S. Department of Commerce, U.S. Census Bureau, Current Population Reports, at http://www.census.gov/population/socdemo/marr-div/p23-180/p23-180/pdf

Ogunwole, S. U. (2002). *The American Indian and Alaskan Native population: 2000* [Electronic version]. Retrieved from the U.S. Department of Commerce, U.S. Census Bureau at http://www.census.gov/prod/2002pubs/c2kbr01-15.pdf

Oliver, M. L., & Shapiro, T. M. (1999). Black wealth/White wealth: A new perspective on racial inequality. In S. J. Ferguson (Ed.), *Mapping the social landscape: Readings in sociology* (2nd ed., pp. 274–287). Mountain View, CA: Mayfield.

Oropesa, R. S. (1997). Development and marital power in Mexico. *Social Forces, 75*(June), 1291–1317.

Ortiz, S. (1993). The language we know. In P. Riley (Ed.), *Growing up Native American* (pp. 29–38) New York: Avon.

Osterweil, Z., & Nagano, K. N. (1991). Maternal views on autonomy: Japan and Israel. *Journal of Cross-Cultural Psychology, 22*, 362–375.

Oyserman, D., Kemmelmeier, M., Fryberg, S., Brosh, H., & Hart-Johnson, T. (2003). Racial-ethnic self schemas. *Social Psychology Quarterly, 66*, 333–347.

Pabon, E. (1998). Hispanic adolescent delinquency and the family: A discussion of sociocultural influences. *Adolescence, 33*(132), 941–955.

Panzarine, S. (1988). Teen mothering: Behaviors and interventions. *Journal of Adolescent Heath Care, 9*(5), 443–448.

Parrillo, V. N. (2003). *Strangers to these shores* (7th ed.). Boston: Allyn & Bacon.

Pearson, J. L., Hunter, A. G., Cook, J. M., Ialongo, N. S., & Kellam, S. G. (1997). Grandmother involvement in child caregiving in an urban community. *The Gerontologist, 37*(5), 650–657.

Perez, L. (1994). The household structure of second-generation children: An exploratory study of extended family arrangements. *International Migration Review, 28*(4), 736–747.

Perez-Firmat, G. (1995). *Next year in Cuba: A Cubano's coming-of-age in America.* New York: Anchor.

Perry, C. (1999). Extended family support among older Black females. In R. Staples (Ed.), *The Black family: Essays and studies* (pp. 70–76). Belmont, CA: Wadsworth.

Perry, H. L. (1993). Mourning and funeral customs of African Americans. In D. P. Irish, K. F. Lundquist, & V. J. Nelsen (Eds.), *Ethnic variations in dying, death, and grief: Diversity in universality* (pp. 51–65). Washington, DC: Taylor & Francis.

Pessar, P. R. (2002). Grappling with changing gender roles in Dominican American families. In Benokraitis, N. V. (Ed.), *Contemporary ethnic families in the United States: Characteristics, variations, and dynamics* (pp. 66–71). Upper Saddle River, NJ: Prentice Hall.

Peters, M. F. (1985). Racial socialization of young Black children. In H. P. McAdoo & J. L. McAdoo (Eds.), *Black children: Social, educational, and parental environments* (pp. 159–173). Beverly Hills, CA: Sage.

Petersen, W. (1978). Chinese Americans and Japanese Americans. In T. Sowell (Ed.), *Essays and data on American ethnic groups* (pp. 65–106). Washington, DC: Urban Institute Press.

Peterson, J. T. (1993). Generalized extended family exchange: A case from the Philippines. *Journal of Marriage and Family, 55,* 570–587.

Phinney, J. S., & Chavira, V. (1995). Parental ethnic socialization and adolescent coping with problems related to ethnicity. *Journal of Research on Adolescence, 5,* 31–54.

Phua, V. C., Kaufman, G., & Park, K. S. (2001). Strategic adjustments of elderly Asian Americans: Living arrangements and headship. *Journal of Comparative Family Studies, 32*(2), 263–281.

Picot, S. J. (1995). Rewards, costs, and coping of African American caregivers. *Nursing Research, 44,* 147–153.

Pidcock, B. W., Fischer, J. L., & Munsch, J. (2001). Family, personality, and social risk factors impacting the retention rates of first-year Hispanic and Anglo college students. *Adolescence, 36*(144), 803–818.

Pleck, E. H. (2000). *Celebrating the family: Ethnicity, consumer culture, and family rituals.* Cambridge, MA: Harvard University Press.

Pleck, J. H., Sonenstein, F. L., & Ku, L. C. (1993). Masculinity ideology: Its impact on adolescent males' heterosexual relationships. *Journal of Social Issues, 49*(3), 11–29.

Portes, A., & Bach, R. L. (1985). *Latin journey: Cuban and Mexican immigrants in the United States.* Berkeley: University of California Press.

Posadas, B. M. (1981). Crossed boundaries in interracial Chicago: Pilipino American families since 1925. *Amerasia, 8,* 31–52.

Purdy, J. K., & Arguello, D. (1992). Hispanic familism in caretaking of older adults: Is it functional? *Journal of Gerontological Social Work, 19,* 29–43.

Pyke, K. (2004). Immigrant families in the United States. In J. Scott, J. Treas, & M. Richards (Eds.), *The Blackwell companion to the sociology of families* (pp. 253–269). Carlton, VIC, Australia: Blackwell.

Qian, Z. (1999). Who intermarries? Education, nativity, region, and interracial marriage, 1980 and 1990. *Journal of Comparative Family Studies, 30*(4), 579–597.

Queen, S., Haberstein, R., & Quadagno, J. (1985). *The family in various cultures.* New York: Harper & Row.

Ramirez, R. R., & de la Cruz, G. P. (2003). *The Hispanic population in the United States: March 2002* [Electronic version]. Retrieved from the U.S. Department of Commerce, U.S. Census Bureau, Current Populations Reports at http://www.census.gov/prod/2003pubs/p20-545.pdf

Rasche, C. (1988). Minority women and domestic violence: The unique dilemmas of battered women of color. *Journal of Contemporary Criminal Justice, 4*(3), 150–171.

Red Horse, J. G. (1980). American-Indian elders: Unifiers of Indian families. *Social Casework, 61*(8), 490–493.

Red Horse, J. G. (1988). Cultural evolution of American Indian families. In C. Jacobs & D. D. Boweless (Eds.), *Ethnicity and race: Critical concepts in social work* (pp. 86–102). Silver Spring, MD: National Association of Social Workers.

Rennison, C. M., & Welchans, S. (2000). *Intimate partner violence* [Electronic version]. Retrieved from the U.S. Department of Justice, Bureau of Justice Statistics Special Report at http://www.ojp.usdoj.gov/bjs/pub/pdf/ipv.pdf

Renzetti, C. M., & Curran, D. J. (2003). *Women, men, and society* (5th ed.). Boston: Allyn & Bacon.

Repak, T. A. (2002). Central American workers: New roles in a new landscape. In N. V. Benokraitis (Ed.), *Contemporary ethnic families in the United States: Characteristics, variations, and dynamics* (pp. 205–211). Upper Saddle River, NJ: Prentice Hall.

Rindfuss, R. R., Liao, T. F., & Tsuya, N. O. (1992). Contact with parents in Japan: Effects on opinions toward gender and intergenerational roles. *Journal of Marriage and Family, 54*(November), 812–822.

Rivera, F., Sweeney, P., & Henderson, B. (1986). Black teenage fathers: What happens when the child is born? *Pediatrics, 78*(1), 151–158.

Roberts, D. (2001). *Shattered bonds: The color of child welfare.* New York: Perseus.

Rodgers-Farmer, A. Y., & Jones, R. L. (1999). Grandmothers who are caregivers: An overlooked population. *Child and Adolescent Social Work Journal, 16*(December), 455–466.

Roldan, M. (1988). Renegotiating the marital contract: Intrahousehold patterns of money allocation and women's subordination among domestic outworkers in Mexico City. In D. Dwyer & J. Bruce (Eds.), *A home divided: Women and income in the Third World* (pp. 229–247). Palo Alto, CA: Stanford University Press.

Roschelle, A. R. (1997). *No more kin: Exploring race, class, and gender in family networks.* Thousand Oaks, CA: Sage.

Rossi, A. S., & Rossi, P. H. (1990). *Of human bonding: Parent-child relations across the life course.* New York: Aldine de Gruyter.

Rubin, L. (1993). *Families on the faultline.* New York: HarperCollins.

Rucibwa, N. K., Modeste, N., Montgomery, S., & Fox, C. A. (2003). Exploring family factors and sexual behaviors in a group of Black and Hispanic adolescent males. *American Journal of Health Behavior, 27*(1), 63–74.

Ruggles, S. (1994). The origins of African-American family structure. *American Sociological Review, 59*(February), 136–151.

Ryan, R. A. (1981). Strengths of the American Indian family: State of the art. In J. Red Horse, A. Shattuck, & F. Hoffman (Eds.), *The American Indian family: Strengths and stresses* (pp. 25–43). Isleta, NM: American Indian Social Research and Development Associates.

Sado, S., & Bayer, A. (2001). *Executive summary: The changing American family* [Electronic version]. Retrieved April 20, 2004, from the Population Resource Center at http://www.prcdc.org/summaries/family/family.html

Sailer, S. (2003). *Interracial marriage gender gap grows* [Electronic version]. Retrieved July 29, 2004 from United Press International at http://www.upi.com/view.cfm?StoryID=20030314–091022–8657r

Salas-Provance, M. B., Erickson, J. G., & Reed, J. (2002). Disabilities as viewed by four generations of one Hispanic family. *American Journal of Speech-Language Pathology, 11*(2), 151–162.

Sanchez-Ayendez, M. (1991). *Puerto Rican older adults: Realities and needs.* Paper presented at a symposium entitled "A People in Two Communities" (Sponsored by the National Puerto Rican Coalition, the Puerto Rico Community Foundation, and the Office of Civil Rights of the U.S. Department of Health & Human Services). Washington, DC: Government Printing Office.

Sanchez-Ayendez, M. (1998). The Puerto Rican family. In C. H. Mindel, R. W. Haberstein, & R. Wright, Jr. (Eds.), *Ethnic families in America: Patterns and variations* (pp. 199–222). Upper Saddle River, NJ: Prentice Hall.

Sanders-Thompson, V. L. (1994). Socialization to race and its relationship to racial identification among African Americans. *Journal of Black Psychology, 20,* 175–188.

Santiago, E. (1993). *When I was Puerto Rican.* New York: Random House.

Schaefer, R. T. (2004). *Racial and ethnic groups* (9th ed.). Upper Saddle River, NJ: Prentice Hall.

Schick, E., & Schick, R. (1991). *Statistical handbook on U.S. Hispanics.* Phoenix, AZ: Oryx Press.

Schoen, R. (1995). The widening gap between Black and White marriage rates: Context and implications. In M. B. Tucker & C. Mitchell-Kernan (Eds.), *The decline in marriage among African Americans: Causes, consequences, and policy implications* (pp. 103–116). New York: Russell Sage.

Schvaneveldt, P. L. (2003). Mate selection preferences and practices in Ecuador and Latin America. In R. R. Hamon & B. B. Ingoldsby (Eds.), *Mate selection across cultures* (pp. 43–59). Thousand Oaks, CA: Sage.

Schwartz, M. A., & Scott, B. M. (2003). *Marriages and families: Diversity and change* (4th ed.). Upper Saddle River, NJ: Prentice Hall.

Scott, J. W. (1999). From teenage parenthood to polygamy: Case studies in Black polygamous family formation. In R. Staples (Ed.), *The Black family: Essays and studies* (pp. 339–348). Belmont, CA: Wadsworth.

Seelbach, W. C. (1981). Filial responsibility among aged parents: A racial comparison. *Journal of Minority Aging, 5,* 286–292.

Segal, U. A. (1998). The Asian Indian–American family. In C. H. Mindel, R. W. Haberstein, & R. Wright, Jr. (Eds.), *Ethnic families in America: Patterns and variations* (4th ed., pp. 331–360). Upper Saddle River, NJ: Prentice Hall.

Seligman, M., & Darling, R. B. (1997). *Ordinary families, special children: A systems approach to childhood disability* (2nd ed.). New York: Guilford.

Seltzer, J. (1991). Relationships between fathers and children who live apart: The father's role after separation. *Journal of Marriage and Family, 53*(February), 79–101.

Serwer, A. E. (1993, April 19). American Indians discover money is power. *Fortune,* pp. 136–142.

Shelton, B. A., & John, D. (1993). Ethnicity, race, and difference: A comparison of White, Black, and Hispanic men's household labor time. In J. C. Hood (Ed.), *Men, work and family* (pp. 131–150). Newbury Park, CA: Sage.

Shin, E. H. (1987). Interracially married Korean women in the United States: An analysis based on hypergamy-exchange theory. In E. Y. Yu & E. H. Phillips (Eds.), *Korean women in transition: At home and abroad* (pp. 249–274). Los Angeles: California State University, Center for Korean-American and Korean Studies.

Shkilnyk, A. M. (1985). *A poison stronger than love: The destruction of an Ojibwa community.* New Haven, CT: Yale University Press.

Shomaker, D. M. (1990). Health care, cultural expectation and frail elderly Navajo grandmothers. *Journal of Cross-Cultural Gerontology, 4,* 1–18.

Silva, J. S. (1995). Mexican-American women: Death and dying. In J. K. Parry & A. S. Ryan (Eds.), *A cross-cultural look at death, dying, and religion* (pp. 102–116). Chicago: Nelson-Hall.

Silverstein, M., & Marenco, A. (2001). How Americans enact the grandparent role across the family life course. *Journal of Family Issues, 22*(4), 493–522.

Silverstein, M., & Parrott, T. M. (1997). Attitudes toward public support of the elderly: Does early involvement with grandparents moderate generational tensions? *Research on Aging, 19,* 108–132.

Simmons, T., & Dye, J. L. (2003). *Grandparents living with grandchildren: 2000* (U.S. Department of Commerce, U.S. Census Bureau, Census 2000 Brief). Washington, DC: Government Printing Office.

Simmons, T., & O'Connell, M. (2003). *Married-couple and unmarried-partner households: 2000* (U.S. Department of Commerce, U.S. Census Bureau, Census 2000 Special Reports). Washington, DC: Government Printing Office.

Simmons, T., & O'Neill, G. (2001). *Households and families: 2000* (U.S. Department of Commerce, U.S. Census Bureau, Census 2000 Brief). Washington, DC: Government Printing Office. Electronic version available at http://www.census.gov/prod/2003pubs/c2kbr-31.pdf

Simon, R. J. (1995). Transracial adoptions: In the children's best interests. *Black Issues in Higher Education, 12*(5), 36–38.

Skolnick, A. (1991). *Embattled paradise: The American family in an age of uncertainty.* New York: Basic Books.

Smith, D. (2001). Romance, parenthood, and gender in a modern African society. *Ethnology, 40,* 129–151.

Smith, M. D. (1990). Sociodemographic risk factors in wife abuse: Results from a survey of Toronto women. *Canadian Journal of Sociology, 15,* 39–58.

Smith, N. (2003). *American empire: Roosevelt's geographer and the prelude to globalization.* Berkeley: University of California Press.

Sonuga-Barke, E. J. S., & Mistry, M. (2000). The effect of extended family living on the mental health of three generations within two Asian communities. *The British Journal of Clinical Psychology, 39*(2), 129–141.

Sorensen, P. (1996). Commercialization of food crops in Busoga, Uganda, and the renegotiation of gender. *Gender & Society, 10*(5), 608–628.

Sotomayor, M., & Curiel, H. (Eds.). (1988). *Hispanic elderly: A cultural signature.* Edinburg, TX: Pan American University Press.

South, S. J. (1993). Racial and ethnic differences in the desire to marry. *Journal of Marriage and Family, 55*(2), 357–370.

Speare, A., & Avery, R. (1993). Who helps whom in older parent-child families. *Journals of Gerontology, Series B: Psychological Sciences and Social Sciences, 48B*(2), S64–S73.

Spencer, M. B. (1983). Children's cultural values and parental child rearing strategies. *Developmental Review, 3,* 351–370.

Stack, C. B. (1974). *All our kin.* New York: Harper & Row.

Stanton, M. E. (1995). Patterns of kinship and residence. In B. B. Ingoldsby & S. Smith (Eds.), *Families in multicultural perspective* (pp. 97–116). New York: Guilford.

Staples, R. (1985). Changes in Black family structure: The conflict between family ideology and structural conditions. *Journal of Marriage and Family, 53,* 221–230.

Staples, R. (1989). Masculinity and race: The dual dilemma of Black men. In M. Kimmel & M. Messner (Eds.), *Men's lives* (pp. 73–83). New York: Macmillan.

Steckel, R. H. (1986). A peculiar population. *Journal of Economic History, 46*(September), 721–741.

Stepick, A. (1998). *Pride against prejudice: Haitians in the United States.* Boston: Allyn & Bacon.

Stets, J. E. (1991). Cohabiting and marital aggression: The role of social isolation. *Journal of Marriage and Family, 53, 669–680.*

Stevenson, B. E. (1995). Black family structure in colonial and antebellum Virginia: Amending the revisionist perspective. In M. B. Tucker & C. Mitchell-Kernan (Eds.), *The decline in marriage among African Americans: Causes, consequences and policy implications* (pp. 27–56). New York: Russell Sage.

Stevenson, H. C., Jr. (1994). Validation of the scale for racial socialization of Black adolescents: Steps toward multidimensionality. *Journal of Black Psychology, 20*(4), 445–468.

Stier, H., & Tienda, M. (1993). Are men marginal to the family? Insights from Chicago's inner city. In J. C. Hood (Ed.), *Men, work, and family* (pp. 23–44). Newbury Park, CA: Sage.

Stockard, J. E. (2002). *Marriage in culture: Practice and meaning across diverse societies*. New York: Harcourt College.

Stoller, E. P. (1990). Males as helpers: The role of sons, relatives, and friends. *The Gerontologist, 30,* 228–235.

Straus, M. A., Gelles, R. J., & Steinmetz, S. K. (1980). *Behind closed doors: Violence in the American family*. Beverly Hills, CA: Sage.

Striegel-Moore, R. H., Dohm, F. A., Kraemer, H. C., Taylor, C. B., Daniels, S., Crawford, P. B., et al. (2003). Eating disorders in White and Black women. *American Journal of Psychiatry, 160*(7), 1326–1331.

Strodtbeck, F. L. (1951). Husband-wife interaction over revealed differences. *American Sociological Review, 16,* 468–473.

Stuart, P. (1987). *Nations within a nation: Historical statistics of American Indians*. New York: Greenwood.

Suarez, Z. (1998). The Cuban-American family. In C. H. Mindel, R. W. Haberstein, & R. Wright, Jr. (Eds.), *Ethnic families in America: Patterns and variations* (pp. 172–198). Upper Saddle River, NJ: Prentice Hall.

Sue, D. W. (1981). *Counseling the culturally different*. New York: Wiley.

Sung, B. L. (1967). *Mountain of gold*. New York: Macmillan.

Sung, K. (1990). A new look at filial piety: Ideal and practices of family-centered parent care in Korea. *The Gerontologist, 30*(5): 610–616.

Suro, R. (1998). *Strangers among us: How Latino immigration is transforming America*. New York: Knopf.

Suro, R. (1999). Mixed doubles. *American Demographics, 21*(11), 56–62.

Swisher, K. (1991). *American Indian/Alaskan Native learning styles: Research and practice* [Electronic version]. Retrieved from ERIC Digests at http://www.ericdigests.org/pre-9220/indian.htm

Szapocznik, J., Kurtines, W. M., & Fernandez, T. (1980). Bicultural involvement and adjustment in Hispanic American youths. *Journal of Intercultural Relations, 4,* 353–365.

Takyi, B. K. (2003). Tradition and change in family and marital processes. In R. R. Hamon & B. B. Ingoldsby (Eds.), *Mate selection across cultures* (pp. 79–94). Thousand Oaks, CA: Sage.

Tanner, J. G. (1995). Death, dying, and grief in the Chinese-American culture. In J. K. Parry & A. S. Ryan (Eds.), *A cross-cultural look at death, dying, and religion* (pp. 183–192). Chicago: Nelson-Hall.

Taylor, R. J., Chatters, L. M., & Jackson, J. S. (1993). A profile of familial relations among 3-generation Black families. *Family Relations, 42,* 332–341.

Taylor, R. J., Chatters, L. M., Tucker, M., & Lewis, E. (1990). Developments in research on Black families: A decade review. *Journal of Marriage and Family, 53,* 993–1014.

Tepperman, L., & Wilson, S. J. (1993). *Next of kin: An international reader on changing families*. Englewood Cliffs, NJ: Prentice Hall.

Thomas, E., Rickel, A. U., Butler, C., & Montgomery, E. (1990). Adolescent pregnancy and parenting. *Journal of Primary Prevention, 10,* 195–206.

Thomas, T. N. (1995). Acculturative stress in the adjustment of immigrant families. *Journal of Social Distress and the Homeless, 4*(2), 131–142.

Thompson, B. W. (1992). "A way outa no way": Eating problems among African American, Latina, and White women. *Gender & Society, 6*(4), 546–561.

Thornton, M. C., Chatters, L. M., Taylor, R. J., & Allen, W. R. (1990). Sociodemographic and environmental correlates of racial socialization by Black parents. *Child Development, 61,* 401–409.

Thornton, Y. S. (as told to Couderet, J.) (1995). *The ditchdigger's daughters: A Black family's astonishing success story.* New York: Penguin.

Thrupkaew, N. (2002). The myth of the model minority. *American Prospect, 13*(7), 38–41.

Tilles, M. C. (1995, May 23). Biracial designation: Will it mean further loss of power for Blacks? *Michigan Chronicle, 58*(34), p. 1A.

Timm, J. T. (1992). Hmong values and American education. *Forward: Wisconsin Journal for Supervision and Curriculum Development, 16*(2), 1–11.

Ting, K. F., & Chiu, S. W. K. (2002). Leaving the parental home: Chinese culture in an urban context. *Journal of Marriage and Family, 64*(3), 614–626.

Tjaden, P., & Thoennes, N. (2000). *Extent, nature, and consequences of intimate partner violence* [Research report; Electronic version]. Washington, DC: National Institute of Justice and the Centers for Disease Control and Prevention. Retrieved from http://www.ncjrs.org/pdffiles1/nij/181867.pdf

Toro-Morn, M. I. (2002). Puerto Rican migrants: Juggling family and work roles. In N. V. Benokraitis (Ed.), *Contemporary ethnic families in the United States: Characteristics, variations, and dynamics* (pp. 232–239). Upper Saddle River, NJ: Prentice Hall.

Toth, J. F., Jr., & Xu, X. (2002). Father's child-rearing involvement in African American, Latino, and White families. In N. V. Benokraitis (Ed.), *Contemporary ethnic families in the United States: Characteristics, variations and dynamics* (pp. 130–140). Upper Saddle River, NJ: Prentice Hall.

Tran, T. V. (1998). The Vietnamese-American family. In C. H. Mindel, R. W. Haberstein, & R. Wright, Jr. (Eds.), *Ethnic families in America: Patterns and variations* (pp. 254–283). Upper Saddle River, NJ: Prentice Hall.

Trent, K., & Harlan, S. L. (1994). Teenage mothers in nuclear and extended households: Differences by marital status and race/ethnicity. *Journal of Family Issues, 15*(2), 309–337.

Tripp, R. (1981). Farmers and traders: Some economic determinants of nutritional status in Northern Ghana. *Journal of Tropical Pediatrics, 27,* 15–22.

Troester, R. R. (1984). Turbulence and tenderness: Mothers, daughters, and "othermothers" in Paule Marshall's *Brown girls, brownstones.* In P. Bell-Scott, B. Guy-Sheftall, J. J. Royster, J. Sims-Wood, M. Decosta-Willis, & L. Fultz (Eds.), *Double stitch: Black women write about mothers and daughters* (pp. 163–172). Boston: Beacon.

Truitner, K., & Truitner, N. (1993). Death and dying in Buddhism. In D. P. Irish, K. F. Lundquist, & V. J. Nelsen (Eds.), *Ethnic variations in dying, death, and grief: Diversity in universality* (pp. 125–136). Washington, DC: Taylor & Francis.

Tseng, V., & Fuligni, A. J. (2000). Parent-adolescent language use and relationships among immigrant families with East Asian, Filipino, and Latin American backgrounds. *Journal of Marriage and Family, 62*(May), 465–476.

Tucker, B., & Taylor R. J. (1989). Demographic correlates of relationship status among Black Americans. *Journal of Marriage and Family, 51*, 655–665.

Tucker, M. B., & Mitchell-Kernan, C. (1990). New trends in Black American interracial marriage: The social structural context. *Journal of Marriage and Family, 52*(1), 209–218.

Tyler, S. L. (1973). *A history of Indian policy* (U.S. Department of the Interior, Bureau of Indian Affairs). Washington, DC: Government Printing Office.

Uchitelle, L. (2003, July 12). Blacks lose better jobs faster as middle-class work drops. *The New York Times*, p. A1.

Ukaegbu, A. O. (1993). Socio-cultural influence on fertility in rural eastern Nigeria. In L. Tepperman & S. J. Wilson (Eds.), *Next of kin: An international reader on changing families* (pp. 118–122). Englewood Cliffs, NJ: Prentice Hall.

United for a Fair Economy. (2004, January/February). Wealth inequality by the numbers [Electronic version]. *Dollars and Sense*. Retrieved from http://www.dollarsandsense.org/archives/2004/0104inequality.pdf

Upchurch, D. M., Levy-Storms, L., Sucoff, C. A., & Aneshensel, C. S. (1998). Gender and ethnic differences in the timing of first sexual intercourse. *Family Planning Perspectives, 30*(3), 121–127.

U.S. Department of Commerce, U.S. Census Bureau. (n.d.). *Sociological comparisons between African Americans and Whites* [Electronic version]. Retrieved from http://www.runet.edu/~junnever/bw.htm

U.S. Department of Commerce, U.S. Census Bureau. (2000a). *Age groups and sex: 2000*. [Electronic version]. Retrieved from Census 2000 Summary File 2 (SF-2) 100-Percent Data at http://factfinder.census.gov/servlet/DatasetMainPageServlet?_program=DEC&_lang=en&_ts=

U.S. Department of Commerce, U.S. Census Bureau. (2000b). *Census 2000 data on aging* [Electronic version]. Available from the U.S. Administration on Aging at http://www.aoa.gov/prof/Statistics/Census2000/minority-sumstats.asp

U.S. Department of Commerce, U.S. Census Bureau. (2000c). *Current population survey* [Electronic version]. Retrieved from the Ethnic and Hispanic Statistics Branch, Population Division at http://www.census.gov/population/socdemo/hispanic/p20-535/sumtab01.pdf

U.S. Department of Commerce, U.S. Census Bureau. (2000d). *Households and families: 2000*. [Electronic version]. Available from Census 2000 Summary File 2 (SF-2) QT-P10 at http://factfinder.census.gov

U.S. Department of Commerce, U.S. Census Bureau. (2000e). *Identifying need: Poverty 2000* [Electronic version]. Retrieved from http://www.census.gov/population/www/pop-profile/profile2000.html

U.S. Department of Commerce, U.S. Census Bureau. (2000f). *Multigenerational households for the United States and for Puerto Rico, 2000* [Electronic version]. Retrieved from http://www.census.gov/population/www/cen2000/phc-t17.html

U.S. Department of Commerce, U.S. Census Bureau. (2000g). *Profile of general demographic characteristics: 2000* (DP-1). [Electronic version]. Available from Summary File 2 (SF-2) 100-Percent Data at http://www.factfinder.census. gov

U.S. Department of Commerce, U.S. Census Bureau. (2000h). *Profile of selected economic characteristics: 2000* (DP-3), QT-P1. [Electronic version]. Available from Summary File 4 (SF-4) Sample Data at http://www.factfinder.census.gov

U.S. Department of Commerce, U.S. Census Bureau. (2000i). *Profile of selected social characteristics: 2000* (DP-2). [Electronic version]. Available from Summary File 4 (SF-4) Sample Data at http://www.factfinder.census.gov

U.S. Department of Commerce, U.S. Census Bureau. (2001a). *The American Indian population: 2000: Percentage of population for one or more races* [Electronic version]. Available from http://www.census.gov

U.S. Department of Commerce, U.S. Census Bureau. (2001b). *The older population in the United States: March 2000* [Electronic version]. Available from the Current Population Survey, March 2000, Special Populations Branch, Population Division at http://www.aoa.gov

U.S. Department of Commerce, U.S. Census Bureau. (2001c). *Statistical abstract of the United States* [Electronic version]. Retrieved from http://www.census.gov/prod/www/statistical-abstract-04.html

U.S. Department of Commerce, U.S. Census Bureau. (2002a). *Current population survey* [Electronic version]. Available from the Ethnic and Hispanic Statistics Branch, Population Division at http://www.census.gov/population/socdemo/hispanic/ppl-171/tab20.1pdf

U.S. Department of Commerce, U.S. Census Bureau. (2002b). *Current population survey* [Electronic version]. Available from the Racial Statistics Branch, Population Division at http://www.census.gov/ Retrieved from http://www.census.gov/population/www/socdemo/race/black/ppl-164/tab21.pdf and http://www.census.gov/population/www/socdemo/race/api/ppl-163/tab22.xls

U.S. Department of Commerce, U.S. Census Bureau. (2002c). *Median household income* (in 2002 inflation-adjusted dollars) [Electronic version]. Retrieved from http://www.census.gov/acs/www/Products/Ranking/2002/R07T040.htm

U.S. Department of Commerce, U.S. Census Bureau. (2003a). *Household relationship and living arrangements of children under 18 years, by age, sex, race, Hispanic origin, and metropolitan residence: March 2002* [Electronic version]. Retrieved from http://www.census.gov/population/socdemo/hh-fam/cps2002/tabC2-api.pdf

U.S. Department of Commerce, U.S. Census Bureau. (2003b). *Projected life expectancy at birth by race and Hispanic origin, 1999 to 2100* [Electronic version]. Retrieved from http://www.census.gov/population/documentation/twps0038/tabC.txt

U.S. Department of Commerce, U.S. Census Bureau. (2003c). *Statistical abstract of the United States* [Electronic version]. Retrieved from http://www.census.gov/prod/www/statistical-abstract-us.html

U.S. Department of Commerce, U.S. Census Bureau. (2003d). *Young adults living at home, 1960–2002* [Electronic version]. Retrieved from http://www.infoplease.com/ipa/A0193723.html

U.S. Department of Commerce, U.S. Census Bureau. (2004). *Historical income tables: Families* [Electronic version]. Retrieved from http://www.census.gov/hhes/income/histinc/f02d.html and http://www.census.gov/hhes/income/ histinc/f02b.html

U.S. Department of Health and Human Services. (n.d.), *At a glance: Suicide among diverse populations* [Electronic version]. Retrieved from the National Strategy for Suicide Prevention at http://www.mentalhealth.samhsa.gov/suicideprevention/diverse.asp

U.S. Department of Health and Human Services, Administration for Children and Families. (2004). *Child maltreatment 2002* [Electronic version]. Retrieved from http://www.acf.hhs.gov/programs/cb/publications/cm02/cm02.pdf

U.S. Department of Health and Human Services, Centers for Disease Control and Prevention, National Center for Health Statistics. (1988). *Vital statistics of the United States, 1984: Vol. III. Marriage and divorce* [Electronic version]. Retrieved from http://www.cdc.gov/search.do?action=search&queryText=Vital+statistics+of+the+United+States%2C+1984

U.S. Department of Health and Human Services, Centers for Disease Control and Prevention, National Center for Health Statistics. (1993). *Morbidity and mortality weekly report 23*(20). Washington, DC: Government Printing Office.

U.S. Department of Health and Human Services, Centers for Disease Control and Prevention, National Center for Health Statistics. (2001). *National linked files of live births and infant deaths* [Data file]. Retrieved from http://www.childstats.gov/ac2004/tables/Health6.asp

U.S. Department of Health and Human Services, Centers for Disease Control and Prevention, National Center for Health Statistics. (2003). *Marriage and divorce* [Data file]. Retrieved from http://www.cdc.gov/nchs/fastats/divorce.htm

U.S. Department of Health and Human Services, Centers for Disease Control and Prevention, National Center for Health Statistics. (2004). *2002 natality data set* [Data file]. Retrieved from http://www.teenpregnancy.org/america/statisticsDisplay.asp?ID=4&sID=39

Vega, W. A. (1995). The study of Latino families: A point of departure. In. R. E. Zambrana (Ed.), *Understanding Latino families: Scholarship, policy, and practice* (pp. 3–17). Thousand Oaks, CA: Sage.

Volkman, T. (2003). Transnational adoption. *Social Text, 21,* 1–5.

Wallace, S. P., Snyder, J. L., Walker, G. K., & Ingman, S. R. (1992). Racial differences among users of long-term care: The case of adult day care. *Research on Aging, 14*(4), 471–495.

Waller, M. A., & Patterson, S. (2002). Natural helping and resilience in a Dine (Navajo) community. *Families in Society: The Journal of Contemporary Human Services, 83*(1), 73–84.

Walters, A. L. (1993). The warriors. In P. Riley (Ed.), *Growing up Native American* (pp. 39–53). New York: Avon.

Warner, R. L., Gary, R. L., & Lee, J. (1993). Spousal resources and marital power. In L. Tepperman & S. J. Wilson (Eds.), *Next of kin: An international reader on changing families* (pp. 216–219). Englewood Cliffs, NJ: Prentice Hall.

Watson, J., & Koblinsky, S. (1997). Strengths and needs of working-class African-American and Anglo-American grandparents. *International Journal of Aging and Human Development, 44,* 149–165.

Weinick, R. M. (1995, April). *Intergenerational exchange over the life course and across generations.* Paper presented at the annual meeting of the Population Association of America, San Francisco, CA.

Weitzer, R. (1996). Racial discrimination in the criminal justice system: Findings and problems in the literature. *Journal of Criminal Justice, 24,* 309–322.

Wellner, A. S. (2000). The money in the middle. *American Demographics, 22*(April), 58–64.

Wen-Shing, T., & Jing, H. (1991). *Culture and family: Problems and therapy.* New York: Haworth.

Werner, E. (1979). *Cross-cultural child development: A view from the planet Earth.* Monterey, CA: Brooks/Cole.

Westoff, C. F., Calot, G., & Foster, A. D. (1983). Teenage fertility in developed nations, 1971–1980. *Family Planning Perspectives, 15*(3), 105–110.

Whitman, D. (1997, May 5). The youth crisis. *U.S. News and World Report,* 24–27.

Wikan, U. (1988). Bereavement and loss in two Muslim communities: Egypt and Bali compared. *Social Science and Medicine, 27,* 451–460.

Wilkinson, H. (1995). Psycholegal process and issues in international adoption. *Family Law Issues in Family Therapy Practice, 23,* 173–183.

Williams, D. R., Yu, Y., Jackson, J. S., & Anderson, N. B. (1997). Racial differences in physical and mental health. *Journal of Health Psychology, 2,* 335–351.

Williams, G. H. (1995). *Life on the color line: The true story of a White boy who discovered he was Black.* New York: Penguin.

Williams, H. A. (1993). Families in refugee camps. In L. Tepperman & S. J. Wilson (Eds.), *Next of kin: An international reader on changing families* (pp. 250–255). Englewood Cliffs, NJ: Prentice Hall.

Williamson, J. (1995). *New people: Miscegenation and mulattoes in the United States.* Baton Rouge: Louisiana State University Press.

Wilson, S. M., Ngige, L. W., & Trollinger, L. J. (2003). Connecting generations: Kamba and Maasai paths to marriage in Kenya. In R. R. Hamon & B. B. Ingoldsby (Eds.), *Mate selection across cultures* (pp. 95–118). Thousand Oaks, CA: Sage.

Wilt, S., & Olson, S. (1996). Prevalence of domestic violence in the United States [Electronic version]. *Journal of the American Medical Women's Association.* Retrieved from http://www.jamwa.org/index.cfm?objectid=5CC90591-D567-0B25-5285BC18E99FF940

Wong, B. (1998). *Ethnicity and entrepreneurship: The new Chinese immigrants in the San Francisco Bay area*. Boston: Allyn & Bacon.

Wong, M. G. (1998). The Chinese-American family. In C. H. Mindel, R. W. Haberstein, & R. Wright, Jr. (Eds.), *Ethnic families in America: Patterns and variations* (pp. 284–310). Upper Saddle River, NJ: Prentice Hall.

Woodworth, R. S. (1996). You're not alone . . . you're one in a million. *Child Welfare, 75*(5), 619–635.

Xia, Y. R., & Zhou, Z. G. (2003). The transition of courtship, mate selection, and marriage in China. In R. R. Hamon & B. B. Ingoldsby (Eds.), *Mate selection across cultures* (pp. 231–246). Thousand Oaks, CA: Sage.

Yanagisako, S. J. (1985). *Transforming the past: Tradition and kinship among Japanese Americans*. Palo Alto, CA: Stanford University Press.

Yancey, G. (2002). Who interracially dates: An examination of the characteristics of those who have interracially dated. *Journal of Comparative Family Studies, 33*(2), 179–195.

Yellowbird, M., & Snipp, C. M. (1994). American Indian families. In R. L. Taylor (Ed.), *Minority families in the United States: A multicultural perspective* (pp. 179–201). Upper Saddle River, NJ: Prentice Hall.

Yeung, W. (1995). Buddhism, death, and dying. In J. K. Parry & A. S. Ryan (Eds.), *A cross-cultural look at death, dying, and religion* (pp. 74–83). Chicago: Nelson-Hall.

Younoszai, B. (1993). Mexican American perspectives related to death. In D. P. Irish, K. F. Lundquist, & V. J. Nelsen (Eds.), *Ethnic variations in dying, death, and grief: Diversity in universality* (pp. 67–78). Washington, DC: Taylor & Francis.

Youth gangs on rise at Indian reservations. (1997, September 18). *Baltimore Sun*, p. 6A.

Zabin, L. S., & Hayward, S. C. (1993). *Adolescent sexual behavior and childbearing*. Newbury Park, CA: Sage.

Zack, N. (1993). *Race and mixed race*. Philadelphia: Temple University Press.

Zhou, M., & Bankston, C. L., III. (1998). *Growing up American: How Vietnamese children adapt to life in the United States*. New York: Russell Sage.

Zsembik, B. A., & Bonilla, Z. (2000). Eldercare and the changing family in Puerto Rico. *Journal of Family Issues, 21*, 652–674.

AUTHOR INDEX

A
Adler, S. R., 220
Agbayani-Siewart, P., 119
Agree, E. M., 140
Aguirre, A., Jr., 235
Ahmed, A. U., 88, 90, 91
Ajrouch, K., 236
Allen, W. D., 84
Allen, W. R., 126, 127
Alvarez, R. R., Jr., 200
Amato, P. R., 120
AmeriStat, 21, 43
Anderson, K. L., 105
Anderson, N. B., 141
Anderson-Darling, C., 167
Aneshensel, C. S., 81
Angel, J. L., 67, 137
Angel, R. J., 67, 137
Angelelli, J., 141
Apospori, E., 127
Aquilino, W. S., 68
Arguello, D., 142
Astone, N. M., 80, 81
Avery, R., 139
Aytac, I. A., 144

B
Baca Zinn, M., 101, 164, 181
Bach, R. L., 77, 195
Bachu, A., 237
Baer, J., 102
Bahr, H. M., 136
Bahr, K. S., 247
Bains, T. S., 52
Baker, S. G., 176
Baldridge, D., 136, 141, 177, 185
Baldwin, A. L., 120
Baldwin, C., 120
Baluja, K. F., 235
Bankston, C. L., 94, 233
Barer, B., 138
Basit, T. N., 114
Bates, D. G., 58, 184
Baumrind, D., 119, 123
Bayer, A., 247
Bean, F. D., 64, 66, 196, 202
Becerra, R. M., 193
Bell-Scott, P., 120
Bengston, V. L., 39, 60, 138
Benokraitis, N. V., 80
Bernal, G., 91, 93, 94
Berry, E. J., 128
Berry, J. W., 232, 233, 235, 236
Biafora, F. A., 127
Bianchi, S. M., 95
Bigfoot, D. S., 148, 185
Billingsley, A., 123, 167
Binh, D. T., 126
Biu, H. N., 105
Blackwell, J. E., 243
Blackwood, E., 89
Blassingame, J. W., 158, 160
Blauner, R., 25
Blee, D. M., 100
Bliatout, B. T., 147
Blumberg, R. L., 95
Bonilla, Z., 237
Borjas, G. J., 27
Boucke, L., 115
Bowman, P. J., 127, 128

Braithwaite, R. I., 101
Bramlett, M. D., 76, 201
Bratsberg, B., 27
Brennan, M., 140
Brokenleg, M., 148, 149, 173
Broker, I., 121, 129
Broman, C. L., 100
Bronzaft, A. L., 101
Brooks-Gunn, J., 68
Brosh, H., 128
Brown, A. S., 143
Brown, L., 99
Bulcroft, K. A., 93, 100, 113
Bulcroft, R. A., 93, 100, 113
Bumiller, E., 53, 89, 95, 130
Bumpass, L., 247
Burgess, N. J., 156, 157
Burr, J. A., 139, 141, 143
Burton, L. M., 80
Burton, O. V., 160
Butler, C., 69

C
Cagney, K. A., 140
Call, K. T., 93
Calot, G., 79
Campbell, D. W., 106, 107
Cantor, M. H., 140
Carmody, D. C., 93, 114
Carr, L., 127
Carter, B. D., 142
Casper, L. M., 67, 68, 82, 139
Cauce, A. M., 100
Cazenave, N., 123
Chan, F., 143, 217, 218
Chan, S., 210, 211
Chase-Lansdale, P. L., 68
Chatters, L. M., 99, 126, 127, 142
Chavira, V., 127, 128
Cheeseman Day, J., 20
Chen, L. A., 128
Cheng, W. J. Y., 127
Cherlin, A. J., 144
Cheshire, T. C., 125
Chiu, S. W. K., 91, 94, 199
Chow, E. N.-L., 107
Christensen, E. H., 90
Chung, H., 167
Clarke, S. C., 41
Clemmons, L., 177
Cleveland, R., 16
Cofer, S., 102, 200
Cohen, P. N., 67, 73, 81, 139
Coke, M. M., 166
Cole, R. E., 120
Coles, R. L., 83, 136, 289
Colleran, K., 237
Comer, J. P., 60, 71, 120, 121, 162
Conover, K. A., 185
Cook, J. M., 67, 68
Cooley, M. L., 69
Cooney, R. S., 236
Coontz, S., 36, 39, 104
Costanzo, J. M., 235
Cotter, C., 182
Courtney, M. E., 124
Coward, R. T., 141, 142
Cox, D., 144
Crawford, P. B., 3, 160
Crawford, S. C., 160
Crimmins, E., 68
Crow Dog, M., 90, 104, 105, 129, 130, 249
Curiel, H., 142
Curran, D. J., 96

D
Dalla, L., 69
Daniels, R., 244
Daniels, S., 3
Darling, R. B., 146
Darrett, B., 37
Das Gupta, M., 94, 238
Davidson, J. R., 246
Davis, C. J., 235
Day, R. D., 122
de la Cruz, G. P., 190
Deater-Deckard, K., 123
Deer, L., 118
DeKeseredy, W. S., 107
Demos, J., 36
DeNavas-Walt, C., 16
Dickson, L., 100, 101
Dill, B. T., 157, 161
Dodge, K. A., 123
Doherty, W. J., 84

Dohm, F. A., 3
Dore, M. M., 99
Dorsey, S., 81
DuBois, W. E. B., 159, 160
Dumois, A. O., 99
Dworkin, A. G., 6
Dworkin, R. J., 6
Dwyer, J. W., 142
Dye, J. L., 145
Dyeson, T. B., 142
Dykstra, R. P., 161

E
East, P. L., 80
Ebomoyi, E., 92
Edwards, M., 89
Eid, N. S., 142
Eisenberg, A. R., 69
Eisenlohr, C. J., 235
Eitzen, D. S., 164, 181
Elder, G. H., Jr., 67, 73
Elliott, S., 198
Emery, J., 227
Erdoes, R., 118
Erickson, J. G., 146
Eshleman, J. R., 19, 28, 94, 162, 168, 244
Espenshade, T., 199
Espin, O. M., 235
Espiritu, Y. L., 103

F
Farzaneh, M., 236
Fennelly, K., 201
Fernandez, M., 243, 244, 245
Fernandez, T., 233
Fielding, W., 52
Fields, J., 39, 43, 68, 75, 77, 82, 94, 190
Fine, M., 166, 167
Finkelhor, D., 123
Fischer, J. L., 94
Flannery, R., 58, 92, 93, 182
Foeman, A., 242, 246, 247
Fong-Torres, B., 103, 131, 210, 233, 237
Ford, B. S., 125
Ford, G. M., 81
Forehand, R., 81
Foroughi, D., 236
Forrest, J. D., 79
Foster, A. D., 79
Foster, G., 60
Fowler, F., 120
Fox, C. A., 81
Franklin, D. L., 161, 162, 163, 164
Fratkin, E. M., 58, 184
Frey, W. H., 74
Fryberg, S., 128
Fu, X., 246, 247
Fuligni, A. J., 112, 238
Furstenberg, F. F., 82, 144

G
Gager, C. T., 93
Gamble, W. C., 69
Gardyn, R., 240
Garner, A., 146
Garrett, M. D., 142
Gary, R. L., 72
Gates, H. L., Jr., 148
Gelles, R. J., 107
Genovese, E., 158
Giarrusso, R., 60, 138
Gil, A. G., 127
Gilligan, C., 99
Giovannoni, I., 123
Glick, J. E., 60, 66, 69
Goldman, N., 79
Gonzales, J. L., Jr., 16, 88, 104, 157, 172, 184, 191, 192, 194, 195, 200, 210, 212, 215, 217, 225, 226, 242
Gonzalez-Mena, J., 114, 115
Goode, W., 60
Gordon, M. M., 232
Grasmuck, S., 102
Green, M. A., 157
Greenfield, P. M., 233
Greif, G. L., 82
Griswold del Castillo, R., 113, 191, 241
Guillemin, J., 183
Gurak, D. T., 237
Gutman, H. G., 158, 159, 160, 161
Guyer, J., 95

H
Haberstein, R., 59
Hachett, S., 167
Haizlip, S. T., 248
Hale-Benson, J. E., 93, 119, 124
Hamer, J., 83, 84, 157, 158, 160
Hamilton, B. E., 77, 79, 115
Hamner, T. J., 120
Hanchard, M. C., 83
Harden, B., 24
Harlan, S. L., 82
Harooytan, R. A., 39
Hart-Johnson, T., 128
Hatchett, S., 167
Hattar-Pollara, M., 119, 121, 238
Hawkins, A. J., x
Hayslip, L. L., 107, 129
Hayward, S. C., 81, 82
Heaton, T. B., 246
Heffer, R. W., 122
Henderson, B., 84
Hennessy, C. H., 142
Henshaw, S., x, 79
Herring, C., 100
Hetherington, P., 60
Hetrick, E. S., 90
Heyle, A. M., 89
Hidalgo, H. A., 90
Hill, M. E., 249
Hill, S. A., 118, 142
Hinrichsen, G. A., 142
Ho, D. Y. F., 120
Hoebel, E. A., 181
Hojat, M., 236, 237
Hollingsworth, L., 251
Holmes, R., 167
Holmstrom, D., 180, 185
Holtzman, J. D., 48, 51, 53, 122
Hondagneu-Sotelo, P., 102
Hopkins, S. W., 149
Hoppe, S. K., 96
Hortacsu, N., 53
Horwitz, A. V., 142
Hossain, Z., 104
Howard, C., 127, 128
Huang, K., 244
Hughes, D. L., 128
Human Rights Campaign, x
Hunter, A. G., 67, 68
Hunter-Gault, C., 59
Hurh, W. M., 104
Hurrell, R. M., 236
Hurst, C. E., 18
Hutchinson, R., 91

I
Ialongo, N. S., 67, 68
Ichioka, Y., 215
Ingegneri, D., 68
Ingman, S. R., 140
Ingoldsby, B. B., 36, 50, 59, 126
Irish, D. P., 146
Iverson, D., 182

J
Jackson, J., 167
Jackson, J. S., 141, 142
James-Myers, L., 166
Jarrett, R. L., 80, 100
Jimenez-Vazquez, R., 236
Jing, H., 58
Jo, M. H., 103
John, D., 100
John, R., 142, 143, 145, 172, 180, 181, 184
Johnson, C. L., 138
Johnson, C. S., 161
Johnson, D., 128
Johnson, D. J., 128
Johnston, H., 52
Jones, L. C., 130
Jones, R. L., 145
Josephy, A. M., Jr., 175
Joyce, T., x

K
Kadi, J., 233
Kaestner, R., x
Kagan, J., 114
Kamo, Y., 66, 68, 138, 139, 142
Kantor, G. K., 107
Kaufman, G., 67, 68
Kellam, S. G., 67, 68
Kelley, M. L., 120
Kellogg, S., 36, 38
Kemmelmeier, M., 128

Kendall, H., 247
Khan, A. N., 91
Kiernan, K., 44
Killian, K. D., 247
Kim, K. C., 104
Kim, U., 233
Kimmel, M., 84
Kimura, N., 60
King, V., 67, 73
Kitano, H. H. L., 214, 215, 216, 244
Kitano, K. J., 214, 215, 216
Kitson, G. C., 167
Knaefler, T. K., 216
Koblinsky, S., 144
Koebel, C. T., 66
Kohn, M., 118
Koltyk, J. A., 70, 113
Korenman, S., x
Korson, H. J., 58
Kotchick, B. A., 81
Kraemer, H. C., 3
Kreider, R. M., 42, 251
Krieder, R. M., 42
Ku, L. C., 81
Kulikoff, A., 160
Kurtines, W. M., 233

L
Laditka, J. N., 142
Laditka, S. B., 142
LaFromboise, T. D., 89, 148, 185
Laird, J., 84
Lam, M., 112
Lamanna, M. A., 93, 173, 184
Lamar, J., 128, 246
Landale, N. S., 74, 201
Landrine, H., 4
Lareau, A., 120
Larson, L. L., 52
Larzelere, R. E., 123
Laslett, P., 36
Lawson, E. J., 101
Lawson, L. V., 150
Le, Q. K., 143, 147
Lee, D., 114
Lee, G., 67, 141
Lee, J., 72
Lee, S. J., 91, 94
Lee, S. M., 243, 244, 245
Lee, Y., 144
Lempert, L. B., 166
Leonard, K., 218
Lerman, R. I., 84
Lessinger, J., 52
Levy-Storms, L., 81
Lewis, E., 99, 246
Lewis, R., 240
Liao, T. F., 90
Lichter, D. T., 74
Liem, J. H., 107
Liem, R., 107
Lin, G., 143
Lincoln, R., 79
Lipsky, D. K., 146
Littlejohn-Blake, S. M., 167
Lobo, S., 183
Logan, J. R., 143
Lomawaima, K. T., 177, 178–179
Lopez, R. A., 200
Lucas, P., 182
Lugaila, T., 75, 76, 125, 144

M
Mabry, J. B., 60, 138
MacCartney, D., 73, 81
Maccoby, E. E., 119
MacDonald, S., 125, 250
Maldonado, M., 233
Malone, N., 235
Manetta, A. A., 106
Manfra, J. A., 161
Marenco, A., 144
Margolis, M. L., 103
Markides, K. S., 67, 96, 141
Marshall, S., 127
Marsiglio, W., 81
Martin, A. D., 90
Martin, J. A., 77, 78, 79, 115, 119
Martin, P., 28
Martin, T. C., 235, 247
Masaki, B., 106, 107
Matthews, S. H., 142
McAdoo, H. P., 157, 167, 168
McCracken, C., 122
McCreary, M. L., 128
McDade, K., 122

McDonald, T. E., 125
McGarry, K., 144
McInnis, K., 70, 114, 150
McKenry, P. A., 167
McKenry, P. C., 120
McKinnon, J., 165
McLanahan, S., 81, 82
McLemore, S. D., 176
McLoyd, V. C., 100, 123
McNall, M., 91
Medora, N. P., 52
Meekers, D., 60
Meleis, A. I., 119, 121, 238
Mena, F. J., 233
Menacker, F., 77, 78, 79, 115
Mencher, J., 95
Messner, M., 102
Middleton, D., 148, 149, 173
Midgley, E., 28, 235
Milkie, M., 95
Miller, D. B., 126
Miller, D. L., 125, 180
Miller, K. S., 81
Miller, L. F., 168
Miller, S. C., 141
Min, P. G., 103, 104, 122, 136, 138, 221, 225, 235, 237
Minde, T., 233
Mintz, S., 36, 38
Mistry, M., 72
Mitchell, J., 143
Mitchell-Kernan, C., 245
Modeste, N., 81
Mok, D., 233
Montgomery, E., 69
Montgomery, R. J. V., 142
Montgomery, S., 81
Mooney, T. M., 93
Moore, C. D., 125, 180
Mor, V., 141
Morash, M., 105
Morrill, D., 48
Mosher, W. D., 76, 201
Mott, F. L., 81
Mui, A. C., 142
Muller, T., 199
Munger, R. G., 220
Munsch, J., 94
Munson, M. L., 77, 78, 79
Murdock, G. P., 49, 56, 58
Murray, C. I., 60
Murray, M. S., 66
Mutchler, J. E., 139, 141, 143
Muzzonigro, P. G., 90

N
Nagano, K. N., 116
Nagata, D. K., 127, 128
Nance, T., 242, 246, 247
National Adoption Information Clearinghouse, 250
Nayerahmadi, H., 236
Negy, C., 247
New York Academy of Medicine, x
Newman, B. S., 90
Newman, D. M., 14
Ng, F., 55, 119, 129
Ngige, L. W., 50, 53
Nock, S. L., x
Norton, A. J., 168

O
O'Connell, M., 237, 242
Ogunwole, S. U., 173, 174
Oliver, M. L., 7
Olson, S., 105
O'Neill, G., 139
Oropesa, R. S., 16
Ortiz, S., 178
Ortiz, V., 236
Osterweil, Z., 116
Overturf, J., 75, 125
Owens, A. S., 125
Oyserman, D., 128
Ozer, E. J., 89

P
Pabon, E., 23
Padilla, A. M., 233
Panzarine, S., 82
Park, K. S., 67, 68
Park, L., 124
Parrillo, V. N., 73, 175, 177
Parrott, T. M., 73
Patterson, S., 146
Pearson, J. L., 67, 68

Peek, C. W., 141
Perez, L., 67, 69
Perez-Firmat, G., 91, 113, 124, 195, 233, 234, 236
Perry, C., 166
Perry, H. L., 148
Pessar, P. R., 102
Peters, M. F., 128
Petersen, W., 120
Peterson, G. W., 122
Peterson, J. T., 59, 70, 116
Phinney, J. S., 127, 128
Phua, V. C., 67, 68
Picot, S. J., 142
Pidcock, B. W., 94
Pleck, E. H., 40, 81, 130, 138, 147, 149, 213
Pleck, J. H., 81
Portes, A., 195
Posadas, B. M., 218, 241
Poussaint, A. F., 120, 121
Purdy, J. K., 142
Pyke, K., 233

Q
Qian, Z., 245
Quadagno, J., 59
Queen, S., 59

R
Ramirez, M., 142
Ramirez, R. R., 190
Rank, M., 144
Rasche, C., 106
Ray, L. A., 96
Red Horse, J. G., 142, 180
Reed, J., 146
Register, J. C., 143
Reinhard, S. C., 142
Rennison, C. M., 105, 106
Renzetti, C. M., 96
Repak, T. A., 99, 102
Rickel, A. U., 69
Riedmann, A., 93, 173, 184
Rindfuss, R. R., 90
Rivera, F., 84
Roberts, D., 124
Roberts-Jolly, J., 96
Robinson, J., 95
Robinson, T. N., 125
Rodgers-Farmer, A. Y., 145
Rogerson, P. A., 143
Rogler, L. H., 236
Roldan, M., 95
Romo, H. D., 176
Roschelle, A. R., 199
Rosner, T. T., 142
Rosoff, J. I., 79
Rossi, A. S., 73
Rossi, P. H., 73
Rubin, L., 94
Rucibwa, N. K., 81
Rudkin, L., 96
Ruggles, S., 155, 161
Rutman, A. H., 37
Ryan, R. A., 120

S
Sado, S., 247
Sailer, S., 243
Sainz, A., 140
Salas-Provance, M. B., 146
Sanchez, L., x
Sanchez-Ayendez, M., 194
Sandefur, G., 82
Sanders-Thompson, V. L., 127
Santiago, E., 101, 199, 238
Sayer, L., 95
Schaefer, R. T., 34
Schick, E., 200
Schick, R., 200
Schoen, R., 100
Schoeni, R. F., 144
Schvaneveldt, P. L., 60
Schwartz, M. A., 184, 185
Schwebel, A. I., 166
Scott, B. M., 184, 185
Scott, J. W., 101
Seelbach, W. C., 141
Segal, U. A., 217, 247
Seligman, M., 146
Seltzer, J., 84
Serwer, A. E., 185
Shafieyan, M., 236
Shapiro, T. M., 7
Shapurian, R., 236

Shelton, B. A., 100
Shin, E. H., 218
Shkilnyk, A. M., 183, 184, 185
Shomaker, D. M., 142
Silva, J. S., 131
Silverstein, M., 73, 144
Simmons, T., 42, 139, 145, 242
Simon, R. J., 251
Skolnick, A., 32
Slavin, L. A., 128
Smith, D., 60
Smith, J., 123
Smith, M. D., 107
Smith, N., 38
Snipp, C. M., 183, 244
Snyder, D. K., 247
Snyder, J. L., 140
Sonenstein, F. L., 81
Sonuga-Barke, E. J. S., 72
Sorensen, P., 50
Sotomayor, M., 142
South, S. J., 101, 102
Speare, A., 139
Spencer, M. B., 128
Spitze, G., 143
Stack, C. B., 70, 71, 166
Stanton, M. E., 56, 183
Staples, R., 100, 101
Steckel, R. H., 157, 160
Steinmetz, S. K., 107
Stepick, A., 238
Stets, J. E., 107
Stevenson, B. E., 158, 159
Stevenson, H. C., Jr., 128
Stier, H., 84
Stockard, J. E., 53, 55, 88, 212
Stoller, E. P., 142
Straus, M., 107, 123
Straus, M. A., 107
Striegel-Moore, R. H., 3
Strodtbeck, F. L., 104
Stuart, P., 172
Suarez, Z., 141, 191, 195, 196, 200
Sucoff, C. A., 81
Sue, D. W., 114
Sung, B. L., 221
Sung, K., 136
Suro, R., 197, 242, 243, 244, 245
Sutton, P. D., 77, 78, 79, 115
Sweeney, P., 84
Swisher, K., 125
Szapocznik, J., 233

T
Takeuchi, D., 100
Takyi, B. K., 49, 60
Talbort, R., 127
Tanner, J. G., 146
Taylor, C. B., 3
Taylor, D., 127
Taylor, R. J., 99, 100, 126, 127, 142
Teno, J. M., 141
Tepperman, L., 137
Thoennes, N., 105
Thomas, E., 69
Thomas, T. N., 236
Thompson, A., 101
Thompson, B. W., 3
Thornton, M. C., 126, 127
Thornton, Y. S., 126, 249
Thrupkaew, N., 114, 220
Tickamyer, A. R., 100
Tienda, M., 84, 196, 202
Tilles, M. C., 250
Timm, J. T., 122
Ting, K. F., 91, 94, 199
Tjaden, P., 105
Tora, J., 247
Toro-Morn, M. I., 72
Torres, S., 106, 107
Toth, J. F., 119
Tran, T. V., 136, 218, 220, 237
Trent, K., 82
Trierweiler, S. J., 127
Tripp, R., 95
Troester, R. R., 166
Trollinger, L. J., 50, 53
Truitner, K., 149, 150
Truitner, N., 149, 150
Tseng, H., 120
Tseng, V., 112, 238
Tsuya, N. O., 90
Tucker, B., 100
Tucker, M., 99
Tucker, M. B., 245

Turnbull, A. P., 146
Turner, J. H., 235
Turner, P. H., 120
Twaite, J. A., 166
Tyler, S. L., 177

U
Uba, L., 244
Uchitelle, L., 42
Ukaegbu, A. O., 16
Umberson, D., 198
Unger, D. G., 69
United for a Fair Economy, 16
Upchurch, D. M., 80, 81
Urey, J. R., 142
U.S. Census Bureau, 68
U.S. Department of Commerce, 2, 18, 20, 22, 24, 25, 65, 66, 96, 98, 137, 140, 155, 198, 201, 209
U.S. Department of Health and Human Services, 41, 75, 79, 97, 117, 123, 124, 143

V
Van Hook, J. V. W., 64, 66
Vega, W. A., 199
Ventura, S. J., 77, 78, 79, 115
Volkman, T., 251

W
Walker, G. K., 140
Wallace, S. P., 140
Waller, M. A., 146
Walters, A. L., 182
Warheit, G. J., 127
Warner, R. L., 72
Watson, J., 144
Weinick, R. M., 73
Weitzer, R., ix
Welchans, S., 105, 106
Wellner, A. S., 16, 26
Wen-Shing, T., 58
Werner, E., 113
Westoff, C. F., 79
Whitman, D., 32
Wikan, U., 147
Wilkinson, H., 251
Williams, D. R., 141
Williams, G. H., 121, 166
Williams, H. A., 220
Williamson, J., 241, 248, 249
Wilson, J. C., x
Wilson, L., 100
Wilson, S. J., 137
Wilson, S. M., 50, 53
Wilson-Sadberry, K. R., 100
Wilt, S., 105
Wong, B., 51, 225
Wong, M. G., 119, 120, 126, 140, 210, 211, 213, 214, 221
Woodworth, R. S., 145
Wright, J., x, 160

X
Xia, Y. R., 60
Xu, X., 119

Y
Yamanaka, K., 244
Yanagisako, S. J., 215
Yancey, G., 240, 246
Yellowbird, M., 183, 244
Yeung, W., 150
Younoszai, B., 149
Youth Gangs, 185
Yu, Y., 141

Z
Zabin, L. S., 81, 82
Zack, N., 248, 249
Zamsky, E. S., 68
Zhou, M., 60, 66, 94, 233
Zhou, Z. G., 60
Zimmerman, R. S., 127
Zinn, J., 141
Zsembik, B. A., 237

SUBJECT INDEX

A
Acculturation issues
  attitudinal changes, 237
  biculturalism, 232–233, 236
  cultural assimilation, 232
  "cyclical migration" concept, 235
  dissonance, 232
  divorce rates, 237
  ethnic identity maintenance, 235, 235*table*
  family life affected by, 237–239
  fertility rates, 237
  gender factors, 236–237
  generation factors, 236
  helping and hindering factors, 234–237
  intergenerational conflict, 237–239
  language facility, 237–238
  marital assimilation, 232
  "museumization" concept, 239
  power issues, 238
  resistance from U.S. society, 234–235
  social support, 235
  structural assimilation, 232
Acoma Indians
  assimilation, 178
  matrilineality of, 183
African Americans
  academic stimulation, 125
  acculturation of, 154
  African heritage, 156
  aging trends, 137
  attenuated extended households, 68
  authoritarian parenting style, 119, 120
  birth rituals, 129, 158–159
  caregiver stress, 142
  child abuse, 123
  civil rights movement, 164–165
  class structure, 166
  in colonial period, 34, 36
  communalism, 166
  corporal punishment, 122, 123
  death beliefs, rituals, 148
  diversity of, 154
  divorce rates, 75–76, 100, 164, 167
  domestic abuse, 105–106
  education levels, 26, 99, 100, 154, 165
  families today, 165–168
  family composition, 154–156, 155fig., 160, 166
  female-headed households, 77, 154–155, 155*fig.*
  fertility rates, family size, 115*table,* 168
  fictive kin, 166
  forced immigration status of, 26
  in foster care system, 124, 124*table*
  free blacks, 156
  gender roles, issues, 93, 99–101, 163
  Great Depression, 163–164
  holiday rituals, 130
  housing, 164, 165
  informal adoption, 166–167
  informal home caregiving, 141
  interracial marriage, 242–243, 243*table*
  Kwanzaa holiday, 130
  life expectancy, 98, 165

marriage, 75–76, 100, 164, 167–168
multigeneration co-residence, 139, 145–146, 145table, 154, 161, 166
nonmarital births, 76, 77–78, 79*table,* 80–81, 168
northern migration, 162–163
nuclear family households, 73, 74
nursing home use, 140–141
"other mothering," 166
poverty, 156, 165
racial-ethnic labels, 8–9
racial socialization, 127, 128
regional population distribution, 165, 165fig.
religiosity focus, 167
sex ratio of, 21, 96*table,* 100
sharecropping, 162
single-parent families, 68, 100, 154–155, 155fig., 159, 160, 161
skintone social status factor, 249
slave marriages, 157–158
slave women, 157
slavery effects, 156–160
after slavery, 160–165, 165*fig.*
social interaction with children, 143
socialization of children, 59–60
teaching coping, defense mechanisms, 121
World War II, 164
See also Black Americans

African society
family structure, 155
genital mutilation, 92

Age structure, 22–23, 22*table*

Agrarian societies, 16

Agricultural era of American families
arranged marriages, 36
co-provider families, 35, 95
divorce, 36
gender factors, 35
health and life expectancy, 35
infant mortality rates, 35, 36
interracial relationships, 157, 248, 249
large families, 35
parenting of children, 36
population diversity, 34
remarriages, 36–37
single-parent families, 36–37, 75

Aid to Dependent Children (ADC), 164

Alcoholism, Native Americans and, 184–185

Alien Registration Act, 217

American family, brief history of
agricultural era (colonial period, 1500–1800), 34–37
industrial era (1800–1970), 34, 37–41
service era (1970s-present), 34, 41–44
contextual nature of, 33
median age at first marriage, 34, 34*fig.*
perceptions *vs.* realities, 32
transition period difficulties, 44
See also Agricultural era of American families; Industrial era of American families; Service era of American families

American Indian Religious Freedom Act, 180

American Indians
age structure of, 22–23, 22*table*
aging trends, 137*table*
child abuse rates, 124*table*
domestic abuse, 105–106
education levels, 19, 20*fig.*
family and nonfamily households totals, 65*table*
fertility rates, family size, 115*table*
foreign born percentage, 235*table*
geographic distribution, 25*table*
grandparents co-residence, 145*table*
income and wealth distribution factors, 17–18, 18*table*
infant mortality rates, 116, 117*fig.*
life expectancy, 98, 98*fig.*
nuclear family households, 75*fig.*
occupational distribution, 21*fig.*
poverty rates by family structure, 76*fig.*
racial-ethnic labels, 9
sex ratios, 96*table*

suicide rates, men *vs.* women, 97
teen births, 79*table*
verbal participation in school, 125
See also Native Americans; *specific tribe*
Apache Indians
death beliefs, rituals, 148
population trends, 173*table*
puberty rituals, 130
Arab Americans
acculturation, 233, 236–237
social support, 235
Arab society, 55
Asian Americans
aging trends, 137
alternative medicine, 146
Asian countries by region, 208, 208*table*
Asian Indian, Filipino, Korean Americans, 216–218, 226–227
authoritarian parenting style, 120
Chinese Americans, 210–214
corporal punishment, 122
death beliefs, rituals, 149–151
discrimination, stereotypes, 225
divorce rates, 76, 221
domestic abuse, 105–106
East Asians, 208*table,* 209–214, 209*table,* 226–227
education gender differentiation, 94
education levels, 19, 20*fig.,* 221, 222*table,* 225–226
elder care, 139, 140
elder respect custom, 136
familism values of, 112
family and nonfamily households totals, 64, 65*table*
family structures today, 221, 222–224*table,* 225–227
female-headed households, 77, 224*table*
fertility rates, family size, 115*table*
"filial piety" custom, 138, 221
folk illness beliefs, 147
in foster care system, 124, 124*table*
gender roles, issues, 93, 103–104
gender sexual behavior, 91
geographic distribution, 24
holiday rituals, 131
homosexuality, 90
income levels, 222–223*table,* 226
interracial dating, 241
interracial marriage, 242, 243–244, 243*table,* 245
Japanese Americans, 214–216
Korean War, 218
life expectancy, 98, 223*table*
lineage social status, 54
"model minority" designation, 209, 226–227
multigenerational co-residence, 138, 139, 144–145, 145*table*
nonmarital births, 77–78, 79*table,* 80–81
nuclear family households, 74, 223–224*table*
nursing home use, 141
population trends, 208–209, 209*table*
poverty rates by family structure, 76*fig.,* 222–223*table*
public displays of affection, 126
racial-ethnic labels, 9
racial socialization, 127
from refugee camps, 219–220
relational harmony focus, 126, 127
sex ratio of, 21, 96*table,* 223*table*
single-parent families, 82, 224*table,* 226
social characteristics, 221, 222–224*table,* 225–227
social harmony focus, 114
Southeast Asians, 218–220, 222–224*table,* 226–227
staring aversion, 126
stem family households, 67, 68
teen years, 114
use of shame, 119
Vietnam War, 208, 218–219
women, 226
World War II, 217
See also Asian and Pacific Islanders; Asian Indians; Chinese Americans; Filipino Americans; Hmong Americans; Japanese Americans; Korean Americans;

Korean society; Laotian Americans; Laotian society; Vietnamese Americans; Vietnamese culture
Asian and Pacific Islanders
age structure of, 22–23, 22*table*
aging trends, 137*table*
child abuse rates, 123, 124*table*
foreign born percentage, 235*table*
in foster care system, 124, 124*table*
geographic distribution, 25*table*
income and wealth distribution factors, 17–18, 18*table*
infant mortality rates, 116, 117*fig.*
life expectancy, 98*fig.*
nonmarital births, 78, 79*table*
nuclear family households, 75*fig.*
occupational distribution, 21*fig.*
population trends, 2*table*
poverty rates by family structure, 76*fig.*
suicide rates, men *vs.* women, 97
teen births, 79*table*
Asian Indians, 216
acculturation, 239
family structures, 218
gender ratio, 217
interracial marriage, 241, 246
population trends, 209, 209*table*
skilled professionals, 225
skintone social status factor, 250
social characteristics, 222–224*table,* 226–227
See also India society
Aztec Indians, Mexico, 190, 191

B
Baby Boomers
aging of population and, 22, 23
eldercare, 137
post war economic boom, 40
Bangladesh, 88
BIA (Bureau of Indian Affairs), 176, 178
Biculturalism. *See* Acculturation issues; Multiracial issues
Bilineal lineage system, 54
Bilocality residence, 56
Black Americans
age structure of, 22–23, 22*table*
aging trends, 137*table*
attenuated extended households, 68
child abuse rates, 124*table*
divorce rates, 75–76, 100
domestic abuse, 105–106
eating disorders, 3–4
education levels, 19, 20*fig.*, 26, 100
elder care, 140
elderly/adult children resources exchange, 143–144
familism value of, 113
family and nonfamily households totals, 64, 65*table*
fertility rates, family size, 115*table*
foreign born percentage, 235*table*
in foster care system, 123–124, 124*table*
gender roles, issues, 93, 99–101
gendered wage gap, 95
geographic distribution, 24, 25*table*
holiday rituals, 130
income and wealth distribution factors, 17–18, 18*table*
infant mortality rates, 116–117, 117*table*
informal adoption concept, 70
informal home caregiving, 141
interracial dating, 241
interracial marriage, 242–243, 243*table,* 245–246, 249
interracial marriage, social acceptance, 246
Kwanzaa holiday, 130
life expectancy, 98*fig.*
multigenerational households, 67, 144–146, 145*table*
noncustodial parents, 83–84
nonfamily households, 84
nonmarital births, 77–78, 79*table,* 80–81, 168
nonmarital births, racial gap, 80–81
nuclear family households, 75*fig.*
occupational distribution, 21*fig.*
population trends, 2*table,* 154–156, 155*fig.*
racial-ethnic labels, 8–9

racial socialization, 127, 128
remarriage rates, 76
sex ratio of, 21, 96*table*
single-father families, 83
single-parent families, 82, 100
sterilizations of, x
suicide rates, men *vs.* women, 97
swapping of resources, 70–71
teaching coping, defense mechanisms, 121
teen births, 78, 79, 79*table*
women stereotypes, 3
Black Muslims, 167
Blackfoot Indians, 173*table*
Blind dates, xii
Bride-price, 53
Buddhism, 149–150
Bureau of Indian Affairs (BIA), 176, 178

C
Cable Act (interracial marriages), 213
Cambodian Americans
social characteristics, 222–224table
social structures, 226
Cambodian society
communism, 219
death beliefs, rituals, 150
Castro, Fidel, 195–196
Cherokee Indians
economy of, 180
population trends, 173*table*
removal, 175
tribal structure, 181
Chickasaw Indians, 175
Child abuse, neglect, 123–124, 124*table*
Chinese Americans
acculturation, 233–234
arranged marriages, 212
Chinese New Year, 131
death beliefs, rituals, 150
discrimination against, 211
gender ratios, 212, 213, 214
Gold Rush, 210
immigration exclusion acts, 211, 213–214
interracial marriage, 212–213, 214
language acculturation, 238
as merchants, 213
naming ceremony, 129
population trends, 208, 208*table*, 209*table*
puberty rituals, 130
railroad construction, 210–211
skilled professionals, 225
social characteristics, 222–224*table*
"split-household" families, 212
urban Chinatowns, 211–212
women, 212–213
Chinese society
adoptions from, 251
age at marriage trends, 60
authoritarian parenting style, 120
dowry custom, 53
female infantcide, 53
"filial piety" custom, 138, 233–234
footbinding, 93
multigenerational family trends, 60
patrilineal, patrilocal family systems, 88
reproduction policy, 57, 251
spirit wedding custom, 52
titles, 55
Chippewa Indians, 173*table*
Choctaw Indians
economy of, 180
matrilineality of, 183
population trends, 173*table*
removal, 175
Church of the Latter-day Saints, 50–51
Civil Rights Act, 164
Colonial period of American families. *See* Agricultural era of American families
Colorblindness, *vs.* diversity celebration, ix
Confucianism, 150
Cree Indians, 182, 183
Creek Indians, 175, 183
Cross-cultural comparisons of family
affinial family systems, 48
arranged marriages, 51–52
bilineal system, 54
"bride capture" mate selection, 42

consanguineal family systems, 48, 51–52
decent and lineage power system, 54–55
family functions, 57–60
family power systems, 54–57
family roles and titles, 55
global context, 48
incest laws, 58
marriage types and choices, 49–51
monogamy *vs.* polygamy, 49–51
patriarchal *vs.* matriarcal societies, 54
patrilineal *vs.* matrilineal lineage systems, 54–55, 88
patrilocal *vs.* matrilocal, *vs.* bilocality residence, 56–57, 88
premarital sex customs, 58–59
reproduction function, 57–58
residence *vs.* families of origin, 56–57, 56*fig.*
resources exchange, 53
sexuality regulation, 58–59
social *vs.* legal marriage, 49
socialization of children, 59–60
"spirit weddings" concept, 42
"transnational motherhood" concept, 60, 113

Cuban Americans
acculturation, 233
American school system, 124–125
Bay of Pigs invasion, 195–196
divorce rates, 202
extended households, 67
fertility rates, 202–203
"freedom flights," 196
gender roles, issues, 236
Hispanic family dissimilarities, 200–203
Hispanic family similarities, 198–200
household, family structures, 201–203, 201*table*
interracial marriage, 243
marielitos boat lift, 196
nonfamily households, 201
political refugees, 195
racial-ethnic labels, 9
Refugee Act of 1980, 197
refugee status, 196–197
single-parent families, 201
social characteristics of, 197–198, 198*table*
Spanish-American War, 198*table*
teaching coping, defense mechanisms, 121
U.S. influence, 194–195
women, 202–203

Cubanacan Indians, Cuba, 190

D

Dawes Act of 1887, 175, 177
Demographic factors
age structure, 22–23, 22*fig.*
geographic distribution, 23–24, 25*table*
sex ratio, 20–21
See also specific racial, ethnic group

Diversity
population trends, 2–5, 2*table*

Divorce
in agricultural/colonial era, 36
"covenant" marriage options, x
of foreign-born, 28
geographic factors, 24
Hispanic Americans, 201–202
in industrial era, 39, 40–41, 42*fig.*
Native Americans, 183–184
in service era, 41*fig.*, 43, 44
See also Marriage; *specific racial, ethnic group*

Domestic violence
of immigrants, 106–107
male victimization, 106
by race, 105–106
structural factors, 107
web site resources, 109

Dominican Americans, 102
Dowry, 53

E

Eating disorders, 3–4
Economic factors
class structure, 16–17
education levels, 15, 19, 20*fig.*
fertility rates and, 16

income and wealth distribution, 16–18, 16*table*
income *vs.* wealth, 17–18
micro *vs.* macroeconomic factors, 15–16
poverty, 18–19
See also specific racial, ethnic group
Education
Asian Americans, 222*table*
attainment levels by race, 20*fig.*
Black women's aspirations, 99
as economic factor, 19
of foreign-born, 28
gender differentiation, 93–94
GI Bill, 40
interracial marriage, 245
parenting styles and the school system, 124–126
public school system, 38
See also specific racial, ethnic group
Education Amendments Act, 179
Endogamy, 240
Equality, *vs.* diversity celebration, ix
Ethnicity
census data, 7–8
cultural heritage as, 7
family *vs.* kin labels, 10–11
minority *vs.* majority labels, 9
vs. race, 7
racial-ethnic labels, 8–9
See also specific ethnic group
Evil eye customs, 126, 129–130
Extended families
arranged marriages, 51–52
attenuated extended households, 68–69
family and nonfamily households, by race, 65*table*
fertility rates, family size, 115–116, 115*table*
of foreign-born, 28
gender roles, 72
in industrial era, 39
laterally extended households, 69–70
multigenerational, 66–69
simple extended households, 67
stem family households, 67–68
as systems of exchange, 70–73
trends in, 60
See also Family structures

F
Families of color
extended households, 66
laterally extended households, 69
pathologization of, x
romanticization of, x
See also Family structures; Gender relations and sex ratios; Race and family, study of; *specific racial, ethnic group*
Family, families
adaptation, reconfiguration of, xii
attachment importance of, x–xi
conflict source of, xi
family *vs.* kin labels, 10–11
fictive kin concept, 10
generalizations *vs.* stereotypes, xi–xii
information misinterpretation, xi
legal issues, ix
political issues of, x
racial factors and, 2–5
social qualitative relationships, 10–11
societal resources distribution, ix–x
See also American family, brief history of; Cross-cultural comparisons of family; Families of color; Family structures; Race and family, study of; *specific racial, ethnic group*
Family structures
of Asian Americans, 221, 223–224*tables,* 225–227
attenuated extended households, 68–69
extended families as systems of exchange, 70–73
extended family households, 64, 65*table,* 66–73
female-headed households, 65*table,* 77–82
female-headed households, outcomes for, 81–82

gay and lesbian households, 84–85
laterally extended households, 69–70
male-headed households, 65*table*, 82–83
multigenerational extended households, 66–67
noncustodial parents, 83–84
nonfamily households, 65*table*, 84–85
nonmarital births, 77–78, 79*table*
nonmarital births, racial gap in, 79–81, 79*table*
nuclear family households, 73–75, 75*fig.*
poverty rates, 74, 76*fig.*
simple extended households, 67
single-parent families, 75–82
stem family households, 67–68
teen births, 78–79, 79*table*
See also specific racial, ethnic group
Female infantcide, 53
Fertility rates
economic factors and, 16
of foreign-born, 28
in service era, 44
Filipino Americans, 251
citizenship, immigrant status, 217
education levels, 225
family structures, 218
gender ratio, 217–218
income levels, 222–223*table,* 226
interracial marriage, 241, 246
social characteristics, 222–224*table*
social structures, 226
See also Philippines society
First Nations, 9
Footbinding, 93
Foraker Act of 1900, 193
Foreign Miner's Tax, 210
Freedman's Bureau, 160–161, 162

G
Gay and lesbian households, 84–85
Gender factors
in agricultural family life, 35
biculturalism, 236
children returning home, 139, 140*fig.*
elder caregiving, 142
of immigrants, 27
in industrial era, 38–39
median age at first marriage, 33, 34, 34*fig.*
See also Gender relations; Gender relations and sex ratios; *specific racial, ethnic group*
Gender relations
in extended households, 72
interracial dating and cohabitation, 240–241
third and fourth gender concept, 89
See also Gender relations and sex ratios; *specific racial, ethnic group*
Gender relations and sex ratios, 21, 96*table*
adult roles, 95–96
African American gender issues, 99–101
Asian American gender issues, 103–104, 223*table*
biculturalism, 236
domestic abuse, 105–107
footbinding, 93
gender as a social construct, 88
gender stereotypes and roles, 89–95
genital mutilation, 92
honor killings custom, 91
interracial marriage rates, 242–244
Latina/o gender issues, 101–103
menstruation isolation, 92
Native American gender issues, 104–105
patrilineal and patrilocal family systems, 88
protecting women's sexuality, 90–94
sex ratios, 96–99, 96*table,* 223*table*
suicide rates, men *vs.* women, 97, 97*fig.*
See also specific racial, ethnic group
Genital mutilation, 92
Geographic distribution factors, 23–24, 25*table*

GI Fianceées Act, 214
Gypsy societies, 52

H
Haitian Americans
 generational power gap, 238
 laterally extended households, 69
Hawaiian society, 66
Health insurance, ix–x
Hindi society, 129
Hispanic Americans
 age structure of, 22–23, 22*table*
 aging trends, 137, 137*table*
 alternative medicine, 146
 attenuated extended households, 68
 caregiver stress, 142
 child abuse rates, 124*table*
 corporal punishment, 122, 123
 divorce rates, 76
 domestic abuse, 105–106
 education gender differentiation, 94
 education levels, 19, 20*fig.*
 elder care, 140
 elder respect custom, 136
 elderly/adult children resources exchange, 143–144
 familism value of, 112–113, 198–199
 family and nonfamily households totals, 65*table*
 fertility rates, 237
 fertility rates, family size, 115*table*
 folk illness beliefs, 146
 foreign born percentage, 235*table*
 in foster care system, 124, 124*table*
 gender roles, 93
 gender roles, issues, 101–103
 gender sexual behavior, 91
 gendered wage gap, 95
 geographic distribution, 24, 25*table*
 grandparents co-residence, 144–145, 145*table*
 Hispanic family dissimilarities, 200–203
 Hispanic family similarities, 198–200
 holiday rituals, 130–131
 homosexuality, 90
 income and wealth distribution factors, 17–18, 18*table*
 infant mortality rates, 116–117, 117*fig.*
 informal home caregiving, 141
 interracial dating, 241
 interracial marriage, 242, 243, 243*table,* 245
 life expectancy, 98, 98*fig.*
 machismo, marianismo customs, 101–102
 multigenerational co-residence, 139, 199
 noncustodial parents, 84
 nonmarital births, 77–78, 79*table,* 80–81
 nuclear family households, 73, 74, 75*fig.*, 199
 occupational distribution, 21*fig.*
 population trends, 2*table*
 poverty rates by family structure, 76*fig.*
 public displays of affection, 126
 racial-ethnic labels, 8–9
 remarriage rates, 76
 sex ratio of, 21, 96*table,* 98
 single-parent families, 82
 social interaction with children, 143
 spoon-feeding children custom, 115
 suicide rates, men *vs.* women, 97
 teen births, 79*table*
 See also Cuban Americans; Latino/as Americans; Mexican Americans; Puerto Rican Americans
Hmong Americans
 academic stimulation, 125
 death beliefs, rituals, 150, 151
 domestic abuse, 107
 education gender differentiation, 94
 extended families, 70
 female marriage age, 91
 illness beliefs, 147
 in Laos, 219
 naming ceremony, 129
 racial socialization, 129
 sleeping customs, 113
 social characteristics, 222–224*table*

social structures, 226
teaching at home *vs.* community, 122
as Vietnamese refugees, 219–220
Honor killings custom, 91
Hopi Indians, 104
matrilineality of, 183
"other mothering" practice, 183
praise of children, 114
"Hybrid degeneracy" biological theory, 246–247

I
Immigrants, immigration
age structure factors, 22
arranged marriages, 52
"brain drain" concept, 27
collective socialization, 121–122
depression, PTSD, 220
domestic abuse, 106–107
education levels, 28
extended households, 66, 67, 72
fertility rates, 28
gender ratio, 27
immigrant status, 27–28
immigration regulation, 25, 197, 211, 212–214, 218
in industrial era, 37–38
laterally extended households, 69
manner of entry, 25–27
mortality rates, 117
nuclear family households, 74
racial-ethnic group management, 58
in service era, 43
"transitional mothering" practice, 113
white *vs.* of color, 26
See also Acculturation issues; Multiracial issues; *specific immigration, ethnic group*
Incest laws, 58
Income and wealth distribution factors, 16–18, 18*table*
Asian Americans, 222–223*table*
See also specific racial, ethnic group
India society
arranged marriage, 52
dowry custom, 53
education gender differentiation, 94
evil eye custom, 129–130
sati custom, 88
working resources of women, 95
See also Asian Indians
Indian Child Welfare Act, 180, 184, 250
Indian Removal Act, 175
Indian Self-Determination and Education Assistance Act, 179
Indochina, 218–219
See also Vietnam War; Vietnamese culture; *specific country*
Industrial era of American families
child labor laws, 38
divorce trends, 39, 40, 41*fig.*
education, 40
family structure changes, 39–40
gender roles in, 38–39, 95
immigration patterns, 37
labor union influences, 38
legal segregation, 37–38
marriage trends, 39
population growth, 37
privacy, 40
public school system, 38
segregation, 41
single-provider families, 38
suburban migration, 40
urban growth, 37
U.S. land expansion, 37
women's roles, 38–39, 95
Infant mortality rates
in agricultural/colonial era, 36
decrease in, 32
of foreign-born, 28
in industrial era, 39–40
by race, 116–117, 117*fig.*
Intergenerational relationships: elderly, adult children and grandchildren
aging of population, 136–138, 137*table*
caregiver stress, 142
caregiving for, 140–143
children returning home, 139, 140*fig.*
death, 147–151
elder abuse, 143

grandparenting, 144–146, 146*table*
illness, 146–147
informal home caregiving, 141
living arrangements, 138–140, 140*fig.*
nursing home use, 140–141
respect, deference, 136
social interaction, resource exchange, 143–144
"verticalization" of population, 138
See also Intergenerational relationships: parent and child

Intergenerational relationships: parent and child
authoritarian parenting style, 119–120
authoritative parenting style, 119, 120
child birthday parties, 113
corporal punishment, child abuse, 122–124, 124*table*
disciplinary tactics, 118
"evil eye" custom, 126, 129–130
extrinsic *vs.* intrinsic behavior appeals, 118–119
fertility rates, family size by race, 115, 115*table*
holiday rituals, 130–131
individual *vs.* communal (familism) orientations, 112–116
infant mortality rates by race, 116–117, 117*fig.*
infant rituals, 129–130
modesty and humility focus, 114
parental praise of offspring, 113–114
parenting styles and class, 112, 117–119
parenting styles and environment, 112, 119–122
parenting styles and school system, 124–126
patrilocality impact on, 56
permissive parenting style, 119
permissive school atmosphere, 124–126
public displays of affection, 126
racial socialization, 112, 126–128
racial socialization, cultural rituals, 112, 129–131
relational harmony focus, 126
self-feeding customs, 115–116
sleeping arrangements, 113
socioeconomic status, 116–126
teaching coping, defense mechanisms, 121
toilet training customs, 115
uninvolved parenting style, 119
See also Intergenerational relationships: elderly, adult children and grandchildren

Internet dating, xii

Interracial marriage
1800s laws against, x
immigration trends and, 25
See also Acculturation issues; Multiracial issues

Iranian Americans, 236, 237

Iroquois Indians
population trends, 173*table*
removal, 176
women in, 181

Islamic society, 58

Israeli society
familistic child rearing, 116
kibbutzim living arrangement, 59

J

Japanese Americans
arranged marriages, 215
Asiatic Exclusion League, 215
biculturalism, 236
divorce rates, 221
immigration restrictions, 214
interracial marriage, 243–244
Issei generation, 215
Nisei generation, 215–216
population trends, 208–209, 208*table*, 209*table*
puberty rituals, 130
racial socialization, 127
relational harmony focus, 127–128
relocation internment camps, 215–216
Sansei generation, 216
social characteristics, 222–224*table*

social structures, 226
tenant farming, 214
Yonsei generation, 216
Japanese society
elder respect custom, 136–137
familistic child rearing, 116
gender role expectations, 90
Jews
death beliefs, rituals, 151
puberty rituals, 130
Jim Crow laws, 163, 164
Jones Act of 1917, 193
Jordanian Americans, 239

K
Kenya society, 50
Korean Americans
divorce rates, 237
education levels, 222*table*, 225
fertility rates, 237
gender ratio, 217, 222*table*
income levels, 222–223*table*, 226
interracial marriage, 244
social characteristics, 222–224*table*
social support, 235
Korean society
elder respect custom, 136
female births in, 88
gender roles, issues, 104
Korean War, 218, 251

L
Laguna Indians, 183
Lakota Indians, 148–149
Laotian Americans
generational power gap, 238
social characteristics, 222–224*table*
Laotian society, 150, 218
Latin American Indian, 173*table*
Latino/as Americans
authoritarian parenting style, 119
from Cuba, 190, 190*table*, 194–198
death beliefs, rituals, 149
evil eye custom, 129
familism values of, 112, 198–199
family size, 202
gender roles, issues, 101–103, 236
generational power gap, 238
godparenting custom, 200
Hispanic family dissimilarities, 200–203
Hispanic family similarities, 198–200
household, family structures, 200–203, 201*table*
in industrial era, 37–38
informal home caregiving, 141
Mexican-American War, 191–192
from Mexico, 190, 190*table*, 191–193
multigenerational households, 67, 199
nursing home use, 141
patriarchal, -lineal, -local society, 191
pesonalismo and *dignidad* customs, 119
population trends, 190, 190*table*
puberty rituals, 130
from Puerto Rico, 190, 190*table*, 193–194
racial-ethnic labels, 9
social characteristics by ethnicity, 198*table*
Spanish slave system, 190–191
See also Cuban Americans; Hispanic Americans; Mexican Americans; Puerto Rican Americans
Life expectancy
aging of population trends, 137, 137*table*
in agricultural/colonial era, 36
Asian Americans, 223*table*
grandparenting opportunities, 144
increase in, 32, 165
industrial era, 37
in service era, 43
sex ratios, 97–98, 98*fig.*
See also specific racial, ethnic group

M
Majority *vs.* minority label, 9
Marital assimilation, 232

Marriage
after WWII, 40
in agricultural/colonial period, 36
arranged marriages, xii, 36, 51–52, 60, 212, 215
bride-price concept, 53
consanguineal *vs.* affinial family systems, 48–49
"covenant" marriage options, x
dowry concept, 53
incest laws, 58
in industrial era, 39
marital satisfaction, 95–96
median age at first marriage, 34, 34*fig.*
monogamy *vs.* polygamy, 49–51
in service era, 42–43, 44
sex ratio factors and, 99, 101
slave marriages, 157–158, 161
social *vs.* legal, 49
See also Divorce; Family structures; Multiracial issues; Same-sex marriage; *specific racial, ethnic group*
Matriarchal societies, 54
Matrilineal lineage systems
of African families, 155
of Native Americans, 55, 104, 183
vs. patrilineage, 54–55, 88
Matrilocality residence, 56–57, 88
McCarran-Walter Act, 214
Menstrual isolation, 92
MEPA (Multiethnic Placement Act, transracial adoption), 250
Mexican-American War, 191–192
Mexican Americans
bracero farmworker program, 192–193
common-law marriages, 191
divorce rates, 201
education gender differentiation, 94
family size, 202
fertility rates, 202
Hispanic family dissimilarities, 200–203
Hispanic family similarities, 198–200
holiday rituals, 130–131
household, family structures, 200–201, 201–203, 201table
interracial marriage, 241, 243
interracial marriage, social acceptance, 246
laterally extended households, 69
marital satisfaction, 96
Mexican-American War, 191–192
Mexican Revolution, 192
nonmarital births, 80–81
racial-ethnic labels, 9
racial socialization, 127
railroads, Gold Rush and, 192
repatriation of, 192
single-parent families, 201
social characteristics of, 197–198, 198*table*
teen birthrates, 201
women, 202
World War II, 192
Micmac Indians, 183
Minority *vs.* majority label, 9
Monogamous marriage, 49–51
Mormon church, 50–51
Mortality rates
in agricultural/colonial era, 36
of foreign-born, 28
infant mortality rates by race, 116–117, 117*fig.*
sex ratios, 96, 96*table,* 97–99, 97*fig.,* 98*fig.*
See also specific racial, ethnic group
Multiethnic Placement Act (MEPA, transracial adoption), 250
Multiracial issues
bi- or multiracial identity, 247–250
biracial labels, 247
colonial interracial relationships, 157, 248, 249
dating and cohabitation, 240–241
vs. endogamy, 240
generation, education, residence factors, 245
"hybrid degeneracy" biological theory, 246–247
"hypodescendancy" concept, 249
international adoption, 251

interracial marriage, 241–242, 245–246
interracial marriage; race and gender issues, 242–244, 243*table*
interracial marriage; social acceptance and outcomes of, 246–247
sex ratios and, 21
skintone social status factor, 249–250
status exchange theory, 246
trans- or interracial adoption, 250–251
See also Acculturation issues

Muslim society
Black Muslims,0 167
death beliefs, rituals, 150–151
divorce, 49
holiday rituals, 131
veiling custom, 91–92

N

National Longitudinal Survey of Youth, 123

Native Alaskans
age structure of, 22–23, 22*table*
aging trends, 137*table*
child abuse rates, 123, 124*table*
domestic abuse, 105
education levels, 19, 20*fig.*
family and nonfamily households totals, 65*table*
fertility rates, family size, 115*table*
foreign born percentage, 235*table*
in foster care system, 124*table*
geographic distribution, 25*table*
grandparents co-residence, 145*table*
income and wealth distribution factors, 17–18, 18*table*
infant mortality rates, 117*fig.*
interracial marriage, 244
life expectancy, 98*fig.*
nuclear family households, 75*fig.*
occupational distribution, 21*fig.*
population trends, 2*table*
poverty rates by family structure, 76*fig.*
sex ratios, 96*table*
suicide rates, men *vs.* women, 97
teen births, 79*table*

Native Americans
adoption, 250
aging trends, 137, 137*table*
alcoholism, 184–185
alternative medicine, 146
American Indian movement, 179
annexation status of, 26
Asian origin, 172
assimilation, 172, 177–179
attenuated extended households, 68, 69
authoritarian parenting style, 120–121
blood quantum, 173
caregiver stress, 142
child abuse, 123, 124*table*
collectivism focus, 182
in colonial period, 34, 36
corporal punishment, 122
cross-cultural variations, 172
cross-gendered persons in, 89–90
cultural values, 182–183, 185
current family trends, 183–185
death beliefs, rituals, 148–149
divorce rates, 183–184
domestic abuse, 105–106, 181
education, occupation, income improvements, 184
elder abuse, 143
elder respect custom, 136
European settlement and, 172, 174–175, 176
familism value of, 112–113, 182–183
in foster care system, 123–124, 124, 124*table,* 184
gambling revenues, 173, 180, 185
gang activity, 185
gender roles, issues, 104–105
health issues, 185
historical perspective, 174–180
Indian Child Welfare Act, 180, 184, 250
informal home caregiving, 141
interracial marriage, 242, 243*table,* 244, 245

land loss, 175–177
matrilineal family systems, 55, 104, 183
menstrual isolation, 92
naming ceremony, 129
nonfamily households, 84
nonmarital births, 76, 78, 79*table,* 183
nursing home use, 141
"other mothering," 183
pan-Indian identity, 181
permissive parenting style, 120, 184
population trends, 2*table,* 172–173, 173*table,* 174*fig.*
praise of children, 114
puberty rituals, 130
racial-ethnic labels, 9
racial socialization, 129
regional distribution, 174*fig.*
relational harmony focus, 126, 182–183
reservations, on *vs.* off, 180–181
reservations, removal to, 175–177
single-father families, 82
single-parent families, 82, 183
skintone social status factor, 249–250
status today, 180–185
sterilizations of, x
substance abuse, 185
suicide, 184, 185
tribal groups, 173*table*
tribal sovereignty, 179–180
tribal structure, 181–182
See also American Indians; Native Alaskans; *specific tribe*

Native Hawaiians
racial-ethnic labels, 9
sex ratios, 96*table*

Navajo Indians, 104–105
death beliefs, rituals, 148
divorce, 184
elder abuse, 143
population trends, 173*table*
puberty rituals, 130

Neolocality residence, 56

Nepal society, 88

Non-Hispanic White Americans
age structure of, 22–23, 22*table*
aging trends, 137*table*
child abuse rates, 124*table*
divorce rates, 76
education levels, 19, 20*fig.*
family and nonfamily households totals, 64, 65*table*
female-headed households, 77
fertility rates, family size, 115*table*
foreign born percentage, 235*table*
in foster care system, 124*table*
geographic distribution, 25*table*
grandparents co-residence, 144–145, 145*table*
income and wealth distribution factors, 17–18, 18*table*
infant mortality rates, 117*table*
interracial marriage, 243*table*
life expectancy, 98*fig.*
nonmarital births, 77–78, 79*table*
nuclear family households, 74, 75*fig.*
occupational distribution, 21*fig.*
poverty rates by family structure, 74
remarriage rates, 76
sex ratios, 96*table*
suicide rates, men *vs.* women, 97
teen births, 79*table*
white ethnic groups, 26
See also White Americans

Nonmarital births
ethnic groups, 76, 77–78, 79*table,* 80–81, 168
of foreign-born, 28
Hispanic Americans, 201
racial gap in, 79–81, 79*table*
in service era, 43, 44
See also specific racial, ethnic group

Nur society, Sudan, 48, 51, 53

O

Obesity, 3

Occupational structure, 16, 21*fig.*

Ojibway Indians
infant rituals, 129
puberty rituals, 130

relational harmony focus, 183
relocation effects, 184
Omaha Indians, 183
"Other mothering" practice, 166, 183

P
Pacific Islanders
family and nonfamily households totals, 65*table*
fertility rates, family size, 115*table*
grandparents co-residence, 144, 145*table*
interracial marriage, 242
nonfamily households, 84
poverty rates by family structure, 76*fig.*
racial-ethnic labels, 9
sex ratios, 96*table,* 98
social characteristics, 222–224*table*
Page Act (Chinese immigration), 212–213
Paiute Indians, 148
Pakistan society, 91
Patriarchal society
in agricultural family life, 35
of Blacks after slavery, 161–162
family power and resources, 54
Latino/as Americans, 191
Patrilineal lineage systems, 54–55, 88
Patrilocality residence, 56–57, 88
Pawnee Indians, 182
Philippines society, 59
See also Filipino Americans
Pima Indians, 185
Polygamous marriage, 49–51
Population trends, 2–5, 2*table*
African Americans, 155*fig.*
aging of population, 136–138, 137*table*
See also specific racial, ethnic group
Potawatami Indians, 143
Poverty
child abuse, neglect, 123
domestic abuse, 107
family structure and race, 74, 76*fig.*
female births, 88
foreign *vs.* native born, 28
lower rates of, 32
racial gap, 80–81
See also specific racial, ethnic group
Prejudice *vs.* racism, 6
See also Racism; Segregation
Premarital sex customs, 58–59
Pueblo Indians
caregiver stress, 142
population trends, 173*table*
Puerto Rican Americans
attenuated extended households, 68
citizenship, 194
common-law marriages, 191
commonwealth status, 194
death beliefs, rituals, 149
divorce rates, 201
family values acculturation, 237
gender roles, issues, 101, 236
generational power gap, 238–239
"Great Migration" era, 194
Hispanic family dissimilarities, 200–203
Hispanic family similarities, 198–200
household, family structures, 201–203, 201*table*
interracial marriage, 243
multigenerational households, 66–67
nonfamily households, 201
nonmarital births, 76, 201
poverty rates, 74
single-parent families, 201
social characteristics of, 197–198, 198*table*
U.S. possession of, 193–194

R
Race
as biological concept, 6
vs. ethnicity, 7
family factor of, 2–5
family *vs.* kin labels, 10–11
minority *vs.* majority labels, 9
pure races and, 6
racial-ethnic labels, 8–9
racial groups, 7
as social construction, 6

See also Multiracial issues; Race and family, study of; Racism; *specific racial, ethnic group*
Race and family, study of
age structure, 22–23, 22*table*
agrarian societies, 16
ascribed statuses, 14
class structure, 16–17
cultural *vs.* structural approach to, 14–15
demographic factors, 20–24
economic factors, 15–20
education, 19, 20*fig.*
geographic distribution, 23–24, 25*table*
historical-legal factors, 24–28
immigrant status, 27–28
immigrants, manner of entry, 25–27
income and wealth distribution, 16–18, 18*table*
income *vs.* wealth, 17–18
macro *vs.* micro economic factors, 15–16
occupational structure, 16, 21*fig.*
poverty, 18–19, 18*table*
roles, expected behaviors, 14
sex ratio, 20–21
social structures, 14–15
See also specific racial, ethnic group
Racial segregation. *See* Segregation
Racism
institutional, 6
vs. prejudice, 6
racial socialization, 126–128
racial socialization, cultural rituals of, 129–131
See also Segregation
Ramssey, JonBenet, ix
Reality television shows, xii
Reconstruction Act of 1867, 160

S
Same-sex marriage, x
Sati customer, India society, 88
Segregation
1800s laws supporting, x
housing, 164
immigration policies and, 25
in industrial era, 37–38
Jim Crow laws, 163
Korean Americans, 235
military units, 217
1950s and 1960s, 41
suburban housing, 164
Seminole Indians, 175, 183
Service era of American families
birth rates, 43
dual-income families, 42
education, wages and jobs, 42
gender roles, 42, 95
marriage, divorce trends, 42–43, 43–44
nonfamily households, 43
racial diversity, 43
single-parent families, 43
Sex ratio structure, 20–21
Asian Americans, 223table
See also Gender relations and sex ratios
Sexuality, regulation of, 58–59
Sharecropping, 162
Sikh society
arranged marriage, 52
Asian Indians, 217
interracial marriage, 241
Single-parent families
agricultural era, 36–37
Asian Americans, 224*table*
attenuated extended households, 68–69
female-headed households, outcomes for, 81–82
Hispanic households, 201, 201*table*
male-headed households, 82–83
matriarchy concept and, 54
noncustodial parents, 83–84
nonmarital births, 77–78, 79*table*
nonmarital births, racial gap in, 79–81
poverty rates, 74, 76*fig.*
in service era, 43, 44
slavery effect upon, 159
teen births, 77–78, 79*table*
See also specific racial, ethnic group

Sioux Indians
culture revival, 185
discipline tactics, 118
elder respect custom, 136
gender roles, issues, 105
infant rituals, 129
population trends, 173*table*
puberty rituals, 130
Smart, Elizabeth, ix
Southeast Asian Americans, 218–220
social characteristics, 222–224*table,* 226–227
See also specific racial, ethnic group
Speed dating, xii
Stereotypes
vs. generalizations, xi–xii
See also Gender relations; Gender relations and sex ratios
Sterilizations, x
Structural assimilation, 232
Suicide
Asian Americans, 221
Chinese Americans, 213
men *vs.* women, 97
Native Americans, 184

T
Taino Indians, Puerto Rico, 190
Taoism, 150
Teen births, 78–79, 79*table,* 201
See also specific racial, ethnic group
Teenage smoking, 32
Thirteenth Amendment, 160
Tibetan society, 50
"Trail of Tears," 175
Transitional mothering practice, 60, 113
Treaty of Guadalupe Hidalgo, 191–192
Turkish society
elder respect custom, 136
evil eye custom, 129
titles, 55
Tydings-McDuffie Act, 217

U
Unilineal lineage system, 54

V
Veiling custom, Muslim society, 91–92
Vietnam War, 208, 218–219, 251
See also Vietnamese Americans; Vietnamese culture
Vietnamese Americans
biculturalism, 233
family values acculturation, 237
immigration waves, 219–220
interracial marriage, 244
social characteristics, 222–224*table*
See also Vietnam War; Vietnamese culture
Vietnamese culture, 126
death beliefs, rituals, 150
elder abuse, 143
infant rituals, 129
See also Vietnam War; Vietnamese Americans
Voting Rights Act, 164

W
War Brides Act, 214
Wealth, *vs.* income, 17–18
White Americans
abortions, 80
age structure, 22–23
aging trends, 137, 137*table,* 138
attenuated extended households, 68
authoritarian parenting style, 119
caregiver stress, 142
in colonial period, 34
corporal punishment, 122, 123
domestic abuse, 105–106
eating disorders, 3–4
education gender differentiation, 94
elder care, 140
elderly/adult children resources exchange, 143–144
ethnicity, 7
in foster care system, 124, 124*table*
geographic factors, 24
guilt references, 119
homosexuality, 90
individualism *vs.* familism, 112–116
infant mortality rates, 116–117
interracial adoption, 250–251
interracial dating, 241

interracial marriage, 242–243, 243*table,* 245–246, 248, 249
interracial marriage, social acceptance, 246
laterally extended households, 69
life value of, ix
marriage, 167–168
minority *vs.* majority labels, 9
multigenerational households, 67, 139, 144
non-Hispanic White label, 8
noncustodial parents, 84
nonfamily households, 84
nonmarital births, 78, 79*table,* 80–81
nursing home use, 140
population trends, 2, 2*table*
poverty levels, 18–19
racial-ethnic labels, 8–9
references to, 4
single-father families, 82
social interaction with children, 143
teen births, 79
teen years, 114
See also Non-Hispanic White Americans

Women
acculturation, 236–237
in agricultural era, 35, 95
female-headed households, 77–82
gender roles, 95–96
immigrants, 27
in industrial era, 38–39, 95
marital satisfaction, 95–96
matriarchy concept, 54
matrilineal systems, 54–55, 88, 104, 183
median age at first marriage, 33, 34, 34*fig.*
monogamous *vs.* polygamous marriage, 49–51
in service era, 42–43, 43–44, 95
sex ratios and, 21
single-parent families, 43
slave women, 157
teen births, 78–79
"transnational motherhood" concept, 60
women's movement, 164
World War II, 164
See also Family structures; Gender factors; Gender relations; Gender relations and sex ratios; *specific racial, ethnic group*

Z
Zuni Indians, 183

ABOUT THE AUTHOR

Roberta L. Coles received her PhD in sociology from the University of Wisconsin at Madison. She first taught a course on race and family while a PhD candidate and has continued teaching a similar course at Marquette University, where she has been on the faculty in the Department of Social and Cultural Sciences since 1995. She teaches courses on family, race and family, race and ethnic relations, gender, social inequality, and urban neighborhoods and serves as an adviser to sociology and family studies majors. Her family-related research has focused on African American single fathers and on Turkish elderly. Her work in these areas has been published in the *Journal of Aging Studies, Journal of Contemporary Ethnography, Families in Society, Journal of African American Men,* and the *Western Journal of Black Studies.*